To The Atwoods ~

God created Soot to be a most
special individual. Then He put
us together so that Fire would
convince me that it was so.
And now we can promise you
a very, very special creature who
will fill your hearts with love
and exceed your expectations.
Ed Hubbard told me at least 100
times, "These horses will change
your life!" So they have ... I
wish for you all every bit of the
magic they have been for me.
Thank you for your faith in
Fire. You will not be
disappointed.

I hope this book becomes well-
used and lovingly dog-eared!
As you are all at different
levels of expertise and knowledge,
I hope you will all find
something of interest in its
pages.

With affection & gratitude,

Sable & Soot
Fall '92

the
ARABIAN
a guide for owners

the
ARABIAN
a guide for owners

by

SHARON BYFORD

illustrated by

KARI ALBIOL

International Standard Book No. 0-931866-27-8
Library of Congress Catalog Card No. 86-72633

Printed in the United States of America.

To Cherylle, for believing

ACKNOWLEDGEMENTS

Deepest thanks to Michael and Ann Bowling, The New Albion Stud, Davis, Calif.; Denise Borg, Four Winds Farm, Santa Ynez, Calif.; James P. "Jimmie" Dean, Tip Top Farm, Sanders, Ky.; Dr. Norman Dunn, California State Polytechnic University, Pomona, Calif.; Linda K. Ehlers, Red Wing, Minn.; Dr. Sam Harrison, Sa-Arabet Arabian Farms, Loudon, Tenn.; Sandra Hugus, Pandemonium Pintos, Promise City, Iowa; Kate Knill, Encore at Vail, Vail, Colo.; Neal and Marj McKinstry, McKinstry Arabians, Craig, Colo.; Dr. Shauna J. Omlie, Winter Park, Colo.; Dr. Richard Perce, Steamboat Springs, Colo.; Dr. Marinel J. Poppie, Alpine Arabian Stud, Tucson, Ariz.; Dr. William A. Schurg, University of Arizona, Tucson, Ariz.; Steve and Sue Sidles (formerly Quadis Arabians), Show Season, Scottsdale, Ariz.

The Arabian Horse Registry of America, Inc.; the Arabian Horse Trust; and the International Arabian Horse Association.

The John Crerar Library, Chicago, Ill.; the W. R. Brown Memorial Library, Arabian Horse Owners Foundation, Tucson, Ariz.; and Librarians Betty Nunn and Virginia Taussig, Grand County Library, Kremmling, Colo.

A special thanks to the various Arabian horse magazines, especially to the *Arabian Horse News*, *Journal*, and *World*, for the information and inspiration their articles provided over the years. Thanks especially to authors Gladys Brown Edwards, Carol Mulder, and Mary Jane Parkinson, who have contributed greatly to the depth of published information about the Arabian breed.

Thanks also to the many experts who added to my knowledge, both directly and indirectly—especially to the veterinarians and professional Arabian horse trainers whose classes and workshops I attended.

To all those who loaned photographs, allowed reprints of previously published materials or helped in other ways.

To Cherylle Bumgarner, who cared for my horses during bitterly cold winters in the Colorado Rockies so that I could sit by the fire and write this book.

CONTENTS

Introduction ix

"Tribute" xi

  1   The World's Oldest Breed 1

  2   Arabian Horse Breeding in America 9

  3   The Versatile Arabian 19

  4   The Influence of Arabian Blood 29

  5   Disposition and Senses 37

  6   Type 43

  7   Conformation 51

  8   Gaits and Action 61

  9   Color and Markings 67

10   Buying an Arabian 75

11   Registration and Transfers 83

12   Stable Facilities 91

13   Stable Management 99

14   Feeds and Feeding 109

15   Health Care 117

16   Parasites 131

17   Hoof Care 139

18   Grooming 145

19   Pedigrees and Strains 161

20   Basic Principles of Genetics 169

21   Becoming a Breeder 177

22   Breeding Your Mare 185

23   Teasing and Breeding 199

24   The Pregnant Mare 207

25   Foaling 215

26   Bringing Up Baby 223

27   Size, Growth and Maturity 231

28   Early Training 237

29   Trailering 249

30   Showing the Arab 255

31   Conditioning for Halter 269

32   Training for Halter Classes 275

33   Showing at Halter 285

34   The Stallion 295

35   Arab Geldings 301

36   The Horse Business 307

37   Future of the Breed 315
Talk Like a Horseman 319
Bibliography and Suggested Reading 323
Other Sources of Information 325
Index 329

viii

INTRODUCTION

When I got my first, long-awaited purebred Arabian horse about ten years ago, I was living in a remote area where Arabians were few and far between. Although I had owned horses of various breeds during the previous decade, I knew that Arabian horses were different.

"Arabs aren't *like* other breeds," a friend confirmed. "Everything is done differently. We don't groom or show them like other breeds, and they require a special kind of handling and training."

Forced by circumstances to learn mostly by doing, I searched in vain for a comprehensive, "handy dandy manual" about Arabian horses. Most books, I found, focused on the breed's history and bloodlines. The few books about Arabian horses that contained information on care, breeding, and training often were oversimplified and outdated. The need for an up-to-date primer that compiled widely scattered information into one convenient source was apparent.

About this time, I met Betty Jo McKinney of Alpine Publications, who encouraged me to write the book that I *wish* had been available when I became the proud owner of my first Arabian horse. Others were probably better qualified to write such a book, and I certainly wish someone else had done it long ago. It would have saved me years of hard work—not just on this book but with my own horses!

Although I had written for horse magazines for almost twenty years, I often felt overwhelmed as I was writing this book. The task involved researching existing literature about horses in general and Arabians in particular, drawing upon my own experience and acquired knowledge, and filling in the gaps by personal interviews with experts.

This book is not about the Arabian horse as portrayed in art and literature but about the flesh-and-blood Arabian horse that has inspired artists and writers throughout history. Because flesh-and-blood horses have real histories, problems, and needs, this book addresses the Arabian breed from a practical standpoint.

Although designed as a basic working tool for Arabian horse owners and breeders, this book is not meant to replace the services or guidance of veterinarians, trainers, farriers, or other skilled professionals. Rather, it provides an overview of the breed and general guidelines for care, breeding, and training. The methods outlined here offer one approach; other ways exist to accomplish the same results. Owners should be open-minded about these and other techniques and find the methods that suit them best.

I hope that the information presented here will prove helpful. The book was a labor of love and is dedicated to all who share an interest in the object of that love—the Arabian horse.

Sharon Byford
1986

Gwalior (*Naborr x Gwaliana).
Sparagowski photo courtesy of Locust Farms, Kirkland, Ohio

TRIBUTE

by Deborah Parks

In his liquid eye is the blackness of desert night
Strewn with flickering campfires.

His two ears, pinnacles on an ivory mosque,
Are formed in graceful symmetry.
The cavernous nostrils convert Kansas breeze
Into hot desert wind.

His voice can be a trumpeted call to war
Or a soft, meandering tune of mystery.
The whole quicksilver image of him
Shimmers like heat waves over scorching dunes.

He is molded of morning mist and rifle smoke—
Of soft, cold ashes and boiling clouds.
He hallows the earth where he stands.
He is mine and I am his.

But I know the Prophet's Thumb cannot save him:
It has no power in Kansas.
When he is gone, the tapestry of my life
Will be torn—a void shall exist—
Where once was an awkward baby,
A willing companion,
A happy friend.

WAR IN THE DESERT

The Arabian has been a favorite of artists for centuries.

I

THE WORLD'S OLDEST BREED

The Arabian horse—romanticized by poets, artists, and writers. The ancient breed whose beauty, intelligence, courage, loyalty, spirit, and nobility have captured the imaginations of so many.

Although not perfect, for the perfect horse has never existed, the Arabian inspires such devotion that the breed's admirers are convinced of its superiority. And, the Arabian *is* different from other breeds in many ways.

The Arabian is characterized by a beautiful, delicate head, often with a "dished" or concave profile below large, prominent eyes; a high-set, arched neck; and a naturally high tail carriage. These points of "type" (which is a term describing the special combination of physical traits that make each breed's appearance unique) give the Arabian its distinctive beauty.

The Arabian's physical stamina and intelligence are legendary, and gentleness is as much a hallmark of the breed as are a dished face and high tail. No other breed can match the vitality, gaiety, and high spirits of the Arabian. None other has its charisma. Called "the proud breed," Arabian horses seem to know they are special.

THE HORSE OF THE BEDOUINS

The Arabian got its name from the country that considered it the world's *only* purebred horse—Arabia. The breed's stamina was tested and proven by the larger and more powerful nomadic Bedouin tribes in the deserts of Syria, North Africa, and Arabia. These tribes were often at war with each other, and horses captured in battles or in raids upon enemy camps provided "new" bloodlines for a tribe's breeding stock. However, all the purebred horses of the desert belonged to the same breed—the *Kehilan* (purebred) of the Bedouins.

The horse-breeding tribes (such as the Anazeh) migrated seasonally between northern and southern pastures, living always in black, camel hair tents. Life was hard for the Bedouins and even more difficult for their horses. Feed and water often were scarce, and temperatures could vary from blazing heat during the day to freezing at night. Long marches under adverse conditions honed the Arabian's endurance to a fine edge.

The Bedouins treated their horses with a strange mixture of love and brutality. According to many accounts, a Bedouin would rather part with his

1

family than with a beloved mare. Bedouin horses were blanketed in cold weather and sometimes slept in tents with their masters. Yet newborn foals (especially colts) born on forced marches were sometimes purposely abandoned, and old horses were no longer fed, if they managed to outlive their usefulness.

This difficult lifestyle provided an automatic means of culling breeding stock, with toughness the standard for survival.

The Bedouin's own survival often depended upon the speed, agility, and endurance of his war horse. The horse's ability to perform, therefore, established its value for breeding, with a mare descended from a family of famous war mares considered a treasure. Since the Bedouins seldom (if ever) rode stallions in battle, they traced their horses' pedigrees through their war mares, whose ability to perform had been proven.

The Bedouins chose their horses on the basis of speed, endurance, loyalty, and other qualities valuable in battle. They apparently paid little attention to the horse's appearance, choosing a successful war mare (or a horse descended from famous war mares) rather than choosing a mare that would be superior (by European standards) in conformation or breed type. Yet some of the Arabian's traits of breed type must have been linked to practical qualities such as stamina and speed, for Arabian breed type has endured to the present.

ORIGIN OF THE BREED

According to Bedouin tradition, their first horses were captured in or near the desert. While most older authorities believed that the breed originated in the Middle East, some modern experts do not agree. Actually, no proof of the breed's point of origin exists.

Horses of Arabian type appear in the ancient art of many countries, including Greece and Egypt. Some people even say that they are identifiable in prehistoric cave drawings.

Although the breed's exact origin is a mystery, it is widely acknowledged that the Arabian is the oldest known breed of horse in the world. Horses of Arabian type certainly date back more than 2,000 years; the breed actually may be twice that old.

Although the Arabian breed may not have originated in the desert, little doubt exists that the Bedouins' harsh life increased the breed's stamina and hardiness. And, by inbreeding their horses, the Bedouins helped set the Arabian's distinctive type even more indelibly.

ISLAM AND THE ARABIAN HORSE

The Prophet Mohammed believed that war was the fastest way to convert the world to his new religion, Islam. After being defeated by cavalry, he began urging his Bedouin followers to acquire Arabian horses and to guard the purity and, thus, the stamina of the breed. The owner who took good care of his horse and was ready for battle in the name of Islam was promised a heavenly reward. Devotion to the Arabian horse, therefore, became part of the new Bedouin religion.

The Legendary Arabian

Bedouin legends about Arabian horses, often entwined with Islamic religion, unfortunately have obscured any solid facts about the breed. The legends, however, are as extraordinary as the horses that inspired them. The famous story of *Al Khamsa* (The Five) tells of a group of exhausted, thirsty war mares turned loose near water. As they eagerly raced toward it, the trumpet sounded a call to battle. Only five of the mares responded to the command, and these were chosen to produce the Bedouins' future war horses. According to some versions of the story, these mares were the founders of five major strains (families) of Arabian horses.

Another famous Bedouin religious legend tells of Allah (God) creating the Arabian horse from a handful of wind. The first horse, legend has it, was the color of a ripe date (interpreted variously as dark chestnut or bay).

LEAVING THE DESERT

Bedouin war horses eventually were discovered by Europeans, who obtained some Arabians to produce cross-bred cavalry mounts. During summers, European buyers travelled to the edges of the Syrian desert to buy horses from Bedouin tribes that had migrated north. Such early breeders as the Weil Stud

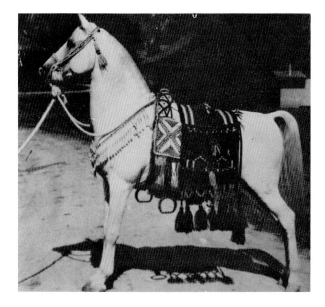

*Mirage, the desert-bred stallion imported by Roger Selby, modeling an imported saddle, bridle, and breastcollar.
Photo courtesy of Arabian Horse Owners Foundation

of Germany and the Sanguzsko family of Poland bought breeding stock directly from the desert. Because of the rugged desert terrain, early Egyptian breeders had a head-start in acquiring horses from the Nejd, a famous horse-breeding area that was inaccessible to Europeans for quite a while.

Arabian and part-Arabian cavalry mounts did battle in most of the world. History was shaped by military leaders who rode chargers of Arabian descent. Such men included Napoleon Bonaparte and George Washington.

In 1877, a wealthy English couple visited some Bedouin tribes and became interested in their horses. At the time, Wilfrid Blunt was thirty-seven years old and his wife, Lady Anne, was forty. Their four-year-old daughter, Judith, remained in England while her parents made the journey that was to change not only their lives but the future of the Arabian horse as well.

CRABBET ARABIAN STUD

Credit for popularizing the Arabian horse throughout the world belongs to the Crabbet Arabian Stud of Sussex, England. Owned and operated by Mr. Wilfrid and Lady Anne Blunt and later by their daughter Judith Blunt Lytton (famous as Lady Wentworth, Arabian horse breeder and authority), the Crabbet Stud was founded on horses personally chosen and imported from the desert and Egypt by the Blunts.

The Crabbet Arabian Stud was operated by this colorful family for almost a century. Its horses were exported worldwide and used for breeding so extensively that the impact of the Crabbet Stud on the Arabian breed has never been equalled.

Throughout history, the Arabian excelled as a war horse. Here, Washington takes command of the U.S. Army in 1775, mounted on an Arabian-type charger.

In November 1877, the Blunts travelled to Syria. At Aleppo they met the British Consul (James Henry Skene) who shared their interest in the Bedouin horses and encouraged them to establish a British breeding farm for purebred Arabian horses. The Blunts bought three Arabian horses in Aleppo: a mare, a young stallion, and a yearling filly (Dajania) that was to be one of their most valuable broodmares. From Aleppo, the Blunts rode horseback to Deyr, Bagdad, Palmyra, and Damascus. They saw many horses, but only one they considered top quality—a brown mare (Queen of Sheba) owned by the Sheikh of the Gomussa tribe of Bedouins. The mare was later bought and imported

to England with the Blunts' other purchases and additional Arabian horses chosen by Mr. Skene.

After their journey, a book of the Blunts' adventures was published. *Bedouin Tribes of the Euphrates* was based upon Lady Anne's diary of the five-month trip, with a chapter about the Bedouin horses added by Wilfrid. A second journey to the desert (December 1878 - July 1879) resulted in another book, *A Pilgrimage to Nejd*. In 1880, the Blunts purchased five more Arabian mares.

In 1882, the Blunts bought the "Garden of Sheykh Obeyd" near Cairo, Egypt. In 1889, they established a second breeding farm there with Arabian horses purchased from Egyptian breeder Ali

One of the most important imports by the Blunts from Egypt to the Crabbet Stud was the stallion Mesaoud (Aziz x Yemameh), purchased from Ali Pasha Sherif in 1889. Mesaoud appears in the pedigrees of many Crabbet-bred Arabians, including the famous Skowronek sons *Raffles, *Raseyn, and Naseem.

Photo courtesy of Cecil G. Covey

Pasha Sherif. One of the first three horses purchased for Sheykh Obeyd was the young, chestnut stallion, Mesaoud, later exported to Crabbet and used extensively in the Blunts' breeding program.

In 1920, after the death of Lady Anne (and after a lengthy legal battle with Wilfrid), Judith (Lady Wentworth) acquired her parents' horses. Unlike her globetrotting parents, Judith seldom left Crabbet where she personally supervised operation of the breeding farm and wrote books and articles about Arabian horses. One of her most important works, *The Authentic Arabian*, combined her writings with previously unpublished manuscripts by both of her parents. When Lady Wentworth died in 1957, the Stud was inherited by its manager, Cecil G. Covey, who operated it on a limited scale until 1971.

Crabbet Stud achieved its greatest fame under Lady Wentworth's management. Her most notable contribution to the Arabian breed was her acquisition of the grey stallion Skowronek. Unlike her mother, Lady Wentworth was fond of greys and hoped that the stallion would pass on his color. He did far more than that, however. Skowronek proved to be so prepotent that he practically reshaped the Arabian breed in his image.

SKOWRONEK—THE TURNING POINT

Lady Wentworth first saw Skowronek at a horse show in 1920. Although small, the stallion was strikingly beautiful. He was pure white with large dark eyes, short "dished" head, arched neck, level topline, and high tail.

Skowronek was foaled in 1908 in Poland, at the Antoniny Stud of Count Joseph Potocki. He was imported to England in 1913 where he was acquired by Arabian horse breeder H.V.M. Musgrave Clark, who registered the stallion and bred him to a few mares. An American secretly working for Lady Wentworth succeeded in buying Skowronek from Clark. (She felt this ruse was necessary to obtain the stallion from her competitor.) Instead of being shipped to America, as Clark expected, Skowronek was transported to Crabbet, where he remained for the rest of his life.

Some early publications say that Skowronek's sire was descended from Abbas Pasha's Egyptian Arabian horses. Lady Wentworth perpetuated this; she may have believed it because of Skowronek's resemblance to horses of those bloodlines. However, Skowronek's sire, Ibrahim, was bought by Count Potocki while the horse was being shipped to Russia "from the desert." Although the names of his sire and dam were provided, no extended pedigree linked Skowronek to the Abbas Pasha bloodlines. This lack of extended pedigree was not at all unusual in the early Arabian horses imported to Europe and England, for the Bedouins did not keep written pedigrees of their horses. The names given to Count Potocki,

Lady Wentworth in front of the Coronation Stables at Crabbet. The mare on the right is Silver Fire (Naseem x Somra).
Photo courtesy of Arabian Horse Owners Foundation

Skowronek (Ibrahim x Jaskolka)—one of the most influential Arabian stallions of all time.
Photo courtesy of Cecil G. Covey

Heijer (Ibrahim's sire) and Lafitte (his dam), might have been a garbling of strain names.

Skowronek's dam was Jaskolka, a Polish mare sired by Rymnik, a champion show horse. Three full brothers were produced by mating Jaskolka to Ibrahim, but Skowronek's brothers were sold to the

*Raseyn (Skowronek x Rayya).
Photo courtesy of Arabian Horse Owners Foundation

Cossacks and lost to the breed. Sadly, both Ibrahim and Jaskolka were believed killed during the Bolshevik Revolution.

Although Skowronek sired only forty-seven foals, this amazingly prepotent stallion left his imprint on the Arabian breed, especially in America, where his bloodlines were inbred.

The Skowronek sons *Raseyn, *Raffles, and Naseem helped make their sire one of the most influential and famous Arabian stallions in the breed's history. All three sons were bred and foaled at the Crabbet Stud in England. *Raseyn and *Raffles were exported to the United States, and Naseem to the U.S.S.R.

*Raseyn

*Raseyn was foaled in 1923. His dam was Rayya (Rustem x Riada). In 1926, he was imported to America by the Kellogg Ranch at Pomona, California. There, *Raseyn was exhibited as a jumper and five-gaited horse at the Ranch's weekly public exhibitions. He became a popular sire, especially in the western United States. His most famous sons were Ferseyn and Sureyn, and a *Raseyn grand-

*Raffles (Skowronek x *Rifala).
Photo courtesy of Arabian Horse Owners Foundation

daughter (Chloette) became a U.S. National Champion Mare.

*Raseyn became sterile in his old age, but sired a total of 135 foals. His final years were spent at the ranch of Alice Payne in California where he died at age twenty-nine of a stroke.

*Raffles

*Raffles was foaled in 1926. He was Skowronek's only inbred son—his dam was the Skowronek daughter *Rifala. *Raffles stood only 13.3 hands tall but gave the impression of being much larger.

Imported from the Crabbet Stud in 1932 by Roger Selby of Ohio, the stallion, at first, was unruly and believed sterile. However, both his disposition and fertility were restored with proper care. American breeders (especially those in the eastern U.S.) used *Raffles so extensively that a high percentage of modern American-bred Arabians have at least one line to him. Some of his famous sons include Azraff, Indraff, and Sotep.

*Raffles sired a total of 122 foals. With *Raseyn, he spent his last years at the Payne Ranch in California where he died at the age of twenty-seven.

Naseem

Naseem was foaled in 1922. His dam was Nasra (Daoud x Nafisa).

The first Naseem bloodlines imported to the United States were his son *Selmian and daughter *Kareyma. Both were imported by Roger Selby, who also imported *Raffles. Naseem was most influential in American breeding through his son Raktha, who sired the full brothers *Serafix and *Silver Drift, both imported to America from the Crabbet Stud. Both stallions are found in the pedigrees of many champions, and *Serafix was the leading sire of Arabian show champions in America for many years.

Naseem was a major sire at the Crabbet Stud in England, and his sons prominent in England include Indian Light, Irex, Raktha, Raftan, and Rissam. Raftan's sire line continues through the stallion Naseel, Rissam's line through *Nizzam, and Irex's through Champurrado.

In 1936, Naseem was exported from England to the Soviet Union. At the age of fourteen, he became one of that country's most influential Arabian sires. His most important Soviet son was probably Negatiw, sire of *Naborr and *Salon (who sired the U.S. National Champion Stallion *Muscat).

With importations in the late 1970s and early 1980s, the Naseem influence on American breeding programs has increased, for many of the Russian imports have a high percentage of Naseem blood.

Like *Raffles and *Raseyn, Naseem lived a long life, leaving many descendants to carry on the Skowronek bloodline.

Naseem (Skowronek x Nasra).
Photo courtesy of Cecil G. Covey

7

American-bred (Domestic): Arn-ett Perlane, U.S. National Champion Stallion, 1983.

Johnny Johnston photo courtesy of Double Z Arabians, Dallas, Texas

8

2

ARABIAN HORSE BREEDING IN AMERICA

Although famous throughout the world, the Arabian horse achieved its greatest popularity in America where it evolved from a war horse to a pleasure and show horse.

A few Arabian horses were imported to the United States during colonial times, but they were used for outcross breeding instead of being bred to each other because of the shortage of purebred Arabian mares. In the mid-1800s, Alexander Keene Richards imported twelve desert-bred Arabians. (This was more than ten years before the Blunt importations to England.) Unfortunately, Richards used his Arabians only for crossbreeding with Thoroughbreds.

The first recorded American breeder of *purebred* Arabians was Randolph Huntington. His main goal, however, was to insure that purebred Arabians would be available for crossing on racing trotters. In 1888, Huntington imported the Arabian mare *Naomi from Roger D. Upton, British breeder and author of *Gleanings from the Desert of Arabia* and *Newmarket and Arabia*. Bred to *Leopard, General Grant's desert-bred stallion, *Naomi produced the first American-bred Arabian horse to be registered by the Arabian Horse Club of America. (The foal, Anazeh, didn't receive the registration number 1 because the numbers weren't assigned in birth order.)

Chicago World's Fair of 1893

*Nedjme, an imported mare, appears as No. 1 in the Arabian Stud Book of America. She was part of a group of desert-bred Arabians featured in a Turkish exhibition at the World's Colombian Exposition (Chicago World's Fair) in 1893. Before the horses could be shipped back to the desert, they were seized by creditors and sold at auction to settle unpaid debts.

Despite the Turkish exhibition's failure, its Arabian horses captured the imagination of many spectators. Most famous among them was Homer Davenport, a successful political cartoonist.

DAVENPORT IMPORTATION

In 1906, with the help of U.S. President Theodore Roosevelt, Homer Davenport travelled to Syria to buy Arabian horses to be used for producing American cavalry horses. A wealthy friend, Peter B. Bradley of the Hingham Stock Farm financed the journey, which resulted in the importation of twenty-six desert-bred Arabian horses. *My Quest of the Arabian Horse*, by Davenport, details his trip.

When Davenport tried to register his imported Arabians in the Jockey Club Stud Book, his plans to breed purebred Arabians hit a serious snag. Registration was refused because he hadn't obtained adequate pedigrees for his new horses and because their purity had not been verified by previous registration in the English General Stud Book. (Most previous imports to America had come via England, but Davenport's were made directly from the desert.)

*Nedjme, Reg. No. 1. Imported in 1893 for the Chicago World's Fair, *Nedjme became the first horse registered by the Arabian Horse Registry of America.
Photo courtesy of Arabian Horse Trust

Davenport solved the problem by starting a new, separate registry for Arabian horses. Until then, they had all been registered in the Thoroughbred Stud Book, Arabian section. The Arabian Horse Club of America, formed by Davenport and some friends, was created in 1908. When it was formally recognized as the official registry for Arabian horses by the U.S. government, Arabian breeders who had previously boycotted the new registry because their horses *had* been registered by the Jockey Club were forced to accept it and resolve their differences with the breeders who had begun the new registry.

OTHER EARLY AMERICAN BREEDERS

The first major importations of Arabian horses to America were mostly from the Crabbet Stud and a few small English breeding farms. Famous early American breeders included W.R. Brown, Spencer Borden, Albert W. Harris, W.K. Kellogg, and Roger A. Selby.

In the early days, Arabian horses were owned by wealthy Americans who could afford to buy or import them. Arabians were expensive because they were scarce, and many breeders idealistically sought to save the breed from extinction.

The early breeders faced problems not shared by modern breeders. Their knowledge of horse management was not as extensive as that available to breeders today. They produced fewer foals because of a lack of scientific advancement in the fields of equine health and reproduction. Few purebred mares were available, so Arabian stallions sired few purebred get. The same horses were bred repeatedly to each other because transporting mares to outside stallions was difficult. Because of their small numbers, virtually *all* Arabians were considered breeding stock, regardless of their individual quality.

Despite these drawbacks, American breeders were able to build a solid foundation for the future of the breed by breeding intelligently. They selected outstanding individuals when they became available

*Hamrah, No. 28, was one of Davenport's imports from the desert.
Photo courtesy of Arabian Horse Owners Foundation

for importation to America and then bred carefully for improvement in conformation and type under conditions that were not always favorable. Today, the United States has more Arabian horses than all other countries of the world combined, and is home to many of the world's finest.

10

THE THREE GRACES—W. K. KELLOGG ARABIAN HORSE RANCH   114108

"The Three Graces" was issued by the W.K. Kellogg Arabian Horse Ranch as a postcard. According to the card, "Arabian horses are fast becoming extinct...." Thanks to the dedication of the early breeders, that statement is now far from true.

TABLE 2.1

APPROVED SOURCES FOR
IMPORTED ARABIAN HORSES*

Country	Studbook Authority	Abbreviation
Argentina	Argentinean Arabian Stud Book	A G S B
Australia	Australian Arab Horse Society	A H S A
Austria	Austrian Arabian Stud Book	A A S
Belize	Belize Agricultural Society (Central America)	B A S
Belgium	Belgian Arab Horse Society	B A H S
Brazil	Brazilian Arabian Stud Book	B R S B
Canada	Canadian Arab Horse Society	C A H R
Denmark	Danish Arab Horse Society	D A H S
E. Germany	Rostock Zoo, East Germany	E G S B
Egypt	Egyptian Agricultural Organization-	E A O
	Private Breeders Section	E A O P B
England	Arab Horse Society	A H S
France	French Arabian Stud Book	F R S B
Germany	German Arabian Stud Book	G A S B
	Marbach State Stud Book	G R S B
Hungary	Babolna State Stud	A S B B
Israel	Israeli Arab Horse Society	I A S B
Jordan	Royal Jordanian Stud Book	J D S B
Morocco	Moroccan Arabian Stud Book	M S B
Netherlands	AVS-Dutch Arab Horse Society	N S B
New Zealand	New Zealand Arab Horse Society	N Z H S
Norway	Norwegian Arab Horse Society	N A H A
Poland	Polish Arabian Stud Book	P A S B
South Africa	South Africa Arab Horse Society	S A S B
Spain	Spanish Arabian Stud Book	S S B
Sweden	Swedish Arab Horse Society	S W S B
Switzerland	Swiss Arab Horse Society	S A H S
USSR	Russian Arabian Stud Book	R A S B

*Every Arabian imported to the U.S. must be individually approved prior to registration. Only those from the listed countries can be considered for registration by the Arabian Horse Registry of America, Inc. (This list is subject to change. Current information is available from the Registry.)

NATIONALITIES

In the United States, Arabian horses are often described according to "nationality." For example, "Polish Arabians" were imported from Poland or trace quickly to Arabian horses bred there, "Spanish Arabians" descend from Arabian horses bred in Spain, etc.

All Arabian horses' roots eventually are traced to the deserts of the Middle East. This means that purebred Arabians of all nationalities are at least distantly related. In fact, many nationalities descend from known common ancestors. The Crabbet Arabians, in particular, can be found in the pedigrees of Arabian horses bred in many different countries.

Determining the nationality to which an Arabian horse belongs therefore can be confusing. Consider, for example, two Arabian stallions of another age—Mesaoud and Skowronek. Mesaoud was bred and foaled in Egypt and was therefore "Egyptian." Skowronek, bred and foaled in Poland, was "Polish." However, when these two stallions were exported from their native countries to England, they sired "English" or Crabbet-bred" Arabians. When their English get were exported to the United States, they founded "American-bred" or "Domestic Arabian" families. Exactly how to identify Arabian horse nationalities is therefore simply a matter of opinion.

Some Arabian horses have been bred "pure in nationality." They are designated "Pure Polish,"

11

"Straight Egyptian," etc. These "pure" and "straight" nationalities preserve a concentrated gene pool for breeding; it is useful for outcrossing with other lines and for inbreeding to concentrate the particular qualities of each nationality.

Until about 1960, most Arabians imported to America were from England. In the early 1960s, breeders began importing Arabian horses from Poland and Egypt. In the late 1970s and early 1980s, Spain and Russia were discovered as sources of "new" blood.

Kellogg's grey stallion, Jadaan, was used for film close-ups of Rudolph Valentino in "The Son of the Sheik."
Photo courtesy of Killiam Shows, Inc.

During the past twenty years, rapid changes in the popularity of the various nationalities have occurred. Whatever is new (most recently imported) becomes fashionable. Only time can prove whether each nationality's initial popularity was justified.

One thing is certain. No nationality is inherently better than another—it is just different. Superior horses and poor horses are found in Arabian horses of all nationalities. The superior individuals of each can contribute their own strengths to Arabian breeding programs. Inferior individuals should be avoided regardless of nationality.

American-bred (Domestic) Arabians

Technically, *any* Arabian horse that is bred and foaled in the United States is an "American-bred." However, the term usually is reserved for Arabians directly descended from the early imports to America (from the late 1800s to the mid-1950s).

Most American-bred Arabs trace back to such horses as Davenport's desert-breds; the early Polish imports by Dickinson and Babson; Babson's Egyptian imports of the same period; and to Arabians imported or bred by such early American breeders as W.R. Brown, Roger Selby, and W.K. Kellogg. American-bred pedigrees often contain the names of such stallions as *Raffles, *Raseyn, *Mirage, *Fadl, *Nasik, *Deyr, *Nimr, *Nurreddin, etc.

American-bred Arabians have become most famous as correct, athletic performance horses but also have contributed their share of halter winners. For example Bay Abi, Khemosabi, Gai Parada and others have achieved the highest national show honors.

American-bred (Domestic): Khemosabi (Amerigo x Jurneeka). U.S. National Champion Stallion, 1973.
Bill Macri photo courtesy of Khemosabi Syndicate

Although American-bred horses often are overlooked because of excitement surrounding the newest imports from abroad, they are among the finest

Arabian horses in the world. Their greater numbers have produced more Class A Arabian show winners than Arabian horses of other nationalities. When inbred, the American-bred horses are as prepotent for their own qualities as recently imported Arabians.

Because of a tendency to emphasize the contribution of the sire while overlooking the importance of the dam, American-bred broodmares have not always received equal credit for the excellent offspring produced by them when bred to stallions of other nationalities. However, foals produced by domestic mares have often been among the best sired by stallions of recently imported bloodlines.

Examples of famous foreign-domestic crosses include Dancing Flame (sired by a Polish stallion), Bint Padron (by a Russian stallion), AN Marieta (by a Spanish stallion), and Ebony Moon (by an Egyptian stallion). All were produced by American-bred mares, and the list of similar successful produce is lengthy.

Influential American-bred sires include Ferzon, Abu Farwa, Ferseyn, and Fadjur. U. S. National

Crabbet: Count Bazy (Count Dorsaz x Al-Marah Ragtime). U.S. National Champion Stallion 1967.
Louise L. Serpa photo courtesy of Al-Marah Arabians

Champion and Reserve National Champion Stallions of American-bred bloodlines include Khemosabi, Gai Parada, Zarabo, Raffon, Afari, Ibn Hanrah, Bay Abi, and Zarr-Hassan.

Crabbet or English Arabians

The term "Crabbet Arabian" or "Crabbet-bred" is reserved for Arabian horses tracing mostly to the bloodlines of England's Crabbet Arabian Stud. Because Crabbet was the largest and most influential English breeding farm, most English Arabians have some Crabbet bloodlines.

Other than *Raffles and *Raseyn, the most influential import to America from the Crabbet Stud was probably the stallion *Serafix (Raktha x Serafina). Imported by John Rogers of California, *Serafix was leading sire of show champions for many years (until displaced by the Polish import, *Bask). *Silver Drift, Serafix's brother, also is found in the pedigrees of many American show horses.

When Lady Wentworth died in 1957, a number of additional Crabbet Arabians were imported by Bazy Tankersley's Al-Marah Arabians, now of Tucson, Arizona. Mrs. Tankersley popularized the "Double R" Arabians (those having *Raffles or *Raseyn plus Rissalix in their pedigrees).

American-bred pedigrees often contain the names of Crabbet Arabians, usually those imported by Selby and Kellogg in the 1920s and 1930s. Importations to America from the Crabbet Stud stretched from the early 1900s into the 1950s.

The most successful halter horse of pure Crabbet bloodlines was Count Bazy, U.S. National Champion Stallion. The Crabbet imports usually have been crossed with other lines, rather than being bred exclusively to each other.

Egyptian Arabians

The first major importations from Egypt to America were in 1932, when W. R. Brown and Henry B. Babson each imported six Arabians. Brown imported the stallions *Zarife and *Nasr along with four mares. Babson imported the stallion *Fadl and five mares.

No additional major Egyptian imports occurred until Richard Pritzlaff of New Mexico imported the stallion *Rashad Ibn Nazeer and four mares in 1958. The following year, Donald and Judith Forbis of Ansata Arabian Stud imported three yearlings by Nazeer, including the influential stallion *Ansata Ibn Halima.

Between 1962 and 1980, Douglas and Margaret Marshall imported over fifty Arabians to their Gleannloch Farms in Texas. Other importations continued during this period. In 1973, Don Ford imported *Asadd, who became U.S. National Champion Stallion in 1975 and U.S. National Champion English Pleasure Horse in 1979.

"Old Egyptian" vs. "New Egyptian" — Horses tracing to early imports such as those of the Babson and Brown importations of the '30s are called "Old Egyptian" to differentiate them from the imports of 1958 onward, the "New Egyptians." Not surprisingly, they share some of the same ancestors.

Famous "Old Egyptian" stallions included *Zarife, *Fadl, and *Hallany Mistanny. Many of the "Old Egyptian" lines also appear in American-bred pedigrees.

The most famous "New Egyptian" sire line is that of Nazeer, a grey stallion by Mansour. His dam, Bint Samiha was by Kazmeen and out of Samiha. Kazmeen (Kasmeyn) was exported to Egypt from the Crabbet Stud in 1920. Famous imported stallions by Nazeer include *Morafic, *Talal, *Ansata Ibn Halima, *Ramses Fayek, and *Fakher el Din.

Egyptian show champions include *Ansata Ibn Sudan (U.S. National Champion Stallion), *Serenity Sonbolah (U.S. National Champion Mare), and *Sakr, (U.S. National Champion Native Costume; U.S. Reserve National Champion Park Horse).

Polish Arabians

The first major importation from Poland to America occurred in 1937 when General Dickinson of the Traveler's Rest Stud in Tennessee imported seven Polish mares. In 1938, he imported more mares and the stallion *Czubuthan. Henry Babson imported a group of Polish Arabians in the same shipment, including the stallion *Sulejman.

During World War II, the United States "liberated" a group of Polish Arabian horses that had been taken to Czechoslovakia by the Germans. In 1945, these horses were imported to America. Included were the stallions *Witez II, *Lotnik, and *Pilot.

Egyptian: *Asadd (*Sultann x Amani). U.S. National Champion Stallion, 1975.
Johnny Johnston photo courtesy of Lancer Arabians

14

In the 1960s, American breeders rediscovered Polish bloodlines when the Polish stallions *Ardahan and *Muzulmanin were imported. When they were shown successfully, American breeders became Poland's largest and best paying market for Arabian horses.

The most famous sire line in Polish Arabians is probably that of Ofir, a son of the desert-bred stallion Kuhailan Haifi, through his three sons: Witraz, Wielki Szlem, and *Witez II. *Witez II was popular for many years, and sired many successful show horses. Wielki Szlem's most famous modern representative is probably *El Paso, U.S. National Champion Stallion. Witraz is best known as the sire of *Bask, also a U.S. National Champion Stallion.

*Bask was imported from Poland in 1963 by Dr. Eugene LaCroix of Lasma Arabians, Scottsdale, Arizona. The next year, he was National Champion Stallion at halter. In 1965, he was U.S. National Champion Park Horse and in 1967 was Reserve National Champion in Formal Driving and also in Formal Combination. *Bask retired from the show

ring but went on to become the leading modern sire of Arabian show champions.

Other Polish imports who became champions in halter or performance include *Aramus, *Elkin, *Buszmen, *Gwalior, *Bajram, *Meczet, and *Prowizja.

Desert-bred Arabians

Modern "Desert-bred" Arabians are those whose lineage can be *proven* to descend directly from desert tribes. (Although all registered Arabians are presumed to have originated from Bedouin foundation stock, documented pedigrees and histories were not always obtained for the early exports from the desert.)

Desert-bred Arabians have a distinctive type which their breeders feel represents the Arabian breed in its purest form. This type has been set even more by inbreeding of Desert-bred lines.

Some breeders of Desert-bred Arabians breed "by the strain," mating individuals of the same strain, which is traced through the bottom female

Polish: *Bask (Witraz x Balalajka). U.S. National Champion Stallion, 1964.

Johnny Johnston photo courtesy of Lasma Arabians

lines of the pedigree (see Chapter 19). Some breeders also avoid horses with Muniqui blood, considering that Bedouin strain to have been impure.

Desert-bred breeders also sometimes specialize in certain bloodlines. The largest and best known group of Desert-breds being bred "pure" are the Davenport Arabians which trace only to ancestors imported to America by Homer Davenport. The largest breeding operation of this kind is owned by Charles Craver III of Hillview, Illinois. Davenport Arabians have also been crossed on other (usually American-bred) lines.

Because of their low numbers, Desert-bred Arabians are more often used for breeding than showing. However, some American-bred champions have a fairly high percentage of Desert-bred bloodlines.

Desert-bred: Monsoon, a modern stallion descending entirely from the 1906 importation by Homer Davenport. By tradition, horses of this breeding are described as "Davenport Arabians."

Photo courtesy of Craver Farms, Hillview, Ill.

Spanish Arabians

The first major importation of horses from Spain to America was by Joseph E. Draper of California, who imported four mares and a stallion in 1934. In the mid-1960s, American breeders rediscovered Spanish Arabian horses.

In 1965, Charles Steen of Nevada imported twenty-six Arabian horses from Spain. (Horses with the "de Washoe" name suffix were Steen imports.) A few small importations occurred in intervening years, with Jay Stream importing *AN Malik in 1972 and *GG Samir in 1976; more importations by American breeders followed in the late 1970s and early 1980s.

The Arabians of Spain trace mostly to desert-bred, Polish, and Crabbet imports to Spain. In recent years, a few Egyptian lines have been added. Horses originally were bred by the Spanish nobility; now private and military breeders exist. Unfortunately, the Spanish Civil War upset the horse-breeding programs of many Spanish breeders. The Duke of Veragua was killed during the revolution, but many of his valuable horses continued to be used for breeding. The Duke was responsible for selecting and importing several important horses to Spain—most notably five Skowronek daughters imported from England.

Spanish imports successfully shown in the United States include *El Moraduke (U.S. National Top Ten Stallion) and *Abha Hamir (U.S. National Champion Mare and Canadian National Champion Mare). WN Mi Kerida, bred and foaled in the United States, was actually "Straight Spanish" because her sire and dam were Spanish imports. She also was Canadian Reserve National Champion Mare.

Russian Arabians

The first Russian-bred imports to the United States and Canada were considered "Polish" because they were imported from Poland, although bred and foaled in the Soviet Union (U.S.S.R.). In 1962, *Naborr (whose name was spelled with only one "r" in Poland and the U.S.S.R.) was the first major Russian-bred imported to the United States. Pietuszok, also bred in the U.S.S.R., was imported to Canada from Poland in 1973.

The first major importation directly from the Soviet Union occurred in 1978, when Howard Kale, Jr. of Arizona imported *Muscat. In 1981, *Muscat became U.S. National Champion Stallion.

The Russian breeding program was based largely upon Polish and Crabbet lines, with some Egyptian and French blood. During World War II, twelve of Poland's best Arabian stallions, and forty-two of its broodmares were "evacuated" to the U.S.S.R. and incorporated into the Russian breeding program.

Russian imports that have been recent show winners include *Pesenka (U.S. Reserve National Champion Mare), *Penalba (U.S. Reserve National Champion Mare), *Napitok (Canadian National Champion Park Horse), *Marsianin (U.S. National Champion Stallion), and *Padron (U.S. and Canadian National Champion Stallion).

Spanish: *Abha Hamir (Bambu x Garbi). U.S. National Champion Mare, 1979.
Judith photo courtesy of La Lomita Ranch

Russian: *Marsianin (Aswan x *Magnolia), U.S. National Champion Stallion, 1981.
Sparagowski photo courtesy of Keg Arabians and Bill Stokes

Zeus, U.S. Reserve National Champion Competitive Trail Horse winning his title on the 1977 IAHA championship ride. Neal McKinstry, up.

Rob Hess photo courtesy of McKinstry Arabians

3

THE VERSATILE ARABIAN

When most people hear "Arabian," they think "show horse." Arabians are equally beautiful under English or Western tack, and no matter how shown, they obviously are Arabians.

America's first Arabian shows were small and informal with no professional trainers or exhibitors. The rider or handler was usually a member of the family, and the horse often was poorly groomed and only partly trained. So few Arabians existed that owners and breeders usually knew each other, and the shows gave them an opportunity to enjoy their horses together. Early Arabian horse shows were social rather than competitive events.

At those first shows, the Arabian breed achieved its reputation for versatility. It wasn't unusual for one horse to be ridden by the entire family, competing in English, western, and gymkhana classes—all at the same show.

With the tremendous growth in the number of Arabian horses and owners, all-Arabian shows grew more sophisticated and competitive. Show horses and their exhibitors now are well-groomed and trained, and amateurs must often compete against experienced professionals.

Increasingly stiff competition has limited the chance for one show horse to demonstrate his versatility by performing in several kinds of classes. To win, the modern Arabian horse must be a specialist.

Although a Park Horse (a flashy, high trotting English horse) may be shown in a related class, such as Formal Driving, the days are nearly gone when a Park Horse also could be a successful Western Pleasure horse.

Despite the emphasis on the individual horse's "specialty," as a breed the Arabian has lost none of its versatility. Arabian shows feature a variety of performance classes, such as English Pleasure, Western Pleasure, Reining, Stock Horse, Trail, Pleasure Driving, Formal Driving, Cutting, Side Saddle, Hunter, Jumper, Park Horse, Equitation, and Native Costume.

USES OF THE ARABIAN HORSE

Modern Arabian horses still have the same qualities that made their ancestors valuable war horses. Their speed, stamina, intelligence and disposition makes them well-suited for most modern equine sports and activities, including racing and trail riding competition.

Arabian Race Horses

Although the Thoroughbred and the Quarter Horse owe their original speed to their Arabian ancestors, they have been selectively bred for racing speed for many generations. Arabians, bred for other qualities, notably endurance and type, cannot beat Thoroughbreds at Thoroughbred racing distances or defeat Quarter Horses at their shorter races. Over very long distances, however, the Arabian's greater stamina overcomes the initial speed of the other breeds.

As with all racing horses, Arabian horses race against other members of their breed, and when a race is well-handicapped, Arabian races offer as much excitement as those of other breeds.

Although the Arabian is smaller than the Thoroughbred and lighter than the Quarter Horse, it can carry more weight over a greater distance than either breed. In 1959, when the first Arabian horse races were conducted in America, long races demonstrated that fact. Unfortunately, the average spectator found the early Arabian races boring because the races were time-consuming, and the horses were spread out at the finish. To add spectator appeal, race distances were shortened, which helped jockeys and trainers used to racing other breeds. And, as more races were conducted, handicapping (the practice of making faster horses carry heavier weights, resulting in a closer finish) became easier. Now, some Arabian horse races have photo-finishes rivalling those of Quarter Horse races, which are famous for close finishes.

Age of Arabian Race Horses — In 1967, a sixteen-year-old Arabian stallion (Julbit) won a race at the Nationals. Another stallion (Al-Marah Ibn Indraff) raced at the age of seventeen. Today, many "open" races still exist, with only a minimum age limit. Although most successful race horses now are much younger, Arabian race horses usually do remain sound under the stress of racing. Many imported Arabians have retired from racing in their native countries and then become halter winners in American shows.

Arabians start racing later in life than other breeds, because of their later maturity. Racing prospects may be started under saddle as late two-year-olds and first race in the spring as three-year-olds.

Length of Races and Weights Carried — Arabian races are from four furlongs (one-half mile) to one mile and five-eighths (1 5/8 mile).

Each horse carries about 119 to 125 pounds. (Mares carry about 5 lbs. less than colts and geldings.)

Major Races — The International Arabian Horse Association (IAHA) sponsors races for young race horses, and other races are sponsored by private racing organizations and individuals. The IAHA Derby (for four-year-old colts, geldings, and fillies,) and the IAHA Oaks (for four-year-old fillies) are the most prestigious races offered by IAHA. The Oaks covers one mile and one-quarter (1 1/4 mile), and the Derby distance is one mile and five-eighths (1 5/8).

Arabians are known for speed over long distances. Kontiki, a successful Arabian race horse, also became known as a sire of winning racers. *Photo courtesy of Kubela Ranch*

Racing Rules, Costs, and Opportunities — Races are held under the rules of IAHA and the racing regulations of the state where each race is held. Arabian race horses must be freeze-marked for identification, and their registration certificates must be at the track where they are racing.

Like show trainers, race horse trainers may be employed by one owner (private trainer) or several (public trainers). Public trainers charge for each horse and also get a share of any winnings. The jockey usually is hired by the trainer and also gets a fee and share of purses. Other costs of racing include entry fees and the usual costs of keeping and transporting horses. At present, it costs about the same to race an Arabian horse as to campaign it on a Class A Arabian horse show circuit.

Arabian racing still offers opportunities eliminated by larger, more sophisticated racing systems. If licensed, owners can train or ride their own horses, and many of the leading Arabian race horse trainers and jockeys have been women. (When the filly Jordana won all her races in 1974, she was owned, trained, and ridden solely by women.)

Racing Arabians in America — In many countries, Arabians always have been raced. Poland, France, Spain, Syria, India, and Egypt have raced Arabian horses for at least half a century.

In *Newmarket and Arabia*, Roger D. Upton wrote:

> "As a racer himself the Arabian possesses every natural gift and qualification—courage, docility, temper, endurance, good and untiring action, great determination, nervous energy, and speed...."[1]

In America, we have been slow to discover just how well those qualities suit the Arabian horse to racing.

For more information on racing Arabians contact the Racing Department at IAHA (see Other Sources of Information).

The Arabian Endurance Horse

When admirers of the Arabian horse brag about its stamina, their claims can be backed up with statistics dating from 1919 when an Arabian horse won the first Cavalry Endurance Ride conducted by the U.S. Remount. That win was followed by others. When W.R. Brown's Arabian horses secured the U.S. Mounted Service Cup by winning three of the cavalry rides, the Arabian horse owners withdrew from further rides "...so that the Army would have a chance of winning the Cup next time," according to Albert W. Harris, one of the winners of the cup.[2]

According to Harris, the Arabians were the most sound breed and the best weight carriers in the cavalry rides. The Arabians carried 26 percent of their own weight while Thoroughbreds carried only 22.1 percent of theirs. The Arabians had a 15 percent rate of lameness on the difficult rides compared to the Thoroughbreds' 85 percent. Interestingly, part-Arabians carried 25 percent of their weight and had 25 percent lameness.

The endurance rides that started with the U.S. Cavalry evolved into two different kinds of modern competition: endurance rides and competitive trail rides.

"Beautiful is the athlete," says Dr. Marinel Poppie, who rode her show and breeding stallion Hai Karatie to successfully complete the grueling Tevis Cup Endurance Ride.
Hughes photo, courtesy of Alpine Arabian Stud

[1]*Newmarket and Arabia*, by Roger D. Upton. Henry S. King & Co., London: 1873. Page 164.

[2]*The History of the Arabian Horse Club Registry of America, Inc.*, by Albert W. Harris. Arabian Horse Registry of America, Inc., 1950. Page 22.

Endurance Rides — The endurance ride takes place over a specified distance within a time limit. The ride covers rough terrain, sometimes requiring the rider to dismount and lead or follow the horse.

Veterinarians monitor the horses' condition along the route. Horses that are "serviceably sound" may continue the ride; those that don't pass the veterinary exam cannot complete the ride.

Endurance horses must be at least five years old, and pregnant mares are not allowed to compete. The rides cover 50 to 100 miles in one day, usually with a 150-pound minimum weight limit to be carried by the horse. The endurance ride is essentially a long-distance race—the first horse to cross the finish line wins.

For information on using Arabians for Endurance Riding, contact IAHA (see Other Sources of Information). For information about all-breed rides, contact American Endurance Ride Conference, 701 High Street, Suite 216, Auburn, CA 95603; (916) 823-2260.

Competitive Trail Rides — Like endurance rides, competitive trail rides monitor the horses' condition and soundness throughout the ride. Horses that fail the veterinary checks are not allowed to continue.

Competitive trail horses are judged on a point system, with the high-point horse in each division winning that division. (Divisions include Heavyweight, Lightweight, and Junior—for riders ages ten to seventeen.) Horses are judged on condition (40 percent), soundness (40 percent), manners (15 percent) and way of going (5 percent). Unlike endurance races, the first horse to finish may not be the winner; the outcome depends on acquired points.

To compete, horses must be at least four years old. Pregnant mares may compete in competitive trail rides, which cover 25 to 40 miles in one day.

The annual U.S. National Championship Competitive Trail Ride for Arabians is sponsored by IAHA. Purebred and Half-Arabians participate in the same ride, but separate U.S. National Championships, Reserve National Championships, and Top Ten awards are given to the winning Arabians and Half-Arabians. For information contact IAHA (see Other Sources of Information).

For information on all-breed Competitive Trail Riding, contact North American Trail Ride Conference, P.O. Box 20315, El Cajon, CA 92021; (619) 588-7245.

OTHER ACTIVITIES FOR OWNERS

Owners of Arabian and Half-Arabian horses are not restricted to activities limited only to their own breeds. Arabians and Half-Arabians can participate successfully in most equine events.

Dressage

Dressage is a style of English riding in which each entry performs individually, following a prescribed pattern in a rectangular arena (*manege*) to test the horse's flexibility, movement, and obedience to the rider. Dressage tests vary by degree of difficulty.

Like other equine events, dressage requires its own traditional attire and a special dressage saddle is used. The dressage rider uses a longer stirrup

Mon-Rey, ridden by Angela Williams, winning in dressage competition at Scottsdale in 1980. *Susan Sexton photo*

Scharif, U.S. National Champion Formal Driving Horse, driven by Dede Bisch-Reeves.

Sparagowski photo courtesy of McKinstry Arabians, Craig, Colo.

length and the saddle places the rider's weight farther back than on a jumping saddle but more forward than on a cutback saddle used for English Pleasure, Equitation, and Park Horse show classes.

Recently, Arabians and Half-Arabians have become more popular for dressage. Dressage classes are becoming more common at Arabian shows, but Arabians can also show in open dressage classes at all-breed shows.

For information about dressage classes at Arabian shows, contact IAHA (see Other Sources of Information), which now sponsors annual Arabian U.S. National Championship Dressage classes. For further information about dressage and all-breed dressage competition, contact United States Dressage Federation, Inc., P.O. Box 80668, Lincoln, NE 68501; (402) 474-7632.

Driving

Like other horse activities, driving can be done on many levels, from pleasure driving (just driving down the road for enjoyment) to international driving competitions based on dressage and patterns in which obstacles must be negotiated. Driving classes at horse shows vary from Pleasure Driving and Formal Driving classes at Arabian shows to open driving classes at all-breed shows.

Local pleasure driving clubs usually exist to provide driving companions for members and to teach new members how to train and drive their horses. Local pleasure driving clubs usually incorporate all breeds and can often be located through notices in tack shops and local newspapers.

For information on affiliated driving clubs, contact American Driving Society, P.O. Box 1852, Lakeville, CT 06039.

Gymkhana

Gymkhanas are equine events consisting of various speed and skill classes. Unlike most horse show classes, gymkhana events mostly consist of horses racing around various obstacles and/or performing specific maneuvers against the clock. Most gymkhana events are timed, with the fastest horse winning. (Tack and attire at gymkhanas usually are western.)

Popular gymkhana races include the clover-leaf barrel race, where the mounted horse races in a clover-leaf pattern around three barrels; the keyhole race, where the horse races through a keyhole shaped pattern, making a small-radius turn before racing back to the starting line; and pole-bending, where the horse races a serpentine around poles set in a straight line.

Gymkhana events are exciting for both the riders and horses. Because gymkhana horses often become nervous when entering the arena, high-strung horses usually are unsuited to simultaneous gymkhana and show ring competition, since the latter requires a quieter, more controlled performance. Although gymkhana events are usually dominated by Quarter Horses, which are bred for quick bursts of speed over short distances, Arabians can

also be successful. Saki, a famous Arabian brood-mare, was once California State Champion Keyhole Racer.

For more information about gymkhanas, contact local gymkhana competitors and clubs.

Sheriff's Posses and Riding Clubs

Local riding clubs usually welcome new members. Popular riding club activities include trail rides, parading, and showing. Riding club announcements may appear in local newspapers and tack shops; local all-breed horse newspapers can often be picked up at local tack or feed stores and are an excellent source of information about local clubs.

Sheriff's Posses provide community services as well as serving as riding clubs. Posses are best known for their search-and-rescue efforts in tracking lost people or locating downed airplanes in remote areas.

Ibn Jurdino (Jurdino x Carinosa), a frequent winner in Working Cow Horse classes at Arabian shows, ridden by Ray Forzani.
Photo courtesy of John Bomarito

24

For information on affiliated groups, contact American Association of Sheriff Posses and Riding Clubs, 3220 North Freeway, Suite 122, Fort Worth, TX 76111.

Parading

The natural beauty of Arabian horses makes them ideal parade horses, and tractable dispositions make them manageable despite excitement, noises, and crowds. Arabians frequently appear in Native Costumes but western tack heavily adorned with silver is also seen. Arabian parade horses frequently are shown in historical costumes (including sidesaddle) or pulling carts or wagons. A *Raseyn daughter, Moneyna, was ridden in California parades during the 1950s ridden without a bridle by her owner, Harvey Ellis.

Small parades are easy and inexpensive to enter. Watch for notices of upcoming parades in local newspapers. Famous large parades like the Pasadena Rose Bowl require an invitation to enter. Most parades give trophies to the "best riding group," "best horse entry," etc. Riding and driving clubs also sometimes participate in parades as a group.

Drill Teams

Mounted drill teams perform various riding maneuvers and patterns to music, often accom-panied by a verbal narrative. Drill teams perform before audiences at horse shows and similar arena events.

Membership in some drill teams is restricted to a specific color or breed of horses, age or sex of riders, or limited to members of a school or organization, while other teams are open to all riders and kinds of horses. Tack and attire vary from all English or all Western to various kinds of costume (Native Costume for Arabians, Indian costumes for Pintos or Appaloosas, historical costumes, etc.). Some drill teams even perform without conventional tack (bareback or bridleless).

If interested in joining a drill team, inquire local-ly about drill teams in your area. If there isn't one for which you qualify, consider forming a new one. Contact existing drill teams for tips on forming a drill team and incorporating patterns for routines.

THE ARABIAN AS PLEASURE HORSE

Many "backyard" Arabian horses are owned mainly as saddle horses. Owners may participate in showing, trail riding, etc., but they own Arabian horses primarily for enjoyment.

The Arabian's stamina, gentleness, intelligence, spirit, and beauty make it an ideal pleasure horse for many.

English Pleasure class.

Arabian Horse Clubs

Arabian Horse Clubs affiliated with the International Arabian Horse Association are located throughout the United States. Membership is open to people of all ages, and it is not necessary to own a horse to join.

IAHA Clubs offer a variety of activities for members including all-Arabian horse shows. The clubs usually have special youth activities for junior members, and often sponsor a Youth (halter) Judging Team. The ultimate competition for judging teams is held at the U.S. National Championship Arabian Horse Show each year.

Members of 4-H Horse Project clubs must be at least nine years old or in the third grade and cannot be older than nineteen. Each member must be responsible for at least half the care of the horse that is his or her project. Careful record books detailing the horse's care and training, and associated expenses, are kept.

The 4-H Club stresses "learning by doing" and promotes having fun and learning good citizenship as well as learning horse management and riding. For more information or the location of your nearest 4-H Horse Club, contact National 4-H Council, 7100 Connecticut Avenue, Chevy Chase, MD

The Half-Arabian at the right is a 4-H project.

Clubs frequently sponsor pleasure trail rides, tours, picnics, lectures, and clinics for members. Contact IAHA (see Other Sources of Information) for the location of your nearest Arabian horse club.

Youth All-Breed Organizations

4-H — The 4-H Club, a national organization coordinated by local County Agricultural Extension offices and land grant universities is partly government funded.

20815; (301) 656-9000 or your local Extension office listed in the telephone directory under the name of your county.

Pony Club — The Pony Club is for young people up to age twenty-one; there is no minimum age, although the youngest riders are usually at least eight years old. The Pony Club was started by a group of foxhunters, so stresses activities like show jumping, dressage, combined training (CT, or "eventing"), fox hunting, and polo but also includes vaulting and competitive trail riding. In addition to riding skills, horse management is stressed.

There is no restriction on the size of the mounts used in the Pony Club. Full-size horses are not barred from participating, and ponies are not discriminated against.

For more information or the location of your nearest club, contact The United States Pony Clubs, Inc., 329 South High Street, West Chester, PA 19382; (215) 436-0300.

OTHER ACTIVITIES

There are many horse activities not listed here in which Arabians and Half-Arabians can be used. Although Arabians are at a disadvantage in some types of competition, due to their small size, they often can compete successfully in the lower levels activities such as combined training, where the extremely high jumps of advanced competitions rule out most horses under 15.3 hands tall. (For more information about CT, contact U.S. Combined Training Association, Inc., 292 Bridge Street, South Hamilton, Mass. 01982; (617) 468-7133.)

An annual "Horse Industry Directory" is available from the American Horse Council, Inc., 1700 K Street N.W., Washington, D.C. 20006; (202) 296-4031. This inexpensive booklet lists additional national horse organizations by category. The International Arabian Horse Association may also be able to provide assistance in locating other organizations of interest to Arabian horse owners.

Neal McKinstry and Ha Rossetta (U.S. National Champion Competitive Trail Horse) cross a creek on his Colorado ranch.

A registered partbred Arabian (Roedean Rhythm 'n Blues) being shown in England.

4

THE INFLUENCE
OF ARABIAN BLOOD

"Gentlemen, you can with Arab blood get immediate improvement in all breeds.... The Arab is a thousand times better than the English Thoroughbred for improving every race, for in him we return to the unmixed purity and power of an original breed."

—Napoleon
quoted in *Authentic Arabian* by Lady Wentworth

All light horse breeds eventually trace to some Arabian blood. The greatest influence upon other breeds began when the Prophet Mohammed ordered his followers to spread the Islamic religion. Armies with Arabian horses moved from the desert into Egypt, Libya, Algeria, and Spain. During the 800-year occupation of Spain by the Moslems, some Arabian stallions were bred to Spanish horses. The Spanish Barb (a hardy, gentle breed from northwest Africa) was probably part-Arabian, and a few so-called "Barbs" later exported to England for breeding Thoroughbreds actually may have been purebred Arabians. The Andalusian breed also received an infusion of Arabian blood during this time.

Arabian Blood in the Thoroughbred

The Arabian gained most of its reputation as the foundation of all light horses through the Thoroughbred breed, which was based largely on Arabian foundation stock. All Thoroughbred horses—including such legendary stallions as Man O'War and Secretariat—eventually trace to Arabian ancestors through three sire lines established by the Thoroughbred stallions Herod, Matchem, and Eclipse. Herod was a great-grandson of the Byerly Turk; Matchem was a grandson of the Godolphin Arabian; and Eclipse was a descendant of the Darley Arabian. Of these three major progenitors of the Thoroughbred breed, the Darley Arabian was definitely known to have been bred by a desert tribe. The other two may have been only part-breds—a controversial subject. The grey color sometimes seen in Thoroughbreds usually is attributed to the Alcock Arabian, another ancestor.

The Thoroughbred even got its name from the Arabian. The Bedouins called their horses "Kehilan," which means thoroughbred, or purebred. Originally, thoroughbred and purebred meant the same thing. Now, however, the term "Thoroughbred" is restricted to horses of that particular breed. Full-blooded horses of every other breed are termed pure-bred.

All American horse breeds trace, in part, to imported Thoroughbreds and, thus, ultimately back to the Arabian breed.

Arabian Blood in the Morgan

The Morgan horse traces to just one foundation sire—a horse named Justin Morgan. Justin Morgan was described by Randolph Huntington as "a pony Arab-bred horse" (small, part-bred Arabian). Justin Morgan probably was sired by the Thoroughbred stallion True Briton or a "Dutch" stallion named Young Bulrock. The latter probably

The Arabian has been called the foundation of all light breeds. One of the newer breeds to which it has contributed is the Morab, a cross between the Arabian and the Morgan.

was a Frisian, a breed based partly on Andalusian and Arabian stock. Justin Morgan's dam was "the Wildair mare," said to be partly of Arabian or Barb descent. Justin Morgan's size, appearance, and remarkable prepotency indicate that he did have some Arabian blood, although the degree is unknown. Although small, Justin Morgan possessed

the versatility typical of the Arabian; he won both races and weight-pulling contests.

The Morgan is second only to the Thoroughbred in adding the blood of the Arabian to other American horse breeds. Morgan blood was added to the early American Saddle Horse (Saddlebred), Standardbred, Tennessee Walking Horse, and Quarter Horse.

Arabian Blood in the Saddlebred

Early Saddlebreds (American Saddle Horses) were a mixture of English, French, Dutch, and Thoroughbred background. In 1908, a Thoroughbred stallion named Denmark was recognized officially as "the" foundation sire for the breed, due to his widespread influence. Denmark had been a successful race horse at distances up to four miles—probably owing to his Arabian progenitors.

The high tail carriage of modern Saddlebred show horses is produced by cutting the muscles of the tail and using a brace (tail set). However, the early Saddlebreds often had naturally high tail carriage, probably as a result of their less-diluted Arabian blood.

Arabian Blood in Other American Breeds

The rest of the American horse breeds also have some Arabian blood. Even the American Quarter Horse, which usually has little physical resemblance to the Arabian, has a much larger amount of Arabian blood than is apparent because of continuing infusions of Thoroughbred blood, especially in Quarter Horse racing stock.

All breeds to which the Arabian has contributed, whether in America or around the world, have received some of its refinement, speed, endurance, and spirit. In the new breeds, Arabian type frequently is masked due to a low degree of Arabian blood or to selective breeding for different traits of type.

HALF-ARABIANS

A Half-Arabian is the result of mating a purebred Arabian with a horse of any other breed or type. Half-Arabians can be registered with the International Arabian Horse Association (IAHA) and

An Appaloosa Half-Arabian, Sanpete Sourdough ("Sardo").
Photo courtesy of Sherry Parker, Rancho Costa Lotta, Bakersfield, Calif.

ond, the registered Half-Arabian is eligible to compete in Half-Arabian classes at Arabian horse shows. Registration also provides a record of the Half-Arabian's pedigree, verifies its age, helps identify the horse by its appearance, and makes it eligible for freeze-marking by the Arabian Horse Registry (see Chapter 11).

Half-Arabian registration certificates are issued by the International Arabian Horse Association (IAHA), which also keeps breeding records and transfers certificates when Half-Arabians are sold. Current applications and fee schedules can be requested from IAHA (see "Other Sources of Information").

The registration application must be signed by the owners of the Half-Arabian's sire and dam at the time of breeding and by its dam's owner when

shown in Half-Arabian classes at Arabian horse shows, as well as competing in open classes and shows.

Norm Dunn, head of the Arabian Horse Department at California State Polytechnic University at Pomona, calls the Half-Arabian "The Arabian's biggest competition." The Half-Arabian can do anything the purebred Arabian can do and sometimes does it better because the Half-Arabian may inherit a specific performance ability from the other breed. An Arabian-Saddlebred cross may have higher action for English classes, for example, and an Arabian-Quarter Horse cross may be a superior stock horse.

In the past, purebred Arabians were scarce and very expensive. The Half-Arabian, which was more common and therefore less expensive, often was called "a steppingstone to owning a purebred Arabian." Today, some people prefer Half-Arabians because they combine the best points of two breeds.

Why Register a Half-Arabian?

Although the Half-Arabian does not belong to a *breed*, in the true meaning of the word (because it can have the type of any breed), several reasons exist for registering it. First, a registered horse is worth more than a grade (unregistered) horse. Sec-

Half-Arabians come in all sizes and colors. This is Pandemonium Angel, a registered Pinto Half-Arabian who has 89 percent Arabian blood. She is owned by Ronald and Fay Robar, Angel Acres Pintos of Whitefield, New Hampshire. *Sandra Hugus photo*

the Half-Arabian was foaled. When the application is received, IAHA verifies that one parent is a registered Arabian, and the Half-Arabian's amount of Arabian blood is recorded. The percentage of Arabian blood appears on the registration certificate, under the registration number. Half-Arabian registration numbers begin with an "A" to differentiate them from purebred registration numbers. A number in front of the "A" indicates the number of crosses to purebred Arabians in the Half-Arabian's pedigree.

No matter how much Arabian blood a Half-Arabian has, it is *never* given purebred status. A purebred Arabian can only result from the mating of two registered purebred Arabians.

To be eligible for registration as a Half-Arabian, one of the horse's parents must be a purebred Arabian horse registered by the Arabian Horse Registry of America or the Canadian Arabian Horse Registry. A foal produced by mating two registered Half-Arabians cannot be registered. A foal sired by a registered Half-Arabian stallion can be registered only if its dam is a registered purebred Arabian. For this reason, Half-Arabian colts usually are gelded.

Unlike its purebred relatives, the registered Half-Arabian can be *any* color. If a "colorful" Half-Arabian meets the registration requirements of a color breed (Pinto, Palomino, Buckskin, etc.), it can be cross-registered in both the Half-Arabian registry and the color breed registry. Cross-registered Half-Arabians can be shown at open shows, Arabian shows, and at shows limited to the color breed. Half-Arabian classes at Arabian shows are limited to mares and geldings, but Half-Arabian stallions can be shown in classes at shows for their color breed.

Other Part-Bred Breed Registries

The Half-Arabian Registry is the largest registry for part-bred horses. However, registries also exist for Half-Thoroughbreds and Half-Saddlebreds. The most recent part-bred registry is the National Show

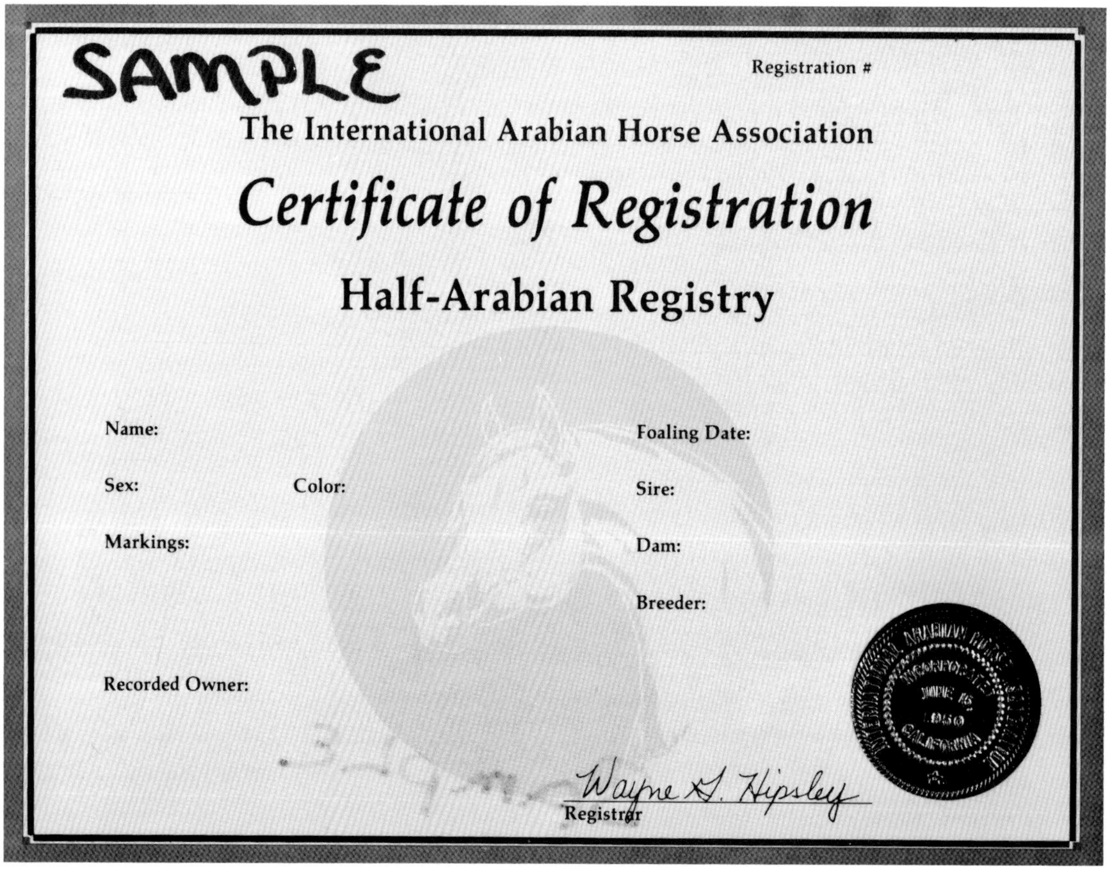

SAMPLE

Registration #

The International Arabian Horse Association

Certificate of Registration

Half-Arabian Registry

Name:

Sex: Color:

Markings:

Recorded Owner:

Foaling Date:

Sire:

Dam:

Breeder:

Wayne L. Hipsley
Registrar

The Half-Arabian registration certificate, issued by the International Arabian Horse Association. Registered horses may compete at shows and other functions sponsored by IAHA.

Horse Registry, which is based on Arabian-Saddlebred crosses from specific bloodlines.

To be eligible for registration as a National Show Horse, a horse must be out of a registered Arabian, Saddlebred, or National Show Horse mare and sired by a stallion whose owner has nominated it with the National Show Horse Registry. (At present, the sire nomination fee is $6,000.) The National Show Horse Registry sponsors special show competitions for the horses it registers, awarding large monetary prizes to the winners and sires. (To be shown at IAHA-approved Arabian horse shows, National Show Horses also must be registered as Half-Arabians. At IAHA-sanctioned shows, National Show Horses compete in the Half-Arabian division against all types of registered Half-Arabian horses.) For more information, contact: National Show Horse Registry, 10401 Linn Station Rd., Suite 237, Louisville, Kentucky 40223; (502) 423-1902.

Morab horses are a cross between the Arabian and Morgan breeds. Like both their Arabian and Morgan relatives, Morabs are versatile riding and driving horses. For more information, contact: North American Morab Horse Association, W3173 Faro Springs Road, Hilbert, Wis. 54129.

Half-Arabian Conformation and Type

Unlike purebred Arabian halter classes, which are judged first on Arabian type, the greatest emphasis in Half-Arabian halter classes is on *conformation* (body structure). Whereas type varies considerably in Half-Arabians (because their "other half" can come from any breed), the rules of conformation are the same for all breeds. No Half-Arabian show horse is supposed to be discriminated against for having type characteristics of another breed. However, a Half-Arabian halter horse with excellent conformation and Arabian type should place higher than an equally correct Half-Arabian that lacks Arabian type.

Although the Half-Arabian that looks like a purebred may have a slight advantage at Arabian shows, it may be at a disadvantage in open shows, depending upon the breed preferences of the judge.

Breeding Half-Arabians

The breeder of Half-Arabians should follow the same rules as the breeder of purebreds, with slightly more emphasis on producing excellent conforma-

tion and less emphasis upon Arabian type. As in breeding purebred Arabians, a superior mare should be bred to a high quality stallion.

Adding the Arabian
by Sue Pettit
(reprinted courtesy of IAHA)

Each breed has its strong points:
Saddler struts, of course.
But add the blood of the Arab
And you get a better horse.

And Shetland's cute and playful,
Though headstrong in addition,
So add Arabian blood
And you add the disposition.

The Quarter Horse is a worker
And capable at his duty,
But if you add the Arab
You get a working beauty.

The Thoroughbred has speed
And runs with self-assurance
But adding Arabian blood
Increases the endurance.

The "Just Horse" may be anything,
From pet to strong wage-earner,
But make him part Arabian
And you've a Registered Hay-Burner.

Anglo-Arab, Morab,
Just Half, or a larger Fraction:
It's still the Arabian blood
That puts you in the action.

Yes, each breed has its strong points,
And its fans who will endorse.
But it's always the Half-Arabian
That is the better horse!

Most often, the registered Arabian parent is the stallion because Arabian mares usually are reserved for producing purebred offspring. The Half-Arabian from a total outcross (mating a purebred Arabian to a horse of another breed) is most likely to resemble its more inbred parent, usually the Arabian. However, a mating of unrelated horses provides more possible combinations of inherited traits, making the result of an outcross breeding less predictable than the result of mating related horses (inbreeding).

Half-Arabians can inherit Combined Immunodeficiency, (CID) a lethal genetic weakness found in the Arabian breed, if both parents carry the recessive gene that causes the problem. Before breeding your mare to an Arabian stallion, be sure he hasn't produced any foals that have died of CID (see Chapter 20).

Cost of Breeding Half-Arabians

It costs as much to produce a Half-Arabian as a purebred Arabian. The costs of board, veterinary care, transporting the mare to and from the breeding farm, and maintaining her until the foal is weaned are the same. However, the purchase price of a grade or Half-Arabian broodmare may be less than that of a purebred Arabian mare. The stud fee to breed a grade, Half-Arabian, or mare of another breed is

often half the fee charged to breed a purebred Arabian mare to the same stallion. However, some owners charge the same fee for *all* mares because the risks and services required are the same.

Magazine advertisements in Arabian horse publications often indicate whether mares that are not purebred Arabians will be accepted for breeding to specific stallions. If the stud fee is shown as "$1,000/$500" it means that the fee is $1,000 for purebred Arabian mares and $500 for others.

Marci Schmidt on Caliente Babe, a Half-Arabian endurance horse.

"Half-Arabian, all-around horse." Jeannie Thompson of Kremmling, Colorado, pole bends on Puden, a Half-Arabian sired by Ramly.

ANGLO-ARABIANS

The Anglo-Arabian is a combination of Arabian and Thoroughbred blood. Anglo-Arabians are registered by the International Arabian Horse Association, which can supply fee schedules and application forms for registration.

To be eligible for registration, the Anglo-Arabian must result from the mating of:

- A Thoroughbred stallion and an Arabian or Anglo-Arabian mare;
- An Arabian stallion and a Thoroughbred or Anglo-Arabian mare;
- Two registered Anglo-Arabians;
- An Anglo-Arabian stallion and an Arabian or Thoroughbred mare.

Only horses whose parents are registered by the Anglo-Arabian Horse Registry (if Anglo-Arabian), the Arabian Horse Registry of America or the Canadian Arabian Horse Registry (if Arabian), or the Jockey Club (if Thoroughbred) are eligible for registration as Anglo-Arabians. In addition, they must not have less than 25 percent nor more than 75 percent Arabian blood.

Breeding Anglo-Arabians

The blood percentage restriction complicates breeding. If the resulting foal has either too much or too little Arabian blood, it is not eligible for registration as an Anglo-Arabian. If it has too little Arabian blood, it's ineligible for registration in any registry. With "too much" Arabian blood, the foal can be registered as Half-Arabian instead of as an Anglo-Arabian. In other respects, the rules of breeding Arabians or Half-Arabians apply. The Anglo should be a good representative of both the Arabian and the Thoroughbred breeds.

What the Anglo-Arabian Can Do

Thoroughbred blood adds size and speed to the Arabian while Arabian blood adds beauty, endurance, soundness, and disposition to the Thoroughbred. Other than racing, Anglo-Arabians can do anything that Thoroughbreds can do, and they also compete at Arabian shows in Half-Arabian classes. Their show record is remarkable considering that there are far fewer registered Anglos than Half-Arabians. Anglo-Arabians especially seem to excel in dressage and jumping.

At the larger Arabian horse shows, the Half-Arabian classes are as varied and competitive as those for purebreds.

Arabian horses make good friends. Ryan Kumerow of Marshall, Minnesota, hugs
the stallion Torabim, a champion stock horse. *Bobbie Lieberman photo*

5

DISPOSITION AND SENSES

The typical Arabian horse thrives on human contact. The breed is gentle, affectionate, and easy to groom, shoe, vet, and train, and its loving disposition, coupled with its greater intelligence, makes the Arabian an ideal pleasure horse and sets it apart from other breeds. The Arabian's affection for people often is attributed to close contact between the desert horses and their Bedouin owners. Foals usually were weaned quite early and were totally dependent upon their owners for care and survival. Bedouin women and children usually raised the young horses, feeding them camel's milk.

Whatever the source of the Arabian horse's "people-oriented" nature, it has been said that they respond more like pet dogs than like other breeds of horses. Arabian horses are likely to nicker a greeting to their owner, to come when called, or to approach strangers in a pasture. They frequently become "one-person horses." They can grieve over the loss of a foal, an animal friend, or an owner with whom they shared a close bond.

The intelligence of the breed also is legendary. Arabians are quick to learn and willing to please. Many amateur owners train their own Arabians with little help or experience. Arabians are natural "trick horses," and by no coincidence many circus and movie horses have been Arabians.

The loyalty of the Arabian horse to its owner was legendary in the desert; a celebrated war mare would not leave her fallen rider. Today, this trait still is seen—if a rider takes a fall, the Arabian usually seems concerned and remains until remounted.

The breed's exceptional curiosity and alertness makes Arabian horses playful. Frequently, they become adept at opening stall and paddock gates, and once out, they often open gates for their less-clever friends. The first sight that greeted me at the old Rogers Ranch was the elderly stallion *Serafix—running and tossing an old tire! Many Arabians never outgrow a need to play.

WHAT IS A BAD DISPOSITION?

A horse with a bad disposition is sullen and aggressive, perhaps biting, kicking, or striking at people or other animals. He is unlikely to be a good show horse and will never be a pleasure to handle. A disposition can be less than ideal or typical of the breed without being truly "bad." An unfriendly Arabian horse shouldn't be labeled "bad tempered" unless he is actually mean. Bad dispositions usually result from neglect or cruelty. In such cases, a bad disposition often can be improved with patience and gentleness. However, some horses simply are bad-tempered from birth, and in those cases, disposition can *never* be improved.

Disposition is inherited just as surely as conformation, type, and color are inherited. *If the sire has a bad disposition, his foals are likely to inherit it.* If a sire's bad disposition resulted from improper handling, his foals will not be "born mean." However, they *may* inherit a tendency to develop a bad disposition from a sire who had the same tendency.

Foals soon exhibit their own personalities and attitudes
This is Raymoniet, courtesy of owner-photographer Karen Kasper, Almond, Wisconsin.

The mare's influence on her offspring is *both* genetic and environmental. Broodmares with bad dispositions usually produce bad-tempered foals. Foals copy their dams' behavior.

SENSES OF THE ARABIAN

The best rule in handling Arabian horses is to treat them with gentleness and patience, as an understanding parent would treat small children. Remember that they are sensitive and intelligent but do not expect them to always understand.

The senses of the Arabian horse may be sharper than those of *cold-blooded* horses (those lacking Arabian or Thoroughbred blood) and are always infinitely keener than our own. Understanding the Arabian's senses of sight, hearing, smell, and touch can help in anticipating the breed's reactions and result in more effective handling.

Sight

All horses have excellent side (peripheral) vision, but the placement of their eyes toward the sides of their heads makes it impossible for them to see directly in front of or behind themselves. Horses therefore are easily startled, if approached directly from the front or rear.

Arabians have broad foreheads and eyes that are set farther apart than the eyes of other breeds of horses.

According to a proverb in General E. Daumas' book, *Horses of the Sahara*, the Arabian horse protects his Bedouin rider from dangers behind them while the rider protects the horse from dangers ahead. This probably refers to the speed of the Arabian horse but may also allude to the horse's vision. The Arabian's prominent eyes are more widely spaced than those of more narrow-headed breeds, which improves the breed's side and rear vision but may slightly reduce his forward vision.

Horses may be partly color-blind, but they seem to distinguish primary colors. They also have excellent night vision, which helped their ancestors avoid night predators.

Because their eyes change focus slowly, all horses are easily startled by moving objects. Slow movements near the ground also recall the dangers of natural predators and may result in instinctive flight. The horse's best protection has always been speed.

The Arabian's alert ears are often in movement, rotating toward sound. In this case, the ears are back because the horse is paying attention to the rider.

Hearing

The Arabian's active ears rotate toward sounds, and can move together or separately. Horses can hear higher and lower tones than people. When a horse's ears are pricked forward, he may be listening to distant sounds. Loud noises may damage horses' hearing.

Arabians have acute senses of touch and smell. They also are famous for their intelligence and affection for people. *Don Sepulvado photo courtesy of Northwestern State University of Louisiana (N.S.U.)*

Smell

The Arabian horse's nostrils flare open wider than those of other breeds. A sharper sense of smell may accompany this increased intake of air. The horse also locates and determines the palatability of feed and water partly through its sense of smell. Horses also identify people and other animals by their characteristic, individual scents.

Sense of Touch

The nerves in the Arabian horse's thin skin transmit even slight sensations. Because of this he responds to light cues from a rider. While some cold bloods might require a kick to obtain speed, light leg pressure may obtain the same results from a more sensitive Arabian.

Arabians usually enjoy being scratched, petted, and groomed. Their heads are especially sensitive, so they should never be patted roughly on the face.

The Arabian horse's lips are thin and sensitive to touch, well adapted for sorting feed. He also examines strange objects by feeling them with his muzzle and lips. Long hairs on the muzzle of the

Most Arabians enjoy being petted and scratched. Breeder Cherylle Bumgarner scratches an itch for Za-Dear (Zajhar x Alure).

An unfriendly Arabian horse shouldn't be labeled "bad tempered" unless it is actually mean. This horse is just expressing displeasure at being taken from pasture.

unclipped horse help him judge distance to and between objects. Arabians often have "busy" lips, touching or biting objects to examine or play with them. This "busyness" results from the Arabian's intelligence, curiosity, and the agility of his sensitive lips.

SUMMARY

Know how your Arabian perceives the world and adapt your handling accordingly. Let him examine unfamiliar objects through his senses of sight, smell, and touch to determine that they are harmless.

Because all horses sense and react to fear or nervousness in the handler, assume a matter-of-fact manner when working around them. Move at a moderate pace; Arabians may be startled by movements that are too fast but become impatient if you are too slow in handling them.

The Arabian horse's senses are ultra-sharp. If an Arabian is fearful or excited for no apparent reason, it may be reacting to something that its senses can detect but yours cannot. Remember the story of the Bedouin's "listening mare" that instead of resting after a long journey stood gazing intently into the distance. To the amusement of the other Bedouins, her owner quickly mounted and left the camp. When an enemy tribe attacked the camp later that night, the sensitive mare—and her understanding owner—were safe.

Although spirited, most Arabians are easily handled. Shawnly McCoy leads El Khyam (U.S. National Champion Jumper, Canadian National Champion Hunter) from pasture to riding ring without benefit of halter or rope. Owner Judi Hook says that "Khy generally led Shawnly in!"

Girl 'Sees' Stallions with Hands
by Dixie Ryan
(reprinted courtesy The Arabian Horse Journal)

It wasn't on the program and few were privileged to witness it, but one event at the 1975 National Show at Albuquerque was probably more beautiful than all the rest.

It came during the stallion finals which were exciting to watch, with the animals all brilliant, stylish and full of fire. Each animal had that something special that only an Arabian stallion possesses. To the eye of spectators not familiar with the breed, the stallions might appear unmanageable.

Suddenly the class was over and the Top Ten horses placed. The National Champion was named, and then the ring was opened to spectators, enabling them to photograph, congratulate, or just admire.

In the midst of this excitement, a young Indian girl approached one of the stallions and asked the handler for permission to view the horse.

Permission given, she approached the animal. Onlookers caught their breath as she seemed to have no fear or show any caution in her movements. The handler (with an obvious expression of concern) looked on, as did many others, as the girl placed her hands on the stallion's mouth.

Her fingers worked with care, traveling up his face, around the eyes, ears, neck and on to his body...

It became immediately apparent to all that the lovely young lady was blind.

The true beauty in the scene was not only the obvious pleasure the young girl felt in what she "saw," but this very excited Arabian stallion suddenly stood completely still as if aware of what was taking place.

Even as the young hands traveled the entire body, even down the back legs, this superb representative of our breed took it all in stride.

The handler stood with tears streaming down his face.

Thanking the man sincerely, the young lady passed to another stallion and another and another. With each new horse came the same unusual but beautiful scene, the breathlessly excited animal with tail high and nostrils flared suddenly standing silent as the girl examined him.

Tears ran shamelessly down the faces of most anyone who watched the scene, and with each tear was a tremendous sense of pride... pride for these wonderful Arabians we own.

There was a thankfulness in our hearts that we can SEE the beauty, but most of all that we can own the greatest breed of all!

Never have I seen more beautiful Arabians in every sense of the word than I saw in Albuquerque on that October day.

The head is the hallmark of the Arabian breed. Ansata Ibn Sudan poses with his sire, *Ansata Ibn Halima. (Ansata Ibn Sudan was U.S. National Champion Stallion in 1971; *Ansata Ibn Halima was U.S. Top Ten Stallion for three years.)

Photo courtesy of Ansata Arabian Stud

6

TYPE

"...an Arabian without type and class is not worth breeding from."

—Lady Wentworth
The Authentic Arabian

WHAT IS TYPE?

Type is the combination of physical traits shared by members of a breed. The following is a description of *ideal* Arabian type. Seen from the side, the head is wedge-shaped (roughly triangular), widest at the cheeks and narrowest at the muzzle. The forehead is broad. In profile, the forehead bulges slightly above the eyes and there is a slight depression ("dish") in the facial bone below the eyes. The eyes are large, protruding, expressive, dark, set low and slightly toward the sides of the head. The hair surrounding the eyes and muzzle is thin, revealing black skin. The nostrils are large. The cheek bones are large and round, with a large space between the jawbones. Overall, the head looks "dry" (well-defined and bony, rather than fleshy).

The head meets the neck at a fine throatlatch and is set on at a wider angle than in other breeds, resulting in higher head carriage. (At speed, the horse's muzzle is thrust upward when the horse moves at liberty.) The neck is curved (arched), rather than triangular in shape, and is attached high on the chest.

The Arabian horse's croup is long and fairly level. The tail is set high and carried at about a 45-degree angle from the body when the horse is alert or moving. The body coat is fine and soft, and the mane and tail hairs are thick, long, fine, and silky.

Arabians that approach this description are called "typey," "extreme," "classic," or "exotic." It should be remembered, however, that few Arabians meet this description of ideal type since type varies, with no two horses exactly identical. Variation in type stems from differences in breeding stock and breeding programs. In the desert, families of Arabian horses differed slightly in appearance, just as they do today. However, in a group of horses, the Arabian should stand out because "he *looks like* an Arabian," being sufficiently typey to be marked as a member of the breed.

The Development of Arabian Type

Whether the Arabian's characteristic type resulted from adaptation to desert conditions or evolved separately before the breed ever reached that

43

part of the world is unknown. However, there is no argument that the features that set the Arabian horse apart from other breeds made it uniquely well-suited to the Bedouin's lifestyle and environment. Because the Bedouin's life made it necessary to breed primarily for strength and endurance, the beautiful Arabian type must have developed for practical (rather than aesthetic) reasons.

The "human eye." The Bedouins were said to prefer this white-rimmed eye, but modern breeders often dislike it because it contributes to a "wild" expression and may make the eye seem smaller. It does not affect the horse's vision and is common in some bloodlines.

Eyes — Typical of desert animals, which have large, bulging eyes, the early Arabian's prominent eyes helped protect it from predators by providing relatively good vision.

Forehead — The Arabian's broad forehead is said to account for its superior intelligence, but this is part of its myth since its brain capacity is no greater than that of other breeds. However, the Arabian's extremely broad forehead *does* provide more sinus space, which contributes to the breed's superior breathing capacity.

Nostrils — The Arabian horse's nostrils flare widely when it runs or is excited, allowing greater intake of oxygen. When at rest, the nostrils partly close, which may have evolved to reduce breathing of dust in a dry climate.

Jawbones — The extra-wide passage between the jawbones of the Arabian provides more room for its large windpipe—probably another adaptation to increase oxygen intake.

Head Carriage — The Arabian's natural head carriage is much higher than that of other breeds, especially when galloping. The Arabian's higher head carriage opens the breathing passage and, along with its expansive nostrils and large windpipe, allows

greater oxygen intake. (The Arabian also has more red blood cells than other breeds. This higher blood count may indicate that the Arabian uses oxygen more efficiently, for oxygen is carried throughout the body by the red blood cells.)

Skin — The black skin of the Arabian is apparent, due to the fineness or absence of hair around the eyes and muzzle. The exposed black skin around the eyes reduces glare from sunlight and reflection, and black skin is also better protected from sunburn. The thinner skin of the Arabian breed probably promotes fast evaporation of sweat to cool the horse more quickly.

Tail — The Arabian's characteristic elevated tail carriage also may enhance the body's cooling system in warm weather. In cold weather, the Arabian clamps its tail like other breeds to retain body heat. The tail's long hairs obviously supply an effective fly swatter.

Mane and Forelock — The mane and forelock usually are fine and long, which shelters the head and neck from direct sun without overheating them. A long forelock also protects the eyes from glare and dust.

Muzzle — The Arabian's small, tapered muzzle also may be a desert heritage. Small amounts of feed and infrequent eating may have gradually refined the muzzle to the "teacup" proportions admired today.

The Arabian's thin, active lips undoubtedly resulted from desert grazing. Bedouin horses were able to graze only sporadically, finding a few blades of grass in one spot and another bite elsewhere. Agile lips can quickly sort small grasses and herbs.

ARABIAN BONE STRUCTURE

It used to be widely believed that Arabian horses have only five lumbar (back) vertebrae instead of the six possessed by other breeds. This missing vertebra supposedly explained the Arabian's shorter back and resultant ability to carry heavier weights in proportion to its size.

Modern Arabian horse authorities like Gladys Brown Edwards, researcher and author, have pointed out that only some Arabians have five lumbar vertebrae while others possess the standard six vertebrae found in other breeds. To date, it is unknown which number of vertebrae is more common in Arabians, and there is no evidence that an Arabian having five vertebrae is more pure or desirable than one having six.

THE ARABIAN HEAD

The distinctive beauty of the Arabian head is one of the hallmarks of Arabian breed type. The profile of a "classic" Arabian head is characterized by two unique breed features: the *jibbah* and the *afnas*.

Jibbah

The *jibbah* is a bulge in the profile of the head. Ideally, this protrusion is above the eyes; a lower *jibbah* appears as a bulge between the eyes and may extend below them. Not all mature Arabians have a *jibbah*, but it is usually obvious in foals. The *jibbah* may result in slightly larger sinus capacity; it is apparently unrelated to the breed's superior intelligence, since the *jibbah* does not provide greater brain space, as was formerly believed.

Afnas

The *afnas* is the "dished face" for which the breed is known. This "dish" is a depression in the front bone of the head, between the eyes and nostrils; it appears as a concave curve in the profile of the head.

Although the *afnas* was admired by the Bedouin as a point of beauty, not all Bedouin horses had dished faces. Not all modern Arabians have a dished profile, either. However, even a straight profile gives

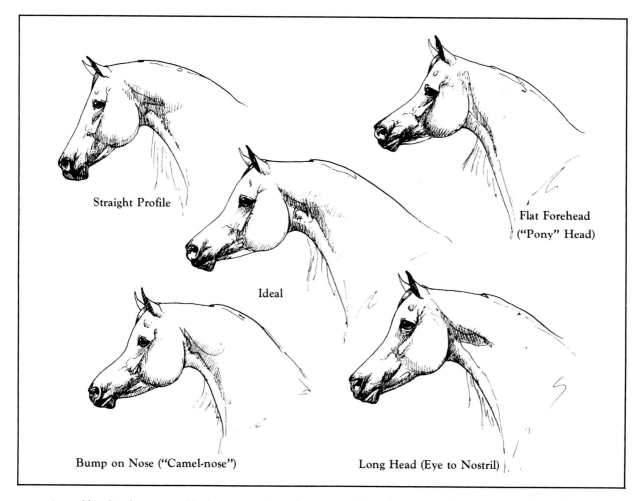

Straight Profile

Ideal

Flat Forehead ("Pony" Head)

Bump on Nose ("Camel-nose")

Long Head (Eye to Nostril)

A good head is characterized by large, prominent, low-set eyes; lack of meatiness; large nostrils; and well-shaped ears. Arabian heads may vary from the ideal but still be "good" heads; however, the more closely the head approaches ideal breed type, the better.

the impression of a slight dish when the nostrils are flared open.

In some Arabians, notably some of the Skowronek bloodlines, a convex "bump" appears on the lower part of the nasal bone, with a dish above it. This kind of profile is sometimes called a "camel nose." It, too, is characteristic of some Arabian horses and seldom seen in other breeds.

Most Arabians do *not* have the classic heads idealized in paintings. A head can be a "good head"—even if it lacks perfect Arabian type—provided that:

- eyes are large, prominent, set low and widely spaced;
- forehead is broad;
- nostrils are large;
- head looks refined and dry;
- general expression is alert, intelligent, spirited, and gentle.

Although many variations from the ideal exist, the more "typey" the Arabian's head, the better since a good Arabian must look like an Arabian and the head is a major point of Arabian type.

The "human eye," in which the white sclera is visible around the colored iris of the horse's eye, was fairly common in desert-bred Arabians. Wilfrid Blunt states, as quoted by Margaret Greeley in *Arabian Exodus*, that the human eye was not a sign of bad temper in Arabian horses and that it was even favored by the Bedouins. Many modern judges and breeders dislike the human eye and penalize Arabian horses having it, despite the fact that it is a trait that appears in certain valuable old Arabian bloodlines.

TAIL CARRIAGE

The Arabian's naturally high tail carriage results from the breed's unique bone structure. The first tail vertebrae, located inside the croup, slant slightly upward in the Arabian instead of being level or slanting downward as they do in other breeds. When the croup muscles tense because the horse is alert or moving, the tail vertebrae raise even higher, which further elevates the tail. Ideally, the tail should be carried at approximately a 45-degree angle from the hindquarters. The angle and height of tail carriage varies in individuals due to differences in conformation.

Wry tails

A tail that is carried to one side, instead of being held straight, is called "wry." Some wry tails deviate only slightly to one side while others are so extreme that the horses' tails touch their hindquarters.

The cause of the wry tail is a mystery. The bones under the croup *may* deviate to one side, causing the tail to be placed slightly off center. A wry tail also *might* result if the croup muscles of one side are stronger than those of the other side of the body.

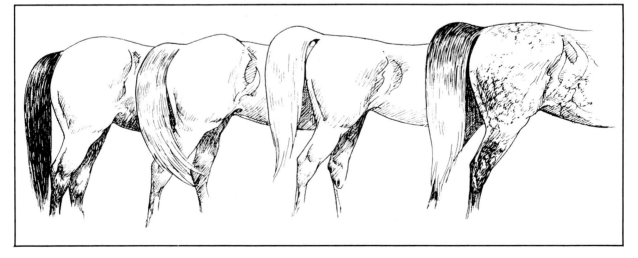

From left to right: an "apple rump" (rounded croup); rough coupling; a croup that slopes upward toward the tail; and the desirable long, level croup. Note all horses have strong hindquarters and long hips, varying only in the topline.

Wry tails were fairly common in early Arabian horses, and considered unimportant by the Bedouins. Today, wry tails are penalized in halter classes. Although wry tail carriage does not seem to affect performance, it is objected to because it detracts from the Arabian's beauty.

The only "cure" for wry tails is to eliminate wry-tailed Arabians from breeding. If that had been done previously, however, stallions like *Rijm and *Raseyn would have been eliminated, which would have been a great loss to the breed. Although wry tails *are* inherited, not all descendants of wry-tailed Arabians inherit them.

illegal. Thermography or other positive tests may soon be available to detect the use of ginger and enforce the "no ginger" rule.

Arabian horse owners and breeders should not allow the use of ginger for any purpose. The Arabian breed must not become dependent upon an artificial aid to produce the illusion of a trait that the breed should possess naturally. Natural tail carriage is inherited but, as trainer Tom McNair says, "ginger does not breed on!"

Besides giving a false impression of high tail carriage and, as a result, a more level topline, ginger causes the horse discomfort.

Naturally high tail carriage is one of the Arabian breed's most distinctive characteristics.
Patti Mack photo of Regal Bee courtesy of McKinstry Arabians, Craig, Colo.

Gingering

"Gingering" is a common unethical practice to artificially improve a horse's tail carriage. Ginger ointment inserted into the rectum creates a burning sensation, causing a horse to raise its tail. It is commonly done for professional photography. It also is sometimes done for showing although it is

REFINEMENT

"Refinement" and "coarseness" are used to contrast desirable and undesirable type. A refined Arabian with a dainty appearance is desirable. Refinement means lighter but proportionate bone, "dryness" or sharp definition of the muscles and tendons, and no excessive flesh on the head and legs. A coarse Arabian has heavy bone, chunky muscling, and looks "meaty" in the head and legs. Coarseness also may be used to describe a horse that lacks obvious Arabian type; especially one with a plain head.

TYPE VS. CONFORMATION

The American Horse Shows Association (AHSA) Rule Book, which contains the specifications for judging Arabian horses, lists type before conformation in the halter class specifications. This means that type receives greater emphasis in judging purebred Arabians at halter. This is because an Arabian horse lacking Arabian type cannot be a superior representative of the breed, even if the horse has outstanding conformation. This does not mean that the conformation of Arabian horses is irrelevant. Both type and conformation are important. Without type, you cannot have a good Arabian; without good conformation, you cannot have a good *horse*.

The Arabian's type results from centuries of development as a breed.
Forrest photo of Aulrab courtesy of Warren Park Stud, Sanger, California

A colt with an abundance of refinement. Zircon Nazeer winning at the Ascot, England national championship show, 1985.

Type varies by breed, but conformation is the same in all breeds. All good horses have good conformation. (This is the Arabian stallion Hai Karatie.)

Photo courtesy of Alpine Arabian Stud, Tucson, Ariz.

7

CONFORMATION

"Anatomy is destiny."

—Sigmund Freud

Conformation is the horse's body structure, determined by the length, angle, density, and size of each bone. Bones both support and move the body.

Early horsemen realized that conformation affected both soundness and performing ability. By comparing the conformation of horses that performed well and remained sound with that of horses that lacked athletic ability or became unsound, they learned which kinds of conformation were desirable and which were faulty.

If a horse's body parts are in proper proportion to each other, the horse is "well balanced." Balance can be accurately judged only in mature horses, because young horses grow into and out of balance many times before reaching their mature height.

W. R. Brown, in *The Horse of the Desert*, stated that Bedouins considered a horse balanced if it could drink from a ground-level stream without bending either foreleg. Generally speaking, a horse is properly proportioned—well-balanced—if the body divides into fairly equal thirds from the side view: one-third forehand, one-third back, one-third hindquarter. Ideally, the body and legs also should fit into an imaginary square. Many Arabians are slightly long in the body, which is fortunately less serious than if the legs are too long in proportion to the length of the body. If the imaginary square is taller than it is wide, the legs are too long for the body. If the square is wider than it is tall, the body is too long for the legs.

JUDGING CONFORMATION

To evaluate a horse's conformation, it must be studied from the side, front, and rear views. Balance and overall conformation are best determined from the side view.

Body—Side View

Neck — The neck should be long, arched, and attached at the top part of the chest. It should be long for good flexibility and balance, and taper so that it is thinnest at the throatlatch.

Faults: 1) neck attached too low on the chest; 2) triangle-shaped neck; 3) thick throatlatch; 4) too-

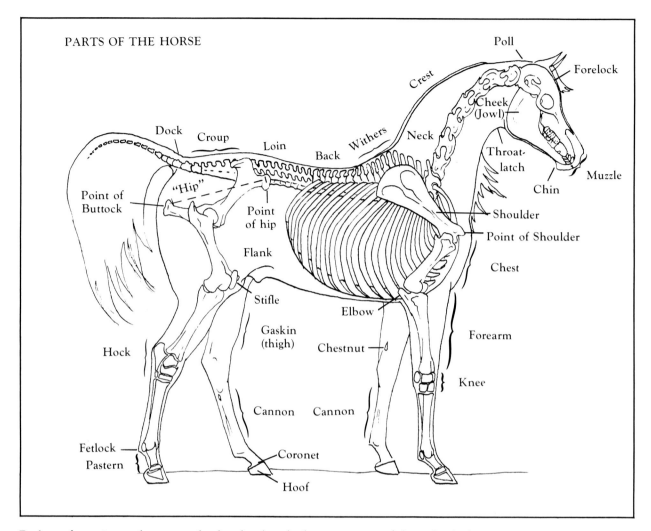

PARTS OF THE HORSE

Poll
Forelock
Crest
Cheek (Jowl)
Neck
Withers
Back
Loin
Croup
Dock
Throat-latch
Chin
Muzzle
Shoulder
Point of Shoulder
Chest
"Hip"
Point of Buttock
Point of hip
Flank
Stifle
Elbow
Forearm
Gaskin (thigh)
Chestnut
Knee
Hock
Cannon
Cannon
Fetlock
Pastern
Coronet
Hoof

Both conformation and type are closely related to the bone structure of the individual.

short neck; 5) ewe neck (looks "upside down" because it's heavier underneath than at the top).

Shoulder — The shoulder should be long and slope back toward the withers at an approximate 45-degree angle. This allows good extension of fore-legs, resulting in a long stride, and helps the shoulder absorb concussion well.

The shoulder's slope depends upon the length and angle of the scapula (shoulder blade), which starts below the withers and slants downward and toward the chest. The true angle may be difficult to judge because the bone is covered by muscle and fat. The angle of the shoulder is not *always* the same as that from the point of the withers to the point of the shoulder.

Faults: short, upright shoulders result in a short stride and greater risk of concussion-related lameness.

Withers — The withers should be wide and well-muscled, and at least as high as the horse's croup. Prominent (high) withers help hold a saddle in place and allow free shoulder action.

Faults: mutton withers are low and rounded. They make it difficult to keep a saddle in place and are related to low action in the forehand.

Back — The back should be short for strength and weight-carrying ability.

Faults: 1) sway back; 2) arched (roached) back; 3) too-long back, which reduces agility and is weak, causing a tendency to swing the body sideways instead of moving straight forward; 4) too-short back creates a tendency to overreach.

Loin — The loin connects the back and the croup. It should be broad, muscular, short, and blend smoothly into the rest of the topline.

The Arabian's neck should be arched (curved, rather than triangular in shape) and set on high, like the neck of the horse at the right. Faults include, at the left, a ewe neck ("upside down neck") and, in the middle, a straight (not arched) neck.

The body of the well-balanced horse is approximately one-third forehand, one-third back, and one-third hindquarters.
Photo of *Podsnejnik courtesy of Karho Farms, Scottsdale, Ariz. and Warren Arabians, Tomball, Tex.

Faults: 1) too long in the loin; 2) loin lower than the front part of the croup, causing horse to be "rough-coupled." Both faults indicate weakness and lack of weight-carrying ability.

Croup — A long, broad, muscular croup increases length of stride and ability to carry weight. The croup should be relatively level and no higher than the withers.

Faults: 1) short croup; 2) steep (very sloping) croup; 3) too-level croup—*only a fault if the level croup is echoed by a hip that is too level. If the horse's hind legs are set properly under the body, the hip is correct and a level croup is not detrimental. If the hindlegs are set too far to the rear, the horse is faulty. If the hindleg stride is shortened due to matching hip and croup angles that are too horizontal, the horse should be faulted.* The level croup may not always be linked to a level hip—it may also be due to the bone structure of the tail vertebrae underlying the croup itself.

Hip — The "hip" is judged from the point of the hip to the point of the buttock. Technically, the hip is part of the pelvis, but the term "hip" is commonly understood to mean this angle. The hip should be long to provide a long stride in the hind legs.

Faults: 1) too-short hip; 2) too-level (horizontal) hip. Both faults shorten the hind stride and contribute to concussion-related injury.

Topline — The topline is the top outline of the horse's back, loin, and croup. These should blend smoothly and be fairly level, with the back slightly lower than the croup.

Faults: 1) back and croup absolutely level with each other; 2) loin or back too long; 3) rough-coupled (back and loin do not join smoothly).

Underline — The underline is the lower outline of the body. The horse should be "deep through the heart" (behind the withers, where the saddle girth fits) and fairly deep through the flank. The underline should be longer than the back and loin portion of the topline.

Faults: 1) shallow heartgirth; 2) "wasp-waisted" or tucked up in the flank area. The first fault reduces lung and heart capacity, and the second leaves less room for the digestive organs.

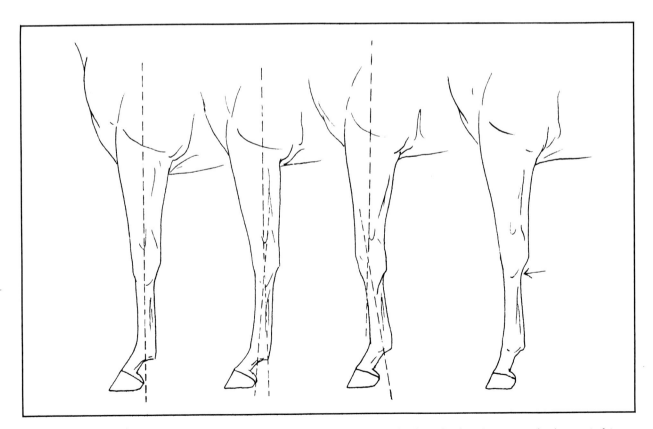

Forelegs, side view. Left to right: ideal placement of forelegs; calf knees (back at the knee); over at the knee; tied in at the knee, upright pastern.

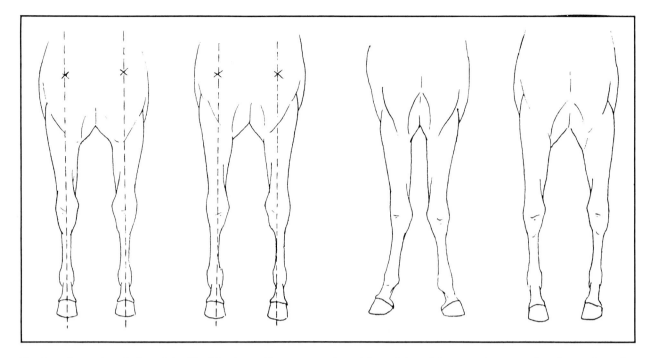

Forelegs, front view. Left to right: ideal forelegs; offset cannons (bench knees); knock knees and toes out; bow legs and toes in.

Forelegs—Side View

More of the horse's body weight is supported by the forelegs than the hind legs, with the forelegs carrying about 65 percent of the total weight. This added weight increases the chance of unsoundness in the front legs, especially if their conformation is faulty.

Forearm — The forearm should be long and well-muscled, for endurance and a long stride.

Faults: 1) undermuscled forearm (cannot lift and extend the forelegs); 2) short forearm (has a short stride).

Cannon Bone — The cannons should look short, flat, and dry (the tendon at the back should be sharply defined).

Faults: 1) fleshy cannon bones—if the cannons look "round" they are either too fleshy or the tendons are not well defined; 2) "tied in at the knee"—the back of the legs look "pinched in" just below the knee because the cannon bone is much smaller than the bone above the knee; 3) calf knees—the cannon bone slants forward from the knee to the fetlock, giving the impression that the front of the cannon bone *curves* forward toward the pastern. Calf knees are a serious fault because they stress the knees at the back of the joint, opposite the normal direction of bend; 4) "over in the knee,"

the opposite of calf knees, is caused by the forearm being farther forward than the cannon bone. This stresses the front of the foreleg but is less serious than calf knees because the leg is stressed in the direction it normally bends.

Pasterns — The pasterns should be long and well-sloped to absorb concussion, but not so long and sloping that they are weak (soft). Their size should be proportionate to the rest of the leg and the horse's body. They should be in harmony with the shoulder angle.

Faults: 1) upright pasterns; 2) too-short pasterns; 3) too-long pasterns.

Proper Placement of the Forelegs

If the front leg is attached to the body at the proper place, an imaginary vertical line drawn from the point of the shoulder will evenly divide the leg into two halves and meet the ground at the back of the hoof. Proper placement of the forelegs under the horse's body allows the horse's weight to be distributed in an even line down through the column of leg bones.

If the leg is set too far under the body, too much weight is thrown to the front part of the horse's leg. If the leg is set too far forward, too much weight is carried by the rear part of the horse's leg. Unequal distribution of the horse's weight causes uneven stress on the leg bones, which can lead to injury.

Front View — Seen from the front, the forearm, knee, and cannon bone should form a straight column. The cannon bones should look narrow, and the knees, wide and well-defined. The pasterns should be straight and the hoofs should point straight ahead.

Faults: 1) wide (round) cannon bones; 2) round, meaty-looking knees; 3) toeing in or toeing out; 4) offset cannon bones (the knee is located toward the inside of the foreleg instead of being centered above the cannon bone, resulting in bench knees that form a bulge at the inside of the foreleg). This fault predisposes the horse to unsoundness from concussion injuries because the leg bones do not form a straight column; 5) base-wide or base-narrow stance (the forelegs either set too close together or too far apart).

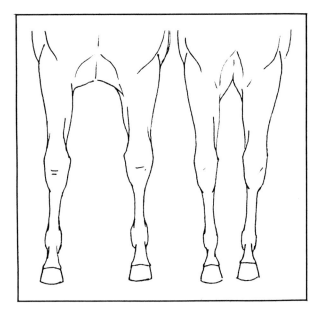

Forelegs, front view. Left: base wide. Right: base narrow (stands close).

Hind Legs—Side View

The hind legs are the propelling force of the horse's body. How well the horse can raise and extend the hind legs depends upon their placement and alignment.

A long distance should separate the hock and the point of the hip. The stifle should be large-

jointed for free action. The gaskin (thigh) should be long and well-muscled but not so muscular as that of a Quarter Horse. The Arabian's longer muscles promote endurance and flexion of the hind leg. The cannon bone of the hind legs should look flat, and short in comparison to the upper part of the hind legs. The hind cannon bones always are longer than those of the forelegs.

The hocks should be large, clean, and smooth looking. From the side view, the hocks of the Arabian should have more angle than those of the Thoroughbred. This increased angle increases the Arabian's weight-carrying ability and endurance, while the Thoroughbred's upright hocks indicate speed.

Faults: 1) short gaskins (reduce stride and propulsion); 2) long cannon bones (add unnecessary weight and are weaker than short bones); 3) sickle hocks—the hocks have *too much* angle—the hind cannon bones appear to slant back toward the hocks instead of being vertical, and the front of the hock looks curved. (This curve resembles the curved blade of a sickle, hence the fault's name.) Sickle hocks are weak and prone to unsoundness; 4) post legged—the opposite of sickle hocks—the legs are too straight in the hock. Propulsion is reduced and there is a tendency to dislocate the stifle. Low action also results from insufficient flexion of the hind leg.

Rear View — The cannon bones of the hind legs should be parallel to each other, and perpendicular to the ground. From the rear view, they should appear thin.

Faults: 1) *extreme* toeing out. The hind legs *always* toe out slightly; in fact, it is a fault if the hind legs stand too straight); 2) cow hocks—the hocks slant inward toward each other instead of being vertical; 3) bowed hocks—the hocks angle slightly outward, rather than being vertical. Both cow hocks and bowed hocks weaken impulsion, reduce hind action, and can lead to unsoundness; 4) toeing in behind. Like extreme toeing out, it reduces the hind stride and may lead to concussion unsoundness.

COMMON CONFORMATION FAULTS OF THE ARABIAN

Conformation faults seen in many of the early Arabian breeding horses were cow hocks, sickle

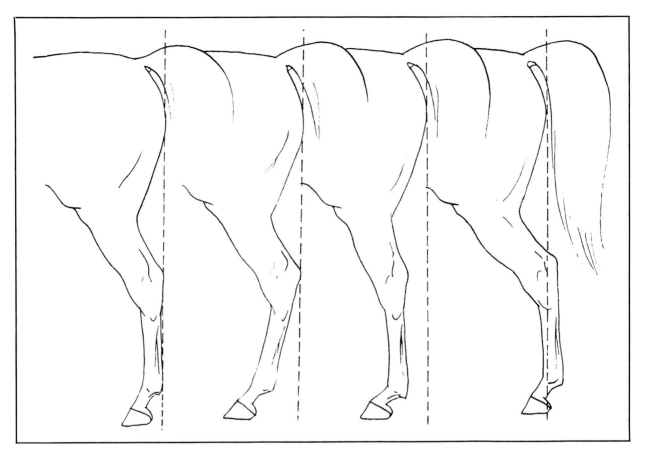

Hind legs, side view. Left to right: ideal hind legs; sickle hocks and stands under; post-legged and weak pastern ("coon-footed"), sickle hocks and stands camped out.

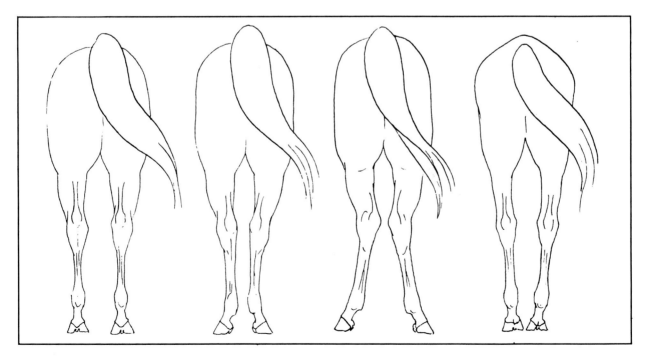

Hind legs, rear view. Left to right: ideal hind legs; hocks too close together and toes out; cow hocks; rafter hips, "cat hammed" (too lightly muscled in the hindquarters and thighs), and base narrow.

hocks, ewe necks, soft pasterns, standing under in the forelegs, and standing higher at the croup than at the withers. Today these faults still are seen but have become less common. Unfortunately, as these faults have been reduced, some "new" problems have become more frequent. Serious faults seen too often in modern show horses are calf knees and upright pasterns.

All conformation faults are inherited, but Arabians with calf knees seem quite prepotent for this particular fault. Because some popular breeding stallions have this fault, more and more Arabians of otherwise top quality exhibit the problem. A horse with calf knees should never be a halter champion and is a questionable choice for a breeding animal.

Upright pasterns not only result in a very bumpy ride because they cannot absorb concussion well but also can lead to incurable navicular disease. A horse with severe navicular becomes useless for performance. Allowing upright pasterns to become common in a breed always famous for its soundness would be unfortunate.

Faults That Go Together

When one part of a horse's body is faulty, related parts are automatically affected. Sometimes, a related part of the body partly compensates for the fault. At other times, one fault leads to another. Because of this, some conformation faults are frequently seen together. These include:

- low-set tail and sloping croup
- too level hip and too level croup
- upright shoulder and shallow heartgirth
- upright shoulder and upright pastern
- upright shoulder and foreleg set too far under the body
- upright shoulder and mutton withers
- short, thick neck and mutton withers
- higher behind and stands under in the forelegs
- cow hocks and sickle hocks
- low-set neck and triangle-shaped neck.

Although faults often appear together, they also can appear independently. Not every horse with cow hocks is also sickle-hocked, for example.

In this book, leg faults are illustrated in pairs. If one front foot toes out, both front feet toe out. Although legs sometimes share the same faults, one leg may be correct and the other may be faulty. Or, each leg may possess different faults. Only one foreleg may have an offset cannon bone, for example, while the other foreleg may toe in. There are too many possible combinations of conformation faults to illustrate them all here.

Relative Seriousness of Faults

The most serious conformation faults predispose a horse to injury or unsoundness. Less serious faults merely reduce athletic ability. The seriousness of a fault also depends upon its degree of deviation from the ideal. A slight deviation is less serious than an extreme deviation. Unfortunately, judges do not always agree upon "rules of relative seriousness." However, the following is offered as a general guideline. *If the faults are equal in degree:*

- Calf knees are worse than being over in the knees.
- Bowed hocks are worse than cow hocks.
- Toeing out is worse than toeing in.
- A short, sloping croup is worse than a long, sloping croup.
- A back that is too short is worse than one that is too long. (If too short, the horse will forge. See Chapter 8.)

IMPORTANCE OF CORRECTLY EVALUATING CONFORMATION

The breeding program that produced the desert-bred ancestors of our modern Arabian horses was totally practical. The Bedouins, although lacking the Europeans' knowledge of conformation, bred tough horses out of necessity.

Today, the show ring determines which Arabians are most valuable. Halter winners become breeding stock, and halter horses are selected on the basis of their beauty (type) and what they look like they should be able to do (conformation). Because today's Arabians are not tested under harsh conditions, their practical value as athletes must be based upon objective and accurate evaluation of their conformation.

UNSOUNDNESSES AND BLEMISHES OF THE LEGS

Unsoundnesses and blemishes can be caused by injury or strain. Faulty conformation predisposes the horse to develop blemishes or unsoundnesses although it is not *always* the cause.

When the hoof hits the ground, the column of leg bones strike each other, transferring the concussion upward through each leg bone in turn. If the leg is properly aligned, this concussion is transmitted through the middle of each bone. If one of the bones of the leg is not properly centered above the next, one side of it receives extra concussion. This extra force can strain muscles or tendons, or chip or break bones.

Unsoundnesses

An unsoundness is any illness or injury that impairs the horse's ability to perform as an athlete. Most unsoundnesses occur in the legs, which must support the weight of the horse and rider as well as propel the horse and control direction of movement.

Curb — A curb is a bump at the back of the hind leg, just below the point of the hock. Curbs result from inflammation and thickening of the plantar ligament. Not all curbs cause lameness, but because they are likely to, curbs generally are classified as unsoundnesses rather than blemishes.

Bone Spavin — A bone spavin is a *hard* bump in the hock joint (visible on the side of the hock). It is caused by excessive bone growth and can be treated only by rest and possibly surgery.

Ringbone — Ringbone is a bony enlargement on the pastern. It causes erosion of the joint cartilage and abnormal growth of bone in the pastern or coffin joint.

Osselets — Osselets first appear as swelling and heat in the fetlock joint, followed by excessive growth of bone in the joint capsule of the fetlock.

Blemishes

A blemish is a visible swelling, bump, or scar that does *not* affect the horse's soundness. Although unsightly, blemishes are not serious defects. If a blemish becomes worse and causes lameness, it is no longer just a blemish but an unsoundness.

Splint — A splint is a bony enlargement on the cannon bone. It occurs when the small splint bone is pulled away from the side of the cannon bone, and the area becomes inflamed. Splints can result from concussion or injury, such as a kick. Crooked legs predispose the horse to develop splints, which often are seen in horses with bench knees (offset cannon bones). A halter horse should be penalized for splints only if they are accompanied by defective leg conformation. Depending upon cause and degree of inflammation, splints can be temporary or permanent. If the splint causes lameness, it is no longer a blemish but an unsoundness. Splints located close to the knee are more likely to result in lameness than splints located lower on the cannon bone.

Bog Spavin — A bog spavin is a soft, fluid-filled swelling in the hock joint, visible at the side of the hock. It is caused by synovial fluid leaking into the joint capsule. Bog spavins usually are blemishes, for they seldom cause lameness. Bone spavins are usually much more serious.

Sidebones — Sidebones are excessive bone growth in the cartilages along the sides of the hoof and over the coronary band. Whether they are a blemish or an unsoundness depends, again, on whether they cause lameness.

Windpuffs — Windpuffs are soft, fluid-filled swollen areas in the fetlocks. They usually get smaller if the horse is rested and usually are not serious.

*Raging Bear.   *Anne Quinn photo courtesy of Fantasy Hill Arabians, Bakersfield, Calif.*

8

GAITS AND ACTION

Gaits are the various ways that a horse moves (kinds and speeds of movement). The Arabian is considered a three-gaited breed. In the show ring, it performs three gaits in performance classes—the walk, trot, and canter.

The *walk* is the slowest gait with four distinct hoofbeats. The *trot* is called a "diagonal gait" because each foreleg moves in unison with the opposite hind leg. The trot is a springy, two-beat gait. The *canter* has three distinct beats and is the Arabian's fastest show gait.

Although the Arabian is considered three-gaited, it also can gallop. However, the gallop (a four-beat gait) is not used in the show ring. The gallop is the horse's fastest gait and generally is reserved for racing and other speed events.

Some performance classes require a hand gallop, which is not a true gallop but an extended canter. It is characterized by a longer stride and less collection than the canter.

Some Arabians have a natural running walk ("single-foot") in addition to the standard gaits. This smooth, natural gait would be discouraged in Arabian show horses but is pleasant for pleasure riding. The Bedouins discouraged their horses from trotting by using pacing ropes, and at least *some* desert breeders may have selected their Arabian horses partly for a tendency to single-foot or rack. If so, the occasional modern Arabian with this trait may be a "throwback" to a smooth-gaited ancestor.

Arabians also can be trained to be five-gaited horses. The Naseem daughter *Kareyma (owned by Roger Selby in the 1930s) won blue ribbons in five-gaited classes, which feature the rack, a fast lateral gait. *Raseyn also was featured at the Kellogg Ranch shows as a five-gaited horse.

ACTION

"Action" describes the way a horse moves, and the trot is the best gait for evaluating action since faulty action becomes exaggerated and, therefore, more visible. Also, horses that trot well also move well at other gaits.

Like conformation, action should be evaluated from the front, rear, and side views.

Action—Side View

From the side view, the trot should be even and balanced. The diagonal foreleg and hind leg should be raised equally high and moved forward at the same time so that they remain parallel to each other. The length of stride of both diagonal legs should be equal.

Faults: 1) unequal diagonals may result from having shoulder and hip angles that are too different. Sometimes a horse has a "lazy leg" with a shorter stride than its diagonal partner; 2) lack of extension or lack of elevation of the forelegs can result from an upright shoulder or forelegs that are set too far toward the rear; 3) overreaching (forging) occurs if a foreleg is struck by the hoof of a hind leg; interfering occurs if the hoof of a foreleg strikes the other foreleg, or a hind leg's hoof strikes the opposite hind leg. Both overreaching and interfering can cause tripping and/or injury to the legs that are struck.

When a hind leg strikes a foreleg when the horse moves forward, it is called overreaching or forging.

Action—Front View

The action of the forelegs is best judged from the front view. As the horse trots toward a viewer the forelegs should move forward in a straight line. Only straight (correct) legs can have ideal, straight-forward action. Defects in conformation are proven—or revealed—by faulty action.

Faults: 1) winging is throwing the forelegs in an *inward* arc (toward each other). It is caused by forelegs that toe out. The seriousness of this fault depends upon the degree of toeing out and how much the legs swing inward at the trot; 2) *paddling* is throwing the forelegs in an *outward* arc (away from each other). It is caused by forelegs that toe in.

Paddling is less serious than winging because the paddling horse is less likely to interfere.

The horse that paddles or wings but appears to stand straight puzzles novices. Toeing in or out can begin as high as the elbow or as low as the pastern. Sometimes the horse toes in or out only from the pasterns down. Skillful hoof trimming over a period of time can help conceal toeing in or out, but the conformation defect is revealed when the horse's trot is seen from the front view. Such a horse invariably wings or paddles.

Other conformational faults are also reflected by action. The base-narrow horse that also toes out is more likely to interfere or stumble because his forelegs are closer together. The horse that is base narrow and toes in will be a "tightrope walker," placing one foreleg directly in front of its opposite as he moves forward. The horse that is base wide will sway sideways as weight is shifted from one foreleg to the other.

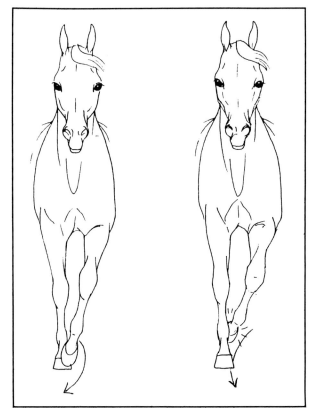

Left: "Rope walkers" paddle so much that they set down the hoof directly in front of the other front hoof. Right: Horses that wing excessively are more likely to interfere (strike the opposite foreleg when moving) than horses that paddle.

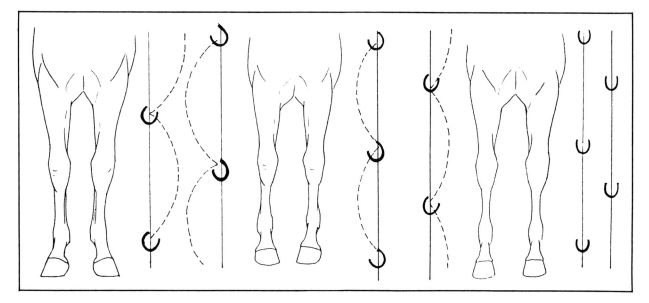

Action, front view. Left to right: Winging (the hoof arcs outward as the leg moves forward); paddling (hoof arcs inward); and ideal, straight forward ("true") action.

Left: Horses that toe out tend to wing when moving forward. Middle: Horses that toe in, paddle. Right: Only horses that stand straight (neither toe in nor out) can move their legs straight forward when in motion.

Action—Rear View

The action of the hind legs is best judged from the rear view. As the horse trots away from a viewer, the hind legs should move in a straight line but angled slightly away from the body. The hind legs should not move as straight forward as the forelegs because horses should naturally toe out slightly behind. As the hind legs move forward, the hocks should be steady and the stride long and powerful.

Faults: 1) cow hocks cause unnecessary sideways motion of the hindlegs and reduce forward stride; 2) bowed hocks wobble. This is one fault that is more apparent at the walk than at the trot; 3) base-wide hind legs are set too far apart, causing them to move straight forward, resulting in stiff action; 4) base-narrow hind legs may interfere. Horses whose hind legs are either base wide or base narrow (too far apart or too close together) lose both agility and propelling ability.

THE ARABIAN: A TROTTING BREED?

The Bedouins preferred the walk or gallop and discouraged trotting by hobbling their horses with

A nicely balanced trot under saddle. Note the extension of the opposite foreleg and hind leg and good flexion of knee and hock. This is Aurik.
Georgia Cheer photo courtesy of Warren Park Stud

pacing ropes. Desert-bred Arabian horses had to cover long distances with speed and endurance. High action (at any gait) was unnecessary.

When the Arabian horse became a superior endurance-ride mount, high trotting action also was unnecessary. In fact, a high trot reduces endurance because it 1) burns more energy; 2) reduces the length of stride, which reduces the amount of ground covered by each step; and 3) increases concussion to the legs, which increases the risk of unsoundness.

Arabian horses have been bred selectively for high-trotting action only in recent years as they have become more popular as show horses. When Park Horse classes became more popular, the desire for higher trotting action increased.

Kinds of Trotting Action

Two major kinds of action are seen in modern Arabian horses: 1) the high, bent-kneed, up-and-down trot and 2) the lower, straight-kneed, "striding" trot. Admirers of the first kind of action say it is correct because that is the way the "trotting breeds" (Saddlebred and Hackney) trot. Those who prefer the second kind of action (with more shoulder action and less flexion of the knees) argue that it is typically Arabian. The Arabian, they maintain, should not be "an imitation Saddlebred."

The Floating Trot — In *every* trot, an instant occurs when all four of the horse's legs are off the ground. This is the point when the horse may "float" at the trot—he springs into the air and seems to remain suspended above the ground for a moment, as though "floating" on air.

Any horse that is feeling energetic and proud will strut and display this floating action at the trot. (Witness the rodeo bucking horse who dumps his rider and proudly circles the arena with an energetic, floating trot!) However, the floating trot is commonly seen in Arabians, which normally exhibit this springy action and vitality.

The Effect of Conformation on Action

A horse's action depends upon his conformation. Thus, a horse's basic way of moving cannot be changed by training, although it can be enhanced.

Unfortunately, the details of bone structure that result in the bent-knee and straight-knee trots have not been identified. Perhaps the joints of the foreleg or shoulder are larger in some horses, allowing the forelegs more freedom of movement than in horses with less open joints. A scientific study of conformation related to action might reveal why action varies so much and finally prove which kind of trotting action is really best. Until then, the controversy will continue concerning just how the Arabian should trot.

For best absorption of concussion (and to reduce the chance of stumbling), *the horse's heel should strike the ground first.* If the toe comes down first on a rock or uneven spot, the pastern will bend forward instead of backward, throwing the horse's weight forward and possibly causing stumbling or a fall.

The *knee should be elevated sufficiently* for the kind of work being done. The hoofs must never scuff the ground.

Barnaby (*Bask x Alondraa), ridden by Tom McNair.
Johnny Johnston photo courtesy of the Barnaby Syndicate, Warren Arabians, Tomball, Texas.

Although halter horses are judged at the trot, the rule book does not specify whether the knee should be bent or straight, how high the knee should be raised, or how much the forelegs should be extended at the trot. The kind of trot desirable for performance classes varies according to class—the Park trot is undesirable in a hunter, and the Western jog isn't wanted in an English Pleasure horse.

Despite individual variation caused by conformation and kind of performance, certain factors always characterize a "good trot." One is *ease of movement.* The action should be smooth and natural for the horse. The gait should be *well-balanced,* with the diagonal foreleg and hind leg having equal length of stride.

Lady Wentworth described the Arabian's trot in *Authentic Arabian:*

"The action should be smart and free and darting from the shoulders, the forefeet dwelling a moment before touching the ground with a semi-floating dancing movement, which suggests treading on air and springs and recalls a deer trotting in fern. The hock action powerful, and the hocks well raised and brought forwards with a swinging stride. The knee action is rather higher perhaps than that of the Thoroughbred, but it is the shoulder action which matters."

Grey horses are born chestnut, bay, brown, or black and turn grey (white) as they mature. There are many greys in the Arabian breed, and many people picture a white (grey) horse when they hear the words "Arabian horse." This is champion KJ Karaff.

Photo courtesy of Laurence Arabians

9

COLOR AND MARKINGS

No typical, or best, Arabian color exists. Pure-bred Arabians can be any shade of grey, bay, or chestnut. Blacks and roans also occur occasionally and while browns are sometimes seen, they are registered as bay.

The Bedouins superstitiously attributed certain traits (speed, endurance, spirit, etc.) to various body colors, but the traits assigned to each color varied from tribe to tribe. And, although Lady Wentworth accused the Prophet Mohammed of inflicting his color preferences upon his followers, she did the same thing when she stated that Crabbet's best horses were chestnuts and greys. What she didn't say was that Crabbet's chestnut Arabians usually were related to Mesaoud and its greys to Skowronek—two outstanding sires!

Each Arabian horse should be judged on its own merits. As the proverb states, "A good horse is never a bad color." And, it should be added, a pretty color cannot make up for faulty type or conformation.

BASIC COLORS

Grey — When most people hear the words "Arabian horse," they visualize a grey or white horse. This probably results from having seen grey

Arabians in art and movies. There *are* many greys in the breed now, possibly because of the widespread influence of Skowronek, Lady Wentworth's grey stallion.

The "grey" Arabian may be born bay, chestnut, brown, or black, greying as it matures. The greying process usually begins first on the head, then the neck and body, with the body coat growing lighter with seasonal shedding and new growth of hair. Dark horses, especially bays, often keep black points (mane, tail and legs) before turning completely grey.

A few Arabians become white by the age of five, but most don't reach this stage until they are much older. Grey horses often become "fleabitten" instead of pure white, with colored hairs scattered throughout the grey coat. The fleabitten hairs are the original color of the coat (usually chestnut).

The rare "bloody shoulder" marking—the shoulder or hindquarter appears stained red—also occasionally occurs in grey Arabians.

Rose grey and *bay grey* describe young, greying horses who still have some of their original coat color mixed in with the grey hairs.

Rose grey is a transitional shade between chestnut and grey and is called rose because of its pink tinge. Bay grey is a transitional shade between bay

All grey horses are born dark and become lighter as they mature. "Rose grey" is a term for a chestnut horse that is turning grey. Zircon Nazeer winning his class at Ascot, England, 1985.

Some greys become "fleabitten" with specks of chestnut, bay or black (depending upon their original coat color). This is Lady Fair (Tripoli x Dharebah).
Charles Craver photo courtesy of Craver Farms, Hillview, Illinois.

Most "white" Arabians were born another color and turned white with age. MS Czarthan 044054 is a rare exception—he was white at birth.
Photo courtesy of Cheryl Demers

and grey and is less pink. The bay grey also has a black mane and tail and black on its legs.

Aged grey Arabians may be milk white, but they are registered as grey. Generally, white horses are born a dark color and lighten with age.

White Arabians — Aged grey Arabians may be milk white, but they are registered as grey. Generally, white horses are born a dark color and lighten with age.

A *few* rare Arabians apparently have been born white. On one of the Blunts' desert trips, Lady Anne awoke to find a *white* foal sharing her pillow. For a while, the Arabian Horse Registry of America allowed a few Arabians to be registered as white, but now any true whites must be registered as grey. A true white has a white coat and dark eyes. Its skin may be mottled rather than solid black. This fact may be linked somehow to the unusual white foal color. However, the white Arabian cannot be albino (have pink body skin and blue or pink eyes).

Chestnuts sometimes have flaxen (blonde) manes and tails. The Bedouins were said to dislike horses with dark coats and white manes and tails, but modern breeders often admire this flashy coloring.

Bay — Bays vary from a light gold to a dark reddish-brown, but they always have black "points" (black mane, tail, and legs). The height of the black on the legs may vary, but it usually extends at least to the knees and hocks.

"Black bay" describes a dark bay or dark brown horse whose coat also contains black hairs. However, it is not a true black because it has tan or brown hairs on its flank or muzzle.

The *brown* horse has a solid brown body, legs, mane, and tail. The Registry does not differentiate between brown and bay, registering brown Arabians as bay, a genetically related color. However, a few Arabians (including the Blunts' Queen of Sheba and

The mane, tail and legs of a chestnut horse are the same color as (or lighter than) its body coat. Pictured in the rain at the 1985 Ascot show is Ralvon Elijah, British National Champion.

The bay color can be distinguished from chestnut by the presence of black "points" (the bay's mane, tail and lower legs are black).
Photo of Lotus courtesy of Craver Farms, Hillview, Ill.

Chestnut — Chestnut consists of various shades of red, including pale (washy) chestnut, liver (chocolate) chestnut and all shades between. However, the legs of the chestnut horse always must match his body color or be slightly lighter. If the legs have black points, the horse is bay instead of chestnut. The chestnut's mane and tail also must match the body color or be lighter. If the mane and tail are black, the horse is bay instead of chestnut.

Davenport's stallion *Haleb, both imported from the desert) are true browns, lacking black points.

Black — Black Arabians are rare and seem limited to certain bloodlines. Some Bedouin tribes treasured the rare black horses while others apparently considered them impure.

Blacks vary from a smokey shade to a true, deep black. If the horse has *any* brown or tan hairs, usually apparent on the flank or muzzle, it isn't black—

The black stallion Cass Ole, ridden by Franny Cuello, was a champion Western Pleasure and Ladies Side Saddle show horse before becoming "The Black Stallion" in films. (In the movies, Cass Ole's white markings were concealed by make-up.)

Photo by Michelle, courtesy of San Antonio Arabians, Inc.

it's *bay.* Sunlight can bleach true black to a dark brown shade with red highlights, so many blacks are blanketed to preserve their rare color.

Roan — The Arabian Horse Registry of America registers an Arabian as roan only if it has an equal mixture of white and solid-color hairs over its body. Because the color is rare in purebred Arabians, color photographs are required when the registration application is submitted. A bay or chestnut Arabian with a sparse sprinkling of white roaning throughout the body coat or only at the base of the tail or the flank is not registered as roan.

Roans are either chestnut roans (red roans) or bay roans (blue roans). There is no such thing as a grey roan although greys sometimes are mistakenly called roans. Roan is a separate color that cannot turn grey as the horse ages. However, the degree of roaning changes with seasonal shedding. The easiest way to tell a roan from a grey is by its head—the head of the roan horse is darker than its body while the head of a horse turning grey is lighter than its body color.

FOAL COAT COLORS

It can be difficult to determine a horse's eventual color by the foal coat, so waiting until the original baby hair is shed is sometimes necessary.

Bay Foal Coat — The bay foal varies from light fawn to dark brown. The legs and muzzle are beige. The legs often have a smokey undercoat with a silver sheen. The mane and tail are darker usually than the body, but the black points don't appear until the foal coat is shed.

Chestnut Foal Coat — Chestnut foals have unpigmented (pinkish) hoofs. The skin around the eyes of the newborn chestnut foal also is pink. The mane and tail are the same shade as the body or lighter. If they're darker than the body coat, the foal is probably bay.

Grey Foal Coat — Grey foals are born grey, chestnut, bay, or black and turn grey with seasonal growth of hair. *A foal cannot be grey unless at least one parent is a grey.* The best clue that a foal will turn grey are grey (silver or white) hairs around the eyes or at the base of the tail. Some foals are born with grey hairs scattered throughout the coat, but others have no grey until they are much older. The muzzles and legs of a grey foal usually are darker than those of foals that will remain their original birth color. Black foals usually turn grey.

Black Foal Coat — The foal that will darken into black is an even, light charcoal with a silvery sheen (from a smokey undercoat like that seen on the legs of bay foals).

MARKINGS

White areas on the face and legs are called "markings." The Registry has carefully charted the locations of the various markings and guidelines appear on the current registration applications. (Markings for Half-Arabians should be described for registration purposes, in the same way as those of purebreds.)

Facial Markings

Star — The star is the most common facial marking in Arabians. It is any white spot on the forehead, from the bottom of the ears to the bottom of the eyes. The star may appear as a single white mark or be connected to a strip.

Strip — A strip is a *narrow* white mark located anywhere between the bottom of the eyes and the top of the nostrils. The strip may appear by itself or be connected to a star. Although a strip that starts above the bottom of the eyes is often called a "blaze," it is correctly described as "a star and connected strip." If the strip begins below the bottom of the eyes, it is just called "a strip."

Blaze — A blaze is a *wide* white mark on the face, starting below the eyes and *covering both nasal bones* at each side of the face. If the mark starts above the bottom of the eyes, it is correctly called "a star and connected blaze." If it begins below the bottom of the eyes, it is simply "a blaze."

Snip — A snip is *any white mark on the muzzle*, between the top and bottom of the nostrils. If it is part of a narrow white mark down the face (from above the bottom of the eyes), the marking is correctly called "a connected star, strip, and snip." If the snip isn't connected to any other white, it is simply "a snip."

Leg Markings

Stocking — A stocking is a white mark extending from the hoof to above the middle of the cannon bone.

Sock — Socks are shorter than stockings, extending from the hoof to at least the top of the fetlock, but no higher than just below the middle of the cannon bone.

Fetlock — A white fetlock describes a marking that reaches above the pastern but below the top of the fetlock joint.

Pastern — A white pastern is a mark found anywhere from more than one inch above the coronary band (just above the hoof) to the bottom of the fetlock joint.

Coronet — This is the smallest leg marking. It extends no more than one inch above the coronary band.

Problems Associated with White Markings

The Bedouins favored white markings for superstitious reasons as well as for beauty. However, certain problems are associated with them.

The horse's skin is black under the body coat, but pink under white markings. Thus, a grey has black skin except where it originally had white markings. The pink skin can be seen when white markings are wet or if the hair has been clipped quite short. Pink skin, which results from lack of pigment, is more sensitive—and thus subject to irritation—than black skin. This means that skin under white markings is more vulnerable.

Problems arise from two sources: sunburn (usually seen on the face) and "scratches" (an irritation of the skin of the legs). Scratches is a skin problem caused by dampness; it is aggravated by dirt and bacteria. It appears as a crusty sore on the legs, and white legs are affected more often than dark legs.

The Registry describes this marking as a star and connected strip. However, it is commonly referred to as a narrow blaze. *Photo courtesy of Craver Farms, Hillview, Ill.*

BODY SPOTS

Occasionally, purebred Arabian horses are born with spots. (All permanent spots should be described on the registration application, as they can help identify the horse.) Spots may occur as dark or light areas on a solid-colored body, or as white spots. Of these, white spots are most disliked. In the past, owners sometimes "cheated" by surgically removing or dying a white spot. Even today, a few breeders sell white-spotted foals without registration papers. These actions stem from the belief that purebred Arabians have no genes for spots and that white spots on the body are proof of impurity.

Spotted Ancestors

Apparently, the white spots that show up sporadically in purebred Arabian foals are throwbacks to some "spotted" ancestors. The Bedouins never allowed pintos to be crossbred with their purebred horses, but they did consider certain kinds of body spots in purebred Arabian horses to be good omens. For example, white markings behind the shoulders were called "wings" and thought to promise speed. There is no indication that Bedouin breeders ever discriminated against Arabian horses that had body spots, or that they considered the spots to indicate impurity.

Body spots and high white (markings above the knees or hocks). Some people dislike these flashy markings, but others find them attractive.

White Spots vs. Pintoism

Body-spotted Arabians seldom look like pintos. True pintos are characterized by large blotches of color distributed over the entire body while purebred Arabians with body spots usually have only one patch or spot of white under the body (belly spot) or a few, small round or oval spots on the side of the body or under the jaw.

Although the Pinto registry *has* registered some body-spotted purebred Arabians, Pinto breeders have been unable to produce a Pinto foal by mating two body-spotted Arabians to each other. The resulting foal is usually a solid color. They've had better luck producing Pinto foals by mating body-spotted Arabians to Pintos. However, it's impossible to tell whether body-spotted Arabians would have produced more Pinto offspring than solid-colored horses bred to the same Pintos.

White Spots and "High White"

Stockings over the knee, especially if combined with a wide blaze, are called "high white." In the 1950s and 1960s, such markings were discriminated against. Although Arabians with high white or spots were not denied registration, such markings were officially ruled "permissable but not desirable" in breeding stock. This statement was removed from the rule book during the 1970s.

High white and body spots usually are thought to be genetically related. However, they don't always occur together.

Bloodlines that Carry Body Spots

Body-spotted foals have been sired by prominent stallions of virtually *all* Arabian bloodlines and nationalities. However, such foals sometimes are sold quietly instead of being shown or advertised. White spots definitely are traceable to some of the Abbas Pasha I Arabians, usually through Crabbet bloodlines. The white spots that sometimes cropped up in the Crabbet horses were attributed by Lady Wentworth to an ancestor of Mesaoud. Mesaoud was one of Crabbet's most successful sires, and his influence particularly permeated the Crabbet mare lines, which were then crossed with the sirelines of such stallions as Skowronek. It may be quickly seen that many of the world's best Arabians carry some of the Mesaoud blood.

Aziz, sire of Mesaoud, traced to one of the "particolored" Arabian mares of Abbas Pasha I, who was reputed to own the best and purest desert-bred Arabian mares of his time. The Blunts, who selected Mesaoud, were known for their determination to use only purebred Arabian breeding stock. There is, therefore, no reason to question the purity of this line of Arabians on the basis of body spots.

This dark bay (commonly called "black bay") has a large star and two visible white fetlocks.
Photo of Schaun courtesy of North Forty Arabians, Kremmling, Colo.

Some believe that body spots result from a recessive gene. If this is true, the characteristic is transmitted by *both* the sire and dam. However, recessive traits do not "breed true" in every generation, appearing only randomly. If body spotting is a recessive trait, concealing a spotted foal or selling it without papers will not insure against future throwbacks in the same family.

While color and markings affect the horse's beauty, they cannot alter its conformation and type. A superior Arabian with extra white markings should not be discarded, and a spot-free Arabian of poor quality is not an asset to the breed.

Evaluating an immature horse is difficult. The young Arabian's personality, disposition, conformation, type, action and athletic ability offer clues as to how it will look and perform at maturity.

10

BUYING AN ARABIAN

Unfortunately, horses are not priced like cars. There is no "blue book" to give a pricing guideline, and basically *a horse's value is determined by what a buyer will pay and by what a seller will accept.*

Many people have the mistaken impression that *all* Arabian horses are expensive. This idea comes from the well-publicized record prices paid at some auctions for Arabian show and breeding stock. However, the average Arabian horse can be bought as reasonably as purebred horses of other breeds. The Arabian horse selection is greater than ever before, and almost anyone can find an Arabian horse to meet particular needs and price range.

Depending upon wants and needs, a buyer can spend either a lot of money or just a little for a purebred Arabian. The price depends on many factors, including the quality of the individual horse and the market demand for that kind of horse.

SHOPPING FOR AN ARABIAN

The keys to successful shopping are (1) knowledge and (2) patience. Take time to study the market. Know what kinds of Arabians are available, and what prices they are bringing. It's up to the buyer to become familiar with bloodlines, type, and conformation. A good shopper must be able to spot a good Arabian—or a bad one.

Age

An Arabian under the age of five is still maturing; a horse fifteen or older is called "aged." A horse is in its prime between the ages of five and twelve years. It usually is better trained and less flighty than a younger horse but still has a long useful life ahead.

There are some advantages in buying a young, growing horse. An owner has more control over its development through careful feeding, deworming, vet care, and training. However, it is difficult to predict how a young horse will mature (the younger the horse, the harder it is to evaluate what it will look like when it is mature). A young Arabian also should not be ridden before it is *at least* 2½-years old. In the meantime, all the expenses of keeping a horse remain. In fact, it can be more expensive to maintain a growing horse than a mature one, due to higher feed costs.

Arabians usually live and remain active longer than horses of other breeds. A healthy Arabian should live to be *at least* twenty years old, and many survive into their early thirties. Longevity varies according to family, but stress colic sometimes kills show horses prematurely. Other serious illnesses or accidents may also shorten life span. Old horses are nearing the end of their useful life and often develop health problems and need special care. However, they often are good "babysitters" for children and novices. Wise old show horses can "teach" new exhibitors. Elderly broodmares may still produce excellent foals but tend to have more breeding and foaling problems than younger mares.

Buying a Foal or Yearling

It is difficult to predict exactly how a young, still-growing Arabian will look when mature, for young horses quickly pass through different growth stages. One week, the young Arabian's neck may appear to be long; the next, it may look short. The true proportions of the horse's body cannot be evaluated until growth is complete.

A young (yearling to three-year-old) Arabian that looks like a mature, well-balanced horse will continue to develop bulk as it matures. A refined three-year-old may develop heavier bone and muscling by the time it is five or six years old. For this reason, an immature Arabian should look slightly long-legged and gawky. As the horse matures, it will usually fill out and lose this appearance.

Many yearlings and two-year olds are higher at the croup than at the withers. The horse's hind end usually grows taller first, then its withers catch up; this growth pattern usually alternates until the horse is finally mature and even in height at withers and croup. However, some mature Arabians are higher at the croup. Whether the young horse is likely to remain higher behind depends upon its bloodlines; if this fault is apparent in some of its mature relatives, it may be shared by the individual.

The young horse's back continues growing in length after the horse has reached its full height. For this reason, a short-backed yearling to three-year-old may gain more length in the back and loin by the time it matures. When an immature Arabian is quite long in the back and loin, its back will be too long when the horse is mature.

As horses grow, bone angles usually change less than bone length. Bench knees or a low-set neck, which are related to bone angles, will not improve with growth. However, a short hip can increase in length. Some young horses whose necks and hips are long at maturity may pass through growth stages when their necks and hips appear short, due to faster growth of other body parts. Whether an individual's neck and hip will be long or short at maturity depends upon its particular genetic programming.

Since all traits are inherited, the best clue to the horse's mature appearance is provided by the type and conformation of its mature relatives; faults and strengths are often shared by family members.

A young horse's aptitude for various tasks may be recognized at an early age. Some horses are more athletic and coordinated than others, depending upon conformation. The immature horse's attitude and personality also indicate its later potential for performance. Intelligence and disposition, which affect later trainability, can be accurately judged in foals and yearlings. The horse's attitude also indicates its possible later use—a calm foal that doesn't spook may eventually be suitable as a Trail Horse; a more spirited foal may be more suited to show classes requiring a more energetic performance.

Before buying, it is wise to have a veterinarian examine the horse for soundness and good health.

Sex

The horse's sex affects its temperament and performance. Powerful sex hormones influence the behavior of stallions. Although many Arabian stallions are gentler than stallions of other breeds, they still require special facilities and special handling, and it is difficult to find boarding facilities for them. Stallions aren't for most beginners, and there is no advantage to owning a stallion except for breeding.

Mares can be used and enjoyed by novices, but open mares come into heat about every twenty-one days and stay in heat for about a week. During the heat period, they often are nervous and difficult to handle. If used for breeding, a mare may not be available for showing or riding. If she is sent to an outside stallion to be bred, she may be gone for several months. A mare in late pregnancy cannot do hard work, and having a foal at side makes it difficult to ride the mare until the foal is weaned.

Unlike mares and stallions, geldings usually are calmer because they are not subject to hormone rushes. This means that they may be more consistent performers. Because they also are usually less expensive than mares and stallions, geldings are the best choice for most uses.

Training

Professional training is expensive, with present costs averaging $250.00 per month and top show trainers commanding much more. A trained horse is therefore usually cheaper in terms of time and money required for training, although an untrained horse may be priced lower.

If you buy a young, untrained horse, choose one with a suitable temperament and conformation for your desired use. If possible, choose one from a family of horses that has produced successful performers in that activity.

Whether to hire a professional or train your own horse depends upon your own experience and skill, and the purpose for which the horse will be trained. It is possible for an amateur to train a horse for pleasure riding, but preparing a show horse for national competition requires more expertise than most amateurs possess.

PRICE RANGE OF ARABIAN HORSES

Arabian horses of average quality often sell for $500 to $5,000. Many well-trained purebred geldings are available from $700 to $2,000. These prices compare favorably with prices of other breeds. In fact, it's often possible to buy a purebred Arabian gelding for less than a Quarter Horse gelding of equal quality. Of course, you will *probably* not find a champion show gelding for only $2,000. Price usually is related to a horse's success in shows or another area of performance.

At the top of the scale, a high-selling Arabian breeding and show horse may sell at public auction for $500,000 or more. The top-selling Arabian stallion sold privately (to date) reportedly brought about $3,000,000; however, the price was not advertised.

The $500,000 Arabian may be better or worse than its sale price would indicate. So may the $500 horse. Price is not a reliable indicator of the individual's quality. For this reason, knowledgeable shoppers sometimes discover very good Arabian horses at comparatively low prices.

An Arabian horse is a bargain when it will meet the buyer's needs and is available at a price that either reflects the horse's quality or is below the selling prices of similar Arabians. If the horse is poor quality, it isn't a bargain at *any* price.

Never buy an Arabian horse just because of its price. A high price is no guarantee of high quality, and a low price is not always a bargain.

Negotiating the Price

Some sellers are offended when offered a lower price for their horse than they are asking while others purposely overprice to allow for bargaining. If the asking price is reasonable and you can afford to pay it, it's probably best to do so. If you want the horse, but cannot afford the price, make a lower offer. Do this tactfully, explaining that the horse is undoubtedly worth the asking price but that you cannot afford to pay that much. If your offer is refused, shop until you find a different Arabian that will meet your needs at an affordable price.

There are also ways to "lower" the price without giving the seller less value. If you're buying a broodmare, the seller may accept a lower price if you promise a future foal (usually the first filly). Arabian horses are sometimes traded rather than sold, or valuable merchandise may be accepted for part of the sales price. Sometimes horse equipment, trailers or vehicles, art, jewelry, or even labor may be accepted instead of money. (If you're in business, consult a tax expert before bartering. Trades *may* be taxable as income.)

WHERE TO SHOP

When shopping for an Arabian or Half-Arabian, read the ads in Arabian horse magazines. Check both the display ads and the classifieds. Less expensive horses usually are advertised in classified ads, and more costly horses, in the large display ads, but this is not always the case. Call or write for more information about any horses that interest you.

Don't overlook local sources. If you can find a suitable horse locally, you will have less expense in transporting it. Contact local Arabian horse clubs and breeders and read the classified ads in your local newspapers.

Sales lists and posters of sale horses are sometimes found in feed and tack stores, and Arabian horses for sale often are found at Arabian horse shows. Lists of a breeder's sale horses often are also available at shows or directly from the breeder, by mail.

in finding good homes for their horses than in getting high prices. The care and training that a privately owned horse has received should be apparent.

The size of a breeding farm does not determine its quality. *Any* breeder may produce excellent Arabians and take good care of them, or the breeder may have a herd of neglected, poor quality horses.

Although a breeder's prices may be higher than those of an individual owner who doesn't raise horses for income, buying from a breeder offers advantages. You usually can compare the sale horse

Shopping for an Arabian at a breeding farm often allows you to evaluate the relatives of the sale horse. This can be an important consideration if you're buying breeding stock or purchasing an immature horse.

Sharon Vander Ende photo courtesy of Warren Park Stud

Whenever possible, see the horse before you buy it since photographs and pedigrees can be deceiving. If you cannot see the horse personally, have a knowledgeable person inspect the horse and report on its good and bad points. Be sure that your agent is a skilled horseperson who is familiar with Arabians, and someone who understands the kind of horse you want.

Buying Privately

Arabians can be purchased from individuals, training stables, or breeding farms. The person who just owns one or two pleasure horses may sell them for lower prices than someone in the business. Private owners also are sometimes more interested

with some of its relatives, which is a definite advantage when choosing breeding stock. The horse's relatives may indicate its own potential for breeding or showing. If the Arabian was bred by the farm that is selling it, you also can see what kind of care it has received from birth.

Buying a horse from a training stable also has some advantages. The horse usually has had professional training and already may have a show or performance record. Higher prices, however, may reflect those facts.

Buying at Auction

Arabian horses are sold through public consignment sales and private auctions. Arabians sold in all-breed consignment auctions often bring lower prices than those sold in all-Arabian consignment auctions. However, the horses frequently are of lower quality and sold without any guarantees.

At Arabian horse consignment auctions, the horses have been put in the sale by various owners. Consigners pay a fee plus a percentage of the sales price to the management of the auction. The horses usually are sold after a veterinary exam, and any health problems are announced. (The veterinarian does not evaluate type and conformation.) Fertility in breeding horses also is usually guaranteed with any known breeding problems announced.

Private, well-advertised auctions by "big breeders" often feature theatrical effects including spotlights. Flowers, music, food and beverages make the event a social, as well as financial, occasion. Such auctions are put on by a breeding farm and usually contain horses owned by that farm; some consignments may come from other invited breeders. A production sale consists mostly of young stock produced by the farm's breeding program although older mares and stallions may be included. A dispersal sale means that the breeding farm is going out of business and its breeding stock of all ages and sexes are being sold.

Arabian horse auctions usually are slower than other horse auctions; each "lot" auctioned is typically allowed between five and fifteen minutes in the ring. To create excitement and encourage higher prices, an especially desirable horse normally is the first animal auctioned. An auctioneer announces the horses and the bids; a pedigree reader describes bloodlines and shows records of the horses being sold; and ringmen watch for and relay bids to the auctioneer.

Auctions are exciting, and it's easy to get carried away by "auction fever." Use the same techniques in buying an Arabian at auction that you would if buying privately. Don't bid on a horse unless you've examined it carefully *in advance* and are reasonably sure it will meet your needs. Decide on a maximum price, and don't bid over that limit.

CASH SALES

If you pay the full price at the time of purchase, the seller will complete and sign the transfer of ownership on the back of the horse's registration certificate. Pay with a certified check so that the seller has no hesitation about transferring the horse's certificate. After completing the buyer's section of the certificate, mail the endorsed certificate to the Registry with the proper transfer fee, and a new certificate will be sent to you, showing your name as

Arabian auctions often feature special theatrical effects. Here trainer Leo Hansen presents Sezabask (*Bask x Sez Afnas) at his Main Attraction Sale in Scottsdale.

Sparagowski photo courtesy of Leo Hansen/The Main Attraction, Scottsdale, Arizona.

the recorded owner of the Arabian. If you're buying a Half-Arabian, the certificate and transfer fee is mailed to the International Arabian Horse Association instead of to the Arabian Horse Registry.

TIME PURCHASES

Arabian horses in all price ranges often are sold on time payments. If the seller is willing to "carry the papers," the horse may be advertised as being for sale "with terms available."

The actual terms can vary greatly. Many sellers require a specified percentage of the purchase price as a down payment. For example, a seller may ask for one-third down and the balance payable over a period of two years at a specified interest rate. The payments may be monthly, quarterly, semi-annual, or annual. Some sellers do not charge interest, but most professional breeders and trainers do.

If you buy a horse on time, get a written contract that clearly specifies all terms, conditions, and guarantees. The buyer usually pays an insurance premium on the horse until it is completely paid off, and the seller holds the horse's registration certificate until the last payment is received.

LEASING ARABIAN HORSES

Arabians of any age or sex can sometimes be leased instead of purchased. Leases usually cover breeding horses although show and pleasure horses also may be leased. The lessee usually pays to lease the horse for a specified purpose and time period; in effect, he is "renting" the horse.

Leasing Arabians for breeding is a very old practice. A form of it existed among the Bedouins; it wasn't unusual for a particularly desirable mare to be owned "on shares," with the share buyer paying in advance to receive one or more future foals.

Mare Leases

Mare leases allow the lessee to breed a purebred Arabian foal without the expense of buying a broodmare. The lease benefits the mare's owner because it saves the cost of maintaining the mare during the lease period and may include income. There are many variations in mare leases. The two most common are the cash lease and the every-other-foal lease. Under the terms of the first, a fee is paid to the owner, and the lessee usually maintains the mare and pays the costs of breeding and foaling; the resulting foal then belongs to the lessee. The "every-other-foal" lease requires no lease fee. Instead, the lessee assumes the costs of rebreeding the mare after the first foal is born; the second (unborn) foal becomes the property of the mare's owner, in payment for the first foal.

Stallion Leases

Stallions usually are leased for cash or a portion of stud fees, or both. Leasing a stallion may be less expensive than paying stud fees for several broodmares, and the mares do not have to be transported to a breeding farm since the lessee keeps the stallion during the lease period.

Performance Leases

A young show rider may lease an experienced show horse for a season or more of competition. (Leases are especially common with equitation mounts, which must be highly trained and can be very expensive.)

Sometimes less expensive Arabians are leased as 4-H projects or as temporary mounts. This can save maintenance costs during a time when the owner cannot use the horse but does not wish to sell.

Most leases require a monthly, quarterly, semi-annual, or annual cash payment. Others only require that the horse be maintained in good condition for a specified period of time with the lessee paying all costs.

EVALUATING SALE OR LEASE HORSES

It is easy to "fall in love with" a beautiful Arabian horse that won't meet your needs. Be careful that you don't become charmed by a weanling stallion prospect if what you really need is an older, well-trained gelding. See as many Arabians as possible before you make your choice, so you will know what kind of horses are available in your price range. When you go to see sale horses, take a knowledgeable horseperson with you if you lack confidence in your own judgement but be sure the individual is knowledgeable about Arabians.

If the horse is trained, having someone else ride it first will allow you to watch the horse under saddle. Then, if you will be riding the horse you buy, try it personally. Are the horse's gaits smooth? Does it have a soft mouth? Does it move freely? Do you feel comfortable on that particular horse? Is the horse willing or temperamental, lazy or nervous? Evaluate the horse's conformation and type very carefully. Be sure the horse can perform in the desired capacity.

When you have found the Arabian you want to buy, be sure that the horse passes a veterinary exam. If the horse doesn't pass, don't buy it. The buyer pays for the health examination, whether or not the horse passes. If it doesn't, paying for the exam will be cheaper than paying future veterinary bills. If buying a breeding horse, have the veterinarian verify that it is reproductively sound.

It is always wise to be cautious when buying or leasing *any* horse. Examine the horse's registration certificate before you buy. Sometimes a seller will advertise "an Arabian" for sale when the horse is actually a registered Half-Arabian, not realizing that there is a registry for partbreds. (Registration certificates for purebred Arabians are issued by the Arabian Horse Registry of America, Inc.; certificates for Half-Arabians, by the International Arabian Horse Association.) You cannot always identify a purebred Arabian by its appearance; some Half-Arabians *do* look like purebreds!

Examine the horse's registration certificate to be sure that the description matches the horse offered for sale. Check the horse's color, age, sex, and markings. A freeze-mark is also entered on the certificate, if the horse has been marked (see Chapter 11). Be sure that the owner's name shown on the face of the certificate is that of the person who signs the transfer of ownership on the back of the certificate.

Getting any guarantees about the purchased horse in writing may provide legal protection if the horse is misrepresented by the seller. Get a written guarantee of a breeding horse's fertility and, before buying an Arabian for breeding, determine whether any inherited lethal defects have occurred in the horse's immediate family (see Chapter 20).

You may wish to have a veterinarian draw blood for a Coggins test, making your purchase contingent upon a negative result. If the test is positive, the horse is a carrier of equine infectious anemia (EIA) and cannot be bred, shown, or even stabled with non-carriers (see Chapter 15).

If buying a pregnant Arabian mare, get a properly signed registration application for the unborn foal. If the mare will foal before she is registered in your name, a signed "Transfer for Eligible but Unregistered Foal" form will also be required to register her foal. It is best to obtain these signed forms at the time of purchase.

Be wary of buying any horse that supposedly "can be" registered, unless it is a foal and a proper "Transfer for Eligible but Unregistered Foal" form accompanies it. Registering an unregistered Arabian or Half-Arabian can be time-consuming, expensive, and difficult. If all records are not in order, the horse may be refused registration despite the seller's claim of its eligibility.

Transfer for Eligible but Unregistered Foal

Arabian Horse Registry of America, Inc.
3435 South Yosemite Street
Denver, Colorado 80231
303 750-5626

the Registry

All transfers of ownership must be recorded with the Registry. The recorded owner of the dam at the time of foaling may transfer an eligible but unregistered foal to another owner at the same time application for registration is made for the foal. To request this transaction, this form must be completed and returned to the Registry with the application for registration and the applicable transfer fee. **Any erasures or alterations on this form will require a separate letter or bill of sale signed by the seller confirming the facts.**

Seller Owner number: 902296

Recorded owner of the dam at the time of foaling: Sharon Byford

Dam name: Bint Arabian   Reg # 0000000

Date of foaling: Month 5 / Day 31 / Year 86

Date of sale: Month 6 / Day 15 / Year 86

I (we) certify that all information on this form is, to the best of my (our) knowledge, true and factual. I (we) do further hereby transfer and assign all right and title to this foal to the person(s) listed below.

Signature of recorded owner(s) of the dam at the time of foaling:

Sharon Byford   Date 6/15/86

Date

To be transferred to:

Buyer Owner number: (if applicable)

Name of new owner: I. M. Buyer

Address of new owner:

Street 1500 Main Street

City Anytown   State California   Zip 93000

Telephone (805) 555-1212

When buying a purebred foal before it has been registered, the buyer must get a signed Transfer for Eligible but Unregistered Foal form from the seller. The buyer then sends the completed form to the Registry along with the registration application and fee. The foal is then registered under the buyer's name.

The Arabian Horse Registry of America, Inc., is the official organization for registering purebred Arabians in the U.S. This is *Druch a champion halter and park stallion.
Photo courtesy of Locust Farms, Kirkland, Ohio

II

REGISTRATION AND TRANSFERS

The Arabian Horse Registry of America, Inc. exists to record and certify the purity of registered Arabian horses in America and to record their ownership. In addition, the Registry compiles and publishes stud books listing purebred Arabian horses registered by it.

The Registry is unique among United States horse breed registries, for it alone performs no "social" functions for the breed it represents—it does not conduct horse shows or promote the breed through literature and advertising. These functions belong to a totally separate organization, the International Arabian Horse Association (IAHA), which also registers Half-Arabians and Anglo-Arabian horses.

The Registry registered its first Arabian horse in 1908. By 1959, only 15,000 Arabian horses had been registered in the United States. By 1973, however, the number of Arabian horses registered since 1908 had risen to more than 100,000. Now, about 25,000 foals are registered annually, with over 300,000 total registrations. Of these, perhaps 250,000 horses are still living. The Registry has grown with the population of the breed. First organized in New York, the Registry later was established in Chicago. In the 1960s it moved to Denver, Colorado, where it currently employs more than sixty people.

SUBMITTING INFORMATION

Breeders are required to keep complete and accurate records and to provide them upon request to the Arabian Horse Registry of America, Inc. Failure to meet Registry regulations can result in the rejection of registration applications or transfers of horses owned by the rule breaker. In severe instances, existing registrations may be cancelled, making the horses' registration certificates invalid.

Throughout the life of a purebred Arabian horse, its owner is responsible for supplying various kinds of information to keep the Registry's records current. This information includes:

Stallion Report

Completed by the owner of the purebred Arabian breeding stallion, this form lists all purebred Arabian mares bred by the stallion during the breeding year (whether or not they conceived or were in foal at the time of the report) and the dates they were bred. The Stallion Report is due by January 31 for the previous breeding year, and the resulting foals cannot be registered unless the report is filed.

Registration Application

Completed by the owner of the Arabian foal. This form is accompanied by a signed "Transfer for an Eligible but Unregistered Foal" form if the owner of the foal does not own its dam.

Castration Report

Completed by the owner of the Arabian colt or stallion when and if the horse is gelded. This form accompanies the original registration certificate so that it can be reissued showing the correct sex. The Castration Report appears on the back of the current registration certificate; separate forms are also available because this information does not appear on older certificates.

Request for Blood Typing Form

At present, this form is required only for Arabian stallions used in breeding purebred Arabian mares. Stallions must be blood typed and the information recorded by the Registry before their foals can be eligible for registration.

Changes in Color, or Corrected Markings

Owners should report any coat color changes or needed corrections to the markings shown on the original registration certificates. Changes are submitted to the Registry with the original registration certificate so that a corrected certificate can be issued. Photographs verifying the changes are also required; the photos should show all white markings and front, side, and rear views of the horse.

Transfer of Ownership

When a purebred Arabian horse is sold, the seller signs the transfer of ownership on the back of the horse's registration certificate. The new owner is usually responsible for sending the certificate to the Registry with a transfer fee. The Registry records the change of ownership and issues another certificate showing the new owner's name.

Death Report

When an Arabian horse dies, the Death Report on the back of the current registration certificate should be completed and the certificate sent to the Registry for cancellation. (Separate forms are also available because this information does not appear on older certificates.) If requested, the unmarred cancelled certificate is returned to the owner. This final report to the Registry should not be overlooked; it completes the horse's record and prevents the possibility that the certificate could be fraudulently used to misrepresent a different horse.

Owner Authorizations

The recorded owner of an Arabian horse can authorize someone else to sign Registry forms concerning that horse for either a specified or indefinite time. Authorization is made by the owner on a special Registry form and revoked by written notice from the owner to the Registry.

Breeder Designation

Until 1986, the "breeder" of an Arabian horse (according to the Registry's records) was the recorded owner of its dam at the time she was bred to produce the horse in question. Now, that person can assign the title of breeder to whomever actually planned the mating (for example, the lessee or installment-payment buyer of a broodmare).

The owner of the dam at the time of service signs the Registry's "Assignment of Breeder Designation" form, which is submitted with the resultant foal's registration application. The person designated as breeder of the foal completes the "Breeder's Certificate" on the application form and will be shown as the breeder of that foal on all Registry records. (Assigning the title of breeder to another does not change the ownership of the foal. The first recorded owner of an Arabian horse is the person who owned its dam at the time the foal was born.)

SERVICES OF THE REGISTRY

Besides keeping records and issuing and transferring registration certificates, the Arabian Horse Registry of America helps guard the breed's purity through freeze marking and blood typing.

Freeze Marking

In 1972, Registry technicians began freeze marking registered Arabian and Half-Arabian horses upon request and payment of a fee. The freeze mark is a permanent, painless means of identification applied with extreme cold rather than extreme heat. This mark provides positive identification, which may be needed when horses are extremely similar in appearance (such as a group of otherwise unmarked grey mares that share a pasture). Freeze marking also increases the chance of recovering lost or stolen horses and may serve as a deterrent to thieves.

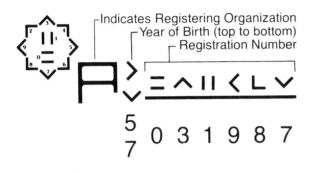

The freeze mark uses Dr. R. Keith Farrell's angle system (above, left) to indicate the year of birth and registration number of the horse. The large symbol at the left side of the freeze mark (a stylized "A") is used for purebreds; the same symbol on its side designates Half-Arabians.

Before a horse can be freeze marked, its original registration certificate must be available; the technician must enter the freeze mark on the certificate at the time of freeze marking. The freeze mark is a series of right angles representing letters and numbers. It shows the year that the horse was foaled, its registration number, and whether it is a purebred or Half-Arabian. The freeze mark is about two inches wide and seven inches long, and is placed on the horse's neck about midway between its poll and withers. The owner decides which side of the neck will be marked. For aesthetic reasons, the mark is usually placed under the mane. However, some prefer that it be put on the opposite side for greater visibility.

Applying the Mark — The freeze-marking iron is cooled in liquid nitrogen while the area where the brand will be applied is clipped and cleaned with alcohol. The iron is applied and held in place on the horse's neck. On horses that are chestnut, bay, or black, the iron is applied for about sixty seconds to destroy pigment in the hair. A few days after freeze marking, the outer layer of skin and hair peels

off. When the hair grows back, it is white where the mark was applied. Because white hair wouldn't be visible on a grey horse, the iron is applied to greys for about ninety seconds to destroy the hair follicles. The freeze mark can be read because the hair does not grow back where the iron was applied.

Foals can be freeze marked with a special, smaller iron. The freeze mark grows with the foal; when the foal is mature, its freeze mark will be the same size as the freeze mark applied to a mature horse. However, to be freeze marked, the foal must already be registered since the registration certificate must be presented before the mark is applied.

On horses of all colors except grey, the freeze mark appears white because hair pigment is destroyed by the cold marking iron. (When the horse has its winter coat, it may be necessary to clip the horse to read the mark.)

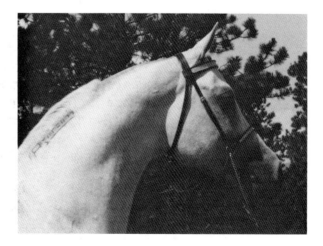

On greys, the freeze mark appears black because the hair is removed (the horse's skin is black).
Photo courtesy of Arabian Horse Registry

The Registry schedules freeze marking trips when there are sufficient requests from a geographical area. To expedite freeze marking, owners in an area sometimes designate a central location and trailer horses there to be freeze marked on a special "freeze marking day" authorized by the Registry. Technicians are also sometimes available to freeze mark horses at large Arabian shows and similar events.

Blood Typing

The Registry now requires that all Arabian stallions used for breeding purebred Arabian mares be blood typed before their foals can be registered. (Two years after the Arabian Registry began mandatory blood typing, it was also instituted by the Thoroughbred Jockey Club.)

Blood typing cannot prove that a particular horse is the parent of a specific foal. However, it can sometimes prove that the horse in question could not be the parent. It is possible to deduce parentage in about 90 percent of the cases when the blood characteristics of the foal are compared to those of its alleged parents. Blood typing can help establish parentage of a foal in case of an accidental breeding or if the Registry's "42-day rule" is broken by breeding a mare to two stallions within that period of time.

Blood typing can also be a tool to help identify a horse. If the blood type of a registered horse is known, it can be compared to that of a blood sample taken from the horse in question.

The Arabian Horse Society of Great Britain requires blood typing of all Arabian horses registered in England, and future mandatory blood typing of all Arabian horses in America is a possibility. If blood typing of foals were required, the Registry's computerized system could easily compare the blood types of a foal and its alleged parents upon application for registration.

Random Blood Sampling — Each year certain number of Arabian foals are randomly selected by the Registry for blood typing. Their blood types are then compared to the reported sire and dam to assist in verifying parentage. This helps prevent misrepresentation of parentage and provides a spot check for mix-ups. If the blood types of the foal and its reported parents are compatible, there is no charge to the foal's owner for the blood typing. The blood

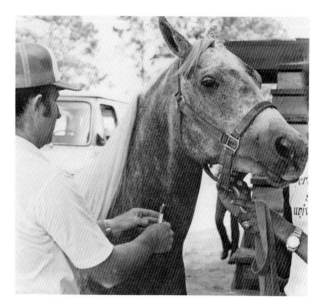

Blood typing helps verify parentage and prove identity. Typing is done by specific labs after a blood sample is taken by a veterinarian. *Don Sepulvado photo courtesy of NSU*

type of all foals sampled is recorded by the Registry for future reference.

The Blood Typing System — Upon payment of a one-time fee, a blood sampling kit is sent by the Registry to the stallion's owner. The kit contains instructions and materials for containing, labeling, and mailing the stallion's blood samples to the lab.

Blood to be used for blood typing must be drawn aseptically and protected from extreme temperatures. If it is contaminated or frozen, the sample cannot be used.

If utilized wisely, blood typing and freeze marking can help insure the present and future purity of the world's oldest breed.

REGISTERING ARABIAN HORSES

The front of the registration certificate of a purebred Arabian shows the horse's name, registration number, color, markings, and foaling date. It also lists the horse's breeder and its recorded owner, who are further identified by "owner numbers." Each ownership is assigned a permanent number which is shown on the certificate of each horse it owns.

At the top of the fold-over registration certificate is a four-generation pedigree that includes names, colors, and registration numbers. If the ancestor was not imported to America, the abbreviation for the foreign stud book in which it was registered is shown in front of the horse's name. (See Chapter 2, Table 1 for a list of the foreign stud books and their abbreviations.)

Just above the pedigree, the individual's markings are indicated on line drawings of a horse's head, legs, and body. Each side of the head and body is depicted, along with front, side, and rear views of the legs.

The back of the registration certificate has separate sections for transferring ownership and reporting the castration or death of the horse.

Like the Registry's other forms, the certificate of registration has undergone several style changes. A horse that has not been sold for many years may therefore have a valid registration certificate that looks different from the current form.

The original registration certificate should be kept in a safe place and a photocopy sent with the horse to shows, breeding farms, etc. If the original is lost, it is possible for the horse's recorded owner

to purchase a duplicate registration certificate. However, the loss of the original must first be proven to the satisfaction of the Registry.

The Registry's computer system contains many listings by subject for every registered Arabian horse. Although it is possible to locate an Arabian horse under several categories, it is easiest for the Registry to locate a horse under its registered name or number. Although the Registry will verify information found in its records, it will not release owner information, which is considered privileged material.

Each new application for registration is subjected to numerous automatic checks against the Registry's existing computerized records. In order to be approved, the application information must agree with all other Registry records. For example, the dam's record is checked to be sure that the breeding dates previously reported on the stallion report are compatible with the foaling date on the application.

When the information on the application agrees with existing records, the horse receives a registra-

REGISTRATION APPLICATION
ARABIAN HORSE STUD BOOK

the Registry

Arabian Horse Registry of America, Inc.
12000 Zuni Street
Westminster, Co 80234
(303) 450-4748

NAME   PLEASE PRINT IN INK

1st Choice	I b n A r a b i a n
2nd Choice	A r a b i a n s o n

Color (check one): ☐ Bay ☒ Black ☐ Chestnut ☐ Grey
Sex (check one): ☐ Mare ☒ Stallion
Date Foaled: Month 5 | Day 21 | Year 86

Sire of Foal: Arabian   AHR No. 0000000   Color (One Only) Bay

Dam of Foal: Bint   AHR No. 0000000   Color (One Only) Grey

I hereby certify that the above pedigree and particulars are correct to the best of my knowledge and belief.

Signature of recorded owner(s) of Dam at time of foaling: *Sharon Byford*   Date: Month 6 | Day 15 | Year 86

Address: 5200 Arabian Place, Mytown, Colorado 80459   Owner No. 0000000

BREEDER'S CERTIFICATE

I hereby certify that I owned the mare named: Bint   AHR No. 00000000

mentioned above at the time she was bred to the stallion mentioned above as the Sire of the foal for which registration is now requested.

Signature of recorded owner(s) of Dam at time of service: *Ex Too Owner*   Date: Month 5 | Day 30 | Year 86

Address: 615 Oats Drive, Anyplace, Arizona 85711   Owner No. 00000000

SERVICE CERTIFICATE

I certify that the stallion named: Arabian

AHR No. 0000000

Bred the mare named: Bint

AHR No. 0000000

BY:

Natural (Hand) Service Dates: 6/24, 6/26/ 6/28

Pasture Exposure From: To:

Artificial Insemination Dates:

} During the year 19 85

Signature of recorded owner(s) of Sire at time of service: *Mr. R. Expensive III*   Date: Month 6 | Day 3 | Year 86

Address: 9 Black Tent Way, Scottsdale, Arizona 85258   Owner No. 00000000

The completed application for registration form.

tion number, and a file is started for the newly registered Arabian. At the same time, the horse is added to the progeny records of its sire and dam and to the ownership record of its owner.

Applying for Registration

Submit the foal's registration application before it is six months old. The registration fee increases when the foal becomes six months old and rises again at twelve months of age. It is possible to register an Arabian after it is two years old, but it is expensive; the Registry currently charges a non-refundable $500 fee to consider late applications.

To get the foal's registration certificate quickly, submit it soon after the foal is born. Waiting until the end of the year results in a backlog of applications and slower processing.

Completing the Registration Application

Type or neatly *print* the application, using ink. After completing the form, verify all information on it, especially registration numbers, spelling, and dates. Be sure that all blocks have been completed. (Items most commonly omitted are markings and correct signatures.)

Name Choice — The application allows room for two name choices for the foal. The foal will be registered under your first choice, provided that no Arabian has ever been registered by the Arabian Horse Registry with that exact name. If the name has already been used, your horse will be registered using your second choice. If both names have been taken, you will be asked to choose another.

Name choices are limited to seventeen spaces and three words for each name. The seventeen spaces include letters and spaces between words. Numerical prefixes or suffixes, punctuation, diacritical marks, and "Jr." or "Sr." are not acceptable as parts of names.

Color — Enter only one color on the application. If the horse is "black bay," enter "bay." If it is turning grey, enter "grey" instead of the original foal color. Arabians must be registered as Grey, Bay, Chestnut, Black, or Roan. No other terms are acceptable.

Sex — Enter the foal's sex as "mare" or "stallion." If the foal already has been gelded, enter "stallion" but submit a completed Castration Report form (available from the Registry) along with the application. The original registration certificate will then show "gelding" rather than "stallion."

Markings — The horse's white markings must be accurately shown on the outline drawings of an Arabian horse provided for this purpose on the registration application. Using the foal as a model, copy its markings as accurately as possible. Never try to draw markings from memory.

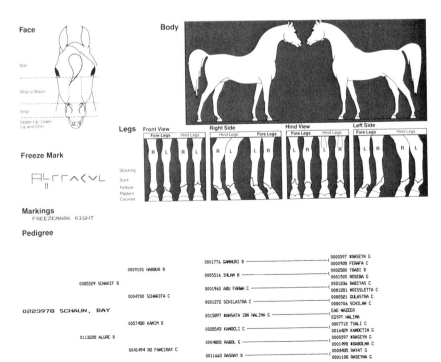

This side of the registration certificate details the horse's markings, pedigree, etc.

The registration certificate now used by the Arabian Horse Registry of America, Inc.

For accuracy, sketch the markings with a pencil first, then trace the pencilled line with dark ink. Your drawing will be transferred directly onto the horse's registration certificate for identification purposes. Make your lines dark, and just outline the white markings—don't fill them in.

Draw all white markings on the application. If the horse has no white markings at all, be sure to check the block labeled "No White Markings" to avoid a delay in processing the application while the Registry verifies that this section was not omitted by mistake.

If the horse is grey (or may turn grey), indicate in the proper blocks whether the skin under each white marking is pink. (Pink skin will show through white markings if the hair is thoroughly wet or clipped quite short.) After a horse has turned grey, the only way to identify it by its markings is to check for pink skin, because its white markings will have blended into the grey coat.

Also indicate whether each hoof is light, dark, or "parti" (striped), marking the appropriate blocks on the application.

Dates — Be sure that correct breeding and foaling dates are entered in the appropriate blocks. The dates shown must agree with breeding dates previously reported by the stallion owner.

Signatures — The registration application must be signed by: (1) the owner of the dam at the time of breeding; (2) the owner of the dam at the time of foaling; and (3) the owner of the sire at the time of breeding. If the same person owned the mare when she was bred and when she foaled, those signatures would be the same. The signatures must be those of the recorded owner in each case. The recorded owner is the person *shown on the Registry's records* as owner at the indicated time.

TRANSFER OF REGISTRATION CERTIFICATE

When an Arabian horse is sold, the seller signs and completes the transfer on the back of the registration certificate. The buyer sends the signed certificate to the Registry with the transfer fee. After the Registry's records have been updated, a new certificate is sent to the buyer, showing the buyer as the horse's current owner.

Mail the transfer fee and certificate to the Registry within two months of the date of sale of the horse to avoid paying a higher fee. The transfer fee rises again if you wait until six months after the transaction to transfer the horse's papers.

When an Arabian is purchased on time payments, the seller usually keeps the horse's registration certificate until all payments have been made. At that time, the seller signs the transfer and gives the certificate to the buyer.

Sale of an Unregistered but Eligible Foal

Arabian foals often are sold before they are registered. In such cases, the buyer sends a completed "Transfer for an Eligible but Unregistered Foal" form to the Registry along with the foal's registration application and fee. This form must be signed by the recorded owner of the foal's dam at the time the foal was born. The registration certificate is then issued directly to the foal's buyer rather than its breeder. The "Transfer for an Eligible but Unregistered Foal" form also is used to register foals from both leased mares and mares being purchased on time payments.

Sale Without Papers

Occasionally an Arabian horse is sold without a registration certificate. By doing this, the recorded owner prevents the horse's future foals from being registered as purebred Arabians, and the horse also cannot be shown at Arabian horse shows. The value of an Arabian sold without papers is therefore the same as that of a grade (unregistered) horse. It is the seller's responsibility to return the registration certificate to the Registry for cancellation.

Whether elaborate or simple, shelters must offer protection from wind and moisture. (This loafing shed also stores equipment safely behind locked doors.)

12

ƒTABLE FACILITIES

Although some Arabian breeding and show barns are equine palaces complete with fountains and chandeliers, simple facilities can meet the needs of the horse quite well. What you *do* with your horses should determine their housing. Pleasure horses and breeding stock are healthier and happier when kept under fairly natural (outdoor) conditions, often needing only a large, safely fenced area and a simple shelter from wind and wet weather.

Show horses are more easily maintained in show condition if they are kept indoors where their feed, exercise, and grooming can be more closely controlled. They, therefore, require more elaborate facilities (stalls, bathing areas, etc.).

Whether elaborate or simple, the facility should be planned for convenience, comfort, and safety.

Before building (or remodeling), visit other facilities used for the same purposes. Ask the stable managers which features of design they like and which they would change. Keep notes and snapshots of ideas for your own facility.

The efficiency of daily routine is directly linked to the lay-out of the stable. Make the area convenient for working by reducing walking, carrying, and door and gate opening whenever possible. Put related areas near each other—the tack room near the saddling area, tools near where they will be used, etc.

Be sure all gates are wide enough to admit tractors, trucks, and trailers. Easy access to barns, corrals, pastures, and arenas makes maintenance, deliveries, and cleaning easier.

When planning your facility, consider ease of future expansion. Even if you never need to enlarge your original structures, this may be an important sales point if you decide to sell the property.

The typical American-style barn consists of box stalls along both sides of a wide center aisle and large doors at each end of the aisle. The doors usually are sliding or overhead (garage) doors that don't block the aisle and can be left open for ventilation or closed in bad weather.

Shed-row stables consist of a long row of stalls with stall doors opening to the outdoors. Shed rows often consist of two rows of stalls back to back, with the back wall of each stall common to the stall on the opposite side of the building.

Wooden buildings make attractive stables and retain warmth well in cold weather. However, lumber is expensive to purchase and maintain—horses chew wood, and it requires frequent repainting or treatment with wood preservative. Wood also presents a fire hazard.

Concrete block or brick barns are expensive to build, and because they tend to be dark, require large windows and doors. They may be cold, damp, and difficult to ventilate. Also, horses can be injured if they kick the stall walls. The advantage of block or brick barns is that they are very durable and easily maintained.

A metal barn with a metal roof is durable, requires little maintenance, and is nearly fireproof. Its major drawback is that it doesn't hold heat well in cold weather. If you're unsure how long you will be at your present location, consider installing portable metal barns. Many large Arabian horse farms use portable stalls or barns as part of their permanent facilities. Portable barns are relatively inexpensive, easily maintained, durable, and safe.

STABLE DESIGN

Stables can be planned for beauty, but safety and comfort of the horses and convenience in caring for them should be the first priorities.

barn walls can be partly open to the outdoors. In cold climates, barn ventilation is a greater problem. Cupolas and vents under the eaves of the roof improve ventilation, and heated barns must have ventilating fans in the ceiling to help remove ammonia and moisture from the air.

Lighting

Good lighting makes the barn more pleasant and convenient to work in and promotes the health of the horses. Windows and skylights admit sunlight, which helps dry stalls, kill bacteria, and add warmth in cold weather. With good *natural* lighting, costs of artificial lighting also go down.

Electric lights in the barn improve visibility. They are convenient for working at night or in the early morning. In addition, they can help control the growth of the horses' hair coats and help regulate the estrus cycles of broodmares (see Chapter 23).

Stables should be planned for convenience and safety.

Ventilation

Good ventilation is a critical element of barn design. The stable must allow circulation of fresh air without being drafty. Drafts along the floor are especially dangerous for foals. Ammonia fumes from manure and urine also can cause respiratory diseases.

Good ventilation is easier in warm climates. Barns can feature large windows and doors, and the

In addition to ceiling lights in the aisles, a recessed and safely covered electrical light in each stall is recommended.

Windows

Ideally, each stall should have a window to provide light and ventilation. Also, stabled horses are more content when they can see outdoors. If the

92

To promote good health, stables should feature good lighting and ventilation.

Tucson Arabian Park Ltd., Tucson, Arizona

window contains glass, it must be covered with wire screening small enough to protect the glass from being struck by a hoof and to protect the horse from broken glass. In cold climates, stall windows must seal well.

Doors

Most modern stables have sliding stall and entrance doors. Sliding doors require no aisle space when open and are safer than dutch stall doors because horses cannot bump into the open doors.

Stall doors must fit snugly. If a gap occurs at the bottom or side of a stall door, a horse's leg can become trapped or a foal may become wedged there, causing serious injury. If dutch doors are used, adding a latch to the bottom of the lower door will prevent it from gapping open at the bottom if the horse leans against it.

Heating

Heated barns are more expensive to build than unheated barns because they require more insulation and must seal well to hold in artificial heat. Barn heating systems are not only expensive to buy, install, maintain, and operate, but may increase the fire hazard.

Ammonia fumes from urine and manure can cause respiratory illnesses in horses. In heated barns, the risk is heightened because fresh air is excluded in favor of warmth. (Ceiling fans improve ventilation and may lessen the problem slightly.) If the horses

are exercised outdoors, the abrupt temperature change may result in chilling and lowered resistance to disease. Despite these drawbacks, show barns in extremely cold climates often are heated to discourage the growth of a thick winter coat.

The horses' own body heat raises the temperature inside an unheated barn. If the barn is too chilly, horses can be blanketed. Where more heat is necessary, heat lamps can be used (e.g., in the wash area or the stalls of foals, sick or old horses, etc.).

Stalls

Box stalls must be *at least* 10 feet by 10 feet. Most stalls are 12 feet by 12 feet. Foaling stalls and stallions' stalls should be 14 feet by 14 feet or larger. Larger stalls are more expensive to build and to bed but provide more comfort.

For optimum safety and convenience each stall should have two doors. The front door of the stall usually opens onto the center aisle of the barn; the back door should open into a fenced area (paddock or pasture). If dutch doors are used, the top door can serve as an open "window" to admit sunshine and fresh air in good weather.

Open grating on the top portion of the front and sides of the stalls is ideal. Metal grillwork allows good air circulation and allows the horse to see its neighbors without being able to fight or chew their manes or tails. Grillwork is preferable to bars because

Flat, closely spaced wire grills on stalls confine horses safely while allowing good visibility and air circulation.

93

a horse can get a leg caught between the bars, and adjacent horses may be able to fight between them. If bars are used, they should be large in diameter and placed closely together. All stall walls must be free from sharp edges or nails that might injure a horse.

Feeders — Feeding troughs can be plastic, fiberglass, or metal. They must not have any sharp or jagged edges. Hay and grain can be fed in separate feeders, or a combination hay/grain feeder can be used. The most popular style is a wall-hung hay rack over a grain trough. Hay spilled from the rack falls into the grain trough, which reduces waste especially when feeding legume hay such as alfalfa.

To prevent accidents or contamination of the feed by manure, the feeder should be hung no lower than the horse's shoulders. This placement also may help develop a more arched neck than if the horse were fed from a low feeder, since it requires the use of different muscles while eating. However, if the feeder is hung too high, dust from the feed may irritate the horse's eyes or aggravate respiratory problems. In foaling stalls, feeders and waterers must be hung higher than normal, to prevent accidents during foaling or to the young foal afterward.

A small opening or trap door in the front wall of each stall, directly over the feeder, makes it possible to feed without entering the stall.

Waterers — The waterer or water bucket should be placed on the wall opposite the feeder to keep the horse from dropping feed into the water. If automatic waterers are used for convenience, they should be checked daily to be sure they are working. Using buckets allows the horse's water consumption to be monitored. These should be hung on the wall at the horse's shoulder height to prevent contamination of the drinking water by manure.

Stall Floors — A mixture of clay, fine gravel, and sand makes an excellent base for stall floors. If the stalls are deeply bedded to absorb moisture, dirt also is acceptable, and laying gravel beneath the dirt floor will improve drainage.

Clay floors quickly become uneven and must be patched regularly to fill holes that will collect moisture and provide uneven footing for the horse. An uneven floor also is uncomfortable when the horse is lying down.

Wood flooring retains warmth and is flexible. However, it cannot be disinfected. It also absorbs

Inexpensive and efficient hay and grain feeder. The grain pan is hung below the hay rack to catch falling hay leafs and help prevent wasted feed.

moisture, resulting in dampness, odor and rotting. Because of possible rotting and collapse, wooden stall floors should be creosoted to prevent rot and laid directly on the ground instead of being suspended on a foundation. Wooden floors also must be replaced periodically.

Concrete floors are durable and easily cleaned. However, they must be deeply bedded since cement is cold and its hard surface can cause leg problems in horses.

Sand floors are absorbent but can cause sand colic if any of the sand is eaten with feed picked up from the stall floor.

Rubber stall mats are desirable over any stall flooring material. Although expensive, mats are durable, cushion the horses' legs, and prevent mud.

For good exterior drainage, stall floors should be at least six or eight inches higher than the ground surrounding the stable. To aid interior drainage of moisture from urine or spilled drinking water, stall floors may slope slightly. However, too great a slope may cause leg strain by shifting the horses' weight unnaturally. Level stall floors are satisfactory if absorbent bedding is used.

Although old stables often contained floor drains for removal of urine, most modern buildings do not. If the bedding material is sufficiently absorbent, floor drains are unnecessary because the absorbed urine is removed with soiled bedding. In fact, drains easily become clogged with bedding, creating a maintenance problem. They must be cleaned out and frequently flushed with water to prevent ammonia fumes from accumulated manure and urine. If drains are present, they should be covered with strong metal grills to prevent injuries resulting from a horse stepping into them.

Grooming Area

A special grooming area with cross-ties and good lighting is a convenience. Rubber trailer or stall mats will cushion the horse's legs and add traction for the hoofs. The area should be located away from stable activity; a special stall is best because it is away from distractions that might upset the horse and protected from drafts by the stall walls.

Horses can be bathed outdoors, but an indoor bathing/grooming stall is more efficient, especially if a large number of horses are bathed frequently. The area usually provides hot and cold running water and a floor drain. If the floor is cement, its surface should be roughened to improve traction for hoofs since cement is slippery when wet.

Cross ties are two tie ropes about three to six feet long that connect to each side of the horse's halter to immobilize the horse for grooming or saddling. Install sturdy eye-bolts for the ties. It is safer to *tie* the horse with a quick-release knot than to use heavy metal snaps that attach directly to the halter. If snaps are used to secure the horse in the cross ties, they should be the quick-release "panic snaps" that are readily available from tack stores.

ARENAS

Arenas are fenced, elongated oval or rectangular areas used for training and exercising horses. An arena should be at least 50 feet by 100 feet. An *indoor arena* may be a necessity for preparing show or sale horses in harsh winter climates. This arena may be part of the stable or a separate building and can be totally enclosed or partially open to the outdoors.

A *round ring* is an enclosed, circular arena used for lunging and training young horses. It is usually 50 to 60 feet in diameter and enclosed by

a wooden or metal fence. For safety and to prevent distractions during training, it is best if the round ring is enclosed by a solid wooden wall about six feet high; however, many round rings use regular wooden or metal pole fencing. The ring may be covered to provide shade and protection from rain or snow, but most are not.

The ground surface of all arenas must be level and neither too hard nor too soft. Wood shavings over sand make a good working surface. Spraying the surface periodically with used crankcase oil will reduce dust and insects, and sprinkling it frequently with water will also help keep down dust.

A round ring at Tucson Arabian Park Ltd., Tucson, Arizona. Its solid walls not only prevent distractions but are safer than pipe or wooden railings, which a horse might get a leg through or over. The walls slant outward, which is another safety feature.

FENCES

Horse fences must be strong but safe, with the bottom of the fence eight to ten inches above ground. This prevents a horse from becoming trapped between the ground and the fence when rolling, etc.

One of the safest kinds of fencing is V-mesh ("no climb") wire. Horses cannot get caught in it or break it easily. If the fence posts are installed about every six to eight feet, V-mesh will remain tight for years. Unfortunately, it is quite expensive.

"Horse fence," which consists of connected rectangles of smooth wire, is also preferred fencing for horses. It is safe and sturdy but less expensive than V-mesh. Horse fence must also be attached to sturdy fence posts that are close enough together to prevent the wire from sagging.

Welded pipe is sturdy and easily maintained but also is expensive. It also is inflexible if the horse hits the fence or gets caught between the rails. If pipe is used, it should be thick pipe for sturdiness, and the rails should be at least ten inches apart.

Wooden fences are attractive but expensive to build and maintain since horses chew wood and it must be painted or treated with preservatives regularly.

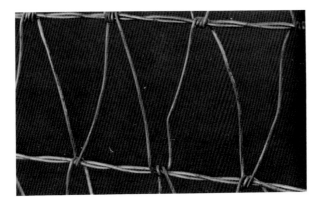

V-mesh wire provides safe fencing for horses.

Although attractive, board fencing is costly to maintain. Wood is satisfactory for building arenas, provided that the horses do not have the opportunity to chew the rails. (Free-standing galvanized feeders are used to feed hay and grain to horses in pasture.)

Single-strand smooth wire fencing sags if horses lean against it and is easily broken. Electric fences are inexpensive but hold the potential of electrocution under such circumstances as lightning, standing water, etc.

Barbed wire is never safe for horses. It is made to hold cattle, which have much thicker skin, and can badly blemish or even kill a horse.

A recent innovation in horse fencing is rubber belting nailed to wooden posts. Rubber fences are inexpensive, resilient, durable, and require no paint or preservatives. However, the rubber must not be the type that will "shed" strings of fiber since horses may eat the rubber and develop colic or impaction.

Heavy-duty plastic fencing that looks like wooden railing is now used at some breeding farms and show stables. Although very expensive, it is said to be easier to maintain than wooden fencing because it does not require painting or replacement.

Fence gates should be sturdy yet safe for horses. If metal gates are used, they should be made of round pipe which will not have edges that can cut horses. As with fencing, wooden gates are more flexible than metal gates meaning they will "give" when horses run into them. A gate having safe wire (V-mesh, horse fence, or chain link) on the side *away* from the animals will prevent a leg from getting caught between the gate cross-bars.

The safest kind of metal gate is made of pipe and has no sharp edges.

STORAGE

Feed Storage

Never store hay in the stable. As it ferments, moldy hay creates heat which can start a fire from spontaneous combustion. Storing hay in a loft also reduces stable ventilation by reducing the amount of air space near the ceiling. The best place to store a quantity of hay is in a separate metal shed with roof, floor, and a windbreak on two sides to keep out wind-blown moisture in wet weather. Good ventilation will help prevent hay mold.

Store grain in rodent-proof containers in a dry area (to prevent mold). Grain containers also should be horse-proof to prevent a horse from reaching the grain supply and eating until it becomes ill or dies. If a quantity of grain is kept in a special room, a horse-proof lock on the door also will help prevent this tragedy.

Storage of Bedding

Keep fresh bedding clean and dry by storing straw and baled shavings in the hay storage area. Loose wood shavings can be piled or stored in a pit, protected from wind and moisture by a heavy tarp or protective walls and a roof.

STOCKS

Stocks are special chutes used for restraining horses during veterinary treatment, palpating or artificially inseminating mares, etc. Each chute is a rectangular box large enough to accommodate a horse comfortably but small enough to keep it fairly immobile.

Stocks usually are made of wide, sturdy pipe which has no rough edges to injure a horse or handler. Most are designed so that the horse enters from the rear, which opens to admit the horse and then closes to prevent it from backing out. Most stocks are partly open in the back, front, and sides to allow easy access to the horse's legs. The front

and sides of the stocks must be tall enough to minimize the risk of a horse getting a leg over them. Well-made stocks not only restrain the horse but help insure the safety of both the horse and its handlers.

HOT WALKERS

A hot walker is a mechanized device used to cool out sweating horses, dry them after bathing, or lightly exercise them. It is convenient when many horses are cared for since several horses can be put on the walker at the same time, and the horses do not have to be individually walked by a handler.

The most common type of walker consists of metal arms radiating from a central point. One horse is tied to each arm of the walker. When the motor is turned on, the arms rotate and the horses are led in a circle around the walker.

Indoor walkers consist of a ceiling track with lead lines hanging from the ceiling of an indoor arena. When the motor is on, the horses are led around the arena by the moving lines. The indoor, ceiling-track walker requires no floor space and is handy in inclement weather. It also is safer than the conventional walker because a horse cannot hit its head or throw a leg over a metal arm.

The footing for the area where the walker is located should be sawdust over sand; it should cushion without being deep enough to strain muscles. Keep down dust by oiling and dampening the surface when needed.

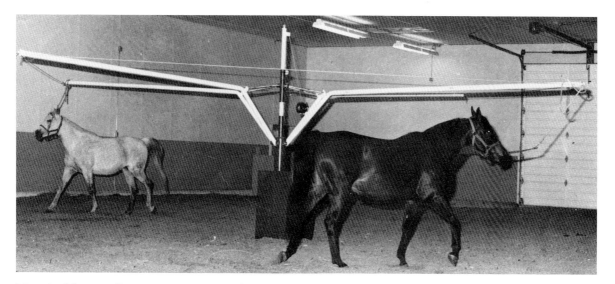

Motorized horsewalkers are a great convenience.

Photo courtesy of Hot to Trot® Horsewalkers

An Arabian in clean surroundings is healthier, happier, and more attractive.
Curt Foss photo of Rolo Allende-B, courtesy of Gossamer Gait Stables, Washington, Missouri

13

STABLE MANAGEMENT

An Arabian horse in clean surroundings is healthier, happier, and more attractive than one kept in a messy stable. Even a well-groomed, well-conditioned horse seems less appealing when viewed in a dirty area. Stable aisles and tack and feed storage rooms should be swept and tidied frequently for efficiency and a more pleasant appearance.

Manure and urine-soaked bedding must be removed from stalls at least once a day, and soiled bedding replaced with clean. Manure should be removed in the morning and afternoon, and more often, if possible.

When tack and equipment are kept clean, they are not only more attractive but last longer. Nylon halters and leads should be washed often to avoid a build-up of dirt and sweat, and leather tack, cleaned and oiled regularly.

Buckets, feeders, and grooming tools should be scrubbed frequently and dried in sunlight to kill bacteria. Washing bits after each use will remove saliva and pieces of hay.

For health reasons, each horse needs its own blankets and halters. Hanging them in front of each stall and putting each horse's name on its things will avoid mixing them. When equipment must be shared, it should be washed between users since diseases can be spread by using the same equipment on more than one horse.

DISINFECTING STABLES AND EQUIPMENT

The best way to prevent disease is to keep horses' vaccinations current; isolate transient or sick horses; supply adequate feed, exercise, sunlight and fresh air; and keep the stable clean. Routine cleanliness prevents disease germs from accumulating in the stable. If, however, contagious disease occurs, the contaminated stall (and perhaps the entire stable) should be disinfected.

Several disinfectants are available from veterinary supply companies, but all are not effective against the same organisms. Consult your veterinarian to see which sanitizing solutions are needed for a particular disease. When using a disinfectant, follow label directions carefully. Some disinfectants can irritate skin or corrode metal, and all are poisonous if taken internally.

Before disinfecting the stable, remove all horses. Begin by sweeping all surfaces (ceilings, walls, floor, windows, doors, stall dividers, etc.) before scrubbing them with soap and hot water. Take particular care to scrape off any accumulated dirt or manure during this preparatory cleaning; to be effective, disinfectants must be applied to a clean surface.

To disinfect a stall occupied by a diseased horse, first remove and burn all bedding or bury it where it will not come in contact with other horses. A hard stall floor such as concrete should be scrubbed. If the surface is dirt or clay, the top four or five inches should be removed and replaced with fresh material. Be sure that all damp flooring is removed and replaced with clean, dry material.

disease to horses or people. Stable cats or mouse traps may eliminate rats and mice. If more stringent measures are required, a pest exterminating company, an agricultural college or extension agent should be consulted for recommendations. If pesti-

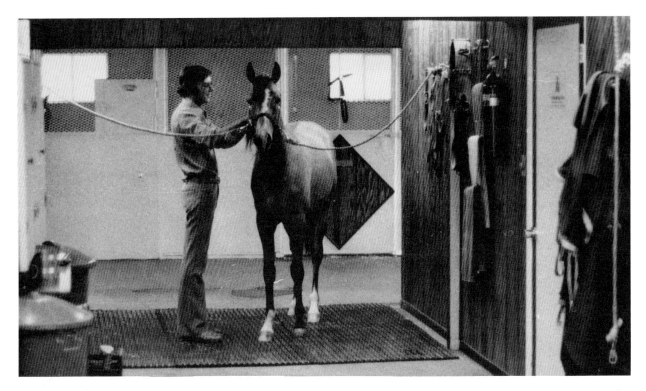

In the well-managed stable, horses are kept clean and healthy and receive individual care each day. Here, Steve Sidles grooms one of his Arabian colts.

After all surfaces have been scrubbed with soap and hot water and allowed to dry, spray on the disinfectant until the entire stall is saturated. Disinfect all stable equipment that has come in contact with the diseased horse, including buckets, grooming tools, feeders, waterers, trailers, etc. When the premises and equipment have been thoroughly disinfected, allow them to dry completely and air out before reuse.

As a precaution against disease, a stable may be routinely disinfected each year. Foaling stalls and isolation stalls for transient or sick horses should be disinfected before each new occupant.

PEST CONTROL

Rats and mice are attracted to stables for warmth, shelter, and food. They also can carry

cides are used, they must be kept away from the horses and measures must be taken to protect their feed and water from contamination. Equal care should be taken when fighting a severe infestation of insects or other pests in a stable. The mildest effective method of control should be chosen, and pesticides avoided whenever possible.

STALL BEDDING

Bedding is disposable material put on stall floors to provide warmth, cushion the horse's body and legs, and absorb moisture from urine and manure. The most popular bedding materials are wood shavings and straw.

Wood shavings are very absorbent and slightly deodorizing. Pine shavings are best. Some woods, notably black walnut, actually are poisonous and must never be used for bedding. Avoid oak shavings, too—they contain tannic acid, which is harmful to hoofs.

Good shavings are larger than sawdust but don't contain large chunks or splinters. Shavings are available in paper "bales" about the size of small bales of hay, which are easily stored. However, loose shavings are usually less expensive.

Good straw is bright yellow and not dusty or moldy. Straw makes a warm bed but is less absorbent than wood shavings. It is preferred for foaling because birth fluids drain through it, leaving a dry bed.

Horses are more likely to eat straw than wood shavings, but eating either material can cause colic and impaction. When first using straw for bedding, watch horses carefully to be sure they don't eat it.

Bedding the Stall

A scoop shovel should be used to put clean wood shavings in the stall. (An aluminum snow shovel is lightweight and holds more shavings than a regular shovel.) Shavings are raked into a thick, even layer over the floor and banked higher along the walls. A bed of wood shavings should be about six inches to eight inches deep.

When bedding with straw, less straw will be required and the bed will be more absorbent if the straw is chopped into shorter pieces before the stall is bedded. Use a pitchfork to distribute the straw in the stall. If the straw bed is cross-layered by first placing pieces of straw parallel to the back wall of the stall and then adding a layer of straw laid vertical to the wall, the bed will be tighter; manure will not fall through the bedding to the stall floor and the bed won't develop "holes" as the horse moves around. The straw bed should be ten inches to twelve inches deep.

Cleaning Stalls

"Picking out" a stall means removing the manure and wet bedding, leaving the unsoiled bedding in the stall. A special manure rake is helpful because it is lightweight and allows dry, clean wood shavings to sift through its narrow tines when manure is picked up. A pitchfork is best for removing soiled straw bedding although the manure rake can be used to remove manure from straw.

Soiled bedding can be put into a wheelbarrow, small trailer, truck bed, garden cart, or large plastic basket (skep) for removal from the stable.

Ideally, stalls should be stripped to the floor weekly and powdered lime put on wet spots as a deodorant and disinfectant. The stall should be aired and dried before rebedding with clean bedding material. Weekly rebedding keeps stalls dryer and warmer and helps reduce worm reinfestation.

Disposal of Soiled Bedding and Manure

A manure pit is a hole in the ground used to store manure until it can be hauled away from the stable premises. The pit is less an eyesore than an above-ground pile of manure. It also kills worm eggs better and reduces the fire hazard because it traps the heat generated by decomposing manure. The pit should be large enough to hold a sufficient amount of manure for disposal and should allow easy access for truck loading.

If manure is piled above ground, the top layer should be turned every few days to help kill worm eggs on top and to avoid hot spots that could start a fire. Spraying the pile with used crankcase oil or

A stall in a well managed stable. The feed record card posted on the front of the stall (just below and next to the small door that opens into the feeder) insures that the ration is always correct, and the blanket bar on the front of the stall door allows handy storage when the horse's blanket is removed.

Courtesy of Tucson Arabian Park, Ltd., Tucson, Ariz.

insecticide will help control flies until it can be transported for disposal.

In suburban areas, horse manure sometimes can be sold as fertilizer. All types of soiled stall bedding can be included with manure in a compost for later sale as fertilizer, but wood shavings take the longest to decay. If desired, wet wood shavings may be dried in sunlight and then used as footing in arenas and other horse exercise areas. If the manure and soiled bedding cannot be recycled for other purposes, they must be dumped where they will not create a health hazard or an eyesore. Most public dumps accept horse manure, and private contractors sometimes are hired to remove manure regularly from suburban horse property.

FLY CONTROL

In *Stable Management and Exercise*, M. Horace Hays states that Wilfrid Blunt allowed spiders to live in the stables at Crabbet Stud to protect his valuable Arabian horses from flies. Fortunately, we now have other, more effective methods of fly control.

Insecticides can be sprayed manually on the stable walls and ceiling or dispensed automatically into the air. Portable, battery-operated fly spray dispensers are available as are elaborate and expensive built-in systems that periodically spray insecticide from ceiling jets.

Sprays and "wipe on" fly repellents for horses are available. These products may cause skin irritation if applied too heavily. If irritation results, the amount used should be reduced. Horses usually stand better for spraying if it is begun at their forelegs and then worked upward to the neck and body, and then to the hindquarters and hind legs. If their hind legs are sprayed first, horses may be startled and jump forward.

Special "fly bonnets" can be used to keep flies from irritating horses' eyes. These usually are made of transparent netting that fits over the top of the head, covering the eyes, and attaches to a halter. Another type of fly screen consists of leather strips connected to a browband; it covers the eyes like an extended forelock.

Chemical fly baits can be used to attract and kill flies. Such compounds are applied to a feed sack in the stable area, etc.

Special devices are available to electrocute flying insects. Although it is unsightly, fly paper can also be used if hung out of the reach of horses.

Finally, modern companies have updated Wilfrid Blunt's approach to fly control by marketing fly predators—insects that eat flies, fly larvae, or eggs.

THE CLOTHES HORSE

The stabled horse needs a "wardrobe" of halters and blankets. Show horses also may require hoods to prevent the growth of long hair on their necks and heads in cold weather. Performance horses need coolers (loose blankets thrown over sweaty horses to prevent chilling and help dry them). Coolers also can be useful when drying bathed horses in cool weather.

The Stable Halter

The stable or work halter is designed for function rather than beauty. Nylon web halters are most popular because they are sturdy and machine washable. They also come in a wide selection of colors and keep their color for the life of the halter. They don't shrink like cotton rope or stretch like nylon rope halters, and they don't have to be cleaned manually or oiled like leather halters. A cotton or nylon lead rope about ten feet long connects to the halter by a sturdy metal snap.

The properly adjusted stable halter provides control but is comfortable for the horse. It should *not* fit as tightly as a show halter. The noseband should fit about an inch below the cheekbone and be loose enough to insert two or three fingers between the noseband and the horse's head. The throatlatch should not fit tightly.

A horse should be haltered before anything is done with the animal (grooming, cleaning out its hoofs, etc.) because even a gentle horse can spook and bolt if improperly restrained. However, a halter should never be left on a horse while it is loose in a stall or pasture. The haltered horse could break its neck if the halter became caught on an object or a leg could be broken if it got caught in the halter. If a halter must be left on a loose horse, a "safety release" halter that automatically releases under pressure should be used.

Tying the Horse

Horses can be restrained by tying them in cross ties or to a fixed object for activities to which they are accustomed and unlikely to resist (grooming, etc.). A horse shouldn't be tied during any activity that is likely to be upsetting, for the animal may pull back or throw itself over if tied. An excited or frightened horse can be seriously injured this way.

If the horse is tied using a regular knot in the lead line or tie rope, the knot will tighten as the horse pulls back, making it impossible to untie the horse quickly in an emergency. Fortunately, the safety release knot is easy to learn. Practice tying this knot on a horizontal surface (such as a fence board) until it is mastered. Once learned, safety release can be used on any surface to which a horse can be tied.

A horse should never be tied to any object that cannot withstand the strength of the animal and never tied with faulty equipment. The tie rope should connect to the halter with a heavy metal snap. If the halter or tie rope breaks when a horse pulls back, the horse is "rewarded" for pulling back by getting free and will probably repeat this negative behavior.

To tie the safety release knot:

1. Form a loose loop around the object to which the horse will be tied, passing the lead rope over and around the object (first away from, and then toward yourself).
2. Pass the loose end of the rope over the loop and to your left.
3. Form a second, round loop by bringing the loose end of the rope up, across the original loop, and back to your right.
4. Pass the loose end of the rope behind the second (bottom) loop and to your left.
5. Pull part of the loose end of the rope through the bottom loop and to your left. (Don't pull the entire loose end through the loop—just a small portion near the bottom loop.)
6. To tighten the knot, pull downward on the part of the lead rope that is attached to the halter while holding the new loop firmly (to prevent it from slipping out as the knot tightens).

When correctly tied, the rope is tight around the object to which the horse is tied. When the end

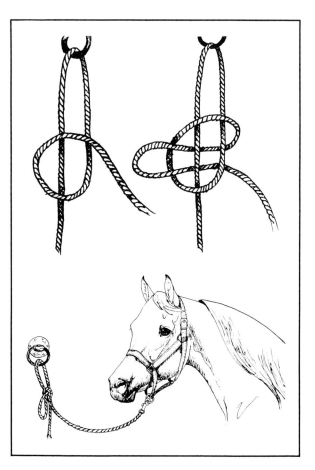

Tie a horse with a safety release knot that can be released quickly in an emergency.

of the rope that connects to the halter is pulled, the safety release knot holds firm. However, when the loose end is pulled, the rope instantly releases. To quickly untie the horse, the loose end is jerked and the rope removed from the object to which it is tied. (Many Arabians are adept at untying knots, so it is best not to leave a tied horse unsupervised.)

If, in an emergency, the tie rope cannot be quickly released, it must be cut to free the horse.

Blankets

Horses are blanketed to keep them warm in cold weather. Show horses also are blanketed to keep the coat short and clean. Every horse needs *at least* two blankets—one to wear while the other is being washed and dried. Before blanketing, the horse and blanket should be clean. Chafed skin results from dirt, dead hair, sweat, or an improperly fitted blanket.

Fitting Blankets — To determine blanket size, one side of the horse's body is measured from the center of the chest to the center of the tail (the length of the body). The resulting measurement (in inches) is the horse's blanket size.

Blankets are available only in even sizes (68, 70, 72, 74, 76, etc.). If the horse measures an uneven number of inches, order the next larger size.

Blankets come in two basic styles: front closure and solid front (which must go over the horse's head when put on and removed). "Regular" cut blankets and "Arab contour" blankets are available. The Arabian contour is cut out at the withers to avoid rubbing the mane and at the back to accommodate the Arabian's higher tail carriage. The regular horse blanket is less expensive and may be sufficient for a pleasure horse; its fuller cut may even provide extra warmth in cold weather. For a show horse, however, the Arabian contour blanket is best.

Blanketing for Warmth — Horses that live outdoors develop long, thick winter coats that usually keep them warm. In extremely cold and wet weather, even a shaggy horse might need a blanket. The long hair that keeps the horse warm in dry weather actually holds moisture next to his skin in wet weather, resulting in chilling. Shivering uses more calories, which means that additional feed is required to keep the horse warm. If a horse shivers, he should be blanketed.

If a blanket is put on a long-haired horse, the animal must be checked frequently to insure that it isn't sweating under the blanket. Sweating can cause chilling and resulting illness. If the horse sweats, the blanket should be removed or a lighter (thinner) blanket used. If the blanket gets wet in damp weather, it should be removed, the horse dried, and a dry blanket put on. A wet blanket should never be left on a horse.

Short-haired horses lack the protection provided by a long winter coat and *must* be blanketed for warmth in cold weather.

The most satisfactory style of blanket for outdoor horses is the New Zealand turn-out rug which is water-repellent and has hindleg straps and a body roller (a girth that fastens over the blanket) to keep the blanket in place.

Blanketing for Show — Show horses usually are blanketed whenever the temperature is less than 70 degrees F. Unless the nights are quite hot, they are always blanketed at night. However, each horse's blanket should be removed at least once daily (for example, when the horse is exercised and groomed).

The blanket's weight, material, and lining determine the amount of warmth it provides. A lightweight blanket or unlined "sheet" should be used in warm weather and a heavier blanket in cold weather. A winter blanket should be two or three plies thick, and a warm pile lining is needed in cold climates. In extremely cold weather, show horses may need to wear two or three lighter blankets at once to maintain enough body heat to prevent excessive hair growth.

When horses are kept blanketed most of the time, their skin can become irritated. A coat dressing, especially one with a silicone base, shouldn't be used under blankets. If a coat dressing is used, the horse should be bathed before reblanketing, to prevent skin irritation.

Coolers

Coolers are longer than regular blankets and do not have body rollers, girths, or leg straps. They cover the horse's neck as well as its body, and are held in place by buckles or Velcro® closures at the neck and chest, an attached browband, and a cord that fits loosely under the tail.

Performance coolers usually are wool; they prevent the sweaty horse from chilling after a workout by keeping it warm and drawing the moisture away from its body. Show coolers may be of nylon, wool, or a blend of the two fabrics and primarily are used to slick down the hair and keep the horse clean before a halter class. A rain cover is a waterproof nylon cooler used to keep the show horse and its tack dry in wet weather prior to entering the arena.

EXERCISE FOR STABLED HORSES

Exercise is critical to equine health. It circulates blood throughout the horse's body (including the legs and hoofs), strengthens the heart and lungs, builds muscles, improves speed and endurance, and stimulates digestion and elimination. It also promotes mental and emotional well-being. Confined without exercise, stabled horses become bored and anxious.

When exercise is irregular or insufficient, horses also may develop physical problems. "Stocking up" is one of them. When exercise isn't sufficient to

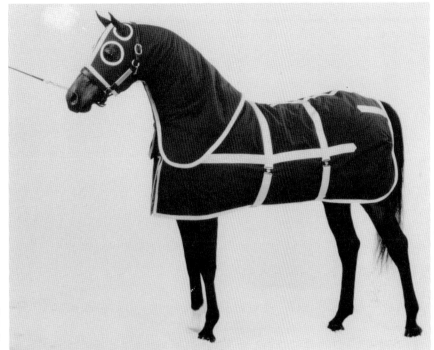

A winter blanket and full hood are modeled by Don Ibn Bask, owned by Widenauer Arabians of White Bear Lake, Minnesota.

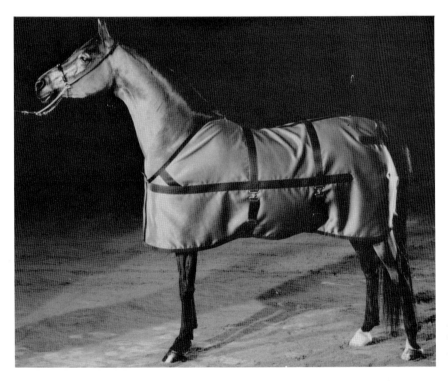

A lightweight sheet keeps the coats of show horses slick and clean.
Photos courtesy of RaDon Horse Blankets, Jordan, Minn.

pump blood from the horse's lower legs, the pasterns swell with accumulated fluid. Stocking up is usually not serious and disappears with exercise. However, it also can be a symptom of serious health problems. If lack of exercise is not to blame, a veterinarian should determine the cause.

Mature horses need daily controlled exercise (riding, driving, or lunging). At a *minimum*, they should be turned loose in a large area for an hour of free exercise. Young horses usually will get enough exercise if turned loose in a pasture or paddock, especially if other playful young horses are present.

Daily exercise is a must for the physical and mental health of stabled horses.

Photo courtesy of Craver Farms, Hillview, Ill.

STABLE VICES

When the Arabian horse—known for its naturally high level of energy—is confined to a stall, it quickly becomes bored and nervous, often resulting in bad habits (stable vices). These include wood chewing; mane and tail chewing; eating bedding; eating dirt, manure, or other non-feeds; tearing the blanket with the teeth; cribbing; weaving; pacing; pawing; and kicking the stall walls. Some horses never develop stable vices while others may have several. Working off the horse's excess energy by sufficient exercise is the best way to prevent *all* stable vices. Other preventive measures also help. Allowing the stabled horse a view of the outdoors and its neighbors helps relieve boredom as do stall toys (such as a tetherball or plastic jug hung from the ceiling). A predictable stable routine also reassures nervous horses; always feed and exercise them at the same time, and in the same order.

In a paddock or pasture, Arabians often enjoy playing with a deflated innertube, gunny sack, partly deflated ball, or highway marking cones. A companion animal—goat, burro, pony, cat, etc.—may help calm a nervous horse. However, the horse can become overly dependent upon its friend and become more upset when they are separated.

When a horse chews or eats wood, manes or tails, dirt, or other non-foods, the cause may be a lack of minerals or fiber in its diet. However, often it is merely a habit resulting from boredom.

The best solution for wood chewing is to replace wooden structures with fences and buildings made of metal or other materials. Coating the wood with an unappetizing (but non-toxic) substance or covering exposed edges with metal also may prevent wood chewing. Some owners use an electric wire at the top of wooden fences to discourage the practice. The best prevention for mane and tail chewing is to separate horses from each other—especially those inclined to chew on their neighbors.

Many horses will bite at a wound or bandage, or tear a horse blanket with their teeth. A neck cradle, made of rods and straps that buckle around the horse's neck to prevent it from lowering or turning its neck to chew the wound or blanket, may solve the problem. A leather or rubber bib that

106

fastens to the halter with snaps and by a strap over the nose also is effective and only covers the horse's chin. While wearing it, the horse can eat and drink but cannot chew bandages or blankets.

Eating bedding can result in impaction, which can be fatal. Straw bedding is especially tempting and substituting wood shavings may stop the problem. However, some horses will even eat wood shavings. A wooden neck cradle, a brace used to keep a horse from biting at a wound or bandage, may keep the animal from reaching the bedding while standing. If that fails, the horse must be kept in a stall without bedding or wear a muzzle in the stall except at feeding time. The best solution is to keep the horse in a paddock or pasture instead of a stall.

In weaving—swaying the head, neck, and body from side to side—the horse may either rock from side to side or alternately step in place. This nervous activity burns calories, which can cause a lack of condition in show horses. Moving the horse to a pasture or paddock may help although some horses will continue weaving along the fence just as they did along the stall wall. The only way to make a confirmed weaver stop the habit is by tying it, but the animal cannot be tied constantly. Pacing is a similar vice, but the pacer walks a path around the stall or back and forth along the wall. Spacing bales of straw around the stall walls may help discourage the habit; otherwise, the treatment is the same as for a weaver.

Kicking stall walls can damage the stable and injure the horse. A length of chain attached to a strap around the pastern of each hind leg can discourage kicking—when the horse kicks, its back legs are struck by the chain. A danger in this measure is that it can blemish the hind legs.

Horses sometimes paw when impatient, a foreleg repeatedly striking the ground with a digging motion. Stabled horses are most likely to paw when anxious to leave the stall or while waiting to be fed, and some horses paw while they eat. Pawing hobbles (two straps, connected by a chain, that fit around the pasterns of the forelegs) may discourage pawing, and Arabians can often be taught to temporarily stop pawing on command.

Cribbing probably is the most serious stable vice, for it may adversely affect the horse's condition and cause digestive problems. Wood chewing is often incorrectly called "cribbing"—the *true* cribber sucks air into its stomach by clamping its teeth on a protruding object, usually a wooden ledge or board. The horse bites the object, arches its neck, and swallows air with a grunting sound. Cribbers are compulsive, and they may even prefer the habit to eating. Because they may teach other horses this dangerous habit, cribbers should be separated from non-cribbers.

Unfortunately, no satisfactory cure for cribbing exists. The best prevention is to keep the horse where there are no protrusions it could use for cribbing. A cribbing strap may also discourage the vice; it is a wide band that buckles snugly around the throatlatch, cutting off the horse's oxygen when its neck is flexed for cribbing. Unfortunately, persistent horses may manage to crib while wearing the strap. A radical surgical procedure can prevent cribbing by removing some of the muscles that flex the neck; however, this ruins the horse's head carriage for riding or driving.

Abundant clean water must be constantly available. Water is necessary for all bodily functions.

Photo courtesy of Ra'adin Arabians

14

FEEDS AND FEEDING

Although Bedouin horses often didn't have enough to eat, their diet was surprisingly well-balanced. Although only scattered pastures with sparse grasses were available, they grew in limestone-rich soils which helped build strong bone. Barley was the only grain the desert horses were fed, but it ranks higher than oats in nutrients. And although water was scarce in the arid deserts, from weaning through old age, the Bedouin horses drank camel's milk, which provided not only moisture but calcium and protein.

Although their ancestors survived on this diet, the needs of modern Arabian horses are better met through scientific feeding.

WATER

Although Arabians may drink less water than horses of other breeds (perhaps because of more efficient use of water, or simply because of their relatively smaller size), they should have a constant supply of clean, fresh water. Water containers should be kept clean; horses won't drink sufficient water if forced to drink from a polluted source, and some algaes are poisonous.

A horse can survive longer without feed than without water. Water is necessary for digestion, transporting nutrients (in the blood), cooling the body (in perspiration), and removing wastes (in manure and urine). Adequate drinking water is needed even in winter; abundant snow cannot provide enough moisture for the horse's body. In summer, of course, the horse will drink more water because of perspiration.

SALT

Salt also should be available constantly since it aids the body functions and is an important part of blood, urine, and sweat. If a horse doesn't have enough salt available, it tires easily and may chew wood or eat dirt. In hot weather, horses consume more salt. A trace-mineralized salt block provides additional minerals, as well as salt.

Loose salt is sometimes preferable to a salt block. A horse that performs strenuous work may not be able to lick enough salt from the block to meet its needs. Also, in very cold weather a horse's tongue can temporarily stick to a frozen salt block, causing a sore tongue and lack of salt consumption.

PLANNING THE RATION

The staple item in a horse's diet usually is hay, which provides nutrients and the roughage needed for efficient digestion and elimination. Hay may be combined with, or replaced by, pasture. To plan a balanced ration, start with excellent hay. Then use grain to add any nutrients not supplied by the hay. If additional nutrients are needed, add mineral or vitamin supplements.

Hay

Two types of hay, grass and legume, are fed to horses. The most popular grass hay is timothy, and the most popular legume is alfalfa.

When available, good quality alfalfa hay is best for young horses and breeding stock, and it is the only feed needed for mature horses that aren't worked hard or used for breeding. Alfalfa has much more protein and calcium than timothy hay. Although grass hay is lower in nutrients and contains more fiber, it is less prone to mold. Its added fiber also creates more heat during digestion, which helps keep horses warmer in extremely cold weather. To provide the benefit of both hays, a combination of alfalfa and timothy can be fed.

The nutritional content of hay crops varies; the only way to be sure of the nutrients in a specific crop is to have it analyzed by a laboratory. Agricultural colleges or extension agents can provide information on hay testing.

Good hay is green and has a fresh, sweet smell. It is leafy, fine-stemmed, and the bales are fairly heavy because fresh hay retains some of its moisture content. The leafier the hay, the better because most of hay's nutrients are in the leaves; stems don't have much feed value.

Bad hay is dusty, brown, weedy, coarse, or stemmy. Bales may be lightweight because hay dries out with age. Moldy hay, however, is extremely heavy. Fungus spores (white powder inside bales) can cause respiratory problems, and black decayed spots or a musty odor indicate mold. Moldy hay must never be fed to horses because it can cause colic.

Hay bales must be kept dry to prevent mold. If a covered storage shed is not available, hay should be covered by a tarp. Bales should be stored off the ground and stacked loosely to promote air circulation. Since alfalfa hay is particularly prone to mold, newly delivered alfalfa should be checked immediately for dampness. Any damp bales should be opened and dried before stacking and moldy bales returned for exchange.

Some parts of the United States have problems with blister beetles in baled alfalfa hay. The dead beetles are highly toxic, and a horse that eats even a little contaminated hay can die. Consult your veterinarian, agricultural college, or agricultural extension agent to learn whether blister beetles occur in the area where your hay is grown.

Pasture

Pasture can supplement hay or replace it entirely, depending upon the quality of the grass. Good pasture always is preferable to good hay of the same kind, because hay loses some nutrients during cutting, drying, and storage. Unfortunately, not all pastures provide good nutrition for horses. Some grasses and weeds are poisonous or cause abortion. "Horse poor" pastures lack nutrients due to overgrazing and lack of refertilization, and grass that is sparse, short, or brown cannot provide proper nutrition.

When good pasture is available, it is the best feed for horses. However, grass alone will not meet the nutritional requirements of mares and foals.
Johnny Johnston photo courtesy of Bentwood Farms, Waco, Texas

Lush spring pasture alone will not supply the percentage of protein and energy required for milk production or growth, so grains and supplements also must be fed to pastured broodmares and young stock. However, rich pasture may meet the nutritional needs of mature riding horses that are not used heavily. Lawn clippings should never be fed to horses because cut grass deteriorates rapidly and can cause colic.

Grain

Oats, corn, and barley are the cereal grains most commonly fed to horses; most prepared grain mixtures contain all three. "Sweet feeds" contain molasses, which prevents powdered nutritional supplements from sifting through the grain and not being eaten. Unless the grain contains such supplements, it probably is better to feed plain grains than to routinely feed sweet feeds, which mold easily and attract flies. Sweet feeds can encourage a sick or finicky horse to eat—if the horse is not accustomed to sweet grain as a regular diet.

Grains should be stored indoors, in a well-ventilated, dry area. Unlike moldy hay, rancid grain may be difficult to detect by its smell or appearance. It, too, can cause severe colic or death. Questionable grain should never be fed to horses.

Good grain is clean, heavy, and not dusty. It smells fresh and tastes sweet.

Horses can be fed whole or processed (cracked or rolled) grains. The nutrients in cracked or rolled grains may be more readily available; whole grains may pass through the digestive tract without being digested, especially if a horse does not chew its feed well.

Oats — Oats are the grain traditionally fed to horses, although they are slightly lower in nutrients than corn or barley. Possibly because of their weight and consistency, oats are believed by many horse owners to be a relatively safe grain that will not contribute to digestive problems when fed in normal quantities. Oats vary considerably in the amount of hulls per pound. Hulls are high in fiber and low in nutrients; heavy oats (weighing more than thirty-two pounds per bushel) supply more nutrition because they contain fewer hulls.

Corn — An energetic horse that is "feeling its oats" might better be described as "feeling its corn," because corn provides twice as much energy as oats.

This makes corn the best choice for fattening a thin horse. Also, corn usually is less expensive than oats.

Corn has an undeserved reputation for causing founder because people who are accustomed to feeding a specific volume of oats tend to feed the same container of corn when changing from a diet of oats to corn. This is a serious mistake. Because corn provides twice as much energy as oats, feeding the same volume of corn is overfeeding. To avoid the problem, feed according to the weight of the grains instead of by their volume. When changing from oats to corn, first weigh the amount of oats the horse was previously being fed. Then gradually switch from oats to corn over several days (to allow the horse's digestive tract to adapt to the change in grain), being sure that the final amount of corn fed weighs only half as much as the oats fed previously.

Barley — Barley is slightly more nutritious and usually cheaper than oats. Unlike corn, barley is similar to oats in weight and texture, so is unlikely to be overfed by accident. (Because barley produces gas during digestion, it may contribute to gas colic in horses with especially sensitive digestive tracts, particularly when fed with alfalfa hay.)

Bran — Bran is the husk of wheat that is removed when flour is milled. It traditionally has been fed to horses as a laxative and to prevent colic and impaction. It also was previously touted as a source of phosphorus when not fed in excessively large amounts. Now nutritionists say that bran is not a true laxative and that its phosphorus is mostly undigestible.

Despite these arguments, bran still is popular. Horses eat bran readily and seem to relish its flavor. It is often fed dry, either by itself or mixed with other grains. In cold weather, horses seem to enjoy a warm bran mash. Sick horses, foaling mares, inactive horses, and horses being transported often are given a bran mash to aid digestion and help prevent colic.

To make a bran mash, boiling water is poured over the bran. The mash is stirred, covered with a towel, and cooled to lukewarm before feeding, allowing most of the water to be absorbed. If the horse isn't drinking enough water, however, extra water may be used. If desired, additional grains may be included in the bran mash. The warm water in the mash increases intestinal motility, which aids digestion.

Pelleted Feeds

Any kind of horse feed—hay, grain, or supplements—can be manufactured into pellets, and they do offer certain advantages. First, pellets always are made by the same formula and should, therefore, always supply the same nutrients. Second, an entire ration can be included in the pellets so that the horse cannot avoid eating the things he doesn't like; thus feed is not wasted. Because pellets are less bulky than hay, horses don't acquire "hay bellies" when fed pellets. Pellets require less storage space and are easier to transport due to their smaller volume. They also are less prone to dust and mold than hays and grains.

Pellets have drawbacks, too. They are expensive (due to processing and packaging costs) and their quality cannot be judged from their smell or appearance. The biggest problem is that horses eat pellets faster than hay, leaving them time to become bored and develop stable vices. For this reason, and to add fiber lacking in pelleted feeds, many owners feed some grass or cereal hay along with the pellets.

SUPPLEMENTS

High-Energy Feeds and Protein

When a horse does hard work, grows, or produces milk for a foal, its energy needs go up. These needs also vary slightly according to the individual's condition and metabolism. In cold weather, *all* horses need more energy to keep warm and maintain weight.

An increased need for energy is met by increasing the feed. If the horse's energy needs are only slightly higher, they may be met by simply increasing the amount of hay eaten. However, a horse whose energy needs are much higher will get full before it can consume enough hay to meet its needs. For this reason, when more energy is required, grain usually is added or increased. Grain supplies up to twice as much energy as hay and is far less bulky.

Broodmares and young, growing horses require more protein in their diets than do mature horses. Hard-working horses do *not* need extra protein (just extra energy), if they are mature and not being used for breeding. The mature horse needs only about 12 percent protein in its entire ration, and this is more than supplied by good alfalfa hay.

A protein deficiency in the diet is less critical in adult horses than in foals. If the mature horse doesn't get enough protein in its feed, its body can manufacture it. However, the foal's body cannot because its digestive system is immature.

Although alfalfa is much higher in protein than other kinds of hay, it alone cannot meet the protein needs of broodmares and growing horses. The *percentage* of protein in the horse's diet can never be raised by increasing the *amount* of alfalfa hay. The additional protein needed by broodmares and young horses must be provided by a protein supplement.

Protein Supplements

The best but most expensive protein supplement is dried milk. Soybean meal is nearly as high in protein and is cheaper. Both dried milk and soybean meal contain lysine, an amino acid that is critical for growth. Although linseed oil meal is a good protein supplement for mature horses whose diets lack protein, it shouldn't be fed to young horses because it lacks lysine.

Feeding horses too much protein is expensive but seldom harmful; the unused protein is merely excreted. Horses fed alfalfa and other high-protein feeds urinate more than horses fed other feeds, but this is not harmful.

Minerals

A mature horse whose diet has a temporary mineral imbalance can draw upon extra minerals stored in its bones to make up the deficiency. However, a fetus or growing horse whose mineral needs are not met may suffer permanent bone deformity.

The most important minerals in the diet are calcium and phosphorus, and these must be in certain ratios to each other. Fortunately, the balance is not a delicate one. The horse is more likely to show visible effects from either too much or too little of either mineral than from slight imbalance. (The desirable ratio of calcium to phosphorus is estimated at 1.1:1 to 1.5:1—up to about 1½ times as much calcium as phosphorus.)

Grain is high in phosphorus, but all hays and grasses are low in it. A phosphorus deficiency will occur if a horse is fed grass hay and no grain (this diet is also low in protein). Hay—especially alfalfa—provides needed calcium. A calcium deficiency will

Broodmares and young (growing) horses need more protein in their diets than do mature idle horses.

result if the horse is fed much grain but very little hay.

A calcium:phosphorus imbalance can occur even if the horse is fed both hay *and* grain, depending on the quality of the feed and how the individual is able to use the available nutrients.

A salt block that also contains trace minerals will supply small quantities of many minerals and can help prevent a mineral imbalance *if* the horse also is fed good alfalfa and grain. If the diet is deficient in either calcium or phosphorus, add a powdered

Chewing wood may simply be a sign of boredom. However, it may indicate a lack of salt or other minerals in the diet.

supplement of the proper mineral to the grain or allow the horse "free choice" access to the mineral supplement, as with salt.

Calcium Sources — The best source of calcium is good, leafy alfalfa hay. By itself, alfalfa supplies enough calcium for the mature horse. Growing horses and broodmares (especially in the last three months of pregnancy and while nursing foals) need extra calcium that can be provided by adding ground limestone, a livestock feed supplement, to the grain ration or offering it free choice.

Phosphorus Sources — Grains are the most common source of phosphorus. If more phosphorus is needed, bone meal or fish meal can be added to the grain or offered free choice.

Dicalcium Phosphate — Dicalcium phosphate is a mixture of both calcium and phosphorus. It contains more calcium than phosphorus, and often is part of commercial grain mixes.

Vitamins

The healthy mature horse can manufacture most vitamins lacking in its diet. If the horse gets good quality feed, supplemental vitamins are seldom needed.

Vitamins A and D are believed to be the most critical in horses. Vitamin A is furnished by green grass and fresh hay. Old hay loses some vitamin A in storage, and processing may reduce the vitamin A in raw grains. Deficiencies of vitamin A are uncommon in adult horses because the vitamin can be stored in the liver for future use. However, a lack of vitamin A in the broodmare's diet may cause weak or crooked legs in her newborn foal.

Vitamin D is necessary for utilizing calcium and phosphorus, and it may help the horse's body adjust slight imbalances between them. Vitamin D deficiencies are rare because the horse's body can manufacture it from sunlight.

Although vitamin E sometimes is given to broodmares and stallions, there is no proof that it boosts fertility. It does add shine to the coat, but soybean or corn oil (from the grocery store) will do the same thing at lower cost.

FEEDING HORSES

Feeding the proper diet and amount will produce a horse with a shiny coat, bright eyes, and

113

enough fat to be attractive without threatening the horse's health.

Feeding is partly a matter of experimentation. Start a horse on an average amount of good quality feed. If the horse maintains condition or improves, continue the same amount and kind of feed. If the horse's condition isn't satisfactory, gradually change the ration or the amount until the desired condition is achieved. If you want to fatten a horse, provide a larger quantity of feed, especially grain (grains are more fattening than hay). If you want to reduce a horse's weight, feed less, especially grain.

Most horses, however, are fed only twice daily—once in the morning and once in late afternoon or early evening. Feeding time ideally should be separated by about twelve hours (e.g., feed at 7:00 a.m. and 7:00 p.m.). If grain is fed, it should be divided equally between the two feedings. The hay ration also should be fed in two approximately equal portions although a little extra hay may be fed at night to occupy stabled horses longer and to provide increased body heat in cold weather.

Horses are creatures of habit and are happiest when fed on schedule. If kept waiting, they become

Old horses may require special diets or extra feed because their teeth and digestive systems may not be as efficient as those of younger horses.

The energy supplied by the horse's feed goes first to maintain its weight. Any energy left over is used for growth or for work. After those needs are met, the body stores the remaining energy as fat.

Show horses always are fed grain to maintain extra weight and promote a slick hair coat. However, from a nutritional standpoint, the mature horse that is worked very lightly probably does not need grain. Its energy needs can be met by good alfalfa hay, and a phosphorus supplement can supply the phosphorus that is present in grain, but lacking in hay.

When to Feed

Under natural conditions, horses graze almost constantly. Their digestion is most efficient when some food is always being digested. For this reason, some people feed horses three or four times daily.

nervous and are more likely to bolt their feed or develop colic. They get hungry at the time they're accustomed to being fed and waiting may cause them discomfort. It also may interfere with efficient utilization of the feed, making it necessary to feed a slightly larger quantity to get the same results.

Amount to Feed

Performance horses, broodmares (especially in the last three months of pregnancy and while producing milk), and growing horses need more feed than idle, mature horses. As the horse's energy needs rise, feed should be increased at the same level. Grain, however, shouldn't make up more than half the ration—it is usually better to feed quite a bit more hay than grain.

As a general rule, a mature horse that is worked lightly (up to about three hours daily) can be fed up to ½ pound of grain for every 100 pounds of its weight daily. A horse worked more than that can be fed up to 1 pound of grain per 100 pounds of its body weight each day. Don't feed more grain than the amount needed to maintain weight and perform the required work.

Hay can be fed at the rate of one to 1½ pounds of hay per 100 pounds of the horse's body weight. Feed less if the horse maintains good condition on less.

If it takes the horse more than 90 minutes to finish a meal, you might be overfeeding. A finicky eater is an exception—it may take hours to finish eating, and overfed show and sale horses may routinely nibble at their feed with lack of interest.

Healthy horses usually are eager to eat. If the horse doesn't finish its feed, check the feed first for palatability (is it moldy, stemmy, weedy?). Then check the horse's teeth and general health (do its teeth need floating or is it sick?).

The best test of a feeding program is the appearance of the horse. If a horse can perform its work (or grow, or produce and nurse a foal) while maintaining its weight and condition at the correct level, it is being fed properly.

Feeding Young Horses

Foals begin nibbling solid feed while quite young (often within a few days of birth). A creep feeder is a device to insure that the foal gets enough grain and supplements without having to compete with its dam. The creep feeder is placed in a corner of

the stall or paddock and a wooden pole is placed across the corner at such a height that the foal can walk ("creep") under it to reach the feeder, but the mare cannot. As the foal grows, the pole must be raised.

Young, growing horses can be fed regular grain or a commercial product specially formulated for growing horses. If a commercial product is used, one that does not contain steroids should be selected. Commercial products used to promote an earlier mature appearance in young horses may contain steroids (male hormones), used to increase weight and muscling. Unfortunately, steroids can seriously impair future fertility of breeding horses and cause stallion-like behavior in fillies and mares.

It is unlikely that foals and weanlings will founder by overeating because their growth rate is so rapid that they need a lot of nutrients and their attention span, even for eating, is short. However, it is wise to stock a young horse's feeder with a safe amount of concentrate rather than allowing it unlimited access to rich feed.

A creep feeder in the corner of a stall or paddock allows the foal access to feed while preventing the mare from reaching it.

DO's and DON'Ts of Feeding Horses

DO feed the best quality feeds possible.

DO feed a ration that supplies the needed nutrients in the proper amounts and ratios.

DO feed by weight rather than by volume.

DO feed equal amounts at each feeding.

DO feed at least twice daily, with twelve hours between feedings.

DO feed at the same times each day.

DON'T change *amounts* fed suddenly.

DON'T change the *kind* of feed suddenly.

DON'T feed grain as more than half the total ration.

Regal Bee running free.   *Patti Mack photo courtesy of McKinstry Arabians, Craig, Colo.*

15

HEALTH CARE

When horses are well cared for, serious illness often can be avoided. Prevention saves emergency veterinary expenses and avoids stress for both the horse and owner.

Preventive care includes an effective program of vaccinations and deworming. Regular dental and hoof care, good nutrition, exercise, cleanliness, fresh air, and sunshine also contribute to good health.

HEALTH RECORDS

Each horse should have its own health record for recording routine and emergency health care. The record should show the date, symptoms, diagnosis, name and amount of medication, and frequency of treatment. Be sure to write down the horse's progress or setbacks during an illness and any allergic reaction to drugs. Record all veterinary treatments immediately, before the details are forgotten. Include deworming and which drugs were used. Keep the original health file at the "home stable" and send a copy with the horse to shows, breeding farms, etc. If the horse is sold, give the health record to the buyer so that its medical care can continue on schedule.

A wall chart showing the health care of all horses in the stable is valuable for quick reference.

Be sure, also, to prominently display the telephone number of your veterinarian in case someone unfamiliar with your operation must summon emergency help.

RESTRAINTS

When the horse is receiving medical treatment, it is the responsibility of the person holding the lead line to keep the horse as still as possible and to protect the veterinarian when stocks are not available. For best control, remain on the same side of the horse as the veterinarian unless requested to do otherwise. If the horse acts up, pull the horse away from the veterinarian. Never let the horse move toward the veterinarian or turn its hindquarters toward him or her. These rules also apply when restraining the horse for a farrier.

Using the Chain Lead

A chain lead under the horse's jaw or over its nose will give extra control, if necessary. The chain is sometimes placed on the upper gums or on the bars of the mouth, where the bit rests, but this is quite severe and can injure the mouth. For directions on using the chain lead under the jaw, see Chapter 34.

HEALTH FORM

NAME:_____ NO.:_____ SEX:_____ FOALED:_____

SIRE: _____ DAM: _____ COLOR: _____

MARKINGS: _____

INNOCULATION HISTORY

YEAR												
TETANUS TOXOID												
INFLUENZA												
ENCEPHALITIS E & W												
VEE												
RHINO												
TETANUS ANTITOXIN												

WORMING

DATE	TYPE MED. USED	DATE	TYPE MED. USED

A health record form used at Denise Borg's Four Winds Farm, Santa Ynez, Calif. Similar forms may be purchased commercially.

118

Using the Twitch

The twitch is usually very effective in making a horse stand still for medical treatment. There are two styles of twitches. The first consists of a round stick with a loop of chain through one end. The exterior of the horse's upper lip is pulled through the loop and the stick is twisted, tightening the loop on the lip. When the twitch is in place, the horse usually stands still. The chain should be tightened when the horse acts up, but loosened whenever possible.

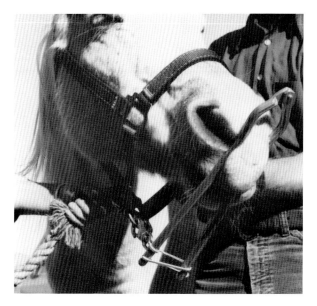

The one-person twitch in place and snapped to the halter.

The twitch is the most common method of restraint for medical treatment, etc.

Don Sepulvado photo, courtesy NSU

The second style is the one-person twitch, sometimes called a humane or clamp twitch. This aluminum, nutcracker-shaped instrument fastens to the halter, leaving the user's hands free to treat the horse. The round part of the twitch clamps around the horse's upper lip and its handles close to tighten the pressure. A cord wraps around both handles to maintain the tension and then snaps to the halter ring to hold the twitch in place.

If the horse must be twitched for very long, periodically remove the twitch and rub the lip. Always rub the upper lip to restore circulation when the twitch is removed. Too much constant pressure on the twitch can damage the nerves or muscles of the upper lip.

For milder restraint, the horse can be "neck twitched" by using a hand to twist a handful of skin on the horse's lower neck, just in front of the shoulder. This isn't as severe or as effective as the mechanical twitch on the lip.

GIVING SHOTS

Most equine vaccines and injected medications are injected in the large muscles of the horse's neck or hindquarters. (The intramuscular (IM) injection is easy to learn; a veterinarian or experienced horseperson can teach you to give IM shots correctly.) However, some medications must be injected beneath the skin, between layers of skin, or into a vein. It is critical that the proper type of injection be used; some medicines that are supposed to be injected in a muscle can kill a horse instantly if injected into a vein.

Only disposable syringes and needles should be used, and they never should be reused. Using the same needle on various horses can spread disease or cause fatal hepatitis. Needles cannot be disinfected by boiling; special medical equipment is needed to sterilize them.

When giving a shot, remove the needle from the syringe and insert it first. Holding the needle, tap the horse with the edge of your hand; the horse will become used to the tapping and will be less startled when the needle is inserted. When the needle is in place, attach the syringe. Before injecting the medicine, pull back on the plunger of the syringe. If blood appears in the syringe, a vein has been hit. Remove the needle and reinsert it elsewhere, again checking for blood in the syringe before injecting. Inserting air or an IM medicine into a vein can cause sudden death.

119

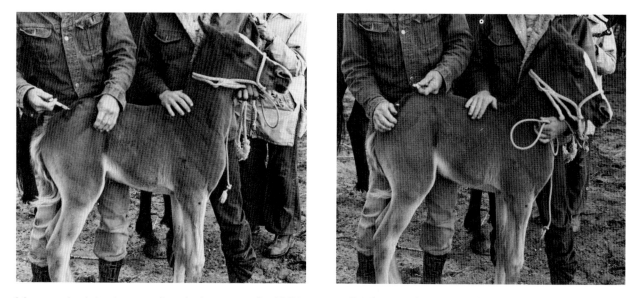

Most vaccine injections are given by intermuscular (IM) injection. IM shots can be given in the large muscles of the croup, hindquarter, or neck. Insert the detached needle first . . . then attach the syringe. Before injecting the medication, pull upward to make sure there is no blood in the syringe. If blood appears, do not inject in that area. Re-insert the needle elsewhere—if medication designed for injection in a muscle is injected in a vein, it can kill the horse. (Consult your veterinarian or an experienced horseman if you want to learn to give your own injections.)

VACCINATIONS

The first year a horse is vaccinated, a series of two shots is required to establish immunity against most diseases. The shots should be given one week to two months apart, depending on which vaccine is used. Each year thereafter, only one annual booster shot of most vaccines will maintain immunity. If the annual booster shot is not received, however, the horse should again be given two shots to reestablish immunity.

If you obtain a horse with an unknown medical history, give it the series of two shots to insure immunity. It won't harm the horse if a series is accidentally repeated.

If horses are sick or under unusual stress, vaccinations should be postponed. Horses also should not be worked hard or transported for the first day or two after vaccinations are given.

What Vaccinations are Needed?

Every horse should receive annual vaccinations to protect it from the following diseases:

Tetanus
Equine Influenza ("flu")
Equine Encephalomyelitis ("sleeping sickness")
Rhinopneumonitis ("rhino")

Vaccines for distemper (strangles) also are available and may be given to horses in greatest danger of contracting this disease. Contact your veterinarian for his or her recommendations.

Tetanus

Tetanus is extremely painful and usually fatal. It is *not* contagious, but the tetanus bacteria that cause the disease are present in soil and manure. The horse gets tetanus when the bacteria enters its body through a cut or puncture wound. The bacteria manufacture a poison (toxin) that affects the brain, causing the muscles of the body to become stiff. The horse may become unable to chew or swallow, and death usually is caused by suffocation because the horse finally cannot breathe.

There are two vaccines against tetanus. The first is *tetanus toxoid*. The horse's annual shot consists of tetanus toxoid, which is manufactured in a laboratory. It protects against tetanus for at least a year, but it takes up to one month to establish immunity.

The second vaccine is *tetanus antitoxin*, which is deactivated toxin taken from the blood of a donor horse. Although it gives immediate protection, it only protects the horse for about ten days.

When a horse that did not get its annual injection of tetanus toxoid becomes injured or has to have emergency surgery, it must be given a shot of antitoxin to establish fast immunity. (The horse could get tetanus before a shot of tetanus *toxoid* would take effect.)

A pregnant mare may be given a booster shot of tetanus toxoid about one month before her foaling date to raise the level of antibodies that will be transmitted to the foal in the colostrum (first milk), or the newborn foal may receive an injection of tetanus antitoxin immediately after birth. (If the mare did not receive her annual tetanus injection she also will require a shot of antitoxin.)

The foal should be given its first shot of tetanus toxoid when it is about three months old, followed by another shot one to two months later. After the initial series of two shots, an annual booster of toxoid is required for all horses.

Influenza (Flu)

"Flu" is a common respiratory infection caused by viruses. Young horses are especially susceptible.

Flu is highly contagious, with symptoms appearing only two or three days after exposure. The symptoms include fever (up to 106 F) and listlessness (depression). The horse may cough, have a watery discharge from the eyes or nostrils, or go off feed because of a sore throat.

Treatment consists of antibiotics and complete rest. Working a horse too soon can cause permanent lung damage; the horse must be rested for three weeks *after* flu symptoms disappear. A stallion's semen also can contain and spread the flu virus. It is easy to see why a simple case of flu can ruin a show or breeding season.

A flu virus is spread by contact with sick horses. It also can be picked up from contaminated feeders, waterers, grooming equipment, tack, trailers, or people who have previously touched sick horses.

The current flu vaccine is effective against the two *major* strains of equine influenza, types A1 and A2. The foal's first flu vaccination can be given when it is four months old; a series of two shots about four to six weeks apart will establish immunity. Booster shots should be given to young horses every six months if the horses are not being transported; they are needed at three-month intervals if horses are being transported or shown. Show, race, and other performance horses that often come in contact with transient horses also need a booster

shot every three months during the performance season. In addition to getting a booster shot every six months, broodmares may be given a flu vaccination one month prior to foaling. All horses should receive a flu shot two weeks before being transported. The idle, mature horse that is not transported needs only an annual influenza booster.

Equine Encephalomyelitis (Sleeping Sickness)

Sleeping sickness is an inflammation of the brain and spinal cord that is caused by a virus passed to horses by mosquitoes or horse flies. These biting insects carry the virus from birds and rodents. (Although these "intermediate hosts" carry the virus, they do not show symptoms of it.) Sleeping sickness also can be spread directly from horse to horse or from horses to people.

There are three strains of sleeping sickness: Eastern (EEE), Western (WEE), and Venezuelan (VEE). All three kinds are deadly. The western strain is most common, killing about half the horses that get it. EEE and VEE are even more deadly, with about an 80 percent mortality rate.

Encephalomyelitis can permanently damage the nervous systems of horses that survive it. Symptoms include nervousness, either a lack of sensitivity or hypersensitivity to touch, lost control of the facial muscles, and wandering in circles.

The foal can receive its first sleeping sickness shot at three or four months old, followed by a second shot one to four weeks later (depending upon the vaccine used). Several vaccines are available: one protects against all three strains of encephalomyelitis, another protects against just the EEE and WEE strains. (Some veterinarians do not recommend vaccinating for VEE because it does not seem to represent a substantial danger in the United States.) All horses require an annual booster of EEE and WEE vaccine about six weeks prior to mosquito or fly season; if used, a VEE booster is given every two years.

Rhinopneumonitis ("Rhino")

Rhinopneumonitis is a highly contagious respiratory disease that has flu-like symptoms. However, it also can cause abortion in pregnant mares and occasionally causes paralysis of the hind legs in horses. Young horses are most susceptible to rhino.

Broodmares exposed to rhinopneumonitis during or after the fifth month of pregnancy may abort in the seventh to tenth month of gestation. To protect broodmares from rhino abortion, any horses kept on the same property with them should be vaccinated on the same schedule as the mares.

Broodmares should be vaccinated against rhinopneumonitis two weeks before shipping or breeding and also in their fifth, seventh, and ninth months of gestation. Only the *killed* virus vaccine is safe for pregnant mares.

Foals can be given their first rhino vaccination when three months old, followed by a second shot one month later. A booster every two to three months thereafter will maintain the foal's immunity. By the time the horse is a yearling, it needs a booster shot only once every six months. However, if kept with broodmares, the yearling must be vaccinated on the same schedule as the mares to protect them from rhino abortion. Show horses and others exposed to transient horses need a rhino shot every three months, and all horses should be given a rhino booster two weeks prior to shipping. Mature, idle horses that are neither transported nor kept with broodmares may be given an annual shot of rhinopneumonitis vaccine if desired.

Distemper ("Strangles")

Distemper in horses is caused by a bacteria. It is seldom fatal and often considered an inevitable foalhood disease. Young, growing horses are most susceptible to distemper. Older horses usually have developed a permanent natural immunity after they have had the disease.

The distemper bacteria (*Streptococcus equi*) is related to strep throat in humans. Symptoms include fever, nasal discharge, and characteristic swelling of glands under the throat. These swollen lumps eventually burst and drain. (Remove the pus with a clean rag, then burn the rag—the pus is highly contagious.)

Horses usually recover after the absesses drain. Rarely, the absesses move inward instead of rupturing on the outside of the body. Such internal absesses are called "bastard strangles" and are a serious complication that can be fatal.

Treatment for distemper is the same as for flu and other respiratory diseases. The best prevention is to isolate sick horses and to disinfect stables and equipment when an outbreak occurs (See Chapter 13). Wash your hands and change clothes immediately after handling a sick horse to avoid spreading the disease to other horses.

Many owners and breeding farms do not vaccinate against distemper; consult your veterinarian for his or her recommendations. If the distemper vaccine is given, the foal can receive its first shot at three months old. Three shots at one-week to three-week intervals (depending on the vaccine used) are required to establish immunity; thereafter, an annual booster is required. A new vaccine (an M-Protein extract of *Strep equi*) can be given to pregnant mares one month before foaling; it is the only distemper vaccine safe for pregnant mares.

Purpura hemorrhagica is a complication that may occur if a horse is given a distemper vaccination after it has been exposed to an outbreak of distemper. It also can develop up to a month following a case of distemper, and may be brought on by discontinuing antibiotics too early or by working the horse too soon after a respiratory disease. Symptoms include fever and swelling (caused by ruptured blood vessels) of the throat, lower legs, and underside of the belly. Although not contagious, purpura requires immediate veterinary treatment because it can be fatal.

Equine Infectious Anemia (EIA, "Swamp Fever")

At present, there is no cure or positive prevention for Equine Infectious Anemia (EIA), a highly contagious disease transmitted by large concentrations of biting insects, especially horse flies. If a horse contracts EIA, it is a carrier of the disease for the rest of its life. However, the horse may not be continually infectious; its ability to spread the disease seems to fluctuate. The disease may or may not kill the horse, but the show, breeding, or performance career of the known carrier comes to a sudden end. The horse must be quarantined forever or destroyed.

The Coggins test determines whether a horse is a carrier of EIA: a positive test result indicates a carrier. Some states require a negative Coggins test for interstate shipment. Often, breeding farms and shows or other horse events require proof of a negative Coggins test before accepting horses. Unfortunately, the Coggins test is not mandatory for all horses, and travelling horses (show and breeding stock, race horses, etc.) are more likely to be tested than backyard pets.

At present, the only controls for EIA are effective insect control and isolation or destruction of carriers.

IDENTIFYING ILLNESS

The better you know your horse's personality and habits, the faster you will be able to spot health problems. Any behavior that is unusual for the individual might indicate illness. Sick horses are often "not themselves" and may show some of the following symptoms:

- going off feed (not eating);
- failure to drink water;
- failure to pass manure;
- straining to urinate;
- diarrhea;
- showing signs of discomfort (e.g., restlessness, looking at its side, pawing, repeatedly shifting the weight from side to side, groaning or grunting, standing with the legs unnaturally spraddled or stretched, stretching the neck upward and curling the upper lip when other signs of illness are present);
- depression (listlessness);
- lying down for a prolonged period;
- repeated or violent rolling;
- repeatedly lying down and getting up;
- lameness (limping);
- coughing;
- drooling;
- discharge from the nose or eyes;
- bad breath;
- tenderness or pain from moderate pressure on part of the body;
- areas that are hotter to the touch than normal (one leg noticeably warmer than the other legs, etc.);
- sweating without exertion;
- shivering when it isn't cold;
- swollen areas;
- shallow breathing;
- panting;
- stocking up or edema (causes vary from heart or kidney problems to simply lack of exercise), always related to circulatory sluggishness.

The best indications of a horse's state of health are its temperature, pulse, and rate of respiration.

Temperature

An adult horse's normal body temperature range is 98°F to 101°F. Foals have a slightly higher normal reading (100°F to 101.5°F). On a hot day, or if the foal has been napping in the sunshine, its temperature may be a degree higher without indicating fever.

Just as all people do not have a normal reading of 98.6°F, all horses do not share the same normal reading; thus, two horses that both have a temperature of 103°F may not be equally sick. You should, therefore, determine your horse's normal temperature range *before* it becomes sick.

To establish a horse's normal range, record the temperature twice a day for three days. Each day, take the temperature morning and evening; temperature tends to be slightly lower in the morning. Take the readings when the horse is calm and rested since the temperature will be higher after exercise. Record all the temperatures, add them together and divide by six to get the horse's "average temperature." For greater accuracy, add the morning readings and divide by three to determine the horse's average morning reading and do the same with the evening readings to get its average evening reading. Record the temperature readings in the horse's individual health record for future reference.

Taking the Horse's Temperature

A livestock thermometer is longer and more sturdy than one used for people, but it is read the same way. Insert a string through the hole in the end of the livestock thermometer for easy retrieval before using it. Shake the mercury down to at least 95°F and coat the bulb end of the thermometer with a lubricant such as *K-Y Jelly®* or petroleum jelly. Insert about 75 percent of the length of the thermometer into the horse's rectum and leave it there for three minutes before removing it to read the temperature.

Livestock thermometers are marked in even numbers, with lines indicating odd numbers. The short lines indicate one-fifth of a degree.

A digital livestock thermometer also is now available. Although much more expensive than a standard thermometer, it records temperature in less than one minute and shows the reading in numerals so there is less chance of error in reading the temperature. In addition, it is more sturdy than a conventional thermometer because it is made of plastic rather than glass.

After use, wash the thermometer in cool water and mild soap, then dip it in alcohol before storing it in a cool—but not cold—place.

In an emergency, you can use a human thermometer to take a horse's temperature. However, it must be held constantly to prevent it being drawn into the horse's rectum, and may not be as accurate as a livestock thermometer because it cannot be inserted as deeply.

Pulse

The horse's normal pulse rate at rest is about 35 to 45 beats per minute. The strongest pulse can be found just under the jaw, next to the jawbone. Stand at the horse's side and put two fingers on the edge of the jaw at the throatlatch, then move your fingers until you feel the pulse; use a medium to light pressure. The pulse also can be felt in the dock of the tail. Count the beats for one minute. If the horse won't stand still, count for twenty seconds and multiply by three to get the pulse rate per minute.

Checking the Respiration Rate

The horse normally takes ten to twenty breaths per minute. (Each breath consists of inhaling and exhaling.) Count the horse's breaths by watching the diaphragm expand and contract.

EMERGENCIES

Colic

Colic is not a specific illness but a symptom. Colic is abdominal pain, usually resulting from a digestive problem—an impaction (blockage) of the intestines, excessive gas, or a twisted intestine. All true colic is serious and can be fatal. Many colic deaths result from shock.

Death can result if an intestine becomes twisted because the blood supply is shut off to part of the body. The tissue in that part dies, resulting in the death of the horse. Impaction can also cause a ruptured intestine, and even gas can rupture the stomach or intestines if the pressure is extreme.

Signs of colic include pawing, repeated rolling, turning to look at the abdomen, kicking toward it, or stretching the neck upward and curling the upper lip as an expression of pain.

Veterinary treatment for colic includes administering mineral oil via stomach tube to lubricate the fecal material and relieve constipation. An injection of Dipyrone or Banamine often is given to relieve spasms and ease pain. Sometimes walking a horse stimulates the passage of gas and manure and "cures" a mild case of colic. A horse with colic should not be exercised at a trot or canter, however.

Stress and worms are believed to be the most frequent causes of colic. Stress is probably the most common contributor to colic in show horses, and worms are suspected when deworming has been neglected.

In severe cases of colic, surgery is necessary. However, surgery cannot always save the horse's life and always entails its own risks.

Laminitis (Founder)

Founder involves the affected horse's digestion, circulation, and—ultimately—hoofs. It causes a breakdown of the hoofs' interior and separation of the wall from the interior tissues. As a result, the coffin bone inside the hoof may rotate and drop toward or even through the sole of the hoof. Because its feet hurt, the foundered horse assumes a characteristic pose with the forelegs stretched forward in an attempt to relieve them of weight. Acute founder results in misshapen hoofs with exaggerated rings in the hoof wall and toes that curl upward.

With careful and expensive farrier and veterinary care, severely foundered horses sometimes can be maintained as breeding stock. With prompt care, a performance horse with a mild case of founder may recover fully. Call the veterinarian whenever founder is suspected.

Research still is being done to determine the exact causes of founder. Causes range from eating too much grain to retaining the placenta after foaling. Founder can even result from being given cold water or grain while overheated. Road founder is caused by too much concussion to the hoofs on a hard surface. At present, the best way to prevent founder is to avoid its known causes.

FIRST AID

Occasionally, the horse owner may have an injured horse that requires treatment before the veterinarian arrives. The most common injuries requiring first aid are cuts and punctures.

Remember that first aid is only emergency "first" aid. Don't attempt to treat the horse completely by yourself. Do what must be done to care for the horse in the immediate situation but have the veterinarian give follow-up medical treatment as soon as possible.

Put together a first aid kit based on your own veterinarian's recommendations and keep with it a concise, easy-to-use book on equine first aid such as *Know First Aid for Your Horse*, by G. Marvin Beeman, D.V.M. (see Bibliography). Contents of a simple first aid kit are listed. The exact drugs and supplies kept on hand for emergencies depend upon your own expertise and situation. People living in remote areas need to know more about first aid than those who live where skilled veterinarians are more quickly accessible.

SAMPLE FIRST AID KIT*

- Livestock thermometer
- Lubricating ointment (K-Y® or petroleum jelly)
- Water-soluble wound ointment (such as nitrofurazone)
- Non-stick *(Telfa)* wound pads
- Veterinary surgical scrub
- Veterinary antiseptic solution
- Rolls of cotton sheeting
- Self-adhering elastic bandage *(Vetrap)*
- Adhesive tape
- Rolls of gauze
- Ophthalmic solution or ointment
- Castor oil
- Iodine
- Bandage scissors

Actual contents should be determined with the help of a veterinarian and based upon the user's expertise and special needs.

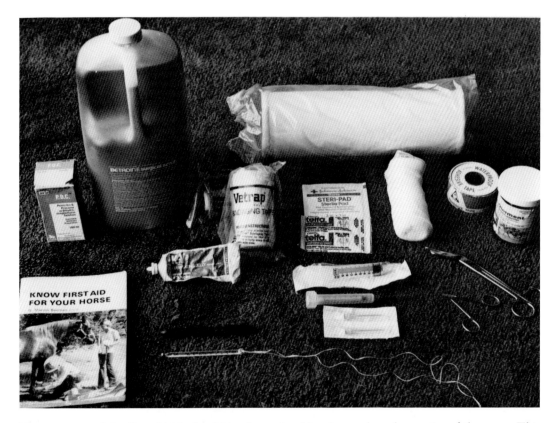

The contents of the first aid kit should be determined by the needs and expertise of the users. This kit includes penicillin, veterinary surgical scrub, sheet cotton, bandaging tape, gauze, non-stick wound pads, nitrofurazone ointment, bandage-cutting scissors, disposeable syringes and disposeable needles, lubricating jelly ointment, livestock thermometer, and a first aid book.

Bleeding

Although it is frightening to see a quantity of blood resulting from an accident, the situation usually is not as serious as it looks because a horse is a big animal containing a lot of blood (about nine percent of its body weight). The horse can lose 30 percent to 40 percent of its blood without serious harm; in a 1,000-pound horse this amounts to about three gallons.

After a certain amount of bleeding occurs, the horse's blood pressure drops, resulting in slower blood flow. This slower rate of bleeding aids clotting. A horse that has lost a lot of blood should not be tranquilized because its blood pressure already has dropped, and tranquilizing the horse can lower it even more, resulting in possible fainting or even death.

Minor bleeding usually will stop without help. Heavier bleeding can be reduced or stopped by using a pressure bandage directly over the wound. If the wound is large, hold a clean towel directly on top of it and then bandage over the towel. Once on, do not remove the pressure bandage. If blood soaks through, add another layer over the original bandage. Never use a tourniquet to stop bleeding; it can damage tissue by shutting off the blood supply to the wounded area.

Body Wounds

If the horse has a body wound with a flap of skin still attached, pull the skin over the wound. Then put the folded gauze over the skin and cover it with a piece of clean bed sheet, tying on the body bandage with rope until the veterinarian can examine the horse.

Puncture Wounds

Puncture wounds can cause serious infection or tetanus; for this reason, a veterinarian should treat them. If a puncturing object is still embedded, wait for the vet to remove it unless there is a danger of it being driven further inward. (When the object is removed, the hole closes quickly, making the site difficult to relocate for later treatment.) If a veterinarian cannot treat the wound right away, it may be necessary to remove the object and clean the area (see "Cleaning the Wound"). A hoof puncture is treated differently than a body or leg puncture; after the object has been removed from the sole of the hoof, pour iodine into the puncture hole and pack it with cotton to keep it clean. (Iodine should be used only on *hoof* punctures, as it can damage body tissues.)

Eye Injuries

When a horse's eye is injured, prevent the horse from rubbing it. Castor oil or a mild veterinary ophthalmic solution can be used to soothe the eye. To reduce discomfort, the horse should be put in a dark stall. If necessary, the injured eye can be carefully covered with a bandage to help prevent pain caused by bright sunlight. If an object is embedded in the eye, it is best to let a veterinarian remove it rather than attempting the delicate task yourself.

Cleaning the Wound

To reduce the chance of infection, clean a wound that is no longer bleeding as soon as it is discovered. First, wet and wash the hair surrounding the wound with veterinary surgical scrub. Then trim off the surrounding hair with scissors, being careful that the cut hair doesn't fall into the wound. After cleaning the surrounding area, flush the wound with water to remove dirt or foreign objects and then apply an antiseptic veterinary solution (such as Betadine Solution) to disinfect the wound.

If you put any medication on the wound before the veterinarian arrives, use only a water-soluble wound dressing such as nitrofurazone. Do *not* put peroxide, iodine, or any oil-based dye medications on a wound. They can damage the tissues and cause proud flesh (an overgrowth of new tissue as the wound heals) and broken sutures if the veterinarian stitches the wound closed. If in doubt, use only water on a wound until it is checked by a veterinarian.

After cleaning a cut, it can be bandaged to keep the wound clean until the veterinarian arrives. Punctures are best left unbandaged to allow oxygen and sunlight to reach the wound, except in the case of hoof punctures, when the bottom of the hoof may be bandaged to keep dirt from being packed into the puncture.

Left to Right: To bandage a leg wound, place a non-stick wound pad and nitrofurazone ointment on the wound, then wrap the leg with gauze tape. Gauze should extend well above and below the wound. Sheet cotton can be applied over the gauze for padding, if desired. Vetrap bandaging tape is applied over the previous wraps. The completed leg bandage keeps the wound clean and prevents further injury.

Bandaging a Leg Wound

A leg bandage should be applied with even tension, making it tight enough to supply adequate support without being so tight that it shuts off circulation and causes swelling. To bandage a leg wound, first coat a non-stick wound pad with water-soluble wound ointment (such as nitrofurazone) and place the pad on the wound. Then wrap the leg with gauze, beginning below the wound and wrapping upward with even horizontal wraps around the leg. The gauze should extend at least several inches above and below the wound; bandaging well above and below the injury helps prevent swelling in the leg. Sheet cotton then is applied over the gauze and held in place by even horizontal wraps of self-adhering elastic bandaging tape (Vetrap). Wrap from the middle of the cotton sheeting downward, then upward, bandaging over and then above the wound. Finish with a strip of adhesive tape applied vertically on the leg bandage.

Shock

Whenever a horse is ill or injured, there is a chance of shock. A rapid pulse (80 or more beats per minute) indicates shock. Another test for shock is pressing on the horse's gums. The pink color should return within three seconds after you stop pushing on the gums; if the gums are white, the horse is already in shock. When a horse is in shock, be sure to *tell the veterinarian* when you call. If treatment is not received immediately, the horse will die.

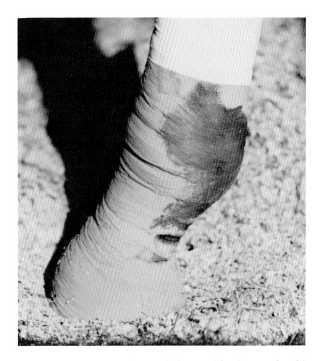

When a bandage is applied to help stop bleeding, it should not be removed until a veterinarian has examined the wound; removing the bandage may increase the bleeding.

127

DENTAL CARE

The mature male horse has forty teeth: twelve incisors (six in the upper jaw and six in the lower jaw); four canine teeth (two upper, two lower); twelve premolars (six upper, six lower); and twelve molars (six upper, six lower). The mature mare usually has thirty-six teeth—most mares don't have canine teeth.

Incisors are found in the front of the mouth. They are used to bite off grasses when grazing.

Canines are the pointed teeth next to the incisors. There is just one canine on each side of the upper jaw, and one on each side of the lower.

The bars of the mouth are the toothless spaces between the incisors and the premolars. (The bit rests on this toothless area when the horse is bridled.)

Premolars (cheek teeth) are the front grinding teeth (used for chewing).

Molars are the back grinding teeth.

Each tooth in the upper jaw is matched by an opposing tooth in the lower jaw. Unlike human teeth, the horse's teeth continue to "grow" throughout its life. They don't actually grow but are forced outward by new bone growth below the roots of the teeth.

Floating the Teeth

Friction from chewing wears down the teeth. If the upper and lower opposing teeth aren't well matched, they wear unevenly. Even well-matched teeth sometimes wear unevenly because the upper premolars always are wider than the lower ones.

Sharp points appear at the edges of the teeth from uneven wear, causing problems with chewing and sometimes cutting the gums, cheeks, or tongue. These sharp edges periodically must be lowered by a veterinarian, who files ("floats") them with a dental file. Older horses usually need to have their teeth floated more often than young horses, but even young, growing horses may require floating.

Tooth Problems

Symptoms of tooth problems include rolling the feed into a ball in the mouth while chewing, drooling, slow (painful) chewing, spilling feed (especially grain) from the mouth, or holding the head sideways while chewing. A horse with severe dental problems will eat less and may even stop eating. Whenever a horse goes off feed, check its teeth to see if they are the cause.

Cavities in horses are rare. Although sweet feeds are sometimes suspected of causing them, infected teeth usually result from injury instead of decay. A foul-smelling discharge from only one nostril may indicate a severely infected tooth.

If a tooth must be pulled by a veterinarian, or is accidently knocked out, its opposite tooth must be floated regularly to compensate for lack of wear from normal chewing.

Cutting and Shedding Teeth

Milk or baby teeth (deciduous teeth) are the first ones cut, appearing within the foal's first week of life. They eventually loosen, fall out, and are replaced by the horse's permanent teeth. The milk teeth consist of twelve incisors and twelve premolars.

The milk teeth are shed at various ages. The first incisors and the second premolars are shed first and replaced by permanent teeth when the horse is about 2½ years old. The rest of the milk teeth are replaced when the horse is between three and 4½ years old. By the time the horse is about five, it has a complete permanent set of teeth.

When the young horse is cutting new teeth, it may chew objects to help them break through the gums. During teething, the gums become sore and red and the horse may eat less or spill feed. If these problems persist, check the young horse's teeth to be sure they are being properly shed and replaced.

Until the young horse cuts all its permanent teeth, it has "teeth bumps" that can be seen along the exterior of its lower jaw. These bumps disappear as the permanent teeth erupt, causing the Arabian's head to become more refined when the horse is about five years old.

Wolf Teeth

A wolf tooth is a small, *extra* tooth sometimes seen in the upper jaw, in front of the first cheek tooth. (Don't confuse wolf teeth with the canine teeth, which are next to the incisors at the front of the mouth.) Wolf teeth are useless, and most horses never have them. If they do, they erupt when the horse is about six months old. Although they usually do not interfere with the bit, wolf teeth can cause discomfort and head tossing. In that case, the

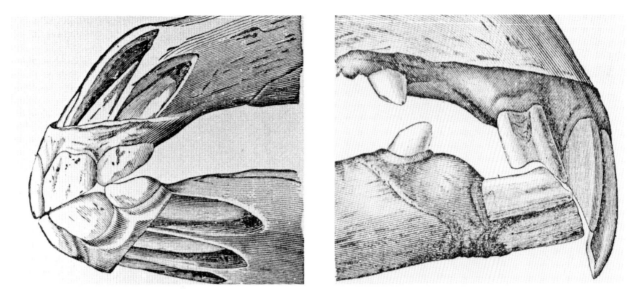

Teeth are important to the horse's health. On the left, an example of a correct bite (alignment of upper and lower teeth) in the young horse. Right: A parrot mouth (overbite) is a grave handicap to a grazing animal. The condition is believed to be inherited from both sides of the family; parrot-mouthed horses will be faulted in halter classes as the condition is inheritable. *Illustration from "The Exterior of the Horse" by Goubaux and Barrier, 1892.*

teeth can be easily pulled by a veterinarian with only minor discomfort to the horse.

Telling Age by the Teeth

As horses age, their front teeth become longer and more angular. They also acquire characteristic worn spots, grooves, and hooks at certain ages. It is therefore possible to estimate the horse's age according to the appearance of its teeth.

According to Lady Wentworth, however, it is more difficult to judge the age of an Arabian by its teeth because they wear more slowly than those of other breeds. (This may be related to the Arabian's denser bone and greater longevity.)

Fortunately, it is unnecessary to "age" a registered Arabian or Half-Arabian by its teeth because its foaling date appears on the horse's registration certificate.

Parrot Mouth

"Parrot mouth" is a deformity of the jaws in which the upper incisors overlap the incisors of the lower jaw. Because this overbite prevents teeth from wearing equally, parrot-mouthed horses must have their teeth floated regularly to prevent excessive growth of the upper incisors. The opposite deformity, with the lower jaw overshooting the upper jaw, is called "monkey mouth." Although much less

common, it is equally serious and also requires careful dental care. Because parrot-mouthed or monkey-mouthed horses cannot graze efficiently, they should never be pastured without supplemental feeding.

If a horse show judge examines the teeth of a halter horse, the horse's bite is being checked. Both parrot mouth and monkey mouth are believed to be inherited as a recessive trait. Because these defects can be passed to descendants, horses with parrot mouth or monkey mouth should not be shown in halter classes. Halter classes are for breeding stock, and horses with these defects should not be used for breeding.

16

PARASITES

Various internal parasites are called "worms." They usually mature inside the horse where they bore into arteries and organs, feeding on the horse's blood. Mature worms lay eggs in the horse's intestines, and the eggs are passed in the manure. When the eggs hatch, the new worms (larvae) enter the horse's body via its mouth. Inside, the worms mature and then lay more eggs to continue the vicious cycle of reinfestation. Unless this cycle is broken, horses host a continually growing number of internal parasites.

Veterinarian Richard Perce says, "We have no way to tell just how much better a certain horse would have been if it had never had worms." Worms can keep a horse from achieving its full genetic potential. They also can kill. Veterinarians say that most cases of colic—the leading cause of death in horses—are caused by worms. Even champion Arabians have died as a result of internal damage caused by worms when they were young.

SYMPTOMS AND TYPES OF WORMS

The severely infested horse has a rough hair coat and a distended abdomen (pot belly), although its ribs may be visible. Wormy horses sometimes lack energy, and young horses may not grow at a normal rate. Worms can cause anemia, diarrhea, and colic. A persistent "cold" with a nasal discharge or cough can result from lung congestion caused by worms. The wormy horse may have a cough and may cough up worm larvae, only to swallow them.

Although the signs of severe worm infestation *are* visible, you cannot tell whether a horse has worms just by its appearance. A bright-eyed, fat, sleek horse also can have worms. Only an extreme infestation is apparent by the horse's appearance.

Strongyles (bloodworms, red worms)

Strongyles are the smallest but most deadly worms infesting horses. The biggest strongyles grow to only three inches in length, and many are so small that they cannot be seen. Strongyles are grey or red in color.

Small strongyles live in the digestive tract, especially in the caecum and colon. Large strongyles are only "large" in comparison to small strongyles—thousands of them can live in the intestines of a single horse. The most dangerous large strongyle is probably *Strongylus vulgaris*, which is carried in the blood to the various tissues and organs where it burrows through their walls. It frequently attacks the intestines but can damage *any* organ—including the heart, liver, lungs, or brain.

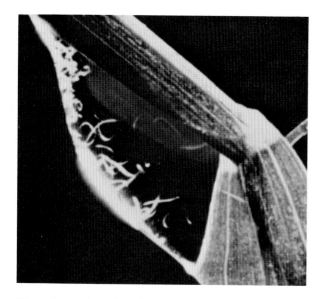

Worm larvae in a dew drop on a blade of grass. Grazing horses swallow the larvae, which migrate through the tissues of their bodies, causing internal damage.
Photo courtesy of Merck & Co., Inc., Rahway, N.J.

Migrating strongyle larvae weaken the blood vessels and can cause blood clots. If a clot breaks loose from the wall of a vessel, it can clog smaller passages, shutting off the blood supply to part of the body. The mesenteric artery, which supplies blood to the intestines, is often attacked by strongyles. If a clot forms and blocks this artery, a section of the intestines will die, resulting in the horse's death. If the blood flow is reduced rather than totally stopped, an impaction or twisted intestine may result; these conditions also can be fatal. Scar tissue from worm damage also can cause a twisted intestine.

Ascarids (large roundworms, white worms)

Ascarids usually affect young horses and may delay growth. Mature horses also can be infested but often seem to have developed some resistance to ascarids.

Ascarids are the largest of the horse worms. They grow to about fifteen inches in length and may be as thick as a pencil. They are white in color.

Ascarid larvae can damage the horse's lungs and other organs as they migrate through the body. Adult roundworms can cause bleeding by eating through the lining of the intestines. A heavy infestation of adult ascarids can cause colic, impaction, or rupture the stomach or intestines, resulting in the horse's death.

Bots

The clusters of ugly, dark-colored larvae often shown in ads for deworming drugs are immature bot flies. They are not really worms but infest the horse in similar fashion.

Adult bot flies lay their eggs on the horse's body especially on the hairs of the abdomen, jaw, muzzle, chest, and legs. The eggs are yellow or black, depending upon the type of bot fly, and hatch when the horse licks or bites at them. Some species even hatch without this stimulation.

When the bot larvae reach the horse's mouth, they burrow into the tongue, gums or lips. When swallowed, they attach to the stomach and intestines. Unlike true worms, bots stay in the stomach instead of being carried throughout the body. New bot eggs are passed in the manure and hatch as mature flies which, in turn, lay eggs to continue the cycle of infestation.

Bots can cause internal bleeding, colic, impaction, or rupturing of the stomach or intestines.

Pinworms

Pinworms live in the horse's large intestines. The female worm crawls through the horse's rectum to lay eggs near its anus and tail. After a few days, the eggs drop to the ground and hatch to reinfest the horse. Pinworms cause itching and resultant tail rub-

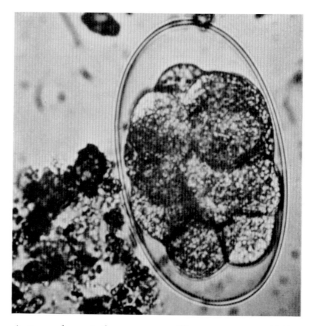

A strongyle egg in horse manure. The eggs are so small that they can be seen only with the aid of a microscope.
Photo courtesy of Merck & Co., Inc., Rahway, N.J.

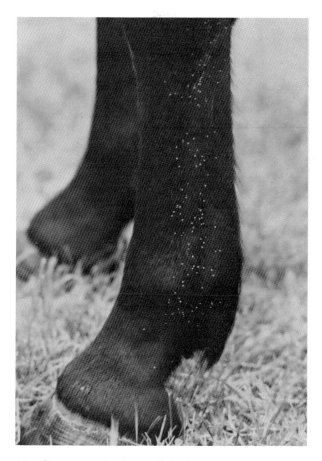

Bot fly eggs on the hairs of the legs.
Photo courtesy of Merck & Co., Inc., Rahway, N.J.

bing. However, they seem to cause little internal damage compared to strongyles, ascarids, and bots.

Tapeworms

Tapeworms are believed to be rare in horses. When present, they infest the intestines. Part of the tapeworm's segmented body contains its eggs, and that part of the body is passed in the horse's manure. If the eggs are swallowed, they develop into adult tapeworms inside the horse. Horses get tapeworms from other species affected by this parasite, usually from grazing in a pasture contamined by feces containing the eggs.

Tapeworms can cause some of the same digestive problems as other worms, including colic or impaction. They also can cause weight loss and lack of condition.

FECAL COUNTS

The kind and amount of worm eggs in manure can be determined by a microscopic exam. The higher the number of a certain kind of worm eggs in a gram of manure, the more severe is the infestation of that particular worm in the individual horse.

Although the fecal count can help evaluate the success of the present deworming program and indicate needed changes in frequency of deworming or drug used, it should not be completely relied upon to indicate when deworming is needed. The fecal count merely determines the kind and number of eggs produced at a given time; it cannot reveal the number of migrating larvae or predict when they will mature and start laying eggs. It is therefore safest to maintain a regular deworming schedule.

Veterinary laboratories can perform fecal analysis to determine egg counts, and one deworming drug company (Farnam Laboratories of Omaha, Nebraska) now offers a mail-in fecal analysis kit.

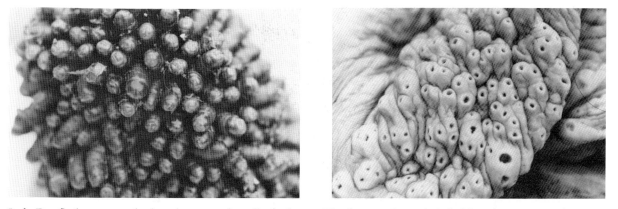

Left: Bot fly larvae attached to the stomach wall of a horse. The larvae release their hold in the spring and are passed in the horse's manure . . . Right: leaving ulcers in the stomach wall. The damage to the horse can be severe if the bots are not removed by deworming.   *Photos courtesy of Merck & Co., Inc., Rahway, N.J.*

DEWORMING

At present, there is no way to completely prevent worms. The best way to control the worm population is to kill the worms while they are inside the horse, to reduce the number of eggs laid to reinfest the horse. To kill the worms, the horse is given a horse deworming drug (a specialized pesticide) by mouth or stomach tube.

Dead worms that were killed by the dewormer are passed in the horse's manure. Ascarids are the easiest to spot, due to their white color and large size. Only the older, larger strongyles can be seen. Many dead worms in the manure indicates a heavy infestation. If dead worms are noticeable, the horse should be dewormed again with a product effective against the same type of worms in two to four weeks. Because some worms killed by the dewormer are too small to be easily seen, a visual examination cannot determine the effectiveness of the treatment.

Deworming Methods

Deworming drugs come in various forms: liquids (for tube deworming); granules, powders, and pellets (for adding to the horse's grain); and as a thick "paste" in a syringe (given by mouth). Of these, the in-feed dewormers are least desirable because many horses refuse medicated grain. The dewormer also can sift through the grain and be left in the feed trough.

In tube deworming, the veterinarian inserts a rubber hose (stomach tube) into the horse's stomach via the nostril and esophagus, and pumps liquid dewormer directly into the stomach. Tubing places the proper dose of the dewormer directly into the stomach, but it is expensive because it involves a veterinarian's charge, and it also stresses the horse. If a horse fights the stomach tube, it can get a bloody nose in the process. The liquid dewormer can drown a horse if it is accidentally put into the lungs rather than into the stomach. Because paste dewormers are highly effective, tube deworming is no longer necessary and is done less often.

Paste dewormers are the most recent development and allow owners to deworm their own horses easily and inexpensively. The paste dewormer is prepackaged in a plastic syringe that is inserted into the side of the horse's mouth (in the gap between the teeth). The syringe plunger then is then pushed, forcing the thick, sticky paste onto the back of the horse's tongue. Before giving the paste, be sure the horse's mouth is empty so the paste cannot be spit out with feed. After administration, keep the horse's head elevated slightly until the dewormer is swallowed.

Deworming Drugs

Dewormers appear under many different brand names made by various chemical companies, but only seven major types actually exist:

Tube deworming. Left: the rubber tube is inserted into the stomach via the nostril and esophagus. Right: deworming liquid is pumped into the stomach.

Photos by Don Sepulvado, courtesy of NSU

avermectins (Ivermectin);

benzimidazoles (cambendazole, fenbendazole, mebendazole, thiabendazole, and oxibendazole);

organophosphates (trichlorfon, dichlorvos);

phenylguanidine (febantel);

phenothiazine;

piperazine;

pyrantel.

These families are *not* equally effective against the same worms. Some are effective against one type of worm, others are more effective against another worm. The following drugs are highly effective against the worms indicated:

Worm	Highly Effective Drugs
Strongyles	benzimidazoles, phenylguanidine, avermectins
Ascarids	piperazine, phenylguanidine
Bots	organophosphates, avermectins
Tapeworms	pyrantel

(Read the label of the dewormer to see which drug it contains.)

The only deworming drug families that will kill bots are avermectins and organophosphates. However, organophosphates are not effective against strongyles. During bot season, use a dewormer effective against both bots and strongyles.

Ivermectin

The newest dewormer is Ivermectin (brand names *Eqvalan®* and *Zimecterin®*), that became available in the United States in early 1983. While other deworming drugs poison worms, Ivermectin kills them indirectly, by paralysis. Ivermectin is the *only* drug that can kill migrating worm larvae—other dewormers kill only the worms that happen to be in the stomach and intestines at the time the horse is treated. Ivermectin is highly effective against most internal parasites, including bots, and also kills blood-sucking external parasites such as ticks and mange mites. However, it is not effective against some developmental stages of ascarids and, like most dewormers, cannot kill tapeworms, which require special treatment by a veterinarian.

If the Ivermectin-treated horse has a heavy infestation of *onchocerca* (threadworm) larvae, edema caused by large numbers of dead *onchocerca* may occur along the underside of the horse's abdomen. If this occurs, the veterinarian should be notified. Fortunately, this is seldom a serious problem and merely reflects the efficiency of the drug in killing the larval stage of this particular internal parasite.

Because Ivermectin affects the nervous system of each parasite, there is little expectation that parasites will develop resistance to the drug if it is used repeatedly. Used regularly, Ivermectin may keep adult horses virtually worm-free. However, there is a danger that a horse kept on a regular Ivermectin deworming schedule may never develop natural resistance to parasites. If the deworming program is discontinued (in the event of the horse's sale, etc.) and the horse is exposed to heavy worm infestation, it may be susceptible to severe worm damage.

Ivermectin is extremely effective against most equine parasites and, when administered properly, safe for most horses (including pregnant mares and foals at least four months old). Consult your veterinarian concerning his or her recommendations for use of this and other dewormers presently available.

Dewormer Dosage

The proper dosage of deworming drugs is based on the individual horse's weight. Recommended dosages are shown on the dewormer label. (Refer to Chapter 27 to estimate an Arabian's weight accurately.)

If a horse is suspected of a heavy infestation of ascarids, *do not give the recommended dosage.* If too many of these large worms are killed at once, they can form a ball and cause impaction, a twisted intestine, or rupturing of the stomach or intestines. To avoid this risk, divide the recommended amount into two or three smaller doses given a few days apart so that the dead worms will be passed in smaller quantities.

PLANNING A DEWORMING PROGRAM

Ask your vet's recommendation as to which dewormers to use, and how often they are needed. Then plan a deworming schedule and follow it conscientiously.

Deworm *all* your horses on the same schedule. If only one horse in a group is dewormed, it can become reinfested from worm eggs passed in the other horses' manure. Horses sharing pastures or pens with wormy horses are quickly reinfested.

Strongyles are the horse's most deadly enemy, so dewormers used should be highly effective against strongyles as well as killing other kinds of worms.

When deworming young, growing horses, use drugs that are highly effective against ascarids as well as strongyles. Deworm for ascarids until horses are at least four years old. For best protection from ascarids, piperazine or febantel dewormers should be included in the deworming program when young horses are being treated. (Ivermectin is effective against some—but not all—stages of ascarids.)

Deworm for bots about two weeks after bot eggs appear, then again about one month after a "killing frost" when temperatures are cold enough to kill the adult flies, stopping bot egg production until the next fly season. If desired, deworm again for bots two months later. Horses in warm or humid climates may need a boticide more frequently because the fly season is longer than in cool, dry areas.

How Often To Deworm

Most horses need deworming every four to eight weeks. Frequency of deworming depends upon the climate and kind of operation. Horses on large

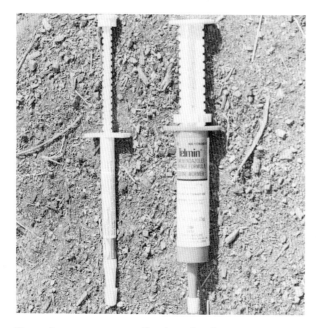

Paste dewormers are easily given by the owner. Several brands and families of deworming drugs are available.

acreages may require deworming less often than those in small paddocks where there is a greater opportunity for reinfestation from manure. In cold, dry climates, horses may require deworming less often than in warmer, humid areas where worm eggs hatch rapidly and worm larvae thrive.

Pregnant mares should be dewormed regularly during pregnancy except for the last two months before foaling. Postpone deworming until a week after the mare foals. Before deworming a pregnant mare, read the label of the deworming product carefully and heed any warnings. Some dewormers are not safe for pregnant mares.

Deworm foals for the first time when they are one or two months old, using a dewormer that is safe for young foals and effective against ascarids. Then add the foal to the same deworming schedule followed for your other horses. Foals, like adult horses, also must be dewormed for bots seasonally.

Postpone deworming if a horse becomes sick and do not deworm when the horse is stressed from weaning, travel, severe weather, etc. Do not work a horse heavily or subject it to other stress for a day or two after deworming.

Rotate Dewormers

When planning your deworming program for the year, *rotate types of drugs*. Research has indicated that small strongyles develop resistance to febantel and benzimidazoles (with the apparent exception of oxibendazole). To prevent this, do not use the same product twice in a row, rotating a *minimum* of two *types* of drugs throughout the year.

Rotate dewormers from different families (types)—not just dewormers with different brand names since there are many brand names for the same drugs. You are not *necessarily* rotating drug types by using drugs made by different companies or even two drugs made by the same company. For example, cambendazole and thiabendazole are from the same family of drugs—benzimidazoles. When rotating drugs, they should not be used one after the other.

OTHER WAYS TO CONTROL WORMS

Since horse manure contains worm eggs, removing manure from the areas where horses are kept will reduce reinfestation. Remove manure from stalls once or twice daily (more often, if desired). Strip

To administer a paste dewormer, insert the syringe between the bars of the mouth (at the side of the mouth, the toothless area where the bit rests), and push the plunger.

the stalls completely once a week and rebed them to reduce reinfestation from worm eggs in the stall bedding. (Strongyle eggs hatch in about ten days.) Clean small paddocks at least twice a week and, if possible, remove manure from pastures weekly.

"Resting" a pasture by removing horses for a year will help reduce the worm problem. During that time, cattle or sheep can be grazed there. Ploughing and reseeding also will help reduce worms. Never use horse manure to fertilize a horse pasture.

Isolate and deworm new horses before putting them with other horses. After they have been dewormed, add them to your regular deworming program. To avoid passing strongyles from mature horses to young ones, pasture young stock separately.

Don't feed from the ground or low feeders, and put waterers high enough to avoid contamination by manure.

Use insecticides in the stable to kill bot flies, and put insect repellent on the horses to discourage bot flies from laying eggs. Remove and burn bot eggs immediately. Electric clippers or special bot egg knives are the most effective means of removal.

EXTERNAL PARASITES

Although not as deadly as the internal variety, parasites that feed on the outside of the horse's body also cause discomfort and carry disease.

Lice and Mange Mites

There are two kinds of lice—those that bite and those that suck blood; in a severe case, the latter can cause anemia. Lice also cause mane and tail rubbing and may cause hair loss.

Mange results from small mites that burrow into the skin and cause itching. The skin becomes more irritated as the horse rubs against fences or trees to scratch; the hair falls out and the bare skin is red and scaley.

External parasites are killed by applying special pesticides in dusting powder or liquid (dip) form. The powder is brushed through the hair; the liquid can either be sprayed or sponged on the horse. Ivermectin also kills external blood-sucking parasites.

Ticks

Ticks are insects that bury their heads into the horse's skin and suck blood. (They also will imbed in other animals and people.) Ticks carry disease and in extreme cases may cause anemia. Unlike tiny lice and mites, ticks are seen easily and can be felt with the fingers. The best time to check a horse for ticks is while grooming.

If an imbedded tick is pulled out, its head may remain in the skin, causing an infection. Instead, apply flea and tick spray to the tick and wait a few minutes for it to die, or encourage the tick to withdraw its head by applying drops of kerosene to its body. Sometimes touching a hot, extinguished match to the tick's body (*instead* of using the kerosene) also will cause it to withdraw. Be careful to avoid burning the horse with the match and never combine the two methods. If you find more than an occasional tick, apply a commercial tick preparation according to the directions on the label.

Ear ticks are especially annoying. The horse may hold tick-infested ears to the side, twitch its ears, or shake its head repeatedly. If a halter horse gets ear ticks, getting it to put its ears forward while showing may be impossible. When treated for ear ticks, the horse may become head shy (moving the head away when you try to reach its head or ears). Ivermectin is effective against ticks and won't make the horse head shy because the ticks are killed without touching the horse's ears.

Summer Sores

Summer sores are non-healing sores that occur when houseflies or stable flies transmit habronema ("stomach worms") to open wounds. The sores also may occur around the horse's eyes. The open sores, which can disfigure or disable a horse, occur mostly in hot climates.

Veterinary application of trichlorfon has proven effective in killing habronema. Ivermectin or other drugs effective against strongyles also kill the parasites so that the summer sores can heal.

137

Farrier John Valdez shoeing Tah Neeka
Photo courtesy of John and Cheryl Casdorph, Bakersfield, Calif.

17

HOOF CARE

Although the Bedouins shod their horses, their shoeing skills were notoriously poor. They used a simple, round shoe and didn't rasp or trim the horses' hoofs, which were worn down by frequent exercise on abrasive ground. The Arabian horses' reputation for soundness and endurance was *not* due to the skills of Bedouin farriers!

The modern Arabian horse cannot fulfill its main function in life—to perform as an athlete—unless it has healthy hoofs. Improper hoof care can cause lameness, even in horses with good conformation.

Although a tendency to certain hoof problems is inherited, good care can prevent many difficulties. Next to a good veterinarian, the horse owner's best friend is a competent farrier.

PARTS OF THE HOOF

The outer hoof consists of the *wall*, a horny shell that protects the sensitive interior tissues and bones of the foot. The underside of the hoof contains the *sole*, a slightly concave plate across most of the bottom of the hoof; the *frog*, a spongey, V-shaped tissue; and the *bars*, which divide the frog and the sole.

When the horse steps forward, the heel of the hoof meets the ground first. Compressed by the heel (from the horse's weight), the wedge-shaped frog pushes against the rest of the hoof. This expands the hoof slightly, forcing blood from inside the hoof upward into the leg.

When the hoof is raised, the horse's weight is removed from it and the hoof contracts, allowing fresh blood to move down inside the hoof. The alternate expansion and contraction of the hoof circulates blood through the horse's hoofs and legs.

The frog does not *have* to contact the ground to do its job. When the hoof strikes the ground, the heel and sole put enough pressure on the frog to expand the hoof. The length of the frog is therefore not as critical as its flexibility, which depends upon moisture. A hard, dry frog will not be flexible enough to circulate the blood properly.

SIZE AND SHAPE OF THE HOOF

Hoofs vary in size and shape, according to the individual's genetic inheritance. Hoof variations found in modern Arabians stem from interbreeding of ancestors having different types of hoofs. The hoof should be in proportion to the rest of the horse.

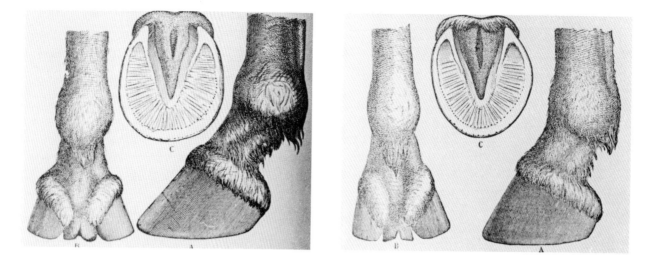

Left: The horse's front hoofs are rounder and slightly larger than the hind hoofs. Right: The hind hoofs are narrower and slightly smaller than the front hoofs. *Illustrations from "The Exterior of the Horse" by Goubaux and Barrier, 1892.*

A small, refined horse should have smaller feet than a larger, heavy-boned horse. Although a small "show hoof" may appear neat and dainty, it may be too small and narrow to properly support the horse's weight and to expand adequately when the horse is in action.

The hoof should be fairly round and not too narrow so that the horse's weight is distributed evenly over the hoof wall. The heel should be wide and open to allow for expansion and contraction. Narrow (contracted) heels reduce the hoof's ability to absorb concussion, resulting in a jolting ride and greater risk of injury to the horse's leg bones. Although the hoofs of the hind legs should be wide at the heel, their shape is more oval than the hoofs of the forelegs.

BLACK HOOFS VS. WHITE HOOFS

Unpigmented (white) hoof walls tend to be softer than pigmented (black) walls. Therefore, black hoofs often are stronger than white ones. However, each hoof should be judged by its condition instead of its color because the hoof wall's strength depends upon its moisture. If it is too moist, horseshoe nails may work loose and the shoe may be thrown. If the hoof is too dry, it may chip or crack.

HOOF CARE

Four factors promote healthy hoofs: cleanliness, moisture, good nutrition, and proper farrier care.

Cleanliness

Use a hoof pick daily to carefully clean out the depressions surrounding the frog. The hoof pick also should be used before and after exercise to remove embedded rocks or other objects that might cause soreness. Use the hoof pick in a heel-to-toe motion.

In the desert, the Bedouins shod their Arabian horses with round iron shoes with a small hole in the center.
Photo courtesy of Arabian Horse Owners Foundation

140

Thrush is a disease that can damage or even destroy the frog. A bad case of thrush can therefore cause lameness. Thrush is caused by bacteria that thrive on dirt, manure, and dampness packed into the hoofs. It usually can be avoided by keeping stalls and pens clean and by cleaning out the hoofs daily.

To treat thrush, pick out the hoof and then scrub the frog and the depressions along the bars with soap and water. Dry the bottom of the hoof and use iodine or a commercial thrush medication to disinfect the frog. Repeat the treatment twice daily until the thrush disappears.

Moisture

Inside the hoof, moisture is supplied by blood. Some moisture can evaporate through the hoof wall, especially if its natural protective coating (a wax-like finish called the periople) is removed by rasping or sanding. If the hoof is sanded for show, extra care must be taken to replace lost moisture. Wood shavings, the most popular stall bedding, also draw moisture from the hoofs.

The hoof also can absorb moisture from the outside. Horses in lush pastures seldom have dry hoofs because their hoofs absorb moisture from grass and damp ground.

One way to replace moisture is to stand the horse in water (free of urine and manure, which are drying to hoofs). Some owners soak the ground next to the water trough to create a mud bath for the hoofs. However, as the mud dries, it also can dry out the hoof. Also, pools of still water can become breeding grounds for mosquitoes, and some horses will reduce their water consumption to avoid walking through puddles. A better way to replace moisture is to apply hoof dressing to the wall and underside of the hoof.

Hoof Dressing — Hoof dressing applied to the walls and undersides of the hoofs helps seal moisture inside the hoof. Although it also may seal moisture out of the hoof by preventing moisture from being absorbed from damp ground, this is not a consideration if the horse is kept in a stall or on dry ground.

Commercial hoof dressings come in liquid and solid form and usually are applied with a brush. To use the dressing, pick out the hoof and apply dressing to the sole and frog, extending it up the heels and into the hairs of the coronary band where hoof growth begins. Then apply dressing to the outer wall, again extending the dressing into the hairs of the coronary band at the top of the hoof.

Apply hoof dressing as often as necessary to add moisture. Soft hoofs never need dressing; it makes them even softer. Most horses benefit from an application of hoof dressing once or twice a week.

When choosing a hoof dressing, avoid preparations with drying ingredients like alcohol and select preparations with lubricants such as lanolin.

Cleaning out the hoofs helps prevent thrush caused by trapped bacteria and avoids lameness from embedded rocks.   *Don Sepulvado photo courtesy of NSU*

Nutrition

Like hair, hoofs are mostly protein. High protein feeds (and supplements such as soybean oil meal or corn oil) will benefit hoof texture as well as hair coat.

Illness or a change in feed can result in rings in the hoof wall, much as rings inside trees reflect years of rain or drought. These rings vary slightly in color, texture, and thickness from the rest of the hoof wall and remain until the hoof wall totally grows out from the coronary band and is trimmed off. Laminitis (founder) causes greater deviation in the rings of the hoof wall, and these characteristic "founder rings" should not be confused with normal variations in the hoof wall.

TRIMMING AND SHOEING

The horse's hoofs grow constantly and wear unevenly, resulting in uneven stress on the bones of the legs. For these reasons, the hoofs must be trimmed approximately every four to eight weeks. Frequency of trimming varies, according to the use of the horse and the amount of hoof growth in the individual. Young, growing horses may need trimming every two to four weeks. Most riding horses are trimmed every six to eight weeks, but broodmares may require trimming only every two to three months. Halter and performance horses can require trimming and shoeing every four weeks or more often to keep them ready to show.

Horseshoes protect the hoof walls from chipping and cracking and can enhance the horse's action. When properly shod, the horse moves as well as its conformation allows. Working horses usually are shod, but breeding stock and young horses often are kept barefoot. Even pleasure horses that are lightly used on soft ground *may* not require shoes, depending upon the condition of their hoofs. Halter horses may be shown either with or without shoes, but most are shod.

Proper Angle of the Hoof Wall

The angle of the hoof wall should match the angle of the pastern. A short, upright pastern should have a matching (upright) hoof wall, and a long pastern should be echoed by a long hoof wall.

Attempts sometimes are made to "improve" the angle of the pastern by changing the angle of the hoof wall. A longer, more angled hoof wall makes the too-upright pastern *appear* less vertical, and a more upright hoof wall helps disguise a pastern that is too long. However, when the angle of the hoof wall is altered, there is risk of injuring the bones of the leg and the interior bones of the hoof. *The hoofs therefore should be trimmed to correspond to the horse's natural pastern angle.*

Corrective Trimming

When the horse is young and growing, its leg bones are soft and easily set. The direction of growth of the foal's legs is affected by the length and balance of the hoof wall. If the wall is shorter on one side than on its opposite side, the foal will toe in or out in that leg. Careful trimming during the first three years of the horse's life often can correct toeing in or out.

"Corrective trimming" never should be attempted on a grown horse because its bones have stopped growing. An attempt to improve the legs of a mature horse with hoof trimming actually can cause serious injuries by throwing the bones out of their natural alignment and increasing concussion on one side of a bone or leg. This excessive jolting when the horse is in motion can strain tendons and muscles, or chip or break bones.

If the foal toes in or out due to an imbalance in the length of the hoof wall, corrective trimming will solve the problem. If, however, the foal was born with crooked legs, corrective trimming will not completely remedy the situation. If the legs are extremely crooked, it may be necessary to surgically staple or cast the leg to straighten the bones.

Hoof Care for Foals

The foal's hoof is naturally longer at the toe ("pointed"), causing the hoof to "break over" to one side as the foal moves. This causes uneven wear of the hoof wall, which results in toeing in or out. Removing the point from the toe of the hoof allows the hoof to break over at the toe rather than to one side of the hoof wall. This results in correct, straightforward action and prevents toeing in or out.

At first, the foal's hoofs only need to be rasped to square the toes. Later, the hoofs may be either rasped or trimmed to prevent the hoof wall from being longer on one side than on the other. To correct toeing in, the inside of the hoof wall is rasped or trimmed. To correct toeing out, the outside of the hoof wall is lowered. These adjustments allow the foal's weight to be evenly distributed over the hoof wall, resulting in straight bone growth of the leg.

The foal's hoofs should be rasped as needed, usually every two to four weeks, beginning when it is just a few weeks old. The faster the foal's growth rate, the more often its hoofs should be checked for uneven wear. Hoof trimming during the first year of life is especially critical, for that is when the foal gets most of its growth.

Like older horses, the foal's hoofs should be cleaned out regularly to avoid disease or injury. Handling the foal's legs and hoofs daily also helps gentle it and prepare it for later shoeing.

Shoeing Show Horses

Although young halter horses are sometimes shown without shoes, most are shod to prevent irregular wear of the hoof wall. Proper trimming and shoeing can enhance or detract from the horse's natural action.

It is against the rules to show Arabians and Half-Arabians with a toe that measures more than 4½ inches long (from the coronary band to the ground, measured at the front of the hoof wall), or wearing a shoe that weighs more than twelve ounces (without nails). The shoes must be standard, bar-less shoes without pads or any other material between the hoof and shoe. To insure that these requirements are met, the National Champion, Reserve National Champion, and one horse chosen at random in each halter, English, and driving class at the Nationals must have one shoe removed for examination and weighing, and the hoof wall measured.

The "floating trot," demonstrated by Aulrab. The float occurs when the horse springs forward and upward, appearing to be suspended in midair for an instant before returning to the ground.
Sharon Vander Ende photo courtesy of Warren Park Stud, Sanger, Calif.

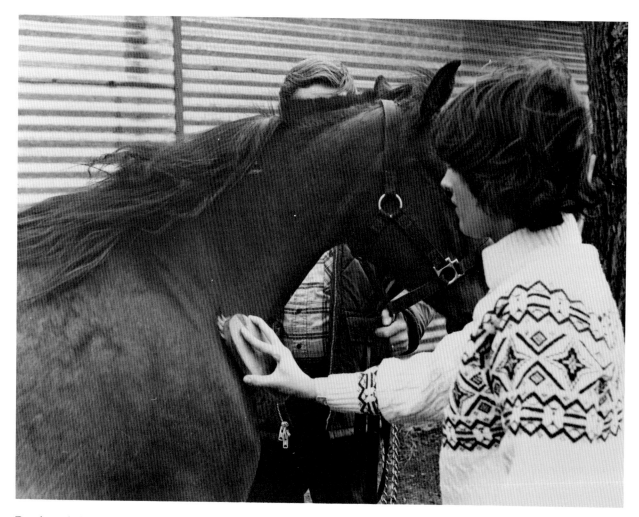

Brushing helps stimulate circulation and remove dust. Brush with the lay of the hair.

18

GROOMING

Grooming a horse properly isn't difficult, but it does take time and lots of "elbow grease." A thorough grooming requires thirty to sixty minutes, and daily grooming is ideal.

Grooming removes dirt, dandruff, and loose hairs and distributes oil throughout the coat. Daily grooming affords a chance to inspect the horse for small cuts, scrapes, swellings, and sore spots that might otherwise be overlooked.

GROOMING EQUIPMENT

Basic grooming equipment consists of a rubber curry comb, a stiff-bristled brush (dandy brush), soft-bristled brush (body brush), cloths (stable rags or rubbers), towels, a shedding blade/water scraper, and sponges. Most people add electric clippers to these basic items, and if the horse is shown, they are a necessity. A special vacuum cleaner made for grooming horses is convenient for removing deep dirt quickly, but cannot replace brushing because vacuuming cannot make the coat shine.

It is important to use clean grooming tools since a horse cannot be kept clean with dirty equipment.

GROOMING THE HORSE

Always use the curry comb first then follow with the brush. Curry with a circular motion to loosen dust, dandruff, and dead hair but always use the brush with the lay of the hair to smooth the coat. You can combine currying and brushing by using the curry comb with one hand and the brush with the other.

When grooming, start at the top of the horse's neck and work toward the hindquarters. Use only a brush or cloth on the head and lower legs where the flesh is thin and the bones are near the surface.

Grooming the Mane and Tail

A long, full mane and tail contribute to the beauty of the Arabian horse. To avoid pulling out or breaking the hairs, the mane and tail can be picked out (untangled) by hand.

To pick out the mane, start at the ends of the hairs and untangle them from the ends to the roots. Do the underside first, then the top hairs. To pick out the tail, hold it in one hand, using the other to separate the tail hairs a few at a time. Hold the tail bone straight out and start with the bottom

Grooming equipment and supplies. Clockwise: electric horse clippers, towels or rub rags, horse shampoo, brushes with bristles of various stiffness, baby oil, rubber curry comb, hoof pick, shedding blade/water scraper, and one-person twitch.

hairs. As the tail is picked out, let the untangled hairs fall.

If the mane or tail is badly knotted, the snarled hairs should be thoroughly saturated with baby oil or a silicone hair polish such as *ShowSheen®*. After they have dried, the stubborn tangles can be carefully picked out with a minimum of hair loss.

If you choose to brush the mane and tail, picking them out before they are brushed will reduce the number of hairs pulled out by the brush. Brush only a small section of the mane or tail at a time, brushing the ends first, gradually lengthening the strokes and finally brushing from the roots.

Finishing Touches

After grooming the body, mane, and tail, wipe the horse's eyes and nostrils with a clean, damp sponge or cloth. Then wipe the dock and area under the tail and, in males, the sheath. Finally, wipe the coat with a clean towel to remove dust and add shine.

Grooming Before and After Exercise

In addition to a thorough daily grooming, the horse should be lightly groomed before and after exercise. After exercise, pay special attention to sweaty areas under the tack (at the poll, back, and girth). In warm weather, rinse off sweat with clear water. Don't let perspiration dry—it dulls the hair coat.

Shedding Out

The horse normally sheds and regrows a hair coat seasonally, developing a thicker, longer winter coat in the fall and shedding it in spring. Early shedding can be stimulated by using artificial lights to simulate long summer days. An ordinary 200-watt electric lightbulb, left on from about 6:00 a.m. to 9:00 p.m., can be used in the stall.

The fastest way to remove long hair is by body clipping. Blanketing also will encourage shedding, but it is a slow process. A horse can wear two or

146

more blankets at once to increase warmth and cause shedding. However, the layers of blankets should be added gradually and care taken that the horse is not allowed to sweat under them.

If an outdoor horse is allowed to shed its winter coat naturally, a shedding blade will help speed up the process and remove "itchy" loose hairs when the horse is groomed.

The tail should be carefully "picked out" from bottom to top. Using the hands helps avoid breaking long tail and mane hairs.

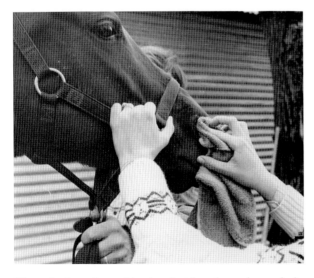

Clean the horse's sensitive head with a clean, damp cloth.

BATHING

Regularly bathing horses makes daily grooming easier. In good weather, horses can be bathed as often as once a week, and manes and tails can be shampooed every other day.

Any mild shampoo designed for human use can be used on horses, and a "no tears" baby shampoo can be used on the face and forelock without irritating the horse's eyes. However, special horse shampoos contain coat conditioners as well as cleaning ingredients, and some even help prevent stains and dust accumulation. For these reasons, a mild horse shampoo is best for frequent bathing or care of show or sale horses.

How to Bathe a Horse

Use warm water from buckets or directly from a hose. If using buckets, you will need three or four—one of soapy water and two or more of clear rinse water.

Curry before bathing to loosen dead hairs, dirt, and dandruff. If the horse is shedding, a curry comb or shedding blade also can be used during the bath to remove long hairs.

Dilute the shampoo in a bucket of warm water. Applying shampoo directly to the hair may make it difficult to rinse out.

It's best to start the bath from the horse's near side since horses are used to being handled from that side. Be sure to be patient with an inexperienced horse, letting it examine the hose first to overcome fear of the snake-like object.

Start the hose bath by directing a gentle stream of water on the forelegs. If you start by wetting the hind legs, a startled horse may kick or jump forward. Wet the legs first, gradually easing the water to the horse's neck, body, back, and hindquarters. Work from front to back as in grooming. Some horses kick when water drips down their hind legs, so stay out of kicking range.

When the horse is wet, apply soapy water with a clean sponge or rag, working up a good lather with a brush.

Dunk the tail into a bucket of soapy water to thoroughly saturate the hairs. Use your fingers to scrub the tail and mane—a brush pulls out hairs.

After lathering and scrubbing, rinse the horse thoroughly because shampoo residue causes dry skin and a dull coat. Shampoo is most likely to be left at the roots of the mane and tail, so pay special attention to those areas when rinsing. Dunk the tail into a bucket of clean water and swish it around to rinse. Finish by pouring clean water over the mane and tail. A vinegar rinse (¾ cup of vinegar to a bucket of water) can be used to help remove any remaining shampoo and add highlights. Be sure to rinse out the vinegar with clear water.

A creme rinse or conditioner (the kind used for human hair) applied to the mane and tail will make them silky and help prevent tangles, as will a spray-on hair polish. If desired, the body can be conditioned or polished, too. (Don't apply a silicone conditioner in the saddle area if you will be riding the horse, as it may cause the saddle to slip.)

Drying the Wet Horse

Squeeze the mane and tail hairs to remove excess water. If the horse will allow it, "spin dry" the tail by holding the tail bone and spinning the hairs a few revolutions like a propeller. It will take about fifteen minutes for the mane and tail to dry.

The water (sweat) scraper, made of aluminum or rubber, may be a separate tool or combined with a shedding blade. Holding the scraper at each end, pull it downward with the lay of the hair so that the smooth edge of the scraper squeezes water from the hairs of the body coat. After using the scraper to squeeze out excess water, rub the horse briskly with a clean towel, if desired.

From this point, the horse can air dry. Lunging in the sunshine will speed drying (Arabians feel

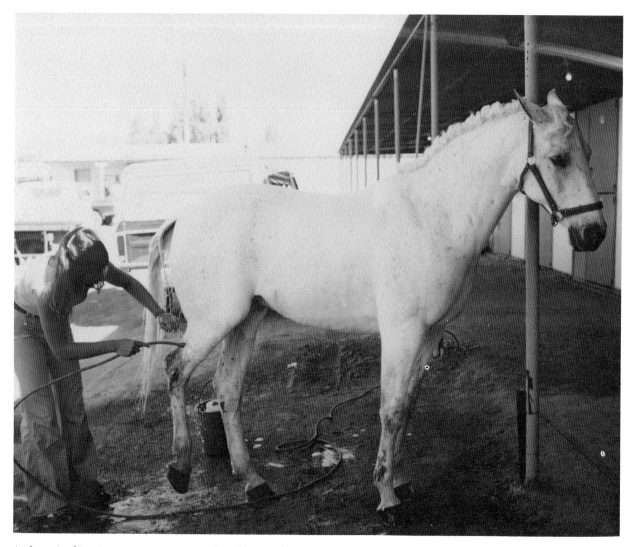

A clean Arabian is more attractive, comfortable, and healthy. Mon-Rey, a champion hunter and dressage Arabian, being freshened up before a class at the Nationals.

frisky after a bath, anyway). Damp horses also can be walked until dry. Never turn a damp horse loose—it will inevitably roll and require rebathing. If the horse isn't lunged or walked, it should be tied to prevent rolling and left in a warm, draft-free area. (Leaving a wet horse in a draft may cause it to catch cold.) If the weather is cool, a wool horse cooler can be thrown over the horse until its body heat causes it to dry.

CLIPPING

Electric clippers are the best and safest way to remove long hairs from the horse and are necessary to create the smooth, finished appearance of a show horse. Choose a well-known brand of large, heavy-duty clippers designed for use on horses. Smaller and quieter ear clippers also can be handy for trimming the ears.

Care of Clippers

If properly maintained, horse clippers will last many years. Before each use, oil the blades at the top and sides. Tube lubricants or light machine oil can be used to oil the clipper blades. A spray lubricant that reduces friction, cleans and cools clipper blades during use also is available.

During a long clipping session, clean the blade by dipping it into kerosene or commercial blade cleaner while the clippers are running. Immerse only the cutting edge of the clippers, being careful to prevent the cord or motor from touching the kerosene. Switch off the motor and dry the clipper head and blade with a clean cloth before resuming clipping.

After each use, loosen the clipper blade and dip the clipper head in kerosene to remove dirt and oil. Then dry with a soft cloth, oil the blade again, and store the clippers in a dry place. (Remember to tighten the loosened blade before using the clippers next time!)

Clipper Blades

Keep clipper blades sharp to insure a neat job and prevent discomfort from pulled hair. Clipper sharpening services are available by mail and through tack stores.

Blades come in numbered sizes; size indicates how closely they cut the hair. The four blades used for clipping show horses are:

Blade Size:	Use:
#10	Blending Clipped into unclipped areas; cheeks (if clipped). May be used instead of a #15 if a slightly longer coat is preferred.
#15 (all purpose)	Body; neck; legs.
#30	Used for same areas as #40; leaves the hair slightly longer.
#40 (close cutting)	Bridlepath; muzzle; inside nostrils; ears; face; under jaw.

To remove unslightly long hairs from a pleasure horse, simply use a #10 or #15 blade. If desired, a show "close shave" can be achieved by using a #30 or #40 on the pleasure horse's muzzle and bridlepath.

General Rules for Clipping

Always bathe and thoroughly dry a horse *before* clipping since dirt dulls the blades and slows clipping. Hold the clippers *lightly*—don't press the blade into the horse's skin. In general, clip *against* the direction of hair growth. (If needed, you can lightly blend the clipped into the unclipped hair by using the clippers *with* the direction of hair growth.)

During clipping, touch the blade frequently to be sure it isn't hot. A hot blade can burn the horse's skin. If the blade feels hot: spray it with a cooling lubricant made especially for cooling hot blades; shut off the clippers until the blade cools; or replace the hot blade with a cool one. Keeping the blade clean and oiled helps prevent overheating.

Training the Horse for Clipping

The horse's first experience of clipping will determine how it will react in the future. The keys to a successful first experience are patience, gentleness, and firmness.

Never try clipping an inexperienced horse alone. Have an assistant hold the lead rope and help reassure the horse. (It is *always* safer to have someone hold the lead rope instead of tying a horse for clipping.)

Remember that being clipped may be an unpleasant experience for the horse. Clippers are noisy and the vibration tickles. Clippers can even cause pain if the blade is dull or hot, or if the horse is jabbed with it. The noise of the motor also may remind the horse of buzzing insects. Make the experience as comfortable and non-frightening as possible.

Before turning on the motor for the first clipping, let the horse see and touch the clippers. Then cover the blade with your hand and rub the horse's neck with the cushioned blade. Next, turn on the clippers to accustom the horse to the sound of the motor. Then, holding the running clippers, again rub the horse's neck to let it feel the cushioned vibration through your hand. After the horse accepts the sensation, clip it first under the chin, putting your free hand on the nasal bone to keep the head from being thrown upward.

Be gentle and patient and don't let the horse avoid the clippers by raising its head or moving around. The horse must learn to tolerate the unpleasant sensations. Follow the horse if it tries to move away from the clippers. (Be sure the cord is long enough; battery-operated, cordless clippers may help for training purposes.) An unruly horse should be backed into a corner against two solid walls. If necessary, restrain the horse with a twitch.

Clipping of Pleasure Horses

Very little clipping is required for pleasure horses, and just how much will be done is a matter of preference. Some owners leave their Arabians completely natural and do not remove any hair by clipping or scissoring, while others clip them like show horses.

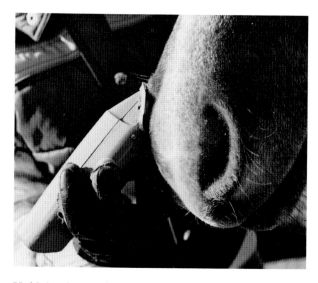

Hold the clippers flat against the horse's skin and use only light pressure to remove the long hairs from the muzzle.

While other parts of the horse's body may be clipped simply to give a neater, more attractive appearance, the bridlepath and fetlocks of pleasure riding horses are clipped for practical reasons. (Although electric clippers are best, scissors may be used to trim these areas.)

Bridlepath — The bridlepath is a "path" cut in the mane at the poll (just behind the ears) to accommodate the top of the bridle. Removing a two or three-inch section of mane allows the bridle to fit evenly (flat) against the top of the head. (For aesthetic reasons, the bridlepath of Arabian show horses has become much longer than necessary for practical purposes.)

Fetlocks — Removing long hairs from the horse's fetlocks does make the legs look finer. However, it also prevents mud and ice from accumulating on the lower legs in bad weather.

Clipping Other Areas — The long hairs on the muzzle and around the eyes (not the eyelashes) usually are removed because they detract from the beauty and refinement of the Arabian's head. Some owners leave the long hairs of the muzzle, which help the horse feel its way in the dark. Loss of these hairs probably is only a minor inconvenience, however. Long hairs extending from the underside of the horse's neck, jaw, and belly also may be removed for aesthetic reasons.

The hair inside the horse's ears serves a very important function, screening out insects, dirt, and wind. To neaten the ear without removing the in-

Hold the leg firmly but gently until the horse relaxes it. Then trim the long hair from the back of the fetlocks, clipping upward against the lay of the hair.

terior hairs, fold the ear together and clip off any long hairs extending from within.

CLIPPING FOR SHOW

Clipping a show horse is much more difficult than clipping a pleasure horse because the show horse is clipped to enhance appearance and give a "better than life" impression. For this reason, clipping show horses is an art.

Body Clipping

The slick, almost "hairless" coat of most show Arabians is achieved by clipping the entire horse. Body clipping usually is started when cool weather triggers the growth of the winter coat, typically in September or October, and continued at two-month intervals during winter and the show season. The coat is kept no longer than about one-quarter inch (Body-clipped horses are kept blanketed to make the short hairs of the clipped coat lie down, as well as for warmth when needed.)

When body clipped, bays become grey-brown and chestnuts fade to an unattractive orange. To recover its color, the hair must be partly regrown.

Although light grey horses can be body clipped just a few days before a show (because their color does not change), all other horses should be clipped at least three weeks before being shown.

When the coat is clipped, it has a tendency to become dry, and the short hair sticks straight out. To soothe the skin and smooth down the coat, the body-clipped horse should be bathed with baby oil and warm water (or the mixture can be sprayed onto the skin and rubbed in). An hour or more of daily grooming improves the body-clipped coat by stimulating regrowth, distributing oil, and helping the hair lie down. Lanolin-based coat conditioners also help restore shine and softness.

A body clip requires about four hours of careful work. Allow plenty of time. (Completing the task in two or three sessions makes it less tiring and stressful for both horse and groom.)

Clipper tracks visible on the horse's body can result from dull blades, a hasty job, or a dirty horse. Be sure the horse is dry and clean before clipping. (Clipping the horse at least three weeks before a show will allow time for partial regrowth, which will help conceal clipper tracks or clipping mistakes.)

Using a #15 blade (or a #10 if a slightly longer coat is preferred), clip the body and neck against the direction of hair growth. To insure a smooth job and to avoid jabbing the horse, hold the skin taut when clipping fleshy areas. Be calm, gentle and patient when clipping, especially if the horse is young or inexperienced. (If necessary, use a twitch or administer a tranquilizer to the horse before body clipping.)

A V-shaped patch of hair sometimes is left on the top of the croup, just in front of the tail. If the horse's body color is about the same as that of the tail, the patch can be slightly larger. The point of the V faces the horse's head and from a distance the croup patch appears to be part of the tail. This makes the topline look slightly more level and the tail set higher. However, it may visually shorten the croup.

Whether a show horse must be body clipped depends upon the level of competition. It may be unnecessary to body clip a horse for a small local show or playday (especially in summer, when the horse's coat is fairly short). At larger, competitive shows, however, most Arabians—especially halter horses—are body clipped.

Even if you do not body clip, you can add refinement and highlight the bone structure by clipping parts of the horse and then carefully blending the clipped and unclipped areas.

Clipping the Head

The head should be clipped about two weeks prior to the show, with follow-up clipping just a day or two before showing.

The current fashion is to "contour" the head, using a series of progressively closer-cutting blades. Each time a change is made to a closer blade, a slightly smaller area is clipped than was covered with the previous blade. This blends the hair, preventing visible lines between the different lengths of hair. By leaving the hair slightly longer in some areas and shorter in others, the bone structure is emphasized and the result is a more refined appearance.

To contour the head, start with a #10 blade on the face, clipping against the direction the hair grows. Clip the face from the muzzle toward the ears. The hair of the cheeks should not be clipped unless it is too long for a neat appearance. In that case,

Gently remove the long hair from above and below the eye. Protect the horse's eyes and eyelashes by covering with your hand.

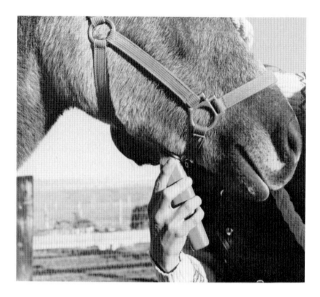

Trim the long hairs under the jaw to make the head look more refined.

it can be trimmed with the #10 blade, also. However, the cheeks should not be clipped again with the closer-cutting blades as longer hair there makes the jowls appear larger.

Clip gently around the eyes, carefully blending the hair to avoid cutting bare circles around the eyes. Clipping off the eyelashes is unnecessary and removes the eyes' natural protection from dust. Also, clipping the eyelids increases the risk of an eye injury from the clippers.

After clipping the entire head (except for the cheeks, if they are to remain unclipped), switch to a #15 blade and clip the head again, this time covering a slightly smaller area and omitting the cheeks. Then change to a #30 and repeat the process.

One or two days before the show, clip the face again. Complete the contour clipping by going over the head (except for the cheeks) with a #40 blade. Pay special attention to removing fine hairs in the nostrils, on the muzzle, lips, and underjaw.

Clipping the Ears

Before clipping a horse's ears for the first time, get the horse accustomed to having its ears handled by rubbing them inside and out. If possible, use special ear clippers that are smaller and quieter than the body clippers. If the horse will not stand still while its ears are clipped, it will be necessary to apply a twitch.

Use a #40 blade, to clip the ear. First, fold its two sides together and clip around the edges of the ear, removing the long hairs that extend beyond the ear's edge. If desired, a small diamond-shaped tuft of hair can be left at the very top, inner edge of each ear to enhance the shape of the ears. Then carefully clip the hairs inside the ear, being careful to prevent cut hairs from falling into the ear, which can cause head tossing or even result in inner ear problems.

Newly clipped ears may be tickled by wind or the forelock brushing against them. To avoid head tossing during show classes, clip the ears far enough in advance of the show to give the horse time to adjust to the sensation.

The Bridlepath

At present, no rule specifies length requirements or limitations of the Arabian show horse's bridlepath. Some people feel that the bridlepath should be only long enough to accommodate the top of the halter, and that very little of the mane should be removed. However, a long bridlepath currently is fashionable in America and Canada, where most Arabian halter horses now have a bridlepath at least eight inches long. The length should be determined by the individual's conformation and type. If the horse has a thin neck, use a short bridlepath to make the horse's neck look heavier.

If the horse needs a thinner, longer neck, a long bridlepath will be more flattering. Removing the mane above the throatlatch visually reduces thickness there. The horse with a heavy, thick mane also will benefit from a long bridlepath. A heavy mane makes the neck look shorter and thick; removing more of the mane visually removes excess weight from the neck. Remember, however, that no judge will be "fooled" about the horse's true length and shape of neck, which can be judged by looking at the side that the mane does not cover.

Before clipping, try out bridlepaths of different lengths by simply flipping different amounts of mane to the opposite side of the neck to see how the bridlepath would look if clipped to that length. Determine the most flattering length of bridlepath by looking at the horse up close and from a distance. Consider head carriage, too. The performance horse usually has his head lower and his neck more arched than the halter horse.

Clipping the Bridlepath — Once part of the mane has been cut off there is no going back; it takes more than a year for it to grow back, so go slowly and pay attention when clipping.

When reclipping, there is a tendency to unintentionally lengthen a bridlepath. Cutting a small nick at the bottom of the bridlepath will help avoid removing too much mane. From that point, clip forward along the crest of the neck and toward the ears. When approaching the forelock, clip the opposite direction (toward the withers) to avoid accidentally removing any of it. To make the mane lie flat at the bottom of the bridlepath, cut the bottom of the bridlepath at a slight angle.

If creating a bridlepath for the first time, use a #15 blade. Then clip the same area again with a #40 blade for a show-ring close cut.

After the bridlepath has been cut, blend the clipped hair of the neck into the unclipped hair by clipping lightly across the bridlepath with a #10 or #15 blade to eliminate a visible clipper blade path.

Clipping the Neck

The neck of a grey or dark bay that has not been body clipped can be subtly emphasized by clipping the entire underside of the neck and then blending the clipped area into the unclipped hair. Don't use this trick on a poor neck, however.

Clip and blend the throatlatch into the rest of the neck for a more refined appearance, lifting the horse's head when trimming the throatlatch.

Clipping the Legs

To refine and call attention to the legs, clip the legs of bays and greys from the knee down. Don't

To clip the bridlepath, begin at the farthest point back on the neck and clip forward. (It is easier to control the length of the bridlepath by clipping forward rather than clipping down the neck.) To even the bridlepath, clip back down the neck. Hold down the long section of mane to make the trim easier.

use this on chestnuts because of the difference in color of the clipped and unclipped hair.

When clipping the legs, carefully remove the long hairs around the coronary band (just above the hoof) and at the fetlock. Be careful when clipping around the ergot that protrudes at the back of the fetlock; don't shove the clipper blade into the ergot. If white-marked legs are clipped too closely, the skin will show through, causing an unattractive pink tinge. If the horse is not already body-clipped, the legs of chestnut horses should be clipped *only* on the white markings.

horse to relax so a straight line exists between the fetlock and hoof before clipping the pastern area.

GROOMING FOR SHOW

Successful show grooming results from months of careful conditioning and grooming before the show. You cannot take an unkempt horse from pasture one day and show it the next. (*If* the horse is basically in good condition, you might be able to put a show finish on it in two or three months.)

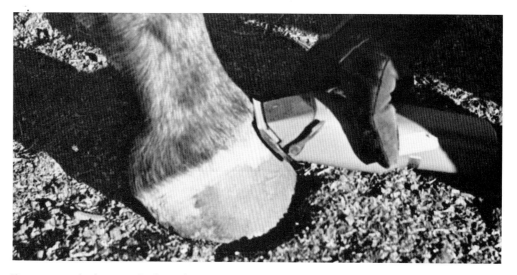

For a neater look, trim the hair that grows over the top of the hoof.

Clipping the foreleg — To trim the fetlock and back of the pastern, stand facing the horse's hindquarters and lift the foreleg. Support it by placing one hand on the front of the cannon bone just above the fetlock. Support the leg's weight with the palm of your hand—don't grip the leg tightly—until the horse relaxes the leg. Then clip upward, against the lay of the hair, at the back of the pastern.

To clip the front of the pastern, face forward and extend the leg slightly. Then clip upward from the coronary band just above the hoof to the fetlock. To complete the foreleg, put the leg on the ground and clip it downward from the bottom of the knee to the fetlock.

Clipping the hind leg — The hind legs are clipped like the forelegs but from the hocks downward.

To trim the back of the pastern, raise the hind leg slightly above the ground. Again, wait for the

After routine daily grooming, the coat of the show horse will benefit from hand massage. This not only distributes the horse's natural coat oils but adds some oils from the groom's hands. It also relaxes tense or sore muscles, stimulates circulation and hair growth, and calms the horse. When you massage the muscles, rub hard and in a circular motion.

The coat of the show horse is kept smooth and clean by blanketing. Blanketing also keeps coat color from fading (see Chapter 13).

Training the Mane

The mane of a show horse must lie neatly to one side of the neck (the side to which most of the mane naturally falls). If it does not, braiding the mane in three-strand braids will help train the mane to fall to one side of the neck and to lie flat; secure each braid with a small rubber band. A mane trainer or tamer is a cover that fits over the mane, fastening under the neck with *Velcro®* fasteners or with straps. It helps make the mane lie down, helps train the mane to one side if it divides into sections falling to both sides of the neck, protects braids from coming unbraided, and protects the mane from being pulled out if the horse rubs it by scratching against objects. (A hood serves the same purposes, and discourages coat growth in cold weather.)

Pulling the Mane

The show horse's mane should appear to flow evenly from just behind the bridlepath to its withers, ideally reaching its longest point just over the shoulder, in front of the withers.

Although the Arabian's mane is never cut (except to trim a bridlepath), it may be desirable to neaten the line of a ragged-looking mane by shortening the longer portions, so that the adjoining parts are about equal in length. This is done by "pulling."

To pull the mane, grasp the ends of some of the hairs that are too long. Holding them firmly, use the fingers of your other hand to "back comb" the hairs, pushing upwards toward the roots. This pushes most of the hairs back, leaving just the longer hairs in your grasp. To remove them, pull just a few hairs (perhaps six) at a time, using a quick downward snap. The hairs will break off or pull out by the roots. Continue this procedure where needed, until the mane has been evened and the desired appearance achieved. If the horse is extremely sensitive, spread the procedure over several sessions instead of trying to do the job at one time.

Pulling also thins the mane and, if done carefully, can improve the appearance of the neck if the horse has an exceptionally thick mane. The forelock can be pulled in the same way, if it is too heavy. When pulling any of the mane, go slowly and stand back to view your progress. Once the hairs are removed, they take a long time to grow back.

Braiding the Tail

The show horse's tail will stay cleaner and lose fewer hairs if it is braided and put up. Oil the tail (using baby oil or a commercial product such as *Shapley's®* oil) to help condition and prevent breakage of hair.

Braid the tail in a simple, three-strand braid from slightly below the end of the tail bone to the tips of the tail hairs. Don't braid too high or too tightly; tight braids can cause loss of blood circulation in the tail. Then pass the braided section through the unbraided part just below the tail bone, forming a flat ball of braided hair. A long tail may have to be passed through the unbraided section of hair more than once.

Wrap the tail with three-inch-wide self-adhering gauze (safety tape) to secure the circle of braided hair into a neatly wrapped package. The gauze bandage is easy to use, won't damage the hair, and does not slip like fabric tail wraps.

A long tail can be braided and taped with self-sticking gauze to keep the tail clean for show. One method is shown here. First the tail is braided from just below the tailbone to the tips of the tail hairs.

The tail hair just below the tailbone is divided into two sections of loose hair and the braided section of tail is passed through it.

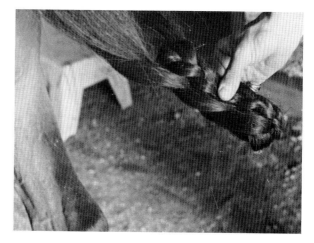

Draw the braided section through the loose hair as many times as necessary, making a loose coil.

Hold the end of the tail against the braided, coiled section so it doesn't come unbraided.

Begin wrapping the tail with gauze. Start at the divided center section of hair, at the top of the braid.

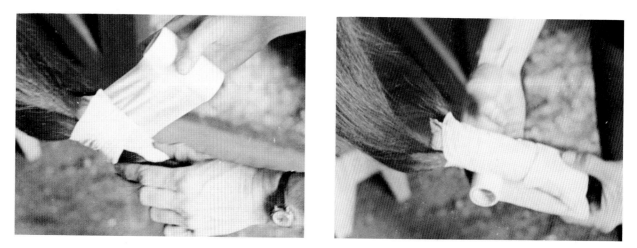

Finish the wrap by wrapping over the end of the braided coil; then cut and secure the gauze.

Grooming the Braided Tail

To groom the tail, remove the gauze, unbraid the hairs, and pick out the tail. If the tail is brushed, do small sections, starting from the ends of the hairs and gradually lengthening the strokes, finally brushing from the roots to the ends. The wavy or frizzy tail sometimes seen in the show ring can result from bathing a horse while its tail is braided or tied in a knot. Avoid a frizzy tail by unbraiding and picking out or brushing the tail *before* bathing. After bathing, the tail will appear fuller if it is picked out while it's drying. (It will take about fifteen minutes to dry.) A braided tail should be taken down and washed about twice a week.

Use of Colored Substances

Present (1986) show rules forbid changing the color of a show horse's "hide or hair" except for mane, tail or hoofs. Apparently this rule originally was designed to let exhibitors brighten yellowed manes and tails of grey horses and to use colored hoof polish. Now, color rinses or even hair dyes are sometimes used on the manes and tails. Some exhibitors interpret this regulation more broadly, alleging that using a colored substance on the horse's skin or coat is legal because it does not *change* the natural color but merely enhances it, provided that the substance is the same color as the horse's skin or coat. Such exhibitors may use black substances on the muzzle and eye skin or even apply color to the legs or body. Other exhibitors feel that the use of any colored substance on the Arabian's head, body or legs is forbidden because it changes the *shade* of the horse's natural color. It is hoped that this controversial issue soon will be resolved by a more specific rule about using cosmetics on Arabian and Half-Arabian show horses.

Exhibitors should refer to current show regulations for the latest rules about grooming of show horses, and be careful to avoid any commercial products which may be against the rules.

Hoof Preparation

If desired, hoof walls can be sanded to remove ridges and give a smoother appearance. Sanded hoofs require extra care and need hoof dressing even more than unsanded hoofs because sanding removes the periople, the hoof's natural protective finish, resulting in drying. However, experienced exhibitors report no *apparent* weakening of the walls caused by sanding the hoofs for show. Naturally, care must be taken to remove a minimum of the hoof walls during sanding.

To sand the hoofs, start a few days before the show, using sandpaper of medium coarseness to smooth the large ridges, and progress to fine sandpaper. At the show, complete the sanding with fine sandpaper and then use fine steel wool to give a soft luster and ultra-smooth surface.

After sanding, apply hoof polish and let it dry while the horse stands on a dust-free surface (a piece of carpet kept just for this purpose is ideal). Hoof polish comes in black for naturally dark hoofs and clear for white hoofs. A striped hoof can be covered with clear polish or the dark parts can be carefully painted with black hoof polish, using a *Q-tip*® applicator.

Hoof polish should be used only for shows or other special events and should be removed afterward because it may keep the hoof from absorbing moisture. A water-base polish can be removed with soap and water; others must be scrubbed off with a wire brush. After removal, apply hoof dressing to moisturize the hoofs.

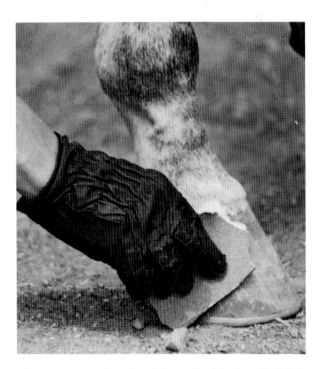

To prepare the show hoof, the wall of the hoof is lightly sanded to remove large ridges before applying hoof polish.

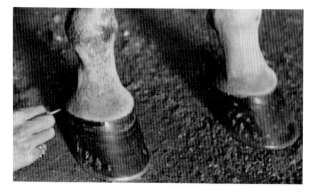

Be careful when applying hoof polish to the top of the hoof, to avoid getting it on the horse's leg. Using a cotton-tipped swab will help you do a neat job.

The rest of the hoof polish can be applied with the applicator from the bottle.

The completed show hoof, at left, versus the natural (unpolished) hoof. (To give a neater appearance, the hairs at the top of the hoof should have been clipped before the hoofs were polished.)

Hoof polish is not required for shows and may be omitted if preferred. Whether the hoofs are polished should make no difference to the judge if the horse is of good quality and otherwise well groomed. (If you wish, apply a light coat of hoof dressing to the walls and buff them with a soft cloth just before entering the class, rather than applying hoof polish.)

Final Touches

The day before the class, bathe the horse with a low-sudsing (easily rinsed out) equine shampoo designed for show horses. Repeat sudsing and rinsing until the horse is completely clean.

Grey horses can be bathed with a special blueing shampoo for horses, which is particularly effective in whitening yellow manes and tails. The blueing shampoo can also be used on the white markings of bays and chestnuts. Be careful to follow the label directions carefully, for it musn't be left on too long. If necessary, reshampoo until the whites are bright.

After rinsing out the shampoo, apply a creme rinse or special mane and tail conditioner. The body can be creme rinsed, also, or use a spray-on conditioning polish while the horse is wet.

Carefully pick out the mane, tail and forelock. When the horse is dry, braid and put up the tail. After a thorough grooming, put a clean blanket on the horse and put it in a freshly bedded stall. If the horse has white leg markings, they can be bandaged to help keep them clean. Be careful not to bandage the legs tightly, however (see Chapter 15).

The day of the class, bathe the horse again. (If the horse is still clean and if time does not allow, you might skip this bath.)

Allow at least an hour before the class to prepare the horse. Complete sanding the hoofs (using fine sandpaper and steel wool). Dust them off and apply hoof polish while the horse stands on a level, dust-free surface. While the hoof polish dries, pick out the mane, tail and forelock; then, if desired, brush them carefully. Curry and brush the body thoroughly, then rub the coat with a clean cloth.

Clear oil slicks down the hair, adding refinement. It gives a soft shine, subtly calling attention to the oiled area. Finally, it makes dark skin appear even darker. For these reasons, apply a light coat of baby oil or *Shapley's®* grooming oil to the bridle-path, muzzle, chin, lips, inside the nostrils and ears, from the hocks and knees down, and around the eyes. If you like, add a touch of clear petroleum jelly on the eyelids, to further highlight the eyes.

If the halter has a browband, wet the forelock with (human) hairstyling gel, pull it toward the mane side of the neck, and tuck it securely under the browband and cheekpiece. If there is no browband and the forelock is too short to tuck under the cheekpiece of the halter, oil the forelock to minimize blowing.

Spray on an equine coat polish to add a brilliant shine to the coat, and use the same product lightly on the mane and tail, lifting the hairs and then letting them fall downward through a light misting of spray. Apply fly spray, if needed, to prevent the horse from fidgeting in the arena.

Finally, just before entering the ring, run a clean towel over the horse, halter, and hoofs to remove dust.

A wise buyer chooses the best broodmares he can afford. Hagunia, Champion Mare, 1985 Ascot Show, England.

Indraff (*Raffles x *Indaia).

Photo courtesy of Al-Marah Arabians

19

PEDIGREES AND STRAINS

A pedigree is a written record of the ancestors of a specific Arabian horse. Most pedigrees are in chart form. In American-style pedigrees, the sire's name and his ancestors appear in the upper half of the chart, and the dam's name and her ancestors are shown in the lower half. (In Egypt, Arabian horse pedigrees reverse these positions.) An example of a partial American-style pedigree is shown below:

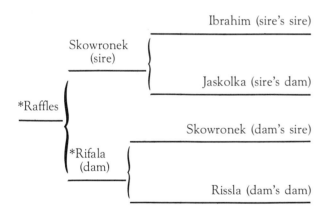

Published pedigrees usually consist of three or five generations. However, the entire pedigree can be traced back to the Arabian's most distant known ancestors which came directly from the desert. The entire pedigree of an Arabian horse can therefore be quite lengthy.

In the American-style pedigree, the very top line of names in the pedigree is called the "tail male" line. Only stallions are included in the tail male line —the sire, his sire, etc., all the way back to the "foundation sire" (the last known stallion in the tail male line). The very bottom line of names in the pedigree is the "tail female" line, and only mares are included—the dam, her dam, etc., back to the "foundation mare" (the last known mare in the tail female line).

The Bedouins had no written literature for many centuries. Instead, history was memorized and passed along verbally. The pedigrees of the Bedouins' horses were remembered and passed along in the same manner. The first *written* pedigrees for desert-bred Arabian horses were prepared for European buyers who wanted a written record of the horses' lineage. To assure sales, the Bedouins produced the desired pedigrees, swearing by *Allah* (God) that the horses they represented were *asil* (purebred). For their own purposes, however, the Bedouins considered written pedigrees unnecessary because their horses' lineage was common tribal knowledge.

The Bedouins did not keep written pedigrees for their horses. However, they were provided upon request to European buyers, with the purity of the Arabian horse being sold duly attested. This is the Bedouin pedigree of Urfah, "The Pride of the Euphrates," a mare imported by Homer Davenport. *Courtesy of Arabian Horse Owners Foundation*

ARABIAN HORSE STUD BOOKS

Like written pedigrees, stud books (used to record the bloodlines and matings of breeding stock) were a European innovation. Stud books were first kept by individual breeders. Later, organizations were formed to record the pedigrees of purebred Arabian horses in national stud books.

Today, the Arabian Horse Registry of America, Inc. keeps the official stud book for Arabian horses registered in the United States. The Stud Book is a set of volumes that lists every Arabian horse ever registered in America. Several volumes of the Stud Book are out of print now, but occasionally can be purchased from private owners. Out-of-print volumes or used sets of Stud Books sometimes are advertised for sale in classified ads of Arabian horse magazines. Volumes that are still in print can be purchased directly from the Registry.

Future Stud Book volumes must be ordered from the Registry *before* publication. However, microfiche copies of the entire Stud Book are sold by the Registry at all times. Microfiche consists of

sheets of microfilm about four by six inches in size, and each sheet contains the contents of several pages of the Stud Book. Although the microfiche version requires less storage space than the printed volumes, a special microfiche reading machine is needed to enlarge the film for viewing. These microfiche "readers" are sold by the Registry and other sources.

PEDIGREE RESEARCH SERVICES

If you don't want to look up a horse's pedigree personally or if you don't have the stud books available, you can order a five-generation computer-printed pedigree from the Registry. A four-generation pedigree also appears on the registration certificates issued since 1984.

Private individuals advertise pedigree research services in classified ads in Arabian horse publications. Prices vary according to the length, style, and amount of information provided by the pedigree. Some pedigrees also show foaling dates, colors, and strains while others list only names and registration numbers. Some are written or printed by hand, others are typed; some pedigrees are elaborate works of art suitable for display, others are notebook or file-sized.

HOW TO LOOK UP A PEDIGREE

You sometimes can research an Arabian horse pedigree by using information from magazine articles, ads, and books. Doing so, however, can result in errors since printed information is not always correct. The best way to trace a pedigree is to use the Stud Book.

Pedigrees are traced from the present, starting with the horse whose pedigree you wish to look up. Start by locating the Stud Book listing for the individual. You probably will find the horse listed in a volume published the year *after* the horse was born. If the horse was registered late, it will appear in a subsequent volume. Imported horses are, of course, listed in the volume published after the date they were imported to America rather than the date they were foaled.

In each Stud Book volume, the horses are listed in numerical order by registration number. However, if you don't know the number, you still can find the horse in the volume's alphabetical index, which shows the registration number.

Each listing for a horse also shows the names and registration numbers of its parents. Write their names and numbers down in pedigree chart format. (The easiest way to do this is using a blank, pre-printed pedigree form. Such forms are available from many tack and gift shops specializing in Arabian horse items, or you can make your own.) It's a good idea to make a "rough draft" in pencil first, and then to copy the entire pedigree after you've looked it up. Print the names neatly to insure correct spelling and verify the information after you've written it down.

To continue tracing the pedigree, look up the horse's grandparents by their registration numbers then look up *their* parents, etc., filling in the pedigree blanks as you go. If you're using the printed volumes, you will be working through older editions as you reach more distant ancestors. By using the American Stud Book, you can trace the pedigree back to the first ancestors registered in the United States. When you reach an entry listing a horse's parents as "Desert Bred," you have traced that part of the pedigree to its end.

When you reach an ancestor that was registered in a foreign stud book, you must go to other sources if you wish to continue tracing the pedigree. The best source—if it's available—is the foreign stud book in which that horse was registered. The Registry now has most foreign stud books on its computer system. (For a complete listing of foreign stud book abbreviations—so you'll know which books are needed to continue tracing the pedigree of your imported Arabian horse—see Table 2.1, page 11.)

If foreign stud books are not available, a reference book about the Arabian horse bloodlines of the particular country may help. Useful books include *Reference Handbook of Straight Egyptian Horses* by the Pyramid Society, *Spanish Arabian Horse Families 1898-1978* by Joanna Maxwell, *Arabian Horses in Poland* by Z. Razwadowski, and *Arab Horse Families* by P.J. Gazder (English bloodlines). *The Crabbet Arabian Stud: Its History and Influence* by Archer, Covey and Pearson also is very helpful in locating ancestors bred or owned by the Crabbet Arabian Stud of England; more than a geneology, this book includes photographs of most Crabbet horses.

Name Changes

Sometimes, when you look up a horse by its registration number, you find the "wrong" name listed with the proper sire and dam. In such cases, the name of the horse probably was changed *after* it had been registered and listed in the stud book. To avoid this problem, the Registry no longer allows an owner to change the name of a registered Arabian.

VALUE OF A PEDIGREE

A pedigree is worth very little to someone who just sees a collection of names. Finding the names of the ancestors is just the first step for serious breeders. Knowing the genetic implications of the individuals in the pedigree makes the horse's pedigree a valuable tool for breeders. Familiarity with the traits and breeding ability of the horse's ancestors is just as necessary as knowing which horses appear in the pedigree.

PEDIGREE PERCENTAGES

The amount of inbreeding in a pedigree is sometimes described by percentage. For example, an Arabian is sometimes described as "50 percent *Raffles blood."

You can determine which percentage of a horse's pedigree consists of a certain ancestor by using the following chart:

Pedigree Percentages

Ancestor in 2nd generation (i.e., the sire or dam)	=	50% of the pedigree
Ancestor in 3rd generation	=	25% of the pedigree
Ancestor in 4th generation	=	12.5% of the pedigree
Ancestor in 5th generation	=	6.25% of the pedigree
Ancestor in 6th generation	=	3.13% of the pedigree
Ancestor in 7th generation	=	1.56% of the pedigree
Ancestor in 8th generation	=	.78% of the pedigree

Count the number of times that the same ancestor's name appears in each generation, then add the percentages. (For example, if *Raseyn appears twice in the fourth generation and once in the seventh, the formula is 12.5 + 12.5 + 1.56 = 26.56. The horse has approximately 27 percent *Raseyn in its pedigree.) This same method can be used to figure percentage of any other factor: nationality, strain, color, etc.

Having a high percentage of the "blood" of a certain ancestor does not necessarily mean that the horse received a greater genetic inheritance from that ancestor. However, it does increase the *odds* that the horse will have inherited more traits from that ancestor than from one that appears only once in the pedigree.

Some authorities argue that the coefficient of inbreeding is much more accurate than pedigree percentages of inbreeding; however, the complex mathematical formula used to calculate coefficients is beyond the scope of this book.

WHAT KIND OF SIBLING?

Horse breeders use various terms to describe closely related horses. The terms *brother* and *sister* are reserved for full brothers and sisters (i.e., those having the same sire and dam). The term *half brother* or *half sister* often is misused. It refers to two horses that have the same dam. Two horses having the same sire but different dams are *not* half brothers; they are just *by the same sire*.

Three-quarter brothers (or sisters) have the same dam. Their sires must be by the same stallion but out of different dams. Examples would be:

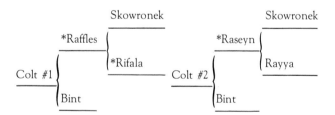

Seven-eighth brothers (or sisters) are even more closely related. Both are out of the same mare, but one is sired by a specific stallion and the other by that stallion's son. Their pedigrees would look like these:

Brothers or sisters in blood do not have the same parents but are quite closely related. When horses are brothers or sisters in blood, the pedigree always is identical beyond the names of their sires and dams. There are several ways to produce two brothers or sisters in blood. One is to breed the same stallion to two mares that are full sisters to each other. Another is to breed the same mare twice to two stallions that are full brothers to each other. Breeding stallions that are full brothers to mares that are full sisters also creates brothers or sisters in blood.

WHAT IS A STRAIN?

Lately, "strain" has sometimes meant "nationality" or "bloodlines" of an Arabian horse. However, the *family strain* is a particular family that can be traced back to the desert. The Bedouins traced their horses' pedigrees through their mares, with every horse inheriting the strain name of its dam. When horses of different strains were bred to each other, the resulting foal always inherited the dam's strain.

The strain names differentiated horses belonging to various maternal families. The strains gave some indication of the history of the horse's family, as well as its reputation. A strain was named for famous ancestors, for certain traits associated with the family, or for the owner/breeder of the particular family strain.

The first Europeans to study Arabian horses in the desert thought that the different strain names denoted different *breeds* of horses. Later, it was realized that the various "breeds" were just different families of one breed—the Arabian.

Strain Names

According to Bedouin legend, there were five major strains of Arabian horses from which substrains derived. These major strains were called "Al Khamsa" (The Five). In *Bedouin Tribes of the Euphrates*, Wilfrid Blunt listed the five strains as Kuhaylan (Kehilan), Seglawi, Abeyan, Hamdani, and Hadban. However, there were additional strains of Bedouin horses and the list of Al Khamsa strains varied according to which tribe supplied the information. Because the Kehilan strain always appeared among the five, it was presumed to be the oldest or even the foundation from which the other strains descended.

The Bedouins suspected any horse designated only by its strain name ("Kehilan," "Seglawi," etc.) of impurity unless the specific branch of the strain also was identified. For example, a Kehilan must be designated as a "Kehilan el Krush," a "Kehilan Jellabi," or as a member of another specific branch of the Kehilan strain. It was important to know whether a "Seglawi" was a "Seglawi Jedran," a "Seglawi Dalia" or belonged to a different Seglawi branch.

The spelling of strain names varies from one source to another because Arabic words can only be translated into English phonetically. Also, in Arabic, the strain names change forms according to the gender of the horse being described. If the horse is a stallion, it is a Saglawi; if a mare, it is a Saglawi*yah*. Masculine and feminine forms of the strains are listed in Table 19.1.

Strain Related to Type and Color

A debate has long raged about whether each strain can be classified by a characteristic physical appearance (type). Lady Wentworth said that the strains did not possess special traits of type, but author Carl (Schmidt) Raswan alleged that they did. Raswan stated that three major strain types existed and that members of each strain shared a characteristic "family resemblance." (He admitted, however, that the horse might *not* resemble the strain whose name it carried, if a different strain predominated in its pedigree. In that case, the horse probably would resemble the strain to which it had a greater relationship.)

According to Raswan, the strain types were:

Kuhilan (Kehilan)	=	Strength
Saqlawi	=	Beauty
Muniqi	=	Speed

The Kuhilan and Saqlawi, which Raswan said were related, had rounded contours while the Muniqi was angular, resembling the Thoroughbred. The Kuhilan was characterized as a "masculine" type and the Saqlawi as a "feminine" type. The Kuhilan was more muscular and athletic while the Saqlawi had more refinement and beauty.

The Polish authority, Dr. Edward Skorkowski, took this one step further. The Kuhilan strain is typically bay, he alleged, while grey is typical of the Saqlawi, and chestnut is the typical Maneghi (Muniqui) color.

Modern breeders in the Soviet Union have taken a practical approach to the type/strain problem. They simply identify the horses by strain *type*, ignoring the actual family strain. Thus, a horse is classed as Seglawi type, if it meets their idea of what a Seglawi should look like. Their idea of type classifications is something like this:

Koheilan	=	Athletic, muscular
Siglavi	=	Small, refined, typey
Hadban	=	Large, Thoroughbred type

To these "strain types" the Soviets have added another: the "Koheilan-Siglavi" that supposedly combines the best points of both types.

Do Strains Vary in Type?

Strains are traced only through the tail female line. Although the tail female line is felt by some Arabian horse breeders to be the strongest and most important part of the pedigree, it seems unlikely that modern Arabians of a certain strain would have inherited a standard, "cookie cutter" appearance handed down through generations from one mare hundreds of years ago. After all, each time a mare of that family strain was bred, the stallion provided one-half the foal's genetic inheritance. To accept the strain/type theory completely, the genetic influence of every outcross stallion in the pedigree must be ignored.

On the other hand, little doubt exists that the strain descriptions that were provided by early observers of the Arabian strains in the desert were accurate—at least for the particular time and place where the descriptions were made. Members of each strain must have had certain traits in common, especially if the family was inbred, since inbreeding fixes type within a family. Of course, any change in a breeding program—especially an outcross to another inbred family—can change the appearance of the future members of that strain. Differences in descriptions of the same strain may be explained by changes in breeding programs.

Strain Breeding

Nothing indicates that Bedouins showed any desire to breed "within the strain" (mate only members of the same strain to each other). In the desert, strains often were interbred. The Bedouins knew the strains of their mares and would not breed a mare of a pure strain to a stallion of questionable purity. However, all asil (pure) strains belonged to the same breed.

When used by modern breeders, the term "pure in strain" does not mean that *all* the ancestors in the pedigree belonged to the same strain. It means that the individual's sire and dam had the same strain name. Thus, both parents eventually trace to the same family in the tail female line. This is linebreeding the mare lines and is believed by strain breeders to intensify the characteristics of the particular strain.

breeds of horses had occurred. Most horse-breeding tribes jealously guarded the purity of their horses.

According to Carl Raswan, one Bedouin tribe had crossed its horses of the Maneghi strain with impure blood. Because of this alleged impurity, Raswan suggested that horses having a high concentration of Maneghi blood be eliminated from breeding programs, and that breeders mate their Arabians having Maneghi blood to Arabians having a higher concentration of the "pure" strains. Some modern breeders have taken this advice while others say it is foolish to avoid a strain because one tribe

Azraff (*Raffles x *Azja IV). *Photo courtesy of Garth Buchanan*

Which Strain is Best?

Although Bedouin individuals and tribes had their own favorites among the family strains, there was no general agreement as to which strain was best. In Bedouin eyes, all strains of Arabian horses were pure so long as no intermixture with other

may have allowed crossbreeding with some members of that strain.

Whether or not the Maneghi strain is less pure than the others, few modern Arabians are completely free of the strain, and no evidence indicates that the breed has suffered in quality because of it. Skowronek—the most influential Arabian stallion of all time—had several Maneghi lines. Many extremely typey modern stallions (including the Egyptian stallion Nazeer) belong to the Maneghi strain, which appears frequently in most nationalities of Arabian horses.

The following table was based upon information in *The Horse of the Desert* by W. R. Brown.

TABLE 19.1

STRAIN NAMES

Masculine Form	Feminine Form
Kuhaylan (Kehilan)	Kuhaylah[1]
Saqlawi	Saqlawiyah
Maneghi (Muniqui)	Maneghiyah
Ubayan	Ubayyah
Hamdani	Hamdaniyah
Hadban	Hadbah

[1]*Exception: Before a vowel, ends in et. Example: Kuhaylet Ajuz.*

STRAINS IN THE STUD BOOK

As of 1944 (Volume 5 of the Stud Book), the Arabian Horse Registry of America stopped including the strains of Arabian horses in its Stud Book entries. This was done so that people would not mistakenly think that *all* the horses in the individual's pedigree belonged to the indicated strain.

It is possible to determine an Arabian horse's family strain in several ways. One way is to find articles or ads in Arabian horse magazines that mention the strain of any mare in the individual's tail female line. Because errors sometimes occur in such sources, however, it is safer to take the strain name from a stud book that recorded it. If the horse was registered in a foreign country, the strain may appear in the appropriate foreign stud book. If the individual traces to Arabian mares that were imported to and registered in the United States before 1937, an old volume of the Stud Book, published between 1908 and 1937, will show the family strain of those mares. The earliest volumes of the Stud Book list the strain under "Family" in each horse's entry; volume 4 (1937) lists the strain name immediately following the Arabian's registration number, name, and color.

VALUE OF FAMILY STRAINS

Studying the Arabian horse strains is rather like studying a dead language. Many modern owners don't even know what family strains are, and the Bedouins who originated the strains are no longer breeding horses. However, knowing the strain of your Arabian horse provides a deeper awareness of its desert heritage.

The horse's body consists of billions of cells, each of which contains genetic programming for an entire body—not just for one cell.

20

BASIC PRINCIPLES OF GENETICS

Genetics is the study of how inherited traits are passed from one generation to the next. Although current knowledge of this very complex subject is limited, understanding the basic principles of inheritance can help breeders produce better Arabian horses.

THE CELL

The horse's body consists of billions of tiny, irregularly-shaped cells. Each cell is made of *cytoplasm*, with a darker and denser area at the center of the cell called the *nucleus*. The cell is a microscopic marvel. Its many substructures produce proteins and other chemical substances necessary to sustain life. The nucleus of the cell regulates the production of the cell's various parts. Coded instructions are transmitted from the nucleus to the rest of the cell by DNA (*deoxyribonucleic acid*), a chemical that contains *all* genetic information for every cell of the body. Each cell of the horse's body therefore contains genetic programming for an entire body— not just for one cell.

Chromosomes

Inside each cell's nucleus are threads of DNA interconnected (complexed) with protein, called *chromatin*. This material is organized into long chains called *chromosomes*—strands that contain the genes in linear array.

The horse has 64 chromosomes, found in 32 pairs. Each chromosome contains many genes that affect various traits. Genes for specific traits are found in the same locations (*loci*) on each chromosome of a pair. Genes on the same chromosome often are inherited together; this is called "linkage."

Genes

Genes are segments of DNA carried by the chromosomes. Each of a foal's traits—from coat color to bone structure—is determined by a specific gene or genes. Many inherited traits result from the influence of multiple combinations of genes. Like chromosomes, genes occur in pairs. Unlike them, genes cannot be seen with a microscope. Their existence is proven by their influence.

DOMINANT AND RECESSIVE GENES

A foal inherits one gene from its sire and one from its dam to make up each of its own gene pairs. Whether the foal will show the trait inherited from its sire or its dam depends upon which of the two genes of each pair is dominant.

When a dominant gene is inherited from either parent, a foal will possess the trait controlled by that gene. The other (unexpressed) gene is called the recessive gene. Although a foal will not have the characteristic controlled by the recessive gene, it may pass that concealed trait to its offspring.

The foal's traits are determined by a random assortment of genes inherited from its parents. Each parent passes along only half of its own genes to the foal, and which they will be is a matter of chance.

All genes are either dominant or recessive. Because a foal inherits one gene from each parent, a gene pair can consist of the following combinations: two dominant genes, one dominant and one recessive gene, or two recessive genes. In the first two cases, a foal will show the trait controlled by the dominant gene. In the third instance, it will have the trait controlled by the recessive gene, because no dominant gene was inherited to mask the influence of the recessive gene.

To complicate matters, some "dominant" genes are not *always* dominant. In some cases, they may be recessive (referred to as "incomplete penetrance").

A dominant trait is not necessarily good or bad, and neither is a recessive trait. A good trait can be masked by a bad trait if the good trait is controlled by a recessive gene and the bad one by a dominant gene.

Inheritance of Recessive Traits

When a foal has a trait that is not seen in either parent, *both* parents must have transmitted a recessive gene for that particular trait. Whenever a foal inherits two recessive genes for the same trait, it exhibits that trait in its phenotype (appearance).

When two carriers of a recessive gene are bred to each other, the resulting foal may or may not inherit two recessive genes. If either parent transmits its dominant gene instead of the recessive gene, the foal will show the trait controlled by the dominant gene instead of the trait controlled by the recessive gene. It is possible to statistically predict the inheritance of foals whose parents both carry a recessive gene for the same trait. Averaged over a large number of matings, the results are predicted as:

1 non-carrier foal	Doesn't have the recessive trait; doesn't inherit the recessive gene; cannot pass it on.
2 carrier foals	Doesn't have the recessive trait; does inherit the recessive gene; can pass it on.
1 recessive foal	Has the recessive trait; inherits the recessive gene; can pass it on.

Thus, three of every four foals produced by a carrier-to-carrier mating probably would not show the recessive trait, but only one foal in four would be incapable of passing the recessive gene to its offspring. (While this is only a prediction of the odds and cannot positively predict the outcome of matings based upon random inheritance of genes, it shows the frequency with which the recessive gene is *expected* to be inherited and passed on.)

HOMOZYGOUS AND HETEROZYGOUS

When a horse's two paired genes are the same, (both are dominant or both are recessive), the individual is *homozygous* for that particular trait. It will be reflected in its appearance and the horse will always pass the gene for that trait to its sons and daughters.

The *homozygous dominant* horse always passes the dominant gene, and its foals always inherit the trait. The *homozygous recessive* parent exhibits the recessive trait and always passes the recessive gene to its offspring.

When an individual's two paired genes are different (one is dominant and one is recessive), the horse is *heterozygous* for that particular trait. The horse can pass along *either* gene with equal frequency although its own appearance will reflect the dominant gene. When the heterozygous parent transmits the dominant gene, the foal will show that trait. If it transmits the recessive gene instead, the foal will show the recessive trait *only* if the other parent also transmits a recessive gene for the same trait.

LETHAL RECESSIVE

A lethal recessive gene causes a fatal weakness in the foal when two recessive genes are inherited (one from each parent). In such cases, the foal will die—either during gestation or after it is born. If a foal inherits only one lethal recessive gene (from one parent), the foal will not show symptoms of the genetic weakness but may pass the lethal gene to its own sons and daughters.

Inbreeding increases the predictability of type and quality in a particular family by reducing the number of genes available for inheritance by the foal. Unfortunately, it also raises the odds that a lethal recessive gene, if present in the family, will be inherited from the foal's parents.

Combined Immunodeficiency (CID)

Combined Immunodeficiency is the best-known lethal trait affecting the Arabian breed and to date has been identified only in purebred and partbred Arabian horses. CID is a deficiency in the immune system of the young foal, causing the animal to die when it contracts its first disease (usually a respiratory infection). Foals having CID always die within the first five months of life.

Because CID results from a simple recessive, the incidence of carriers and CID foals from various matings is the same as that for other recessive traits. As a result, an average of one in four foals from a carrier-to-carrier mating will die. Two of the four will show no symptoms but will be carriers of the

recessive. The other foal will be normal and cannot transmit the recessive to its offspring.

Since CID is not a disease, it has no cure. The only prevention is to avoid mating known CID carriers to each other. Unfortunately, approximately half the foals from carrier to non-carrier matings also will carry the CID recessive gene. A CID carrier shows no signs of disease or weakness—the only proof that a horse is a carrier is the death of one of its foals from CID.

Because a stallion may sire twelve or more foals annually while a mare usually produces only one, it is easier to identify a carrier stallion than a carrier mare. However, it is possible that a carrier stallion might *never* be detected if the recessive lethal genes do not happen to be inherited by any of his foals. Because the lethal CID recessive genes must be inherited from both parents, the best test of a stallion's status is to breed known carrier mares to him. The more foals a stallion sires without producing a CID foal, the more likely it is that he is not a carrier. However, until laboratory tests to identify CID carriers is discovered, there is no way to be absolutely sure about the CID status of any Arabian or part-Arabian.

Some popular bloodlines are rumored to carry CID, but it is difficult to learn which individuals are carriers. Breeders are especially reluctant to publicize that a valuable and popular stallion is a CID carrier because of potential income loss. Rumors about reputed carriers may be based upon fact or result from malicious gossip.

Breeders approach the CID problem in various ways. Some geld stallions that have sired CID foals. Others feel it is worth losing an occasional foal from CID to produce Arabians that otherwise have very desirable characteristics. Some breeders advertise that their stallions have never sired any foals that have died of CID. Concerned Arabian breeders can support CID research and cooperation among breeders to solve lethal genetic problems by joining the FOAL program sponsored by the International Arabian Horse Association (IAHA).

Since the CID recessive lethal is passed at random, there is no way to know which of the CID carrier's living relatives also might be CID carriers. There also is no way to determine which ancestors passed down the recessive gene. The best attitude is that a horse is innocent until proven guilty.

Recently, it became possible for breeders or purchasers to find out whether (according to IAHA's records, at least), a specific horse is a known CID carrier or the offspring of known carrier parents. The information is provided by an independent trustee, the CID Fiduciary, from laboratory reports diagnosing CID in foals.

To get a CID report on a specific horse, you must submit a request form and processing fee, along with an affidavit form signed by the horse's owner which states that, to the best of the owner's knowledge, the horse has never produced any CID foals and its parents have not produced known CID offspring.

The necessary forms and further information are available from IAHA and the CID Fiduciary, P.O. Box 1178, Broomfield, CO 80020.

Although the presence of the CID recessive does not, at present, appear to be a threat to the popularity of the Arabian breed, financial and emotional losses occur each time a foal dies as a result of it.

GENDER

The sex of a foal is determined by the sex chromosomes it inherits from its sire. The mare has only two "female" chromosomes (XX) while the stallion has two different chromosomes—one "female" (X) and one "male" (Y). The dam can only pass the "female" X chromosome to her foals because she is homozygous. The stallion, on the other hand, is heterozygous. This means that he can transmit the "male" and "female" chromosome at random. Statistically, he will transmit the two with equal frequency, which means that an equal chance exists of getting *either* a colt or filly from *every* mating.

Occasional foals are born lacking one sex chromosome. Instead of being XX (female) or XY (male), the foal might be considered "XO." Such foals are female but have very small reproductive organs, resulting in complete infertility. Fortunately, this genetic defect is uncommon.

Sex-Linked Traits

The X (female) chromosome is large and also carries other genes not related to the foal's sex. Because these other traits are inherited with gender,

they are called "sex linked." Sex-linked traits are passed from the carrier female to her sons. Although the female doesn't show the trait, her sons will.

Few traits are carried on the Y (male) sex chromosome. However, since the Y is found only in male offspring, any traits carried by that chromosome are seen only in the males. Such traits (called *holandric*) are extremely rare.

Sex-limited traits affect males and females differently. They are called sex-limited because whether or not they are expressed is determined by the foal's gender.

COLOR-LINKED TRAITS

Horses in a family often vary from each other in both type and color, with certain traits apparently associated with a specific color. For example, grey members of a family may inherit one set of type and conformation traits, while the chestnuts appear to inherit a different set of traits. The specific qualities associated with various colors differ by family. In such cases, the chromosome that carries a particular color also may carry genes for other traits, and the foal inherits both its color and other traits of type and conformation as a package. Although research on color-linked inheritance by family is lacking, breeders including Lady Wentworth have noted the phenomenon.

PHENOTYPE AND GENOTYPE

While *phenotype* refers to a horse's appearance, *genotype* refers to the individual's particular genetic inheritance. The phenotype cannot reveal the entire genotype because not all of the horse's genes are expressed in its appearance.

Although the normal foal receives the proper number of chromosomes (32 pairs) to insure that it will have the proper organs and body parts, predicting the particular assortment of traits it will inherit is impossible. It inherits each chromosome (and the genes it happens to carry) at random, receiving only one chromosome of each pair of chromosomes possessed by each parent.

Because each foal inherits traits from its parents at random, it is possible for full siblings to differ considerably in both phenotype and genotype. A mind-boggling number of possible combinations of traits can be inherited from the same parents.

INHERITANCE OF COLOR

A foal gets a set of color genes from each parent. The foal's own color is determined by which two colors are inherited. The following rules apply:

1. Grey prevents the expression of any other color. If a grey gene is transmitted by either parent, the foal will turn grey.
2. All other colors prevail over chestnut. For example, if one parent transmits genes for bay and the other transmits genes for chestnut, the foal will be bay.
3. If both parents transmit genes for the *same* color, the foal will be that color.

Grey

Whenever the grey gene (G) is inherited, the foal gradually will turn grey. Horses that are not grey have the non-grey allele (gg).

To be grey, the foal must have at least one grey parent. The grey color cannot skip a generation, for it is never recessive. If grey Arabians were no longer used for breeding, the color would disappear from the breed and could never be restored.

If a grey parent is *homozygous grey* (has two grey genes), it always will transmit the grey gene and all its offspring will be grey. Homozygosity can never be proven, but a horse is presumed to be homozygous grey if it has two grey parents and always produces grey offspring from matings with all colors.

A *heterozygous grey* parent has one grey gene and one non-grey gene. It can produce foals of other colors, as well as producing grey offspring. It can pass on either the grey gene or the alternative with equal frequency.

Bay

If a horse is *homozygous bay* (has two sets of genes for the bay color), it can only pass the genes for bay (or another related dark color). Unless its offspring inherit grey genes from the other parents, the foals

To be grey, a horse must have at least one grey parent. The color is never recessive (it cannot skip a generation). This famous grey stallion is Sotep, youngest son of *Raffles.

Johnny Johnston photo, courtesy Lancer Arabians

of the homozygous bay will be bay or a variation of bay.

A *heterozygous bay* is a bay horse that also has genes for chestnut. It can pass on its bay and chestnut genes with equal frequency to its offspring. The heterozygous bay can produce bay, chestnut, or grey foals, depending upon the genetic contribution of the foals' other parent.

Chestnut

All other colors prevail over chestnut. If the chestnut color genes are inherited with another set of genes for any other color, the foal will not be chestnut. To be chestnut, it must inherit the chestnut color from both parents.

The surest way to produce a chestnut foal is to mate two chestnut horses. They carry only the chestnut color genes, so they can only pass their own color to their offspring.

Two bay or two grey parents also can produce a chestnut foal if each has and transmits chestnut color genes to the foal. However, if either parent transmits genes for any other color, the foal will not be chestnut.

Chestnut is recessive to all other colors. In order to be chestnut, a horse must inherit the genes for chestnut from both parents. Spearmint, winning at the 1985 Ascot Show, England.

Black

Black Arabians are rare, but the color appears most frequently in certain bloodlines (mostly in some

Egyptian and Polish families). The black color does not breed true; two black Arabians may produce a foal of a different color, depending upon which color genes are transmitted to the foal. Because black genetically is closely related to bay, "black bloodlines" (a family that previously has produced some black horses) also can produce other dark colors instead of black.

Because the chestnut color is not expressed unless two sets of chestnut genes are transmitted to the foal, chestnut horses often are bred to black Arabians in hope of producing the rare black color. If the black parent transmits the genes for black, the resulting foal will be black. However, if the black parent also has genes for chestnut, half the foals produced by such a mating probably will be chestnut. The rest will be brown, bay, or black.

"The Black Stallion" of movie fame, Cass Ole. The stallion was bred by Donoghue Arabians of Goliad, Texas.
Photo courtesy of San Antonio Arabians, Inc., San Antonio, Texas

Black-to-black and chestnut-to-black matings *sometimes* produce black foals. Depending upon which genes are transmitted to the foal, other matings also can result in black foals. Even grey horses from "black bloodlines" sometimes may produce black foals. A chestnut bred to a grey, bay or brown also may produce a black foal.

Predicting Color Inheritance

To predict the odds of producing foals of specific colors from parents of certain colors, the color genotype of each parent must be determined. It is easy to identify the horse's dominant color genes from its color. For example, a bay horse has dominant bay genes. Its other set of genes may either be bay (in which case the horse is homozygous, or pure for bay) or chestnut (the horse is heterozygous and can transmit the chestnut color genes as often as it transmits bay genes). The bay horse's other genetic color cannot be grey; if the horse had a grey gene, it would not be bay.

It may be difficult to tell whether a horse carries color genes for chestnut because the recessive chestnut genes may be transmitted for many generations without producing a chestnut foal. However, in the following cases, the horse *does* carry genes for chestnut: the horse is (or was born) chestnut; one of the horse's parents was chestnut; or the horse has sired or produced a chestnut foal.

When the parents' color genotype is known, the odds of producing each possible color from the mating can be figured. However, although one chestnut foal out of four foals from a specific mating might be predicted, it is possible to "beat the odds" and to produce four chestnut foals instead. It is just as possible to produce no chestnut foals from the same four matings. No matter how many times a mating is repeated, the odds of producing a given color are always the same. You cannot "improve the odds" of producing a specific color by repeating the mating.

DETERMINATION OF COAT COLOR

Seven genes are known to control coat color in horses, but only three are considered here. They are gene B, which controls the ability to form black pigment; gene A, which determines the pattern (location) of the black hair; and gene G, which causes greying.

If the horse inherits a dominant B gene (B), it will have some black hair. If the alternative (bb) is present instead, the horse has black pigment in the skin but not in the hair, which will look red. The horse with bb as part of its genotype will therefore be some shade of chestnut.

If the dominant gene A (A) is present along with the dominant B (B), the horse's black hair will be confined to the points (mane, tail, and legs), creating a bay. If the dominant B and the recessive allele (a) are present, the black won't be limited to the points and the horse will be black.

A Western Pleasure horse needs a smooth trot so its rider can sit the jog trot comfortably. KJ Karaff, ridden here by Bubbles Slolum, is a Western Pleasure and halter champion. *Johnny Johnston photo courtesy of Laurence Arabians*

The best way to produce uniform foals is to choose mares of similar type, conformation, and bloodlines and breed them to comparable stallions.

21

BECOMING A BREEDER

Modern breeders of Arabian horses have received a legacy that has been passed down through history and must be carefully guarded. The breeder of Arabian horses has a heavy responsibility: to preserve the superior qualities of the breed and to lessen its faults. This requires large amounts of time, money, work, and commitment and should not be undertaken lightly or without a great deal of study.

Before selecting foundation breeding stock, read existing Arabian horse literature. Start with books by early authorities and study modern books and articles in Arabian horse magazines.

Visit Arabian horse shows and breeding farms, seeing a wide variety of types and bloodlines. Analyze the faults and good points of Arabian horses of various bloodlines, discovering what qualities frequently are shared by members of a specific family. After studying photographs, movies (when available), and written descriptions of influential ancestors of modern Arabian horses, you will realize that each horse resembles some of its ancestors in various characteristics. In fact, you sometimes may be able to identify the bloodlines or nationality of an Arabian horse by its appearance.

When you are familiar with the various Arabian bloodlines and types, form your own preferences and opinions. Decide which points of type and conformation are most important *to you* and where you are willing to compromise. (Every breeder must make some compromises because the perfect Arabian horse does not exist.) When you've done your homework, you will know which bloodlines are likely to produce the kind of Arabian horse that appeals most to you.

ESTABLISHING THE BREEDING FARM

Most people put the cart before the horse (or, actually, the horse before the facility). Things run more smoothly if you begin with a facility that is carefully planned for economy and convenience as well as beauty and *then* add the horses (see Chapter 12).

Acquiring Breeding Stock

Studying the breed *before* buying Arabian horses will save time and money in the long run because you will *know* at the start the kind of Arabian horses you want to produce. When you have your ideal Arabian firmly in mind, select foundation breeding horses that are as close to that ideal as possible. Choose animals that look, move, perform, and behave like the kind of Arabians you hope to produce.

A breeding program is simply a plan to reach your breeding goals. The program must be based upon mares, because no stallion can "do it all." Having a solid base of good broodmares allows some flexibility in finding stallions whose qualities and bloodlines will complement them. Start with quality broodmares of similar type and bloodlines. The "ideal" broodmare band would probably consist of full sisters of excellent quality (see Chapter 20).

One way to find stallions whose bloodlines mesh well with your broodmares is to breed each mare to a different stallion for the first two or three years. When a superior foal results, send all your mares to the stallion who sired the outstanding foal. If the rest of his foals from your mares are uniformly good, continue breeding to the same bloodlines, keeping the fillies to eventually replace their dams and selling the colts. When the replacement fillies have produced satisfactory foals, sell their dams and keep these younger mares as broodmares.

Breed these mares to a stallion who seems compatible in bloodlines, type, and conformation to your mares. The more uniform your mares, the easier it will be to find one stallion to complement them all (see Chapter 22).

By always keeping fillies that are as good as or better than their dams, you will maintain high quality in your broodmare band and keep young mares that tend to have fewer breeding problems than aged mares. You also will be culling your older mares while they still will bring good prices.

Quantity and Quality

It is possible to start breeding Arabian horses with only one or two mares, but it takes much longer to be sure of the results and you have a smaller foal crop from which to obtain replacement broodmares. If colts are produced rather than fillies, you may not be able to cull and upgrade your mares for many years. Also, when you have few mares, producing an inferior foal or losing a horse is a much greater setback than if you have a large herd.

The more good mares you have, the greater are the odds of someday producing an Arabian that approaches your ideal. Volume *with* high quality is an advantage to the breeder; volume *without* high quality is wasteful. You can breed good Arabians without owning a lot of horses, but you cannot breed good Arabians unless you have breeding stock of good quality.

Changing a Breeding Program

Any breeder who continually changes direction by following the latest fashion in Arabian bloodlines doesn't *have* a breeding program. Fashions change rapidly, but breeding horses is a long-term project. Never breed to a stallion just because he is popular at the moment. Consider the long-term effects of doing so on your particular breeding program. Breeding to a currently popular stallion may help your present sales of foals, but the breeder must also consider future sales. On the other hand, if the stallion fits well into your program, don't hesitate to breed to him just because he is popular and you are afraid his popularity will fade. The name of the stallion is not the most important factor—what is important is whether he will benefit or damage the chance of reaching your breeding goal.

Quality is more important than quantity. With the present abundance of horses, it is critically important to breed fewer, but better, Arabians.

Although it is important to breed with a plan toward a desired result, it is foolish to adhere to an intricate breeding program just because you already have invested several years in it. If your plan isn't working—or if your own goals change—alter your breeding program.

If you breed the kind of Arabian horse that *you* like, there always will be some other people who also like them. If your horses are good, knowledgeable people will recognize their worth. Poor Arabians *must* be carefully promoted; to some extent, good ones "sell themselves."

Don't be "Barn Blind"

Barn blindness isn't an equine illness. It refers to horse owners who refuse to see their horses' faults. The barn-blind owner can see faults in other people's horses but is deluded about the quality of his or her own. (Sometimes owners who appear to be barn blind are merely ignorant and cannot recognize faults in anyone's horses.) Breeders must be more critical of their horses than anyone else would be. They must know their horses' faults, or they cannot breed for improvement. Barn-blind breeders merely reproduce faults present in their breeding stock.

BREEDING THEORY

The oldest proverb about horse breeding is "like produces like." This means that traits are passed down from one generation to the next. The parents' characteristics often are echoed in their offspring. The best chance of producing a foal of good quality occurs when two parents of good quality are mated. The best way to produce a foal of predictable type is to breed two similar horses to each other.

Breed Type to Type

When horses of different types are bred to each other, the resulting foal is seldom a perfect blending of the two types. The foal probably will resemble one parent more than the other, but it may combine features of both in an undesirable way. For example, a foal may inherit the small size of its dam and the coarseness of its sire, when the breeder hoped to get the mare's refinement and the stallion's greater size.

When the breeder says "breed type to type," this does not mean that a plain mare should be bred to a plain stallion. In that case, you are most likely to produce a plain foal. Instead, if the mare has a plain head, breed her to a stallion with a typey head and hope that the foal's head will resemble that of its sire rather than the head of its dam. However, you have a better chance of producing a foal with a typey head if that characteristic is shared by both parents.

Linebreeding

Linebreeding means mating two individuals that, although related, are not related in the first few generations. This means that the name of at least one common ancestor will appear in the pedigree of the sire and the dam but that it will be four or more generations back in the resulting foal's pedigree.

Linebreeding is done to set family traits by reducing the number of genes that are available for inheritance by the foal. The linebred foal is more likely to inherit traits of the ancestor to which it is linebred than to inherit traits from an ancestor that appears in its pedigree only once. However, there is no *guarantee* that the ancestor to which the foal is linebred will have passed along a greater genetic legacy since all genes are inherited at random.

Inbreeding

When linebreeding becomes inbreeding is a matter of interpretation. To the Arabian breeder, inbreeding means mating two *closely* related horses. Breeders of other horse breeds often consider many "linebred Arabians" to be inbred rather than linebred because such horses may have so many lines to the same ancestors. To the American breeder of Arabians, inbreeding often means incestuous breeding (breeding sire to daughter, dam to son, brother to sister).

Because the parents of the inbred Arabian horse are more closely related than the parents of the linebred Arabian, inbreeding sets family traits more quickly than does linebreeding. Fewer traits can be inherited by the inbred foal because its parents share more of the same genes and have fewer different genes. For this reason, members of inbred families usually have a strong "family resemblance" and usually are able to pass on their own traits to their offspring.

Because inbreeding concentrates genes, it can set bad traits as well as good ones. It sometimes has been accused of reducing vitality, size, disposition, intelligence, and fertility. It also can increase the inheritance of recessive genes for such lethal factors as CID (lack of immunity to disease) and cerebellar hypoplasia (degeneration of the brain) that sometimes occur in Arabian foals. Proponents of inbreeding argue that inbreeding is not the problem—but that the wrong individuals were chosen to inbreed. One thing is certain: only superior Arabian horses should be used in an inbreeding experiment, and if any degeneration occurs in the foals, inbreeding should be discontinued.

Outcrossing

Outcrossing means breeding two unrelated horses to each other. Obviously, all Arabian horses must eventually be related. Outcrossing means that the two horses mated are not *known* to be related, and if any relationship exists it is quite far back in the pedigree.

Outcrossing results in *hybrid vigor*. Foals usually are strong and healthy, but they may be less prepotent breeding animals because they can inherit a more diverse group of genes than linebred or inbred horses.

Using Inbreeding, Linebreeding, and Outcrossing

All three breeding techniques are of value, but most new breeding programs are based upon linebreeding. Later, as the breeders gain experience and familiarity with their horses' bloodlines, inbreeding is sometimes used to set traits within the breeding program. Outcrossing can introduce desirable traits that are lacking in the linebred or inbred horses. Sooner or later, every breeder must outcross, for no family of horses is perfect.

Nicks

Not all Arabian bloodlines blend equally well. Some usually do not cross well with certain other Arabian bloodlines while others may blend to produce consistently good foals. When two bloodlines cross well, they are said to be "a good nick." When the offspring are truly outstanding, the combination may be called "a golden cross."

Discovering a good nick takes experimentation and luck. Occasionally, two families combine better

in one way than another. For example, the daughters of Stallion A may produce excellent foals when bred to Stallion B, but the daughters of Stallion B may produce disappointing foals when bred to Stallion A.

Breeding Up

Most breeders try to improve their horses with each generation. If successful, breeding for improvement is called "breeding up." This usually is accomplished by breeding mares to stallions of better quality than the mares and then retaining their improved daughters as replacement broodmares. If this is repeated with each generation, the quality of the breeder's horses gradually improves. However, it is faster, surer, and less expensive in the long run to start with superior mares. Then a breeder can achieve, in only one generation, foals that could be produced only after decades of breeding up from average mares. As one breeder asked, "Why try to make a positive from a negative when you can start with a positive?"

Family Resemblances

Foals usually resemble each of their parents in some ways. However, traits also can skip a generation or more. A grandson or granddaughter often resembles a horse more than do its own sons and daughters. If the foal doesn't resemble any of its immediate family, it has inherited recessive traits that were not visible in its relatives. Photographs of ancestors that appear farther back in the pedigree often will reveal the same traits present in the foal (see Chapter 20).

Breeding Arabians Isn't Easy

Breeding horses combines science and art with gambling. No matter how carefully the breeder approaches the task, luck is always a factor, for the horse inherits its traits at random from the genes available. Although the traits of Arabian type have been established through centuries of inbreeding and linebreeding, it is surprisingly difficult to breed Arabians of consistent type and quality. This is because the Arabian horse must combine so many traits. The superior Arabian must not only have good conformation but must have a typey Arabian head, arched neck, and high tail carriage. The more traits the breeder tries to incorporate into one individual, the greater the chance of failure.

Nevertheless, the hope of producing one's ideal Arabian horse keeps the serious breeder involved in a long-term effort despite disappointment, failure, and tragedy. It has been said that the Arabian horse breeder is an artist whose materials are flesh, bones, and blood. There is always the hope that the next foal produced will be that elusive ideal Arabian.

SELECTING BROODMARES

Most breeders believe that the mare contributes at least 60 percent to the resulting foal because she can influence it in several ways while the stallion's influence is only genetic. In addition to the mare's *genetic influence*, she has a *physical influence* on her foal. The mare's body nourishes it during pregnancy and afterward through her milk. The foal's development is therefore influenced by the mare's health, nutrition, and the foal's position in the uterus during gestation. The mare also has an *environmental influence* on her foal. They are together constantly during the foal's early life, and the foal learns some behavior from its dam. Because of these multiple influences on their foals, careful selection of broodmares is critical. If you need help choosing broodmares, ask an experienced breeder for assistance.

Evaluating Broodmares

The best measurement of a broodmare's worth is the quality of her foals. Carefully analyze the mare's conformation and type, first. Then analyze each of her foals and compare them to the mare. Which of her own traits did they inherit? Which traits did she fail to pass to her foals? Don't forget to allow for the sires' possible contributions, however.

The superior broodmare produces foals that inherit her best qualities without her faults. The good broodmare produces good foals but sometimes passes along her faults. The poor broodmare always passes her own faults to the offspring, and her foals are no better than she is. Unless her faults are minor, avoid the broodmare who consistently reproduces them. Likewise, avoid the broodmare who does not seem to pass on her strong points consistently to her foals.

The good broodmare produces breeding stock —not simply horses that can reproduce, but Arabians that can improve (or at least maintain) the quality of the breed. If the mare cannot *produce* broodmares, she should not *be* one. The excellent broodmare produces colts that are superior enough to be worthy stallion prospects.

"Incubator mares" are those whose foals always resemble the sires instead of resembling their dams.

When a mating results in superior offspring, it is said to be a "good nick." The bay stallion Fadjur and the grey mare Saki were such a good nick that they repeatedly produced champions. *Photo courtesy of Jack Tone Ranch, Stockton, Calif.*

When bred to an outstanding stallion, a poor-quality incubator mare may produce outstanding offspring. However, the resulting horses are unlikely to pass their good qualities to their own foals. Because inheritance often skips generations, later descendants of a poor-quality incubator mare may resemble her. In the final analysis, an incubator mare is an asset to a breeding program *only* if she is a quality individual.

Fertility — Before buying a broodmare, check her production record to see how many foals she has produced. If she hasn't produced foals regularly, find out whether she was bred and failed to produce a foal or if she simply was left open (not bred).

The broodmare should not have a record of infection or abortion. She should come in heat regularly, show strong signs of estrus, be easy to breed, settle (become pregnant) quickly, and foal without difficulty.

Conformation — Since foals often inherit their dams' traits, broodmares should have the kind of good conformation needed by any performance horse, plus a few special conformation traits particularly valuable in broodmares.

The broodmare should be deep through the heartgirth to allow plenty of space for the heart and lungs, especially when the area becomes crowded by a growing fetus.

Mares tend to be slightly longer in the back than male horses probably to allow room for a fetus. However, if a mare's back is too long, repeated pregnancies can cause ligaments suspending the uterus to stretch downward excessively, increasing pressure on the intestines and uterine arteries.

It is very important that the mare's vulva be vertical, instead of sloping inward. A tipped or sunken vulva makes the mare prone to infection from contamination of the reproductive tract by bacteria and fecal matter (see Chapter 22).

When evaluating broodmares, remember that few of them are kept in show condition. Most are pastured and get minimal grooming and conditioning. In judging the broodmare's conformation, consider how she looked when she was young and how her offspring look. Don't penalize an older mare because she "looks like a broodmare." As a result of repeated pregnancies and lack of conditioning, old broodmares develop pendulous abdomens. Their croups often look steeper, and their hip bones more prominent. If the basic bone structure is correct, the mare has good conformation.

Type — Select broodmares that approach *your* ideal Arabian type to increase chances of producing foals of the type you desire. (See Chapter 6 for a description of Arabian breed type.)

Action — The broodmare should move with great extension and freedom of the shoulders, and her hocks should be lifted high and well flexed at the trot. Remember that action can be inherited from either side of the family. Don't choose a broodmare whose trot you dislike—her foals *may* trot just like her. Because most of the mare's foals will be ridden, she should have smooth and comfortable gaits.

Pedigree — When choosing between broodmares of equal individual quality, always select the one with superior ancestors. A mare's foals may inherit traits from *any* of her ancestors—not just from her.

Although a mare's *entire* pedigree is important, many breeders feel that the presence of excellent mares in the family is even more important than having excellent stallions as ancestors. Some carry this one step farther, placing greatest importance on the tail female line of the pedigree. As an example, *Raffles and *Raseyn are best known as sons of the stallion Skowronek. However, neither would have been produced without the mare who appears in the tail female lines of each of their pedigrees—Rodania. (*Raffles traces to Rodania through Rose of Sharon, and *Raseyn through Rosemary.)

Producing ability often runs in families. Choosing a broodmare whose relatives have produced good-quality horses is a better bet than choosing a broodmare from a family of poor producers.

Type, conformation, and performing ability are all inherited. Choose a broodmare from a family that has excelled in a certain activity. For example, if you hope to produce a future Park Horse, select a mare from a family of Park Horses.

Disposition — Mares that do not bite or kick are much safer and more pleasant to handle than untractable mares. Also, foals are likely to inherit their dams' dispositions. (See Chapter 5.)

The ideal broodmare should *like* motherhood. If she does, she will raise healthy and well-adjusted foals. She will be patient and protective, yet she will trust people and teach her foals to do the same. She also will make them behave, which will make her offspring easier to discipline later. Mares that do not seem to love their foals are not meant to be broodmares—no matter how good their conformation, type, or performing ability.

Show Record — A show record does not affect the producing ability of a broodmare. It always is safer to buy a mare who has *produced* champions than to buy a mare who was herself a show champion. The champion mare may not pass on her own good qualities to her foals. Remember, too, that show wins are based upon the opinions of judges and may not be the best indication of the mare's true quality or ability. However, from a commercial standpoint, the successful show record of a broodmare *will* help sell her foals.

Health — Producing and raising foals is a physical strain. If the mare hasn't had proper care, her health may have been weakened. Before buying a broodmare, insist that she pass a veterinary exam. The veterinarian should palpate the mare and do a uterine biopsy to verify that she is reproductively sound. Ask whether the broodmare has had a history of infection or abortion, whether she has had any breeding or foaling problems, and if she produces enough milk.

Age — The mare's prime producing years are between the ages of five and fifteen. It is safest to buy proven broodmares within that age range, although they are generally expensive.

Maiden mares have never produced a foal; thus, no proof of their breeding or producing ability exists. Check the fertility and producing ability of the maiden mare's family, especially that of her dam, as an indication of her expected performance as a broodmare.

If buying a young filly, remember that she is still growing. See as many *mature* female relatives as possible to predict what she may look like when mature. Find out, too, what her female relatives have produced and whether they've had breeding problems.

If the young filly is bred while she still is growing, the foal will take some of the nutrients that her body needs for its own growth. Breeding a filly before the age of three may endanger her health and sometimes is suspected of shortening her life. Some breeders prefer to wait until a young mare is four or five to breed her for the first time since Arabians mature later than other breeds.

Elderly mares sometimes are difficult to settle and may produce less regularly than younger mares. If an old mare doesn't settle, she may remain barren for the rest of her life. Foaling also is more dangerous for old mares. If the old broodmare's uterus is scarred, her foals may be undernourished or aborted. Despite these greater risks, many Arabian mares *do* remain fertile well into old age.

There is no indication that the first foal of a mare—or foals produced late in the broodmare's life—are of less quality than the foals produced during the "prime production years." The first foals of some mares have been outstanding, as have some produced by elderly Arabian mares.

BUYING BROODMARES

It is helpful to obtain foundation broodmares from knowledgeable breeders. Experienced breeders usually are glad to discuss bloodlines and favorable nicks with buyers. Starting with the end product of a long and successful breeding program can save the new breeder years of hard work and experimentation. Quality broodmares, however, are where you find them. If the mare meets your standards of quality, the "name" of the breeder and the sales price are irrelevant.

Cost of Broodmares

An expensive mare of good quality *may* pay for herself and even produce a profit from the sales of her good-quality foals. An inferior mare never is a bargain at any price. The first rule of buying broodmares is to start with the best mare(s) you can afford. If you start with good mares, your first foal crop will be a good one.

Regardless of the purchase price, a handy rule of thumb states that you should be able to "pay for" the mare with the sales of three foals. For example, if the mare cost $4,500, her foals need to average $1,500 each. After the mare's initial purchase price has been recouped, the breeder can hope to make a profit from sales of additional foals or resale of the broodmare.

The best broodmares come from a family of exceptional broodmares. Breeder Frank McCoy is shown with his premiere broodmare, Bint Sahara (at left) and her famous daughters.

Photo courtesy of McCoys Arabians

184

22

BREEDING YOUR MARE

REPRODUCTION IN MARES

The Reproductive Organs

Ovaries — A mare has two bean-shaped ovaries, each containing fluid-filled sacs called follicles. Each follicle contains one immature egg. When an egg matures, the follicle ruptures, releasing the egg (ovulation).

Fallopian Tubes — When the mare ovulates, the egg is transported through one of the fallopian tubes, where it is fertilized if it is penetrated by the sperm of a stallion. The fertilized egg travels from the fallopian tube to the uterus.

Uterus — The uterus is a hollow organ that contains and nourishes the unborn foal (fetus). The uterus is shaped somewhat like a "T," with its body forming the vertical line and the two horns of the uterus forming the cross bar.

Cervix — The cervix connects the uterus and the vagina. It is open during heat and foaling but tightly closed at all other times to protect the uterus from contamination.

Vagina — The vagina is the entrance to the reproductive tract. Sperm reaches the uterus via the vagina, which is also the birth canal through which the foal passes.

Vulva — The vulva is the outer entrance to the vagina. It is relaxed and appears swollen prior to foaling.

ESTRUS CYCLE

From about February through October (or year-round in warm, mild climates), the mare has regular, recurring heat periods when she is receptive for breeding. A mare in heat (estrus) is said to be "in season."

Each heat period lasts approximately five to ten days. Then the mare is out of heat for about fifteen days before coming back in season. Thus, an average mare is in heat for about one week and then not in heat for about two weeks. A normal mare begins her next heat period approximately twenty-one days from the first day of the previous heat period.

Just because a mare is in heat does not necessarily mean she is fertile. A mare can be in heat but fail to ovulate. To conceive, a mature egg must be released from an ovarian follicle.

Sometimes pregnant mares act as though they are in heat during early pregnancy. The only way to determine whether a mare is really in heat or pregnant is to have her examined by a veterinarian. A pregnant mare that is showing signs of estrus should not be rebred, even if she will accept the stallion.

The filly's first heat period occurs when she is about eighteen months old. However, she should not be bred until she is at least three years old. It is important to segregate colts and fillies at an early age since a weanling or yearling colt could possibly impregnate a mare, and a filly can become pregnant on her first heat period or any subsequent heat.

PRODUCTION OF FOALS

Breeders sometimes think they are being kind to a broodmare by giving her a year or two of "rest" between foals. In fact, it seems to be easier to settle

A good broodmare is motherly. She breeds and foals easily, produces plenty of milk, and takes good care of her foals.

mares if they are bred every year, and remaining pregnant for much of her life does not seem to harm the healthy broodmare. Aged mares are especially likely to "shut down production" if they are not bred regularly. Leaving an old mare open for a year might mean she will never settle again. If a mare's body is not ready for pregnancy, she will fail to settle or will abort.

Lifetime Production Record

A mare cannot safely begin producing foals until she is four or five years old, and elderly broodmares usually produce irregularly. Since each pregnancy lasts eleven months, the prime producing years of the average broodmare are limited to an approximate ten-year period (between the ages of five and fifteen). Some mares produce much later in life than fifteen, but the average elderly broodmare produces foals less regularly than during her prime years.

Even during their ten-year "prime time" span, few mares produce a foal every year, even if bred annually. The average broodmare would be doing well to produce ten to twelve foals during her lifetime. Exceptionally fertile (and long-lived) Arabian mares have produced as many as seventeen or eighteen foals, but few approach this number of offspring.

EXAMINING THE REPRODUCTIVE TRACT

To view the mare's vagina and cervix, the veterinarian inserts a speculum (a tube containing a battery-operated light) into the vagina. A visual

The best test of any broodmare is the quality of her produce.

186

examination can provide information about the health of the reproductive tract and indicate whether or not the mare is pregnant.

When a mare is in season, the cervix and vagina are moist and pink, and the cervix is relaxed (open). When not in heat, the cervix is pale and closed. It also is closed if the mare is pregnant. If the vagina is red (inflamed) or contains pus, the reproductive tract is infected.

Palpating

By palpating (inserting a sterile, gloved hand and arm into the mare's rectum), the veterinarian can feel the reproductive organs.

A follicle is felt as a bulge on the ovary; its size indicates the approximate time of ovulation. After the mare has ovulated, it is possible to feel a depression where the follicle ruptured. A mature (breedable) follicle is about half the size of the ovary. If two mature follicles are detected at the same time, the decision is sometimes made to wait until the next heat period to breed the mare, to avoid the possibility of conceiving twins. However, twins do not always result when a mare is bred on a double ovulation.

The muscle tension of the uterus also is revealing. If the uterus is firm and tense, the mare is probably in heat; if it is relaxed, she is not in heat.

"Palping" is not foolproof. The veterinarian must do a blind examination based upon the way the internal organs feel. It is impossible, for example, to tell whether the bulge felt on an ovary is a maturing follicle or an ovarian cyst that can interfere with fertility. (The cyst too can rupture but contains no egg.) A large follicle also can recede rather than ovulating. Two nearby follicles on the same ovary may feel like one mature follicle.

Mares that are palpated frequently during estrus may be more difficult to settle than those that are not palpated or palpated less often. However, frequent palpation may be necessary if 1) the mare doesn't show signs of estrus; or 2) a large number of mares must be bred by one stallion.

Culturing

Culturing can determine whether the mare's reproductive tract is infected and what type of bacteria is the cause. The specific medical treatment depends upon the bacteria causing the infection. Culturing is done when the mare is in heat since

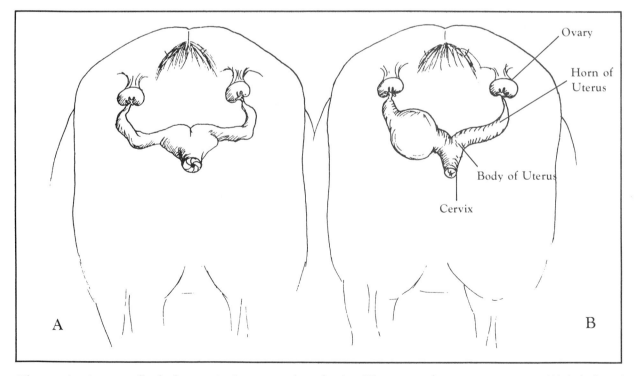

The veterinarian can tell whether a mare is pregnant by palpating. The uterus of an unpregnant mare (A) feels flaccid and the cervix is loose. The uterus of the pregnant mare (B) has a tightly closed cervix and the fetus can be felt as a bulge in the pregnant horn of the uterus.

187

the cervix is open at that time, making insertion of a sterile swab into the uterus easier. There also are additional secretions from the uterus and if a deep-seated bacteria exists, it is more likely to be found in the sample of liquid that is removed from the uterus. When the sample (smear) has been incubated in the laboratory, it is examined for bacterial growth (culture).

Biopsy of the Uterus

A uterine biopsy reveals whether the mare's uterus is able to sustain a pregnancy. A small piece of tissue is removed from the uterus and examined under a microscope to determine the condition (class) of the lining of the uterus (the endometrium). The uterine class helps predict the mare's chances of producing a foal; if the uterus cannot sustain a fetus, breeding is a waste of effort, time, and money.

The uterus is rated as Grade 1, 2, or 3, as shown:

Uterine/Class	Probable Ability to Produce
1	70 percent to 90 percent chance of fertility. (Best rating; should be able to produce a foal.)
2	50 percent to 70 percent chance of fertility. (Might produce a foal.)
3	Less than 50 percent chance of fertility. (Unlikely to produce a foal.)

To biopsy the uterus, the mare's tail is wrapped in plastic and tied to one side to prevent contaminating the reproductive tract.

The grade assigned depends upon the condition of the lining of the uterus.

HORMONES

The estrus cycle, pregnancy and birth are controlled by hormones produced by the mare's body.

Follicle Stimulating Hormone (FSH) — In spring, increasing hours of daylight stimulate the mare's pituitary gland to produce FSH, the hormone that causes follicles to develop.

Estrogen —Estrogen prepares the mare's uterus for pregnancy and may protect it from infection during estrus and foaling, when the cervix is open and vulnerable. Estrogen also surrounds the egg inside the follicle. As the follicle enlarges, the estrogen level in the mare's blood rises. As this estrogen increases, the pituitary stops producing FSH so that no additional follicles will form.

Lutenizing Hormone (LH) — Lutenizing hormone, also produced by the mare's pituitary gland, causes the mature ovarian follicle to soften and rupture. It also controls the development of the *corpus luteum*, which prevents abortion during early pregnancy.

Progesterone — The *corpus luteum* (yellow body) is tissue that forms on the ovary after ovulation. It produces the hormone progesterone, which prevents the pregnant mare from coming into heat. Additional follicles also form to produce more yellow bodies and thus boost the level of progesterone. (It is at this point in the pregnancy that some mares show signs of estrus, even though they are pregnant.)

REGULATING THE ESTRUS CYCLE

Artificial Lights

Mares come in heat in the spring because of increasing daylight hours. Ultraviolet light somehow causes the production of FSH, which results in estrus. Breeders sometimes induce an earlier than normal heat period (in order to get mares bred earlier in the year) by simulating the lengthening days of spring. This is done using artificial light. A standard 200-watt light bulb is left on in the broodmare's stall from before sundown until about 11:00 p.m. to create about 16 hours of "daylight" each day.

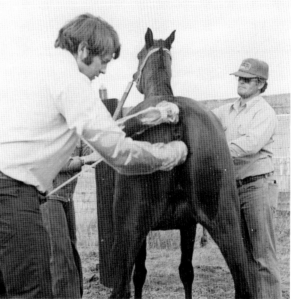

Continuing with the biopsy, the area surrounding the vulva is thoroughly scrubbed with antiseptic and the veterinarian (wearing a disposable plastic palpating glove) then clips off a small piece of uterine tissue for laboratory examination.

Mares that are kept under lights every day starting in November should first come in heat in January or February.

Mares kept under lights have a shorter winter coat and shed out earlier than they would under natural conditions, so they may require blanketing. They also may need an extra feeding of hay at night to keep them occupied and help maintain their body temperature.

Hormone Shots

Regulating estrus and pregnancy with hormone injections is "a blessing and a curse." Mares that otherwise might be unable to produce foals may do so with the help of hormone shots. However, their original breeding problems may be inherited by their offspring, creating a continuing need for hormone injections in order to increase fertility.

Some breeders routinely use hormone shots to induce heat, stimulate ovulation, etc., while others refuse to use them at all. Most veterinarians recommend avoiding hormone injections when possible, but using them when necessary to achieve pregnancy.

Prostaglandin — Prostaglandin shots induce heat in open mares and labor (or abortion) in pregnant mares. Sometimes an open mare has a *corpus luteum* secreting progesterone just as though she were

pregnant, which keeps her from coming in heat for breeding. A shot of prostaglandin will stop the secretion of progesterone and cause the mare to come back in heat.

Prostaglandin also is useful in synchronizing heat cycles in a group of mares, which is necessary for artificial insemination and embryo transfers (see Chapter 23).

Prostaglandin is often used near the end of the breeding season because it can shorten the time between heat periods. If a shot of prostaglandin is given about six days after ovulation, a mare should come back in heat within the next three to five days.

Lutenizing Hormone (LH) — Although an abnormally long heat period can be caused by such things as ovarian cysts and infections, it also may result from the failure of a mature follicle to rupture. This is particularly common early in the breeding season, and is most often seen in maiden mares. Most mares will ovulate normally later in the year. If necessary, a shot of LH can cause ovulation within 48 hours—provided that a mature follicle is present.

Progesterone — Progesterone shots sometimes are given in hope of sustaining pregnancy in mares having a history of abortion. However, opinions vary as to the effectiveness of this progesterone therapy. If it is used, the pregnant mare receives the first progesterone shot about eighteen days after the final ovulation, and shots continue at three-day intervals until 110 days gestation. At this point, the fetus should have implanted in the uterus, lowering the risk of early abortion, and the mare is re-examined to determine whether she is still pregnant. Injections sometimes are continued at 10-day intervals through the seventh or eighth month of gestation.

Because progesterone keeps mares from coming in heat, progesterone shots also are used in synchronizing estrus cycles (for artificial insemination and embryo transfer). The mares are first given progesterone to keep them out of heat, and then given prostaglandin to induce heat (see Chapter 23).

DETERMINING PREGNANCY

Teasing a mare (by bringing her near a stallion to determine whether she is receptive for breeding) can provide a clue as to whether a bred mare is pregnant, but the only way to be sure is with a pregnancy exam or laboratory test.

Palpating

The most common way to tell if a mare is pregnant is by rectal palpation. If no bulge in the uterus is felt, the mare is probably open.

The veterinarian also can estimate the length of gestation by the size and shape of the fetus. At approximately forty days, the fetus is a round bulge about the size of an orange in one horn of the uterus. After fifty days, the fetus has a more oval shape and starts growing down into the body of the uterus.

Mares usually are palpated for pregnancy about forty-five days after they are bred. They can be examined at anytime after twenty days, but it is more difficult to tell whether the mare is pregnant.

Between about forty-two and sixty days' gestation, mares often abort or resorb (the mare's body apparently absorbs the fetus). The greatest risk of either appears at the time mares normally would come back in heat and their hormone balance changes slightly. Because of this, a mare can be pronounced pregnant at forty-five days after breeding but not be pregnant when a later examination is done.

Because of the frequency of early abortions, mares usually are examined again at 110 days gestation or later, after the fetus has become implanted.

Mares pregnant at this time are considered "safe in foal" and usually carry to term.

Pregnancy Tests

The most common lab test done to determine pregnancy is the Mare Immunological Pregnancy Test (MIP test). The MIP checks for a hormone found only in the blood of pregnant mares (pregnant mare serum gonadotropin, or PMSG). The MIP test is almost 100 percent effective in verifying pregnancies of forty-five to one hundred and fifty days gestation.

It is also possible to measure the progesterone in the mare's blood, although this is not done routinely. (The progesterone level drops after ovulation if the mare isn't pregnant, but remains high if she is.)

Ultrasonic Testing

Ultrasound machinery now is being used to detect early pregnancies. Ultrasound equipment bounces sound waves at the mare's abdomen, and the sound waves are converted to a television picture. The fetus (if any), detected by its density, is visible on the TV screen and can be shown on a print-out picture.

Ultrasonic testing undoubtedly will become more common in the future as equipment is made available at lower cost and more people are trained to use it. Ultrasound testing requires less skill to determine pregnancy in its early stages than palpating. Pregnancy can be verified by ultrasound as early as sixteen days gestation. It also can be used to identify a twin pregnancy early enough for the veterinarian to induce abortion or to crush one twin (to improve the other twin's chances of being carried to term).

CHOOSING A STALLION

In theory, every mare has many potential mates. But choose a stallion very carefully since he will provide half the genetic inheritance of your mare's foal. Start with a list of prospective sires and narrow the list according to how well the stallions meet the following criteria.

Evaluating a Stallion

Quality of Get — The best test of any breeding stallion is the quality of the horses he has sired (the stallion's *get*). See as many of the stallion's get (sons and daughters) as possible.

Are the stallion's get uniform? Do they look like him or their dams? If they consistently resemble their dams, the stallion isn't prepotent. Don't breed to him unless you want a carbon copy of your mare.

Which faults and weaknesses seem to appear regularly in the stallion's get? Which strong points does he consistently pass on?

If possible, choose a stallion that already has sired the kind of foal you hope to produce.

The best test of a breeding stallion is the quality of his get. This is *Sultann, sire of *Asadd (U.S. National Champion Stallion) and *Sakr (U.S. National Champion Native Costume, U.S. Top Ten Park Horse).
Johnny Johnston photo courtesy of Lancer Arabians, Reddick, Fla.

Type — The Arabian stallion should have an abundance of Arabian type—whatever his blood-

lines, he should be instantly recognizable as an Arabian. Because Arabians vary somewhat in type, choose a stallion that approaches *your* ideal of Arabian breed type. The stallion seems to greatly influence the type of his get. However, since all characteristics can be inherited from either side of the family, it is easier to predict the type of the resulting foal if your mare's type is similar to that of the stallion.

Conformation — The breeding stallion should have excellent conformation. Avoid a stallion with major defects (such as calf knees, short hip, or bad legs). When defective stallions are used heavily for breeding, conformation faults easily become set in the breed.

Action — Action can be inherited from either side of the family. Choose a stallion that has the kind of action at the trot that you hope your foal will have. Some stallions seem more prepotent for passing along their action than do others, so evaluate how a stallion's get move.

Disposition — Disposition *often* is inherited from the stallion. Foals sired by a bad-tempered stallion often share their sire's disposition. A man-made bad disposition cannot, of course, be transmitted genetically. If in doubt as to whether the stallion's bad disposition was natural or acquired, it is safer to breed to a stallion known to have a good disposition.

Pedigree — The stallion must be a good individual who comes from a family of good individuals. The more horses of good quality there are in the first three generations of the stallion's pedigree, the greater is the likelihood that the stallion's get also will be good.

Compare the stallion's pedigree to that of your mare. Which ancestors appear in both pedigrees, and how good were they? (Remember, if you mate these two horses, you will be linebreeding to mutual ancestors.) To determine whether the mating would be a good nick, evaluate horses that have similar bloodlines. If you need help, consult a breeder who has successfully bred from broodmares whose bloodlines are similar to your mare.

Never choose a breeding stallion solely on the basis of pedigree. However, remember that a good individual that does not have a good pedigree will seldom be a sire of quality foals.

Show Record — A successful show record doesn't guarantee that a stallion will be a good sire.

Champions of outstanding quality do not always sire outstanding foals. A successful show record also is not a guarantee of the stallion's own quality. Show wins depend upon the expertise and preferences of each judge. An outstanding stallion *may* therefore have a mediocre show record while a stallion of less quality has high-level championships.

To decide whether a stallion's show wins were deserved, you must be a good judge of type and conformation and trust your own evaluation of the stallion (or know that the judges who placed the stallion were competent and honest). The best "successful show record" is one achieved under a variety of judges.

Marketability of the Stallion's Foals — If you plan to sell the resulting foal, it is wise to consider the marketability of the stallion's get. The stallion's show wins often are linked to the marketability of his get, so a successful show record can help sell foals.

Marketability comes from the stallion's fame, which also can result from his success as a sire or from clever advertising and promotion. Even the inferior get of a well-known stallion sell more quickly, and for higher prices, than superior foals sired by an unknown stallion. As one breeder said, "It doesn't have to be *good* to *sell*."

If you plan to sell the foal, consider the way the stallion is promoted. Is he heavily advertised? What is his present reputation and future potential? Is there a "marketing program" for his foals produced by client's mares?

Each breeder must decide whether he or she is willing to compromise quality for marketability, or if the two factors can be combined by careful selection of the stallion.

Fertility — A highly fertile stallion will settle mares quickly. As a mare owner, this means lower costs (for veterinary and mare care at the breeding farm) and earlier foals. Poor management, old age, or illness of the stallion can reduce the stallion's fertility.

As in mares, "fertility is inherited." Some families of Arabian horses are less fertile than others. A highly fertile stallion is likely to sire horses that also will be reliable breeders.

Check to see how many mares were bred to the stallion in the last breeding season, and how many foals actually were born. Breeding many mares means nothing if few of them settle. Ask about the stallion's "conception rate" (technically, it's the con-

ception rate *of the mares* bred to the stallion). And look up the stallion's registered get in past volumes of the stud book. How many registered foals has he averaged per year?

One factor to consider in choosing a stallion is type, exemplified by *Ansata Ibn Halima.

Sparagowski photo courtesy Ansata Arabians

Age — Most breeders feel that the quality of a stallion's get is not affected by the stallion's age. The Blunts, however, believed that their stallions sired better foals when the stallions were fully mature than when first used at stud. Some breeders believe that the quality of a stallion's foals declines in the stallion's old age. This may result, however, from breeding mares of less quality than when the stallion was in his prime and at the peak of his popularity as a sire.

Fertility usually does decline with old age. Check the fertility of an elderly stallion before booking to him. An old stallion may offer the advantage of having excellent old bloodlines "close up" in his pedigree, which may strengthen the genetic inheritance of his foals.

The breeding ability of a young, unproven stallion is unknown. It is safer to breed to a proven sire

Choose a sire who has the kind of action you prefer. This is Scharif (U.S. National Champion Formal Driving, U.S. Reserve National Champion Formal Combination, U.S. Top Ten Park Horse several times).

Foucher photo courtesy of McKinstry Arabians, Craig, Colo.

than to an unknown quantity. However, young stallions usually stand at lower "introductory" fees than established breeding stallions, which makes them attractive from the standpoint of the stud fee. If the young stallion becomes popular, the resulting foal may be worth a great deal of money. If the stallion doesn't, however, the foal will be worth less money than the foal by a well-known sire.

Combined Immunodeficiency (CID) — Unless you are willing to breed on a dangerous recessive and risk the death of your foal, do not breed your mare to a known carrier of CID (see Chapter 20). If a stallion's owner does not advertise that his stallion has *not* produced any CID foals, ask whether any of the stallion's foals have died of CID. Get a written statement that the stallion has not produced any CID foals *before* you book your mare to him.

Blood Typing — Purebred Arabian foals cannot be registered unless their sire's blood type is recorded with the Arabian Horse Registry. Established stallions whose foals have been registered previously already have been blood typed. If breed-

ing to a young stallion, be sure that the owner has blood typed him so that the resulting foal can be registered.

CROSS-FAULTING THE MARE AND STALLION

When you have found possible stallions for your mare, evaluate the faults and strong points of conformation and type of each stallion. Then compare each stallion's strengths and weaknesses to those of your mare. Choose the stallion whose strong points best compensate for the weak points of your mare. For example, if your mare's neck is too short, look for a stallion who has a superior neck. If your mare's hip is too short, find a stallion who has a long hip.

In trying to compensate for your mare's faults, do not choose a stallion with the opposite fault. If your mare's back is too long, for example, don't choose a stallion whose back is so short that he forges (strikes the forelegs with the hind legs when moving). The foal from such a combination of parents seldom will inherit a back of the correct length. Instead, it will be too long or too short. To

TABLE 22.1

RESULTS OF A SAMPLE BREEDING

QUALITIES OF SIRE AND DAM		
Dam's Bad Points	Sire's Good Points	Good Points Shared by the Dam and Sire
Short hip	Long hip	
Sloping croup	Level croup	Typey head
Short neck	Long neck	Good shoulders
Triangular neck	Arched neck	Good action
Offset cannon bones	Correct forelegs	

RESULTING FOAL:	
Good Points	
Typey head	Good points possessed by both the sire and
Good shoulder	dam
Good action	
Arched neck	Improvements in the foal—good traits of the
Correct forelegs	sire that are not present in the dam.
Bad Points	
Short hip	Lack of improvement—faults possessed by the
Sloping croup	mare and passed by her to the foal. Not compensated for by the stallion's genetic contribution although he possessed strengths in these areas.

193

compensate for your mare's long back, choose a stallion whose back is the correct length.

Double as many strengths as possible. If a good point is possessed by both parents, the foal is more likely to inherit it. *Never double a fault.* If the same fault is possessed by both parents, it also is likely to be inherited by the foal.

BREEDING TO AN OUTSIDE STALLION

Breeding to someone else's stallion involves expenses for the stud fee, transporting the mare, and board, veterinarian and farrier charges while she is at the stud farm.

Transporting the Mare

The cost to transport the mare to and from the stallion depends upon the distance and the means of transport. Personally hauling the mare insures that she will be carefully transported and usually is cheaper. The alternative is to hire someone. You can either pay an individual who already is going to that area and has time and space for your mare, or you can hire a commercial horse van. Hiring space on a large van means that your mare probably will be in transit longer because trips are planned to pick up and deliver other horses on the same trip. When hiring anyone to transport your mare, check references to be sure that the driver is experienced and responsible and that the van or trailer is safe. You may wish to insure your mare during transport.

Stud Fees

The stud fee is the charge for breeding your mare to a specific stallion. Stud fees vary greatly, due to the reputation, pedigree, and show record of the stallion. The "name" of the owner and special breeding guarantees also affect the cost of the stud fee.

Most stud fees range from $500 to $2,000 but they can go to $10,000 or more for a popular champion. Stud fees in the $1,500 to $10,000 range usually are commanded by well-known stallions. However, a high stud fee does not necessarily indicate that a stallion is of superior quality or sires superior foals. The stud fee is set by the owner. Stud fees usually are published in the breeding farm's advertising and brochures. If not, inquire.

Some stallions never are bred to outside mares ("stand at public stud"). They are bred only to mares owned by the breeding farm or by the syndicate members, if the stallion is owned by a syndicate. (It is sometimes possible to buy breeding shares from a member, however.)

Sometimes a stallion is advertised at "Private Treaty." This means different things to different breeders. It can mean that the stud fee varies, depending upon circumstances (the quality or show record of the mare, what the mare owner plans to do with the resulting foal, or even the mare owner's ability to pay). It can indicate that the stallion is seldom bred to outside mares, but the matter can be negotiated. It also may mean that the stallion owner doesn't want to advertise the amount of the stud fee—either because it is extremely high or because he feels that advertising a low fee may "cheapen" his stallion. If you want to know what the breeder in question really means by "Private Treaty," ask.

Some Arabian stallions are offered at stud to any mare whose owner will pay the fees. Some are limited to purebred Arabian mares while others also are available to grade mares and mares of other breeds.

Most stallions stand "to approved mares only," giving the stallion owner the right to refuse the mare because of lack of quality or lack of bloodlines that nick well with the stallion, etc. Actually, few mares are not "approved" because refusing to breed a mare can cause bad feelings.

Some breeding farms require the entire stud fee in advance. Most require half the fee when the mare arrives and the balance before she leaves the breeding farm. A few do not require payment until the mare is pregnant. Before booking, be sure you understand the payment requirements of the particular breeding farm.

MARE CARE

While your mare is at the breeding farm, you will pay board, or "mare care." This varies from a low maintenance charge barely covering the cost of her feed to a substantial amount that includes costs of labor, etc. Veterinary and farrier charges are seldom included in the cost of mare care. Some farms bill the mare owner; in other cases the veterinarian or farrier bills the owner directly.

Currently, mare care charges vary from about $3.00 to $10.00 or more per day. The charge is higher if the mare has a foal at side when she goes to be bred.

Expect your mare to remain at the breeding farm at least two or three months. If there are any problems in settling her, she will be there longer.

Importance of High-Quality Mare Care

It's possible to pay for months of expensive mare care, only to have your mare returned in poor condition and not in foal. The usual cause is simply poor management. Choose the breeding farm as carefully as you choose its stallion.

Ask other owners and breeders about the farm's mare care. One bad report may be "sour grapes," but several negative opinions may mean that the farm's poor reputation is justified. In such a case, consider sending your mare elsewhere. Why risk loss of a breeding season, reduced resale value, infertility, or even a dead horse?

Visit the stud farm personally before booking your mare. Pay special attention to the care of the visiting mares and foals. How conscientious and expert are the people who care for them? Find out exactly what you'll be getting for your mare care dollars. Where will your mare be kept? Will she be exercised or groomed? What will she be fed and how? What watering facilities are available?

A leading race horse and sire of racers, Kontiki, winning a halter class for horses in racing condition.
Johnny Johnston photo courtesy of Kubela Ranch, Seguin, Texas

Adequate mare care is not guaranteed simply because the stallion is famous or the breeding farm is well known. In fact, some of the largest farms have bad reputations for the quality of their mare care.

Breeding Contracts

Most stallion owners require that the mare owner sign a breeding contract before the mare arrives. The contract specifies the terms under which the mare will be bred and is designed to settle any disputes that arise between stallion and mare owners. A good contract protects both parties. Both the owner of the stallion and the owner of the mare sign the contract, and each keeps a copy.

The breeding contract should state clearly the terms of your agreement. It should identify the stallion and mare by name and by registration number and include the names and addresses of the horses' owners. The contract also should specify the kind of care the mare will receive (whether she will be in a stall, private paddock, pasture, etc.). It should state the season during which the mare will be bred and describe breeding guarantees in detail. It also should cover information regarding veterinary exams or certificates required for the mare prior to breeding, possible substitutions of stallion or mare (and under what circumstances they may be made), the amount of stud fee and amounts of other charges, and when the various charges are due.

Breeding Guarantees

Like stud fees, guarantees vary. Some breeding farms guarantee only that they will breed the mare under the terms of the breeding contract. Others guarantee that the mare will produce a live foal. If she doesn't, she is rebred without an additional stud fee.

A live foal guarantee may be shown in ads as "LFG." Under the usual terms, the mare who aborts or delivers a dead foal is rebred "free." (Mare care is extra.) Most stallion owners allow a rebreeding under these terms if the foal is unable to stand and nurse, even though it is born alive. Some will rebreed if a weak foal dies within a week or so of birth, but they are not legally obligated to interpret a live foal guarantee so liberally unless their breeding contract spells it out this way.

Some stallion owners now advertise a "live filly" guarantee. If the foal is a colt, the mare is rebred free or at a reduced stud fee. Others offer a free or reduced rebreeding if the mare produces a colt that is gelded.

Breeding farms that do not offer a live foal guarantee usually allow "a return in season." If a mare fails to settle, she can be returned for rebreeding later

in the same season. Some permit rebreeding in the following breeding season or substitution of another mare if the first fails to settle.

The Breeding Season

The horse's natural breeding season is spring and summer. In cold climates, mares come into heat later in the year and have fewer heat cycles each year while mares in warm, mild climates come in heat earlier in the year and have more heat periods each year.

Because mature-looking young horses may have an advantage over smaller, less mature horses when shown or offered for sale, the breeding season has been artificially extended to allow production of foals earlier in the calendar year. Although a January foal has an initial advantage over a May foal in the show ring, the advantage disappears when both horses are mature.

The extended breeding season starts in February. Show foals cannot be born before January 1 because they are deemed to be yearlings on January 1 of the year after their birth. A December foal would therefore be considered a year old when it's really only one month old or less.

It isn't natural for mares to conceive early in the year, especially in cold climates. Producing early foals is therefore difficult. Mares often stay in heat longer during the first few estrus cycles of the year, and they may not ovulate early in the "breeding season." Even using scientific breeding methods, it often is impossible to get a mare settled early in the year. Until she does, the frustrations—and the costs—mount.

Because of problems associated with breeding so early, some owners wait until later in the season to send their mares to the breeding farm. Doing so usually results in lower bills because the mare is more likely to settle quickly in spring or summer, resulting in a shorter stay at the breeding farm.

PREPARING YOUR MARE FOR BREEDING

Recent studies indicate that mares in show condition (but not too fat) conceive most readily. Never send a thin or sick mare to the breeding farm since she is unlikely to conceive until she is in good health and condition.

If possible, send your mare to the breeding farm before she comes in heat. She should arrive at least a week before her estrus period. Mares settle more quickly when they are relaxed and in familiar surroundings—give her time to adjust to her new quarters.

What to Send with the Mare

Many states require a hauling permit or brand inspection (whether or not the horse is branded) before horses can be transported. Find out which identification papers are required for each state your mare will travel through and get them. Some states require a veterinary health certificate and negative Coggins test certificate; others do not.

Send a copy of the mare's health record to the breeding farm. Be sure that it is current and lists dates of deworming and medical treatment and medications used. If she has any special health problems, call them to the attention of the farm before your mare is shipped. Put it in writing and keep a copy.

If you are familiar with your mare's heat cycle, send written records (dates and lengths of previous estrus periods). If possible, advise the breeding farm of the expected date of your mare's next heat cycle.

If your mare has any vices (especially if she bites or kicks), warn the breeding farm. Be sure that any special requirements for caring for your mare are understood.

Send a photocopy of the mare's registration certificate with her. The breeding farm also might like to have a copy of the mare's pedigree, if you did not send one previously.

Send a clean blanket, halter, and lead rope with the mare, putting her name on each to help insure that they will be returned with the mare.

Preparation for Shipping the Mare

Three Weeks Before Shipment:

1. Review the mare's health record. Give any vaccinations due.
2. Prepare all paperwork to accompany the mare.

Two Weeks Before Shipment:

1. Deworm the mare.
2. Add bran to the grain ration. (Continue the bran during shipment to aid digestion and elimination.)

One Week Before Shipment:

1. Trim the mare's hoofs.
2. Remove the mare's shoes, if shod. (To reduce slipping in the trailer or van and to protect the breeding stallion from injury.)

Three Days Before Shipment:

1. Bathe and clip the mare.
2. Wash a blanket, nylon halter and lead to accompany the mare. When dry, write the mare's name on them in indelible laundry ink. (If the mare is transported in summer, a blanket may not be necessary.)

Mares and foals at pasture.

Johnny Johnston photo courtesy of Bentwood Farms, Waco, Texas

23

TEASING AND BREEDING

"Teasing" (or "trying") means bringing a stallion and mare near each other to determine from the mare's reactions whether she is ready to be bred. Any mare that is hostile to the stallion and shows no outward signs of estrus probably is at the wrong point in her estrus cycle to become pregnant and should not be bred. A mare can conceive only if she is bred near the time of ovulation. Most mares are receptive to the stallion only when they are forming a follicle.

Teasing Methods

Most Arabian horse breeders use the breeding stallion for teasing, which acquaints the mare with the stallion prior to breeding. However, a special "teaser" stallion sometimes is used instead to prevent possible injury to a valuable breeding stallion.

The teaser usually is controlled by one handler, and the mare by another (both stallion and mare are haltered). A solid partition (teasing wall) that is about the same height as the horses' withers helps prevent injury by separating the mare and stallion. (If not in heat, the mare may kick toward the stallion.)

Some breeders prefer to tease mares by leading the stallion to the mare's stall or paddock and teas-ing over the door or fence. This isn't as safe as having both horses haltered and under control, however.

It's also possible to tease several mares at once by leading the stallion to the broodmares' pasture or paddock. However, with more than one mare to observe, it is easy to overlook a "shy mare" whose signs of estrus are subtle.

Signs of Estrus

In teasing, the stallion and mare face each other and are allowed to become acquainted over the partition. They may nicker, squeal, sniff, or touch each other. If the mare is in heat, she usually will show an interest in the stallion. If she isn't hostile toward him, she may be turned away from the stallion. Indications that the mare is in heat and receptive for breeding include raising the tail, opening and closing the vulva ("winking"), urinating, and the presence of a discharge from the vagina. Mares vary in their responses and may show only some of these indications.

If the mare is not in heat, she usually reacts with disinterest or violence. She may pin her ears back, squeal, strike, bite, or kick toward the stallion.

When to Tease

Open mares should be teased every other day, and a written record kept of each mare's daily response (in heat or not in heat). After the mare has been bred and has gone out of heat, she should be teased through two more estrus cycles, starting about fifteen days after she goes out of heat. If the mare shows signs of estrus, she should be examined by a veterinarian before rebreeding because some pregnant mares act as though they are in heat (some even allow breeding).

Teasing helps determine whether or not a mare is pregnant although the only way to be positive is to do a pregnancy exam or test. Teasing also helps determine the best time to breed the mare to achieve pregnancy.

Teasing Maiden Mares

Maiden mares (those that have never had a foal) sometimes have irregular heat cycles. This is especially true early in the breeding season when mares tend to remain in heat longer. Maiden mares that have never been bred should be handled especially gently and patiently. The stallion should not be allowed to frighten or injure them during teasing or breeding. Mares that are afraid of the stallion may not show signs of estrus even when they are ovulating and physically ready for breeding.

Teasing Mares with Foals

During teasing, a foal can be accidentally injured by its dam. For the foal's safety, it should be removed to an adjoining area that is safely enclosed. The mare will be more content if she can see and hear the foal, but she shouldn't be able to touch it during teasing.

The Shy Mare

Mares that do not "show to the stallion" (show signs of estrus when teased) should be checked by a veterinarian to be sure they are reproductively healthy. If a mare is producing a normal follicle and ovulating, her problem may be psychological. If she fears or dislikes the stallion, she may not show to him. In such cases, using *two* stallions to tease the mare may help—the mare may show signs of estrus when teased by one stallion but not by the other.

If the mare doesn't show signs of estrus because she is not ovulating, hormone shots may induce a heat period (depending upon the reason for lack of ovulation). If the mare *is* ovulating, palpating can pinpoint the time to breed.

Most nursing mares do show signs of estrus. However, some fail to ovulate while nursing foals, and some other nervous mares do not show signs of heat even when they are ovulating because they are worried about their foals' welfare.

BREEDING

Under natural conditions, a stallion runs with a band ("harem") of mares. The experienced breeding stallion senses when one of his mares is ready

Left: The stallion in the process of teasing the mare. Right: If she is not in heat, she may respond by squealing, kicking, or striking. (Note the danger of using an open-railed fence during teasing; a solid partition between the horses is safer. Also, both stallion and mare are usually controlled by handlers.)

to be bred, and the act is accomplished without human interference.

Some Arabian horse breeders imitate this natural order of things by allowing a stallion to be pastured with a group of broodmares that he breeds as they come in heat. Nervous mares may be more relaxed under such conditions, and calm mares are more likely to settle than anxious ones. Also a stallion may service each mare more often than he would if hand breeding were used. These factors contribute to the high conception rate usually claimed for pasture breeding.

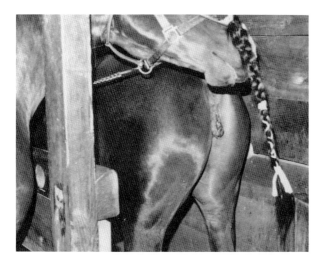

A mare that is ready to be bred will "wink" (open and close the lips of the vulva) when teased by the stallion.
Photo courtesy of Locust Farms

On the other hand, pasture breeding has some drawbacks. It can result in injuries and blemishes to valuable breeding and show stock. Also, pasture breeding may be impractical if a large number of mares are to be bred to one stallion. If several mares come in heat at once, the stallion may be unable to settle them all. In fact, he may not even service them all—a stallion often has favorite mares, repeatedly breeding them and ignoring ones he dislikes.

Hand Breeding

Hand breeding ("breeding in hand") prevents injuries because both the stallion and mare are restrained. It also restricts the number of services per mare. (Mares usually are bred once every other day during each heat period.)

Hand breeding sometimes is blamed for low conception rates. Restrained horses may be more nervous than those breeding under natural conditions, and this may lower fertility. Due to poor management or poor judgment, mares are sometimes restrained and bred when they are unlikely to conceive. Palpating before hand breeding can determine when the mare has a breedable follicle and help prevent unnecessary services; however, frequent palpating is believed to contribute to lower conception rates.

WHEN TO BREED

To become pregnant, the mare must be bred within approximately forty-eight hours of the time she ovulates. Ovulation occurs about two days before the end of the heat period. Mares usually are bred on the third day of the heat period and then every other day until they go out of heat. If the mare becomes pregnant, the length of gestation is figured from the last date she was bred by the stallion.

The first heat period after foaling is called "the foal heat." It usually occurs five to twelve days after the foal is born. Many breeders and veterinarians

Prior to breeding, the stallion approaches the mare from the side. The mare is restrained by a handler who stands to the side, out of the way in case the mare strikes or bolts.
Photo courtesy of Locust Farms

consider this a "cleansing" period after foaling and advise against breeding the mare on the foal heat. They believe that mares bred during this heat are less likely to settle than if they are bred during a later heat period. Mares that do settle on the foal heat are believed to have a greater risk of resorption or abortion.

When the foaling mare is rebred depends also upon the ease with which she foaled. If tearing or infection occurred, breeding must be postponed until she has recovered.

BREEDING METHODS

Infections of the reproductive organs can be caused by uncleanliness. To reduce the risk of infection, the stallion and mare usually are washed before and sometimes after breeding.

Wash and rinse the mare's vulva and hindquarters with warm water and a veterinary surgical scrub or mild soap, then wrap the mare's tail to keep dirt or hair from entering the vagina during breeding. Use clean cotton to clean the area and throw it away after use.

Wash and rinse the stallion's penis with clean warm water and cleansing solution. Rinse the mare's and stallion's genital areas thoroughly to remove all residue of the soap or scrub, which can kill sperm.

to prevent kicking, be careful that the stallion's legs don't get tangled in them during breeding.

The stallion must be controlled by a sturdy halter. If needed, a chain lead can be passed over his nose for extra control. If the stallion becomes unruly during breeding, a whip may be needed for discipline.

The stallion must not be allowed to mount until he has a complete erection, and he must not rush toward the mare. When ready, he should be led toward the mare, approaching from the rear and slightly to the mare's left side, so she can see him.

The stallion rises onto his hind legs and mounts the mare from the left side, placing his forelegs on her back or around her sides for balance. Be sure that the penis enters the mare's vagina instead of the rectum, guiding it by hand if necessary.

During intercourse, the stallion thrusts his penis into the mare several times, flagging his tail when the semen is ejaculated. He then dismounts and should be led away from the breeding area. Watch the mare carefully as the stallion dismounts, for this is when some mares kick. After breeding, walk the mare for a few minutes to keep her from urinating and washing out some of the semen.

When the mare is receptive and the stallion is ready, he is allowed to cover the mare.
Photo courtesy of Locust Farms

The stallion and mare are best controlled by separate handlers. A third assistant should stand by to help if needed. Restrain the mare with a twitch. If breeding hobbles are used on her hind legs

The First Breeding

A young horse's first breeding is very important, for it will influence the individual's future breeding behavior. If bred to difficult mares, an inexperienced stallion may become a shy (unwilling) breeder. Choose older, receptive mares that are unlikely to resist or injure the young stallion.

Don't let the stallion rush or attack the mare. Although a firm hand is required, the stallion must be disciplined tactfully. If too strongly reprimanded, he may refuse to breed.

Always handle an inexperienced mare with gentleness and patience. Don't let the stallion hurt or scare her. If forcefully bred by a stallion, a frightened young mare may not show signs of estrus when she is teased for rebreeding. A mare who is injured by a stallion may retaliate when rebred, injuring a valuable stallion.

Artificial Insemination (AI)

An old legend tells of a Bedouin using stolen semen from an enemy tribe's famous stallion to impregnate his mare. Despite this apparent use of artificial insemination in Bedouin horses, it is only in recent years that the Arabian Horse Registry of America has allowed breeding farms to use the technique. Arabian horses produced by AI still are ineligible for registration in some other countries.

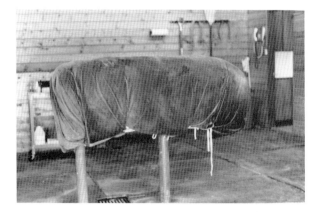

A phantom (dummy) mare used for collecting sperm. A mare in heat is brought near the stallion, who is taught to mount the phantom and ejaculate into an AV. The sperm can then be evaluated and/or used to artificially inseminate several mares.

To use AI, breeding technicians must undergo special training. Expensive equipment also is required to handle the semen. The stallion and mare must be kept at the same stud farm during breeding because it is against Registry rules to transport semen.

A device called an artificial vagina (AV) is used with "a phantom mare" to collect the semen. The stallion is trained to mount a dummy mare, which is a sturdy object that approximates the shape and dimensions of a mare's body, and ejaculate into the AV. The ejaculate is examined under a microscope and divided into several portions for artificial insemination.

In AI, the semen is directly inserted in the mare's uterus while the mare is in heat. Mares are inseminated near the time of ovulation, which is determined by palpating.

Careful use of AI can improve conception rates and make it possible for one stallion to service more mares than he could by natural service, for each ejaculation can impregnate several mares.

Embryo Transfers

It is now possible to transfer a fertilized egg from one mare to another. The recipient mare serves as an incubator, giving birth and nursing the foal. Because the foal is not genetically related to its birth mother, it receives nothing but nourishment from her; its traits were inherited from its sire and the mare that produced the egg. Because of this, the recipient mare can be of any breed but the foal resulting from an Arabian stallion and an Arabian donor mare is an Arabian. Recipient mares usually are large (to provide room for a large foal) and are proven broodmares with no history of breeding or foaling problems.

Hormone shots are used to coordinate the estrus periods of the donor and recipient mares. A week after the donor mare is bred, the fertilized egg is flushed from her uterus with a special liquid solution. The egg then is implanted in the uterus of one of the recipient mares.

Embryo transfer is not an exact science. The donor mare may fail to settle or the recipient mare may abort the embryo during gestation. The process also is very expensive because three or more recipient mares may be kept for each donor mare so that the heat cycles can be coordinated closely enough to make the transfer possible. Hormone injections required to synchronize the heat cycles of the mares also add to the costs, as does the transferring procedure. (The embryo is transferred surgically or by pipette directly into the uterus of the recipient mare.)

Only one foal from a donor mare can be registered each year, although several foals might be produced by her via embryo transfer. When all the foals have been born, the breeder must decide which foal will be registered (possibly the best foal or the one of the desired sex).

BREEDING RECORDS

All breeders of Arabian horses are required to keep accurate breeding records, which must be made

Four Winds Farm

Mare _____ AHC No. _____ Color _____ Age _____

Markings _____

Owner _____

Address _____

Telephone: Home _____ Business _____

In 19___ booked to _____ Results of last year's breeding _____

	1	2	3	4	5	6	7	8	9	10	11	12	13	14	15	16	17	18	19	20	21	22	23	24	25	26	27	28	29	30	31
Jan.																															
Feb.																															
Mar.																															
Apr.																															
May																															
June																															
July																															
Aug.																															
Sept.																															
Oct.																															
Nov.																															
Dec.																															

B = bred   / = in season   v = vet call   F = foaled   W = wormed   H = hoof trimming

A = arrival   D = departure

Date of arrival _____   _____ (sire)

                                of _____ (name)

Date of departure _____   _____ (dame)

Feed ration _____

Comments upon arrival at farm: _____

Comments on foaling (and the foal) _____

The foal: date due _____ Date dropped _____ sex _____ color _____ health _____

Comments on breeding: _____

Expenditures

Date: _____ description _____ charge _____ sub-total _____ total _____

_____

_____

_____

_____

_____

All breeders are required by the Registry to keep accurate breeding records. This is a form developed by Denise Borg, breeder of Polish Arabians, for use at her Four Winds Farm in Santa Ynez, Calif.

Embryo transfer is administered strictly, with advance authorization and detailed reports to the Registry required. Nevertheless, embryo transfer may offer hope to owners of valuable broodmares unable to carry a foal to term due to old age or reproductive problems. It also may allow a two-year-old filly to safely produce foals or make it possible for a mare to continue a show career while a surrogate mare carries, gives birth to, and raises her foal.

available to the Registry upon request. Each year, each stallion owner must supply the Registry with a list of all purebred mares serviced by that stallion and the dates that they were bred. If the Stallion Report form is not on file, the resulting foals cannot be registered.

Individual records also should be kept for each broodmare. All teasing and breeding procedures should be noted, with the results of each. Veterinary exams and pregnancy tests also should be recorded. A handy wall chart for keeping track of breeding activities at the stud farm also is available from the Registry.

Daurita, owned by Warren Park Stud, Sanger, California.
Sharon Vander Ende photo

206

24

THE PREGNANT MARE

When a stallion services a mare, thousands of sperm enter her vagina. Some move into the uterus and into the two fallopian tubes where they can live for about two days. After the ovarian follicle ruptures, the mare's egg travels through one of the fallopian tubes, and if the egg is penetrated by a sperm, conception occurs. At that instant, the mare's chromosomes combine with those of the stallion to form the new life, and the unborn foal's characteristics are set.

When the egg is fertilized, cell division (growth) starts. The single cell of the egg divides into two cells, which divide into four cells; the four cells divide to make eight cells, etc. From the fallopian tube, the fertilized egg moves into the uterus where the unborn foal grows until it is fully developed. The fetus has all its internal organs and the approximate shape of a horse when it's only twenty days old.

In the mare's uterus, the foal is cushioned by fluids inside a membrane called the amniotic sac. The fetus and the amniotic sac are inside another membrane, the chorion. For about 100 days after conception, the fetus is not attached to the mare's uterus. It floats freely inside the uterus until the chorion finally attaches to one horn of the uterus and becomes implanted.

As the foal grows, the placental membranes grow with it, gradually moving into the body of the uterus, which stretches as the foal grows. The placenta also eventually is pushed into the non-pregnant horn of the uterus as the foal grows larger.

LENGTH OF GESTATION

Mares carry their unborn foals for about eleven months. The Arabian Horse Registry of America considers a range of 310 to 362 days to be normal for Arabian mares. In a study, Arabian mares at California Polytechnic University at Pomona averaged 338 days of gestation.

It is impossible to accurately predict when a mare will foal since length of gestation varies greatly. Factors affecting gestation may include the age and health of the individual mare, nutrition, genetic inheritance, and even climate and geography.

Maiden mares often have a slightly shorter gestation period, and aged broodmares tend to carry their foals slightly longer than mares in their prime. Also, foals born early in the year may be carried slightly longer than those foaled later. Colts may be carried slightly longer than fillies, probably because male sexual organs develop more slowly.

Unfortunately, the length of gestation can vary for *each* pregnancy. Estimated due dates shown in the gestation table (Table 24.2, page 213) therefore are merely a general guideline.

Premature Foals, Abortion

It has been said that a premature foal is really a late abortion. Foals *may* survive when born as early as 300 days' gestation. Foals born before that cannot live. Premature foals have a low survival rate because a foal's internal organs aren't completely functional until it is carried full term. Born before it has completely developed, a premature foal is smaller and weaker than a full-term, healthy foal.

Infections of the mare's reproductive tract can cause abortion by destroying part of the mare's uterine tissue or by attacking the placenta or fetus. Infections can be viral, bacterial, or fungal. The most common cause of viral abortion is Rhinopneumonitis (see Chapter 15). *Streptococci* bacteria can cause abortion in early pregnancy, and *E coli* bacteria are frequently the cause of a late gestation abortion. Rarely, fungus enters the mare's open cervix during heat or foaling. The fungus grows slowly, gradually spreading over the placenta until it causes abortion in late gestation.

Abortion can occur in early pregnancy without warning. In late gestation, abortion may be signalled by premature udder development and dripping milk.

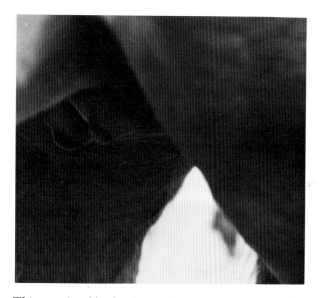

This mare's udder has barely begun to enlarge, and the flat ("dimpled") teats indicate that foaling probably is not imminent. When the teats appear round and protrude from a greatly swollen udder, the mare will be ready to foal. Drops of white milk will appear, and milk may drip or stream from the udder.

The act of aborting doesn't harm the mare. If the abortion was caused by a temporary condition (twins, rhino, etc.), the mare should return to productivity with no ill effects. If caused by a chronic infection or the inability to sustain a foal (due to an unhealthy uterus, etc.), the mare may have continuing problems.

If the mare aborts, store the aborted fetus and membranes in a covered container, out of reach of other animals, until the veterinarian can examine them and possibly order a lab test.

Since abortion often results from infectious disease, the aborting mare should be isolated from other horses. Disinfect her stall and equipment and burn the bedding from her stall, along with the aborted fetus and membranes after the veterinarian has examined them. Thoroughly wash your hands and change your clothes before touching other horses.

CARE OF THE PREGNANT MARE

Water

Plenty of fresh, clean water is critical for a pregnant mare since extra fluids are required for the placental membranes and the tissues of the developing fetus. Water also aids the mare's digestion and elimination, and helps cool her body in hot weather. To prevent the discomfort caused when a fetus becomes active after a pregnant mare drinks cold water, take the chill off cold drinking water by adding warm water to it first.

Feed

In early pregnancy, the mare's nutritional requirements are about the same as those of an open mare. As the pregnancy progresses, however, the mare's appetite increases greatly. An ample supply of high-protein feed and balanced minerals is required (see Chapter 14).

There is a tendency to overfeed pregnant mares since determining how much weight belongs to the unborn foal and how much to the mare is difficult. Judge the mare's condition by feeling her neck and hindquarters; both areas quickly show weight loss or gain.

Mares enjoy a warm bran mash daily during the last two or three months of pregnancy, it aids digestion and elimination and increases water intake (see Chapter 14).

Exercise

Daily exercise is important for the pregnant mare. During the last five months of gestation, the mare should be exercised only at the walk and trot. During the last two or three months, she should be ridden only at the walk or not at all. During this period, free exercise in a large paddock or arena is best.

Pregnant mares tire easily and never should be overheated or exhausted. They become less active as their unborn foals grow larger, and they are uncomfortable in late pregnancy. However, moderate to light exercise each day helps maintain muscle tone and avoid circulatory problems.

Rest

Pregnant mares generally take frequent naps during the day, often lying down in the afternoon. (A *sleeping* mare's legs rest on the ground and she looks relaxed. A mare *in labor* braces her legs stiffly.)

Sleeping mares often groan while breathing. This doesn't indicate illness or labor *unless* other signs of discomfort are apparent. The groaning is caused by the closure of the *epiglottis*, a valve-like tissue in the throat.

Heavily pregnant mares may avoid lying down to sleep because getting up and down is awkward and lying down may be uncomfortable. Because horses' knees have a special "locking mechanism," they can sleep while standing.

Companionship

Pregnant mares should be pastured only with other pregnant mares. They are more sedate than open mares, geldings, and young stock, and as a result some horses may tease or herd pregnant mares and keep them from feed and water. A kick from another horse can cause a pregnant mare to abort. Also, if she foals in pasture, other horses may attack or try to steal her foal.

PROBLEMS

Abortion

Abortion is the premature birth of the immature fetus. Usually, a dead or dying fetus triggers the abor-

tion. However, a healthy foal can be aborted if the mare has a serious hormonal imbalance or becomes quite ill. Severe physical or psychological stress also may induce abortion.

In the first 100 days, when the fetus is floating free in the uterus, there is a greater risk that the early pregnancy will be either aborted or resorbed. If resorption occurs, the tiny embryo apparently is absorbed into the mare's bloodstream and "disappears," but little is known about resorption in mares.

The most common causes of abortion in mares are twins and infections. The uterus usually is not big enough for twins to grow to healthy maturity. One twin frequently weakens and dies, triggering the abortion of both unborn foals. When twins are delivered, one or both may not survive.

Colic

The large, growing foal can cause gas pains (colic) and constipation from constriction of the digestive tract. If a pregnant mare colics, call the veterinarian and watch her closely. As with edema, it simply may be caused by the pregnancy *or* may indicate a more serious problem.

Edema and Stocking Up

Edema is fluid-filled swelling. Mares sometimes develop areas of edema in the abdomen during late gestation. The usual cause is a large fetus that restricts the mare's blood circulation. The condition usually is not serious, but it should be evaluated by your veterinarian since edema also can be a symptom of other serious health problems.

Broodmares also tend to stock up in the legs. This edema in the pasterns also is caused by reduced circulation; mild exercise usually relieves the condition.

COUNTDOWN TO FOALING

In the final weeks before foaling, the mare's body reflects hormonal changes that indicate the approach of delivery. Although a "normal" pattern of changes in the pregnant mare's appearance occurs during the final weeks of pregnancy, few mares foal "by the book." Even if the mare displays none of the usual signs of foaling, she must be watched carefully during the last month of pregnancy. Foaling is the culmination of more than a year's work and planning, and both the mare and foal are irreplaceable.

Although the physical changes outlined here usually occur over a few weeks, some mares pass through them in only a few hours before foaling. Maiden mares are the most likely to do so, but any mare can foal without warning signs. Mares can foal up to four weeks before their expected due date. However, most foals are born within two weeks before to two weeks after the due date.

Four Weeks Before Foaling

As much as four weeks before foaling, the muscles around the base of the mare's tail start to lose tone. The croup and muscles of the hindquarters relax and "sink," making the mare appear rough coupled. A vertical groove appears in the muscles of the hindquarters, and the tail may look lower set than usual. This progressive softening of the muscles reaches an extreme just before foaling. The croup becomes jelly-like and the mare's hind legs may wobble when she walks.

During the last month of pregnancy, the udder starts to enlarge as it fills with milk. (The udder often grows bigger and then smaller several times before foaling; it is usually larger in the morning than evening.) The large milk veins leading to the udder on both sides of the abdomen also enlarge.

Two Weeks Before Foaling

From two days to two weeks before foaling, "wax" forms on the tips of the nipples, forming a sticky, yellow-gold plug. This substance appears before the mare's milk. Mares can wax as much as a month before foaling, but most do so in the final week.

Preparations:
1. Remind your veterinarian of your mare's estimated due date;
2. Post the veterinarian's telephone number conspicuously near the telephone(s);
3. Remove the mare's shoes; shoes can cause slipping on a wet surface or injure a foal;
4. Give the mare a booster shot for tetanus, flu and sleeping sickness to increase the immunizing ability of her colostrum (first milk) (see Chapter 15);
5. Prepare a foaling kit and store it in a handy spot.

One Week Before Foaling

During the last week of pregnancy, the mare's body changes shape. From the side view, it is apparent that the foal has moved downward. From the rear, the mare's body looks pear shaped instead of round. The rib area is thinner and the bottom of the abdomen is wider.

The mare's vulva softens and lengthens. It may "swell" so much that it is level with the hindquarters by the time she foals.

Preparations:
1. Review foaling procedures;
2. Prepare the foaling stall;
3. Check the mare morning and night, more often if it appears she will foal soon.

Three Days Before Foaling

The "dimples" previously visible at the base of the nipples disappear when the nipples fill with milk. The nipples look round and protrude from the full udder. When the wax on the nipples is replaced by drops of milk, foaling is imminent (usually within 24 hours; often sooner).

PREPARATION FOR FOALING

Put foaling supplies together and keep the "foaling kit" near the foaling area (see Table 24.1).

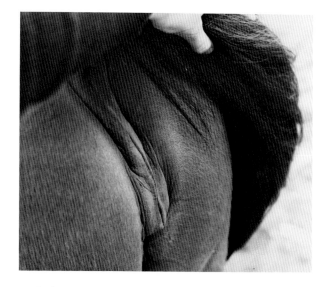

As foaling time approaches, the mare's vulva softens and lengthens to allow easier passage of the foal. By the time she gives birth, the vulva may be swollen almost even with the hindquarters.

TABLE 24.1

FOALING KIT

ITEM	USE
• self-adhering gauze	to wrap mare's tail before delivery
• surgical scrub	to clean hands and arms prior to correcting a malpresented foal
• lubricating ointment	to lubricate hands, arms and birth canal to correct malpresentation
• 7 percent iodine and small paper cup	to treat foal's navel stump
• self-contained phosphate enema (4-ounce)	to give the foal an enema
• covered container	to store afterbirth until the vet can examine it
• towels	to dry foal

THE FOALING STALL

If a normal birth could be assured, it would be best for the mare to foal on clean pasture. However, death of the mare or foal is more likely to result from an unattended birth if foaling problems occur. Because Arabian mares have a high value (both financial and sentimental), they usually foal indoors where the birth can be monitored, and help is available if necessary. If the mare will foal in a paddock, she should be isolated from other horses.

The foaling stall should be at least 20 by 20 feet (the size of two small box stalls put together). It cannot be too large. The stall should be well-ventilated with no drafts—especially along the floor where the foal will be. (Foals can get pneumonia from poor ventilation *or* drafts.)

If feeders and water containers are attached to the walls of the foaling stall, they must be placed high enough to avoid accidental injury to the foaling mare or newborn foal. No projections (nails, wires, boards) that could injure the foal or mare should exist. Dutch doors or other swinging doors must not gap at the bottom since a foal can become wedged between the door and the ground. Adding a bolt to the bottom of stall doors, on the outside of the door will prevent this tragedy.

Newborn foals are wet and easily chilled. If the weather is cold, infrared heat lamps may be used

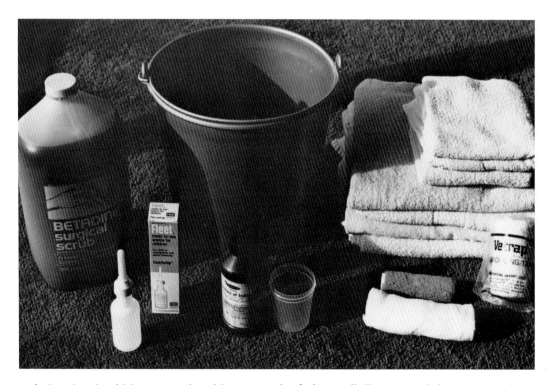

A foaling kit should be prepared and kept near the foaling stall. Recommended contents include: veterinary surgical scrub, a self-contained phosphate enema for children, 7% tincture of iodine, a paper or plastic cup, a container for the afterbirth, bandaging or safety tape, and plenty of clean towels.

to warm the stall. (Be sure to buy infrared lamps—ultraviolet tanning lamps give no heat and can damage horses' eyes.) Keep all light bulbs, cords, and wiring out of reach of both the mare and foal.

If the stall is heated, be sure it isn't too warm. It is better to have a stall slightly too cool than too hot, for a drastic temperature change when the mare and foal are turned outdoors can result in illness.

Preparing the Stall

Bed the foaling stall deeply with straw. Fluids drain better through straw, leaving a warm bed for the mare and foal, and straw also is less likely to be inhaled by the newborn foal than are shavings. Wheat or rye straw is ideal; avoid oat and barley straw, which are more likely to be eaten by the mare. (Eating straw can cause the mare to colic or become impacted.) If you prefer, the bedding can be changed

from straw to shavings when the foal is a few days old.

Bandaging the Mare's Tail

The mare's tail can be bandaged to keep it clean during foaling and prevent contaminating the reproductive tract. A thick tail can be braided and wrapped (see Chapter 18). A thin tail can be wrapped downward from the dock to just below the tail bone, the tail hairs folded up, and the bandage wrapped over them. Self-adhesive gauze holds better than fabric tail wraps and is inexpensive, clean, and disposable.

Prior to foaling, the tail bandage should be replaced as often as necessary to keep it clean. The tail should be unbraided and brushed before rebraiding and bandaging.

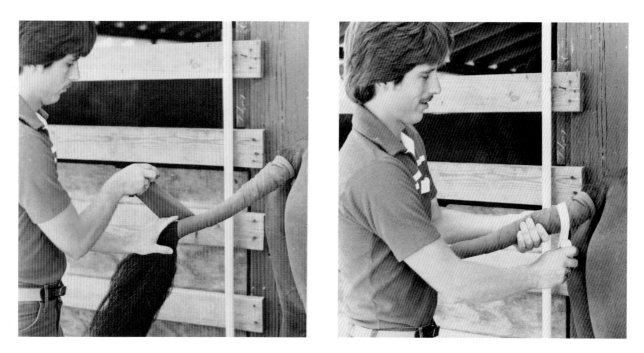

Left: The mare's tail can be wrapped to keep it clean and out of the way during foaling. It may be braided or wrapped loosely, depending upon its length and thickness. Right: Adhesive tape will help hold the tail wrap in place. Care must be taken when wrapping the tail that it is not done so tightly as to interfere with blood circulation in the mare's tail.

Don Sepulvado photos courtesy of N.S.U.

212

TABLE 24.2

Gestation Table for
Arabian Mares
(based on average gestation of 338 days)

date bred	foaling date	date bred	foaling date	date bred	foaling date	date bred	foaling date	date bred	foaling date	date bred	foaling date	date bred	foaling date	date bred	foaling date	date bred	foaling date	date bred	foaling date	date bred	foaling date	date bred	foaling date
JAN.	DEC.	FEB	JAN.	MAR.	FEB.	APR.	MAR.	MAY	APR.	JUNE	MAY	JULY	JUNE	AUG.	JULY	SEPT.	AUG.	OCT.	SEPT.	NOV.	OCT.	DEC.	NOV.
1	5	1	5	1	2	1	5	1	4	1	5	1	4	1	5	1	5	1	4	1	5	1	4
2	6	2	6	2	3	2	6	2	5	2	6	2	5	2	6	2	6	2	5	2	6	2	5
3	7	3	7	3	4	3	7	3	6	3	7	3	6	3	7	3	7	3	6	3	7	3	6
4	8	4	8	4	5	4	8	4	7	4	8	4	7	4	8	4	8	4	7	4	8	4	7
5	9	5	9	5	6	5	9	5	8	5	9	5	8	5	9	5	9	5	8	5	9	5	8
6	10	6	10	6	7	6	10	6	9	6	10	6	9	6	10	6	10	6	9	6	10	6	9
7	11	7	11	7	8	7	11	7	10	7	11	7	10	7	11	7	11	7	10	7	11	7	10
8	12	8	12	8	9	8	12	8	11	8	12	8	11	8	12	8	12	8	11	8	12	8	11
9	13	9	13	9	10	9	13	9	12	9	13	9	12	9	13	9	13	9	12	9	13	9	12
10	14	10	14	10	11	10	14	10	13	10	14	10	13	10	14	10	14	10	13	10	14	10	13
11	15	11	15	11	12	11	15	11	14	11	15	11	14	11	15	11	15	11	14	11	15	11	14
12	16	12	16	12	13	12	16	12	15	12	16	12	15	12	16	12	16	12	15	12	16	12	15
13	17	13	17	13	14	13	17	13	16	13	17	13	16	13	17	13	17	13	16	13	17	13	16
14	18	14	18	14	15	14	18	14	17	14	18	14	17	14	18	14	18	14	17	14	18	14	17
15	19	15	19	15	16	15	19	15	18	15	19	15	18	15	19	15	19	15	18	15	19	15	18
16	20	16	20	16	17	16	20	16	19	16	20	16	19	16	20	16	20	16	19	16	20	16	19
17	21	17	21	17	18	17	21	17	20	17	21	17	20	17	21	17	21	17	20	17	21	17	20
18	22	18	22	18	19	18	22	18	21	18	22	18	21	18	22	18	22	18	21	18	22	18	21
19	23	19	23	19	20	19	23	19	22	19	23	19	22	19	23	19	23	19	22	19	23	19	22
20	24	20	24	20	21	20	24	20	23	20	24	20	23	20	24	20	24	20	23	20	24	20	23
21	25	21	25	21	22	21	25	21	24	21	25	21	24	21	25	21	25	21	24	21	25	21	24
22	26	22	26	22	23	22	26	22	25	22	26	22	25	22	26	22	26	22	25	22	26	22	25
23	27	23	27	23	24	23	27	23	26	23	27	23	26	23	27	23	27	23	26	23	27	23	26
24	28	24	28	24	25	24	28	24	27	24	28	24	27	24	28	24	28	24	27	24	28	24	27
25	29	25	29	25	26	25	29	25	28	25	29	25	28	25	29	25	29	25	28	25	29	25	28
26	30	26	30	26	27	26	30	26	29	26	30	26	29	26	30	26	30	26	29	26	30	26	29
27	31 Jan.	27	31 Feb.	27	28 Mar.	27	31 Apr.	27	30 May.	27	31 June	27	30 July	27	31 Aug.	27	31 Sep.	27	30 Oct.	27	31 Nov.	27	30 Dec.
28	1	28	1	28	1	28	1	28	1	28	1	28	1	28	1	28	1	28	1	28	1	28	1
29	2			29	2	29	2	29	2	29	2	29	2	29	2	29	2	29	2	29	2	29	2
30	3			30	3	30	3	30	3	30	3	30	3	30	3	30	3	30	3	30	3	30	3
31	4			31	4			31	4			31	4	31	4			31	4			31	4

Most mares instinctively protect their foals and show affectionate concern for them.
Photo of Adriana and her filly, Our Quest, courtesy of Craver Farms, Hillview, Ill.

25

FOALING

Arabian mares have a reputation for foaling quickly and without help. If foaling proceeds normally, observe quietly from the sidelines.

To tell whether the mare needs help, you must know what happens during a *normal* birth. When problems occur, you must personally assist the mare or get help from a veterinarian or experienced foaling attendant. If you're not *sure* whether a problem exists, call the veterinarian. *Doing the wrong thing is often worse than doing nothing.*

FIRST-STAGE LABOR

During pregnancy, the foal is carried upside down, with its head toward the mare's hindquarters. When labor begins, the mare's muscles contract to rotate the foal. During labor, its backbone is in line with that of the mare and its forelegs are extended. While the foal is being turned, the mare's cervix dilates so that the foal can be pushed from the uterus into the birth canal (vagina).

During this first stage of labor, the mare's muscle contractions are not visible. She may seem uncomfortable and show signs of colic. Prefoaling behavior may include tail switching, kicking toward the abdomen, curling the upper lip and stretching the neck upward (flehmen posture), stamping the feet,

or flexing a hind leg toward the abdomen. The mare may look at her sides, lie down and get up several times, paw the bedding, or sweat on the flanks and chest. She may pass manure and urinate frequently. If in labor, the mare soon progresses to the second stage of labor—delivery.

DELIVERY

Delivery starts when the mare's water breaks. Several gallons of amniotic fluid gush from the mare's vulva when the outer sac of the placenta is punctured as the foal is pushed toward the mare's hindquarters by contractions. (The amniotic fluid that cushioned and protected the fetus during pregnancy also lubricates the birth canal for easier passage of the foal.) The mare's water can break while she is standing or lying down.

After the water breaks, the amniotic sac containing the foal should appear between the lips of the vulva within five minutes. The sac, which contains more fluids, resembles a water-filled balloon.

Most mares lie down on one side and brace their legs stiffly during foaling. The foal is born with its forelegs stretched straight out and its head resting on top of them. One leg should be slightly ahead of the other, which makes it easier for the foal to be squeezed through the mare's pelvis. This narrows the shoulders of the foal—the widest part of the foal's body and, therefore, the most difficult part of the birth. When the foal's neck can be seen, its shoulders have successfully been pushed through the mare's pelvic bones. After the shoulders have been passed, the mare may rest for a few minutes before the foal's hind legs are delivered.

The newborn foal is delivered inside the amniotic sac, which must be broken so that the foal can start breathing. A foal normally breaks the sac shortly after it is born.

The newborn is attached at its navel to the placenta that is still inside the mare's uterus. Through the umbilical (navel) cord that connects the foal to the placenta, the foal gets a transfusion of additional blood, which gives it more strength. When the foal struggles toward the mare's head or tries to stand, the navel cord normally breaks about two inches from the foal's navel.

The mare usually licks the foal, drying its coat and stimulating blood circulation. When she rises (usually twenty to sixty minutes after foaling), the amniotic sac that contained the foal hangs from the vulva and still is connected to the placenta inside the mare's uterus. The placenta gradually loosens and is passed as the afterbirth.

MIDWIFERY

Some Arabian mares like human companionship when foaling; they seem reassured by the presence of familiar people. Others prefer that everyone stay at a distance. As far as possible, honor the preferences of the foaling mare.

Let the mare choose her own spot to lie down, as long as about eighteen or more inches of clearance exists between her hindquarters and the wall or fence. If she is too close to it, try to move her away from it before she foals.

Normal delivery usually occurs in about twenty minutes but may take longer. If the foal has not been born within twenty minutes of the time that the water breaks, call the veterinarian. If the foal is born when the veterinarian arrives, the mare and foal can be examined. If not, the veterinarian can determine the problem and assist.

If the foal is not produced as expected, halter and walk the mare slowly while waiting for the vet-

erinarian. When the mare rises, the foal moves back inside her, and a malpresentation may "correct itself." If the mare is ready to give birth, you won't be able to keep her up and walking.

If things proceed normally, don't interfere with the foaling or try to speed things up by pulling on the foal. (Foals cannot be "pulled" from the mare. People accustomed to pulling calves sometimes try the same approach with foals—doing so may *seriously* injure the mare.)

When the foal is delivered, the amniotic sac should break. If it isn't torn open by the foal, break (or cut) the sac and remove it from the foal's head to prevent suffocation. Some of the fluids from the

The amniotic sac, which looks like a water-filled balloon, appears between the lips of the mare's vulva.
Foaling photographs courtesy of Locust Farms

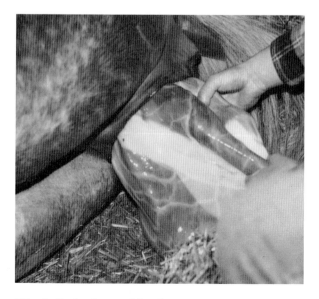

The foal's forelegs and head appear.

216

amniotic sac will drain from the newborn's nostrils. Move the foal's head to a vertical position for easier drainage, but be sure its nostrils aren't blocked by bedding or the ground. Rub the damp newborn foal with clean towels to dry it and stimulate its circulation for warmth.

The sac must be broken so the foal can breathe.

The foal's body has been delivered, but the hind legs are still in the birth canal (normal while the mare rests during delivery).

The foal is allowed to rest as blood is pumped into it from the placenta. This transfusion (via the umbilical cord connected to the foal's navel) is needed to give the foal added strength.

The afterbirth is connected to the sac in which the foal was delivered. The umbilical cord is at the top of the photo; the darker membrane at the bottom of the picture is the afterbirth. The amniotic sac mirrors the shape of the pregnant uterus (the pregnant horn is at the left of the photo).

MALPRESENTATIONS

Difficult births usually are caused by one of the foal's forelegs being out of the proper position, causing the foal to become "stuck" when it reaches the mare's pelvic bones. If this happens, it's necessary to reach inside the birth canal to identify the problem by feel and to correct the foal's position.

When malpresentation occurs, call the veterinarian immediately. It is hard physical work to straighten one foreleg, and a severe malpresentation will require veterinary experience in addition to strength. As soon as the veterinarian has been summoned, wash your hands and forearms *thoroughly* with veterinary surgical scrub. Then apply a lubricant ointment to your hands and arms and inside the mare's birth canal before reaching into the vagina while the mare is resting *after* a contraction. It is safe to reach inside for ten inches or so.

If you can feel only one foreleg and the foal's muzzle, the "missing" leg probably is bent at the knee toward the foal's body. It can be found toward the mare's legs, if the foal is otherwise in proper position. It may be necessary to push the foal slightly backward (into the mare) to straighten the bent leg.

If you can feel only the muzzle, both the foal's legs are bent and must be straightened.

If both forelegs and the muzzle can be felt in proper birth position (head resting on the forelegs), the foal's shoulders may be stuck. Move one of the forelegs forward a bit to narrow the width of the shoulders for easier passage.

If the water breaks and the mare's rectum bulges as she has contractions, but the amniotic sac containing the foal doesn't appear, one of the foal's forelegs may be wedged against the top of the mare's vagina. To protect the vagina from tearing, cup your hand over the unborn foal's hoof to deflect it downward.

Breech Birth

A breech birth occurs when the foal is presented backwards (hind legs first). The foal can suffocate if its navel cord becomes pinched against the mare's pelvis, shutting off blood and oxygen.

The breech birth position is an exception to the rule of not pulling on the foal. The foal must be delivered quickly. Pull only if you are sure that the foal is breech, and pull with the contractions. Use a smooth, continuous pull in a half-circle toward the mare's hocks. Pull the foal upward and then in a downward arc because the mare's pelvis is wider at the top than at the bottom.

Serious Malpresentations

When the forelegs of the foal can be felt but the muzzle cannot, the foal's head is turned. It must be located and put on top of the forelegs.

If all four legs are either in the birth canal or turned away from it, the foal cannot be delivered. This rare presentation usually results in a dead foal.

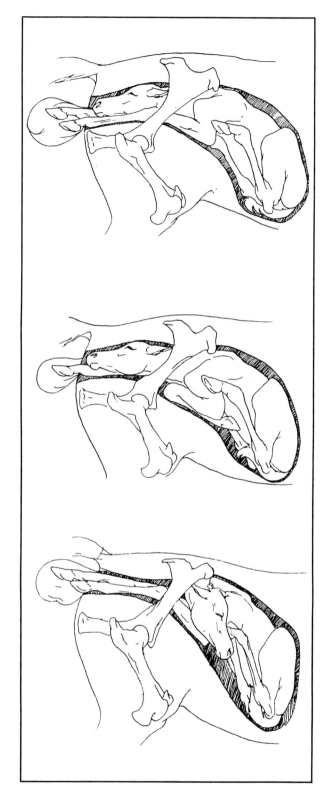

Top: Normal delivery position, one leg slightly ahead of the other and the head immediately following. Middle: One leg is bent backward. It must be found and straightened so the foal can be born. Bottom: Legs in proper position, head bent back. Experience, strength and good luck are needed to correct this dangerous problem.

218

Other Foaling Problems

If the mare's contractions totally stop before the foal is born, a *gentle* tug on the foal's legs may stimulate contractions to start again. If not, the veterinarian can stimulate contractions with an injection.

Although quite rare, the afterbirth can be delivered *before* the foal is born. If the foal isn't delivered quickly, it can suffocate. The delivery should be treated like a breech birth.

During labor, it is possible, but fortunately unusual, for the uterus to prolapse—to be turned inside out and squeezed through the birth canal after the foal is born. If this happens, support the uterus in a sling made from a clean sheet until the veterinarian arrives. Letting the uterus hang from the vulva can cause hemorrhaging and death of the mare. Keep the uterus clean and the mare quiet. The veterinarian can replace the uterus, close the vulva, and pump in sterile liquid to weigh down the uterus and hold it in place. The mare may require a transfusion in addition to antibiotics (to prevent infection).

If the foal's leg tears the roof of the mare's vagina and the lining of the rectum during delivery, the vagina can become infected. Treatment consists of antibiotics and repairing the torn tissue about a month after foaling.

During foaling, great pressure is put on the mare's uterine arteries. This can cause an artery in the uterus or in its supporting ligaments to rupture, especially in an old broodmare or one who has suffered severe strongyle damage. The mare will seem normal immediately after foaling but may colic, sweat, and appear weak eight or more hours later. The gums will be pale from blood loss. The mare must be kept quiet and given coagulants to help the blood clot; the condition usually is fatal.

Caesarian Delivery (C-Section)

A Caesarian operation usually is done only to save a mare's life during a difficult delivery (the unborn foal usually is dead). A C-section does not necessarily mark the end of a mare's breeding career, but a veterinarian should be consulted before rebreeding.

CARE OF THE NEWBORN FOAL

The Navel Cord (Umbilical Cord)

The foal's navel cord usually breaks when the foal stands for the first time. It should break naturally at the proper distance from the navel (about two inches). Do not cut or break the cord unless it fails to break when the mare rises. To allow for the needed blood transfusion to the foal, the navel cord should not be broken for at least fifteen minutes after foaling.

If an exceptionally tough cord must be broken manually, use both hands to pull the cord apart (one hand pulling away from the foal, the other toward the foal). Never pull on the cord without offsetting the pull—you can *severely* injure the foal. If necessary, cut the cord.

Be sure that the newborn foal can urinate, and that the urine is not coming from the navel (leaky navel). If it is, your veterinarian should immediately correct the condition by surgery.

Treating the Navel — If the navel is not disinfected as soon as the cord breaks, there is a risk that bacteria entering the foal's abdomen through an opening in the navel stump will cause a severe infection (navel ill or joint ill). This infection often is fatal.

If the navel is disinfected when the cord breaks, chances of infection are slim. Totally saturate the navel stump and surrounding area with 7 percent iodine, obtained from your local pharmacy or veterinarian. An easy and safe way to do this is to first dunk the navel stump in a small paper cup filled with iodine and to then pour the iodine over the navel.

Injection

After foaling, give the mare and foal a shot of tetanus antitoxin. Penicillin or penicillin-streptomycin also can be given to the foal, if desired, to help prevent disease until the foal gains immunity from its dam's colostrum (the first milk, which contains antibodies to protect the foal). The usual dosage is 5 to 6 milliliters of pen-strep daily for three days.

Enema

The foal's first bowel movement should occur within one hour after nursing for the first time. The foal's first manure is *meconium*—waste material that filled the intestines before birth. The colostrum stimulates the foal's intestinal tract to pass the meconium.

If the foal doesn't have a bowel movement within an hour of nursing, give it a four-ounce, self-contained phosphate enema (such as *Fleet®*, obtainable from a pharmacy). If unavailable, an enema of warm water and glycerine can be given instead.

Retained meconium (constipation) is painful and dangerous. The foal will die if the meconium is not passed for several days. Giving an enema to a newborn foal is therefore standard practice among most breeders.

AFTERBIRTH

The amniotic sac hangs from the mare's vulva after foaling. Its weight helps loosen the placenta from the walls of the uterus. *Never pull on the sac.* Pulling can cause hemmorhaging, scar tissue, or severe infection.

To keep the mare from stepping on the sac, tie it in a knot above her hocks. Let it hang there until the placenta separates naturally from the uterus and plops to the ground.

The placenta usually is passed within an hour of foaling. It may be expelled while the mare is either standing or lying down.

The white side of the placenta usually is turned outward when it is passed as afterbirth. During pregnancy, the white side—an intricate network of veining that resembles the veins of a leaf—was nearest the foal. The other side of the membrane is bright red and was attached to the mare's uterus. Occasionally, if the placenta separates from the uterus earlier than usual, the afterbirth may be presented with the red side outside and the white veining inside. If the entire membrane is passed, it doesn't matter.

When the afterbirth is passed, put the entire membrane (the amniotic sac, the umbilical cord, and the placenta, or chorion) in a clean, covered container with a little water to keep it from drying out until your veterinarian can examine it to be sure there are no missing pieces retained inside the uterus. (Leaving the placenta on the ground can cause it to become damaged so that the veterinarian cannot tell if any of it is missing, and it can contaminate the area.)

If the afterbirth is not passed within two hours after foaling, summon your veterinarian. Although symptoms may not appear for up to twenty-four hours, a retained placenta decays rapidly and can cause serious infection and foaling founder (laminitis), which can cripple or kill a mare. Even a *small* piece of the placenta can cause a bad infection. The most common spot for a piece to be retained is in the non-pregnant horn of the uterus.

Retained placentas might result from a lack of good nutrition or other health problems of the mare. It has been suggested that a tendency to retain the placenta may even be inherited. Some mares always retain the placenta and must have veterinary treatment after each foaling. Others never have the problem. Many mares retain the placenta only once or twice in their lifetime. There is no way to predict whether or not the mare will retain the placenta after foaling.

Treatment consists of an injection of oxytocin to stimulate contractions of the uterus and antibiotics to combat infection.

THE MARE'S FIRST MILK

The mare's first milk is called the *colostrum*. It contains antibodies for the diseases to which the mare is immune. The foal has absolutely no immunity from bacteria or viruses at birth, so it is unprotected from disease *until* it drinks the colostrum. It is critical, therefore, that the foal receive its colostrum within twenty-four hours of birth. If it doesn't, the veterinarian must supply other protection from disease (see Chapter 26).

As soon as the foal is up, it will search (probably unsuccessfully, at first) for the mare's udder. Gently direct the foal toward the udder. Once it has been located, the foal usually has no trouble nursing and can find the milk bar faster the second time.

Most mares allow their foals to nurse without objection. At birth, the udder is painfully swollen, and the mare will be more comfortable when some of the milk is drained by the foal. However, some mares must be restrained before they will allow their foals to nurse. Usually, the mare will accept the foal after it has nursed once.

Hemolitic Anemia

Despite the importance of colostrum, there is one instance in which the foal is actually harmed

220

by it. Hemolitic anemia occurs when the foal's blood type is incompatible with that of its dam. In such cases, the pregnant mare's body manufactures antibodies to destroy the red blood cells of the unborn foal as though it were a disease. Fortunately, the unborn foal is safe because antibodies cannot enter the placenta.

However, the same lethal antibodies are found in the mare's colostrum. When the foal nurses, the antibodies start to destroy the foal's red blood cells, causing anemia. The more colostrum is consumed, the weaker the foal grows. At first, its gums and inner eyelids look pale. Later they become yellowish (jaundiced). If hemolitic disease is not detected and treated within forty-eight hours, the foal probably will die.

When the navel cord breaks, gently squeeze a few drops of blood from the open end of the foal's navel stump onto a glass plate. Add a few drops of colostrum milked from the mare and stir the blood and milk together.

If, after a few minutes, the mixture still is blended, there is no danger from hemolitic anemia. If the blood separates from the milk and clumps together, the blood types of the foal and dam are incompatible. Call the veterinarian and separate the mare and foal so that the foal cannot nurse. (A partition that allows the mare to reach over and touch the foal but prevents the foal from nursing is best.) The mare must be milked and the colostrum discarded until it is replaced by regular milk (in about three days). During this time, the foal must be cared for like an orphan (see Chapter 26).

Colostrum is thick and has a yellowish tint, while mare's milk is whiter with a slight bluish tint. A laboratory test is the best way to be sure the milk no longer contains antibodies. As soon as the colostrum is replaced by regular milk, the foal can begin nursing safely.

After the foal has nursed and the afterbirth has been passed and removed from the area, clean the mare and the stall. If the weather is cold, blanket her. If the mare is wet from sweating, dry and brush her. Then offer her lukewarm water (cold water can cause abdominal cramps), hay, and a bran mash. (See Chapter 14 for instructions for making a mash.)

Watch the mare after foaling for signs of colic. Colic after foaling usually results from uterine contractions as the uterus returns to its normal size. The degree of discomfort varies. If the mare shows signs of colic, she should be examined by a veterinarian to be sure the cause is merely after-foaling discomfort and not a serious complication.

It is normal for foaling mares to have a thick, brownish discharge from the vulva about three to five days after foaling. If the discharge is greenish or smells foul, the mare probably has an infection.

Many breeders keep the mare and newborn foal indoors for the first one to three days after foaling. By the third or fourth day, both mare and foal will benefit from light exercise.

This part-Arab foal was sired by a Pinto stallion and out of an (unregistered) Arabian mare.
Photo by Sandra Hugus

Cal-O-Fiesta, owned by North Arabians of Ramona, California.

Photo by Joe Saccoman

26

BRINGING UP BABY

HEALTH CARE OF FOALS

The greatest dangers to healthy young foals are accidents and illness. Serious illness usually starts with a cold, which can become pneumonia. To prevent respiratory infections, foals should be kept dry and protected from wind and wet weather. In good weather, be sure each foal gets plenty of exercise and fresh air with its dam.

Ammonia from manure and urine can lead to respiratory problems, especially in a dirty or poorly ventilated barn. Foals are more susceptible than mature horses because their immune systems are just starting to work.

Signs of Good Health

The healthy foal is bright-eyed, alert and has a shiny, silky coat. It is playful and energetic although it naps often. (As the foal grows older, naps will be less frequent.) Newborns nurse frequently and for short periods of time. Older foals start eating solid food and nurse less often. Like older horses, foals usually are more active in the morning than in the afternoon.

Signs of Illness

Watch for the following danger signs, which indicate illness in foals:

- failure to eat or nurse;
- listlessness (depression);
- yellow, red, or pale mucous membranes of the eyes or nostrils;
- diarrhea ("scours");
- constipation;
- fever (temperature over 101° F.);
- subnormal temperature (below 100° F.)
- heat in the joints;
- swelling;
- runny nose or eyes;
- loss of weight;
- stiffness;
- swollen lymph glands (under throat);
- dehydration.

Scours (Diarrhea)

Diarrhea often occurs in the foal when its dam has her first heat period about six to ten days after foaling. Foal heat scours may result from a change in the mare's milk, caused by a change in hormones related to estrus. A more recent theory is that ascarids (round worms) may first upset the foal's digestion then (see Chapter 16).

Scouring at the foal heat is considered normal if there are no other signs of illness. The foal should appear otherwise normal and energetic. If it doesn't, call the veterinarian.

Diarrhea in foals can be quite serious because of rapid dehydration. The veterinarian should determine whether scouring is caused by illness or another cause so that the foal can be treated.

Combined Immunodeficiency (CID)

It is estimated that 2 percent to 3 percent of all Arabian foals born each year die as a result of CID. Both purebreds and Half-Arabians are affected by this genetic weakness, which results in a total lack of immunity to disease.

Foals get their initial protection from disease from their dams' colostrum. Eventually, the normal foal's body starts producing its own antibodies. The CID foal, however, cannot manufacture certain white blood cells and therefore is completely helpless against even a minor illness. The first time the foal gets sick, usually with a respiratory disease, it grows continually weaker and eventually dies. CID is always fatal (see Chapter 20).

The only way to tell if a sick foal has CID is by a blood smear and blood serum test.

Tissue samples from dead foals also can be tested for CID.

The following labs test for CID:

1) University of California, Davis
   Clinical Veterinary Immunology Laboratory
   Veterinary Medical Teaching Hospital
   Davis, Calif. 95616
   (916) 752-7373

2) Colorado State University
   Veterinary Diagnostic Laboratory
   Fort Collins, Colo. 80521
   (303) 221-4630

3) University of Florida
   College of Veterinary Medicine
   Clinical Immunology Laboratory
   Box J-126-JHMHC
   Gainesville, Fla. 32610
   (904) 392-4751

4) Veterinary Medical Research & Development, Inc. (VMRD)
   P.O. Box 502
   Pullman, Wash. 99163
   (509) 334-5815

CID isn't the only immunodeficiency found in horses. Similar deficiencies are found in other breeds of horses, but CID is believed to exist only in Arabians and Half-Arabians.

ORPHAN FOALS

People must assume the responsibility of supplying a newborn foal with colostrum or milk if its dam dies, doesn't produce enough milk, or refuses to nurse it. Thanks to modern feed and health care, such foals need not be at a great disadvantage, as Zarr Hassan proved when this former orphan foal became U.S. Reserve National Champion Stallion in 1982.

If a new foal is able to nurse for the first two days of its life, it probably gets enough colostrum to protect it from disease. If not, colostrum should be provided. Some organizations keep "banks" of frozen mare colostrum for emergencies. Check with your veterinarian about the availability of such colostrum.

If no colostrum is available, the newborn foal must be given antibiotics. A plasma transfusion also may be needed to boost immunity. To make up for the laxative effect of colostrum, the foal may need more than one enema.

The best source of milk for an orphan foal is another lactating mare; however, not all mares will nurse a strange foal. If a nurse mare isn't available, use a commercial product designed to replace mare's milk (such as *Foal-Lac*). In lieu of that, the following recipe is one of several recommended by Colorado State University Agricultural Extension Service, Fort Collins, Colorado:

Foal Formula

1 can evaporated milk
1 can water
4 Tablespoons lime water (from a drug store)
1 Tablespoon corn syrup (or sugar)

Warm the formula to about 100° F. and put it in a baby bottle (after enlarging the hole in the nipple) or in a livestock nursing bottle with a sheep nipple.

It may take a while to get the foal to nurse from the bottle. Be patient. If the foal cannot or will not nurse, your veterinarian can supply nutrition intraveneously or pump the foal formula directly into the foal's stomach using a stomach tube.

The newborn orphan should be bottle fed every two hours at first. As it gets stronger, feedings can be spread farther apart. By the time the foal is about a week old, it should only require four to six nursings daily.

During the first week, introduce foal pellets. The new foal should be eating quite a bit of solid feed by the time it is a month old. At three months old, it can be "weaned" from the milk replacement formula and put entirely on solid feed (hay and grain).

Nurse Mares

Whether a lactating mare will nurse a strange foal depends upon her mothering instinct. Many mares will refuse a strange foal, and some will attack it.

If a nurse mare's foal is old enough to wean (three months old or more), the orphan foal can be substituted for her own foal. If a mare's foal died, but she still has milk, she may accept the new foal as a replacement. A mare with a strong desire to mother will raise an orphan along with her own foal. In this case, be sure she has enough milk for two foals and that her diet supplies adequate nutrition for increased milk production.

Breeders sometimes try to make a strange foal more acceptable to the nurse mare by altering its scent. This can be done by rubbing some of the mare's own milk on the foal, or by rubbing the mare with a towel and then rubbing the towel over the foal's body to transfer the mare's scent to the orphan. Smearing the foal with another substance that has a strong scent (such as oil of wintergreen) and then putting the same substance on the mare's nostrils may help cover up the foal's scent.

Even if the nurse mare seems friendly, she should be haltered and held the first time the foal nurses. If she is nervous, a mild tranquilizer before introducing the foal might help. If the mare threatens the foal, put a twitch on her. Holding up one of the mare's forelegs on the side the foal is on will make it more difficult for her to kick.

After the mare has accepted the foal and will let it nurse, watch them closely for a few days to be sure she allows it to nurse and does not harm it.

A mare that has successfully served as an adoptive mother can be a good "insurance policy" for a breeding farm.

Free exercise helps build muscle and improve lung capacity.

FOAL REJECTION

Most Arabian mares show affectionate concern for their foals and instinctively protect them. However, occasional mares will reject (refuse to nurse) or even attack their own foals. Arabian horse breeder Linda K. Ehlers studied this problem after her own mare rejected a foal. Later, she shared her experience and that of forty-five other breeders who also had dealt with the problem of foal rejection or attacking in a series of articles in *Arabian Horse World* magazine.

From descriptions of mares that had rejected or attacked their foals, Ms. Ehlers concluded that such mares often had similar personality traits. By knowing which kinds of mares are more likely to reject their foals, breeders can anticipate (and prepare) for possible rejection or attack by the mare.

Mares that actually attacked their foals often were described as spoiled, "people oriented" horses that received a lot of attention from their human owners and often little discipline. Ms. Ehlers theorized that they might attack their foals out of jealousy, feeling that the foal endangered their own status. Often such mares were raised separately, so they never learned to adjust to other horses. Mares that attacked their own foals usually disliked and sometimes attacked other animals, including dogs.

On the other hand, mares that refused to nurse their foals but did not try to hurt them usually were aloof and indifferent toward people. Often, they were described as clumsy and not intelligent.

Ms. Ehlers pointed out that other possible causes existed for a mare to reject her foal. If the foal became accidentally separated from the mare shortly after birth, the foal might be rejected later. (This might happen if the newborn foal rolled under a fence and into a different pasture, etc.) A painful birth also might be a factor in rejecting the foal.

Ms. Ehlers believes that foal rejection or attack might be discouraged by disciplining spoiled mares before they foal. These mares must learn respect for people and other horses, must be made to behave, and must be disciplined appropriately when they do not. The also can be introduced into a group of domineering, aggressive horses and then be moved to a new group of equally bossy horses before the spoiled mares can assert their own dominance. This approach may teach the mare to be less aggressive with other horses, which may carry over into her relationship with the foal.

Ms. Ehlers suggests that, if a mare has a previous history of foal rejection, additional precautions might be taken. Birth might be induced to be sure that the mare is not alone when she foals. A shot of estrogen a week before foaling may stimulate mothering instincts, and an injection of oxytocin to stimulate milk production after foaling may help. (Some mares may refuse to nurse their foals because they don't have much milk.) A painkiller given after a difficult birth may prevent rejection due to pain, and the mare may be tranquilized after foaling to make it easier for the foal to nurse.

If, despite every precaution, the mare cannot be restrained and made to accept her foal, it must be separated from her and raised like an orphan. Once a mare has rejected a foal, she always should be watched carefully with subsequent foals although most mares seem to gradually adjust to motherhood with subsequent foalings.

When a foal is frightened, it performs "baby talk"—opening and shutting its mouth soundlessly. This behavior indicates submission and helplessness.

FOAL BEHAVIOR AND HANDLING

The best indication of anxiety or fear in the foal is "baby talk"—the foal repeatedly opens and shuts its mouth as though trying to make a sound. It is, however, a silent gesture of surrender and humility that says to other horses, "Don't harm me. I am helpless. I am a baby." (This submissive behavior is similar to a small dog rolling onto its back when challenged by a larger or older dog.)

Always try to avoid frightening the foal. Whenever the foal begins "baby talk" in a stressful situation, try to gently reassure and calm it. "Baby talk" is eventually outgrown. When the foal will stop using it depends upon its self-confidence.

Handling the Newborn Foal

Accustom the foal to being touched from the time it is born. Be gentle and speak quietly to the foal. Remember that everything is new—and may be frightening—to the baby. Each time you handle the foal, you are teaching it something that will be with it the rest of its life. For better or worse, early lessons are never forgotten.

Restraining the Foal

Hold a young foal still by encircling its chest with one arm and lifting slightly upward on the dock of the tail with your other hand. With this method, one person can easily restrain the foal while someone else treats an injury, gives the foal a shot, halters it, etc. This method of restraint is outgrown in a couple of months. When the foal is too strong to be held this way, hold the foal by a halter rope.

Discipline

Foals often test people by biting or kicking to see whether they can get away with it, determining their place in the "pecking order" as they do with other horses. At first, foals don't associate biting or kicking with misbehavior, they merely are feeling experimental or frisky. In a herd, one foal will bite or kick another to encourage it to run or to start a mock battle.

However, foals must soon learn that people must be treated with respect. If they get away with biting or kicking as foals, they will repeat the behavior later. Each time a foal nips or kicks at a person, it must be instantly punished. The sooner the

A young foal can be safely restrained by encircling its chest with one arm and pulling upward on its tail with the other hand.

foal learns to behave properly toward people, the safer and more pleasant it will be.

Biting — When the foal bites, respond immediately with a quick, hard slap on its chest and a loud "No!" Repeat the same treatment every time it nips. In effect, you are establishing your superiority and authority and taking your place in the pecking order (at the top).

Instead of slapping the foal, some people recommend pulling its whiskers. A foal that continues to bite after having learned that biting is not allowed may require more severe action. One method is to carry a piece of wood with a tack attached to it, point outward. When the foal tries to bite (foals usually nip the hand or arm), let it prick itself with the tack instead.

Kicking — Discourage kicking by whipping the foal's hindquarters when it kicks. Punishment must be immediate. Delayed punishment or excessive whipping won't teach the foal anything.

EVALUATING FOALS

Foals grow rapidly and can change greatly in one week's time. Yet the breeder often must evaluate the quality of foals early to decide which will be sold. Sometimes, breeders make the wrong choices. Nobody would knowingly sell a future National Champion!

Members of different bloodlines grow at different rates. Knowing growth patterns of certain families of Arabian horses helps the breeder predict how the foal will look when mature.

When to Evaluate Foals

Most breeders try to estimate a foal's potential during the first month of its life. Lady Wentworth suggested that the best time to evaluate foals is when they are about ten days old. By this age, the foal's tendons are stronger, and it will have put on some weight and muscle but won't yet have begun growing out of balance.

At one week old, it is possible to judge the balance and general proportions of the body—the length and angle of the shoulder and hip, the length of the back, and the general shape and set of the neck. The *length* of the neck may change as the horse matures, but the *placement* of the neck cannot change. The shape of the neck also changes little. If the foal has a thick throatlatch, it will remain thick as the foal matures.

Although the foal grows into and out of balance as it goes through various growth stages, its basic bone structure cannot change. Conformation faults will *not* improve with time. If the week-old foal stands under because the shoulder is upright, it will always do so.

Some things can improve as the horse matures, but they are points of *type* rather than conformation. For example, the horse's head will appear more refined (smaller and smoother) when the permanent teeth erupt and the "teeth bumps" of the lower jaw disappear (see Chapter 15). The "dish" in the facial profile may or may not deepen with maturity. The actual proportions of the head change very little, however. Eye shape, placement, and prominence do not change.

The croup *may* become more level as the foal matures. However, tail set and carriage remain the same.

Evaluating the Foal's Legs

Many foals are born with crooked legs. If caused by muscle and tendon tone, the legs will straighten within a few weeks. However, if the leg bones are crooked (if the cannons are offset, etc.), no amount of muscle development will improve the legs. Many foals are born "down on the pasterns," and this weakness usually corrects itself within the first few weeks of life.

The Disappointing Foal

At some point, every breeder produces a foal that doesn't meet his or her standards. Some choose to put such a foal on the market at a high price, hoping that someone else will like the horse better than they do. Others price a disappointing foal low or give it away (for a 4-H project, etc.). Others take the foal off the market for a while, hoping that it will improve in time.

Before keeping an ugly duckling in hopes it will become a swan, carefully figure the costs. If the cost of maintenance will exceed the horse's eventual sale price, it may be better to take an early but smaller loss and to invest your money and time in a more promising animal.

WEANING

Weaning is the process of separating the foal and its dam so that the foal can no longer nurse. The physical separation also helps overcome the psychological dependency of the mare and foal upon each other.

When to Wean

Breeders formerly weaned foals at six to twelve months of age, thinking that the foals needed the "superior nutrition" of mare's milk. It now is realized that mare's milk actually is lower in nutrients than most horse feeds. Foals that are weaned earlier, given good feed and dewormed regularly, develop faster and adjust better to weaning than foals that remain with their dams longer.

Most Arabian foals are weaned at four or five months of age. Some are weaned at three months, if the mare is in poor condition, sick, or not giving enough milk, etc.

Early weaning is nothing new. In the desert, the Bedouins sometimes weaned foals at only a few days of age, substituting camel's milk for mare's milk. This was necessary because of warfare and migration, and may have helped to create the special bond that exists between people and Arabian horses.

Weaning Methods

The method of weaning depends upon available facilities, the number of foals to be weaned, and the preferences of the breeder. When separating the mare and foal, it is best to remove the mare and to leave the foal in familiar surroundings. Putting

Newly weaned foals and their dams may whinny to each other for the first day or two of separation. Both will adjust better to weaning if they have other horses for companionship.

the mare in pasture promotes self-exercise, which helps reduce the udder. When the foal is weaned, the mare's grain should be stopped or drastically reduced to decrease milk production.

Both mares and foals are comforted by the presence of other horses during the weaning period. If they cannot be pastured with horses of their own age, they should be able to see them nearby. Large breeding farms usually pasture weanlings together for companionship. Foals may adjust better with playmates of similar age. However, some breeders prefer to separate weanlings so they do not have to compete for feed and water.

"A clean break" between mare and foal usually is recommended for weaning, with the mare totally removed from sight, sound, and smell of her foal. However, breeders with limited facilities often have had good results by putting the mare and foal near each other. In such cases, the fences must be safe and solid to prevent injury. If mare and foal are kept in adjoining paddocks or pastures, be sure that the foal cannot reach through to nurse! Some small breeders report that the mare and foal seem less upset by the separation if they remain near each other.

Reactions of the mare and foal to weaning vary. Sometimes the mare is upset, and the foal is not; sometimes the foal panics, and the mare is calm. Sometimes there is a lot of fuss, and sometimes both the mare and foal accept the separation well. Mares often seem relieved at no longer having the responsibility of nursing a foal. Expect the mare and foal to call to each other for the first day or two. However, they soon adjust to their new situation.

Most Arabians are between 14.1 and 15.1 hands in height, but individuals vary. *Zahid (Anter x Zahda) is almost 16.1 hands—one of the tallest Arabians ever.

Johnny Johnston photo courtesy of Antara Arabians

27

SIZE, GROWTH AND MATURITY

A horse's height is expressed in measurements called "hands." Each hand is four inches. A horse that is 56 inches high is therefore 14 hands tall. A horse that is 58 inches tall is 14 hands, 2 inches, or simply "fourteen-two" (written 14.2). If the horse is 59 inches tall, it is 14 hands, 3 inches tall, or "fourteen-three" (14.3).

Confusion arises if the decimal point is incorrectly read as indicating tenths. The decimal merely separates the number of hands from the number of inches over an even number of hands. Sometimes a horse is incorrectly described as "14.5" hands when it is really 14½ hands tall (14.2). If the horse really *were* "14 hands, 5 inches," it would be 15.1 hands.

HEIGHT OF ARABIANS

Mature Arabians vary greatly in size. Most are under 15.2, with the average height of the breed probably at 14.2 or 14.3 hands. Arabians often look taller than they actually are because of their high head and tail carriage. Owners tend to overestimate the height of their Arabians, either through ignorance or sensitivity about their horses' small size. The only way to be sure about the horse's actual height is to measure it.

With experience, after measuring a number of horses to see what a 14-hand horse "looks like" compared to a 15-hand horse, it is possible to accurately estimate height. Seen in the flesh, a 13.3 hand horse is obviously not 14.2, and a 16-hand Arabian seems gigantic!

Measuring Height

The easiest way to measure a horse's height is with a special measuring stick marked in hands. The kind with a level is most accurate. A regular tape measure or yard stick also can be used to measure height (by dividing the total height, in inches, by four to get the measurement in hands.)

To measure the horse, be sure that it is standing squarely, with the forelegs directly under the shoulders and the head in the normal position. (If the head is lowered, the withers may be raised slightly.) Measure the horse on level ground to get an accurate height. Measure from the highest point of the withers straight down to the ground, with the measuring stick or tape resting on the ground just behind the heel of the foreleg. The measurement from the withers to the ground (i.e., the bottom of the hoof) is the horse's height in inches.

SIZE RELATED TO TYPE

Historically, the Arabian has been a breed of relatively small horses, although occasionally Arabian horses of 15.1 hands or taller were found among the desert tribes.

There is some disagreement about whether large or small Arabians are best. Some people allege that small Arabians generally have more breed type, while large Arabians tend to be coarse. Others argue that larger Arabians are more desirable than small ones because a large rider is more comfortable and appears in better proportion when mounted on a tall horse.

When two halter horses of *equal* type and conformation compete, selecting the larger horse is justified. However, a tall Arabian with inferior type and conformation should never win at halter, regardless of its large size. Likewise, a small Arabian should not be discriminated against in the show ring merely because of its smaller size. (Because of the breed's superior endurance and soundness, a small Arabian can probably carry more weight than an equally small horse of a different breed.) Each Arabian horse should be evaluated according to its individual qualities, of which size is only one consideration.

*Raffles, one of the breed's most famous and popular sires, was only 13.3 hands. (Due to the Arabian's superior strength and endurance, small Arabians can carry more weight than equally small horses of other breeds.)
Photo courtesy of Arabian Horse Owners Foundation

GROWTH RATES

All Arabian horses do not mature at the same rate. Growth patterns vary according to genetic inheritance, nutrition, health care, and even sex. All horses grow most during the first year of life. A California Polytechnic (Cal Poly) University study at Pomona, California, recorded the growth of twenty-five of its Arabian foals. During their first year, they grew anywhere from 12½ to 18¾ inches; average growth was about 16 inches during the first year of life.

According to the Cal Poly study, an Arabian foal can be expected to grow about four inches during the first month of life. During its second month, it should grow about three inches. During the third month, the foal may gain another two inches. After this point, growth slows. Even so, the foal may easily gain another four inches in height by the time it is six months old, and about the same amount of growth should occur during its next six months.

The Cal Poly Arabians studied averaged the following rates of growth over five years:

Growth Year	Growth (in inches)
first year	16.13
second year	3.35
third year	.95
fourth year*	.62
fifth year*	.28

Only seven of the original twenty-five horses were available for measuring from the ages of forty-eight to sixty months.

Foals grow in spurts, with various parts of their bodies growing at different rates. Because of this, they usually grow into and out of balance several times before they are mature. Newborn foals are usually about the same height at the withers and croup, but they are much taller than long because of their long legs. (The cannon bones of most Cal Poly Arabian foals studied grew less than an inch during the five-year growth period.)

Most 12-month-old Arabians are taller at the hindquarters than at the withers. Two- and three-year-olds usually are longer in the body than they are tall. By the time a horse is fully grown, these imbalances should have disappeared. However, some mature Arabians are higher at the croup or too long in the body. Of these faults, the former is more serious (see Chapter 7).

A young, growing horse should look immature. The slightly weedy two- or three-year-old generally will fill out as it matures, whereas the two- or three-year-old that looks like a mature horse often will become coarse by the time it is grown.

Epiphyseal Closure Stops Growth

The horse's growth in height stops when the epiphyseal plates of the leg bones fuse together. The epiphyseal closure occurs in the radius of the long bones above the knees and is best determined by x-rays.

Until this closure occurs, the legs are likely to be injured by too much work. The legs of an Arabian horse between the ages of two and three should be x-rayed to be sure the plates have fused before subjecting the horse to strenuous training for performance.

Growth patterns vary according to genetic inheritance, nutrition, health care, and even the sex of the horse. *Sharon VanderEnde photo courtesy of Warren Park Stud, Sanger, Calif.*

MATURITY

Arabian horses grow over a longer period of time than horses of other breeds. This slow development is related to late closure of the growth (epiphyseal) plates of the leg bones and may be related to the longevity associated with the breed. (Animals that mature over a longer period of time usually outlive those that grow more rapidly.)

Arabians reach their mature height at about five years of age but may continue to develop weight, bone, and muscle beyond the time their mature height is achieved. Arabians from families that are "late bloomers" may not reach their final appearance until age seven or older. However, conformation is apparent early in life and does not change after mature height is attained.

Because closure of the epiphyseal plates is related to hormones, gelding a colt early in life may delay closure of the plates and allow him to reach a greater height than he would have attained if gelded later. This theory seems probable but cannot be proven because there is no way of knowing what height the horse actually would have reached if he had been gelded later. (See Chapter 35 for the results of a study on the effect of early gelding.)

BIRTH SIZE RELATIVE TO MATURE SIZE

At birth, most Arabian foals are between thirty-four and forty-one inches tall at the withers. Fillies usually are shorter than colts at birth and often mature to less height. Small birth size does not

It is difficult to judge the balance and conformation of young horses because their body parts grow at various rates.

always mean that the foal will be a smaller mature horse than the foal that is large at birth. The small foal may (or may not) catch up in height by growing more than the large foal.

Small Foals

Small birth size is related to many factors, only one of which is genetic inheritance. A small foal may be produced by a mare that is unable to adequately nourish the unborn foal because of illness, age, or malnutrition. Foals born early in the year may be smaller than those born late in the year, especially if the late-foaling dams have access to rich spring pasture during late gestation. A mare's first foal also may be smaller than subsequent foals because of the mare's tighter ligaments and muscles, which allow less room for the unborn foal to grow.

Many small Arabian mares produce foals that mature to larger size. This may be because the small mare was stunted by poor nutrition during her own growth years. More frequently, the small mare possesses genes for both small and large size—*either* of which may be inherited by her foals.

ESTIMATING MATURE HEIGHT

According to *The Horse of the Desert*, by W. R. Brown, the Bedouins sometimes estimated the mature height of their Arabian foals by two methods:

> *"One is to throw a cord over the foal's head, so that it rests on the neck behind the ears, and bring the two ends together on the upper lip just below the nostrils. Another is, to measure with a cord from the centre of the knee to the crest of the hoof (beginning of the hair above the coronet), and three times this measurement extended upwards from the centre of the knee will be the mature height at the wither."*

Cal Poly University's growth study indicated that, based on the group average, the height of their Arabian horses at birth was about 63.56 percent of their height at maturity. Based on this information, the mature height of a foal might be estimated by using the following formula:

Birth Height (BH) = 63.56 percent of
Mature Height (X)
Therefore, BH ÷ .6356 = X

For example:

Birth Height = 38 inches
38″ ÷ .6356 = 59.79″
59.79″ ÷ 4″ = 14.95, or
15 hands at maturity

This formula is not infallible in predicting mature height, for no studies relate pedigree to birth height or eventual mature height. However, the formula is based on the only Arabian growth rate statistics available.

WEIGHT OF ARABIAN HORSES

Most Arabian horses weigh between 700 and 1,100 pounds at maturity. The horse's weight varies according to its bone structure and condition. The only way to be sure of an individual horse's weight is to weigh the horse on a livestock scale. Since this is impractical, it is possible to estimate weight with sufficient accuracy to administer medications whose dosage is based upon the horse's weight.

A special horse "weight tape" sold by tack and feed stores estimates a horse's weight by its girth measurement. To use the tape, place it around the horse's body where the saddle girth or cinch would fit. The tape should rest just *behind* the withers.

Table 27.1 is a chart to estimate the Arabian horse's weight according to its girth measurement. Use an ordinary cloth tape measure to measure the horse's girth circumference.

TABLE 27.1
ESTIMATING WEIGHT
BY CIRCUMFERENCE OF GIRTH*

Girth Circumference (in inches)	Estimated Weight (in pounds)
64	770
65	795
66	823
67	850
68	878
69	906
70	933
71	960
72	987
73	1013
74	1039
75	1065
76	1092

*This table was based on figures from a 1970 study by California Polytechnic University at Pomona, California. Estimated weights proved to be within 50 to 100 pounds of actual weight of the Arabian horses studied.

A small Arabian mare may produce a large foal. The foal's size at birth and maturity depends upon the genes it inherits from both parents.

The foal should be accustomed to the halter before its first lesson in being led. The lesson must be accomplished without frightening or hurting the foal.

28

EARLY TRAINING

Arabian horses are different than other breeds not only in appearance but in behavior and their response to people. As a breed, they are energetic and high-spirited yet sensitive, gentle, affectionate, and have a strong desire to please. Although docile, they react quickly to everything around them.

Arabians are intelligent, curious, and generally learn faster than horses of other breeds. Most of them also are playful. If you can convince Arabians that work is a game, they love to work.

It has often been said that "the horse trainer must be smarter than the horse." With Arabians, that may not be as easy as it sounds!

PRINCIPLES OF HORSE TRAINING

Horses cannot reason like people do; they learn by doing. You must therefore *show* the horse what you want it to do. If your Arabian seems slow to learn, the problem may lie in communication. Your Arabian cannot obey if it doesn't understand what it's supposed to do.

Horses are trained by punishment and reward. They are punished when they *purposely* do something wrong and rewarded for good performance whether or not it was intended. Proper behavior is reinforced by rewards.

Horses must be trained to perform with one side of their bodies at a time. Everything that the horse learns to do on one side must be repeated for the other side. The horse cannot learn to perform one activity with the left side of its body and then automatically transfer that knowledge to the right side. The lesson is first taught on the near (left) side of the horse because it is accustomed to being led from that side. After the lesson has been learned, it is repeated for the off (right) side.

Lessons should be short enough that the horse does not become bored, for a bored horse will not pay attention and therefore cannot learn. Young horses have a shorter attention span than older ones. A foal, for example, may only be able to pay attention for five minutes at a time.

Begin each training session by repeating a previously learned activity. This serves as a refresher and usually begins the session on a note of cooperation and success because the horse already knows what you want it to do. When your Arabian performs correctly, reward it. Then introduce a new lesson.

Do not let the horse become too tired during training sessions. If tired, your horse will become resentful. The object is not only to train the horse but to keep it enjoying the activity. If your Arabian enjoys learning, it will learn faster and perform better. Try to avoid fighting with the horse during a training session, and always end the lesson before the horse becomes restless.

End each lesson when the horse does *something* right. If it has trouble learning to do something new, go back and repeat something already mastered so that the lesson will end on a successful note. Ending the lesson is the *best* reward for good performance.

Rewards

Arabian horses are more likely to repeat actions that are rewarded. When training the Arabian, reward it when something is done correctly. Arabians quickly associate the reward with the action that immediately preceded it.

A "reward" does not mean that you should give the horse something to eat. Giving a carrot for good performance may result in the horse demanding a carrot before it will perform. The horse may lose interest in performing if its mind always is on the snack it expects to receive.

In the beginning, reward good performance with words of praise and with petting. Later, either will do. The Arabian soon learns that "Good boy!" or "Good girl!" means it has performed correctly. Perhaps more than other breeds, Arabian horses like to be praised. When training, be sure to reward good behavior to let the horse know it did something right—don't just punish the horse when it does something wrong.

Punishment

Punishment varies in degree, and severity of punishment should match the infraction. If the horse in training performs incorrectly (because it hasn't yet mastered the activity, or because it doesn't understand what it's supposed to do), the horse is "punished" merely by being required to repeat the activity. If the horse that already has mastered an activity purposely misbehaves, challenging the trainer's authority, it is punished more severely.

When punishing the horse that has behaved badly, use only the amount of force necessary. Shouting at an Arabian often is sufficient for minor infractions. Arabian horses get their feelings hurt easily and may sulk when punished. Punishment can range from a slap with the hand or leg pressure (if the horse is being ridden) to use of a whip or spurs.

Arabian horses are smart enough to know whether they deserve to be punished. When punishment is unfair, they may fight back or wait for a chance to get even. They do not easily forget or forgive abuse.

Arabians seldom are naturally afraid of people. In fact, they often will take advantage of someone who lacks firmness. They will test a new handler to see just how much they can get away with, and they appreciate having firm lines drawn regarding behavior. The handler must show the horse what kind of behavior is desired and what kind of behavior is not allowed.

Be consistent in punishment. Do not allow the horse to sometimes get away with a certain behavior and punish it for the same behavior at other times. Always punish the horse quickly when punishment is deserved and try to use the same degree of force each time a specific misbehavior is corrected.

The Bedouins subjected their horses to short rations and exhaustion, but they were remarkably patient in handling them. Spurs and whips were seldom used, for Bedouin riders preferred tact to force. Modern Arabian horses have, to a large extent, inherited the temperament of their ancestors. They, too, are more easily trained with persuasion than with force.

HALTER BREAKING

It's easiest to accustom a foal to wearing a halter during its first day of life. If this important lesson is delayed until the foal is older, it will be stronger and more active, making it more difficult to catch and restrain. However, the halter should never be left on the foal because a foal can break its neck if the halter gets caught on an object. Let the foal wear the halter for a short time each day to accustom it to being caught, haltered, and petted, but remove the halter before leaving the foal.

Begin halter breaking (teaching the foal to lead) when it is about one week old. By that time, it will be fairly steady on its legs but not as strong and aggressive as it soon will become. Be gentle, patient, and careful when working with a foal. The young foal is likely to be frightened, and its bones are finer than an older horse, so they are more easily damaged.

Teaching to Lead

A soft, thick cotton rope can serve as both a lead rope and "come along" (rump rope). Snap or tie the rope to the foal's halter and pass the rope around its hindquarters so that the "come-along" forms a loose loop around the foal's buttocks about midway between its tail and hocks. If your lead rope is too short to use as a come-along, use a separate rope for this purpose.

At first, encourage the foal to step to one side by first pulling gently to one side with the lead rope. Follow that with a *slight* tug on the come-along to encourage the foal to step to the side. When it takes one or two steps, pet and praise the foal. Then repeat the lesson in the opposite direction.

At first, teach the foal to lead in circles. It can be trained to walk straight forward later. At first, the lesson is simply to *move* beside the handler, and it is important to avoid any direct forward pull on the lead rope. Pulling on the halter may cause the foal to pull back against the pressure, which can cause a serious injury. Small foals often are frightened of being separated from their dams, so never try to lead the foal very far from its dam.

Limit the foal's halterbreaking lessons to five or ten minutes once or twice each day. Foals have a very short attention span, and boredom leads to bad behavior and possible injury. After the first lesson or two, you probably won't need to use the come-along; you can go back to it if the foal becomes stubborn.

Apply gentle pressure on the halter to turn the foal. Never exert a strong pull, as the foal could be injured.

Walk beside the foal with the lead rope in your left hand (loosely coiled and out of the way). Tell the foal to "walk" and apply gentle pressure with your right hand on the foal's hindquarters. During halter breaking, the foal will be calmer in familiar surroundings, with its dam nearby.

A "come-along" (rump rope) teaches the foal to move away from pressure on its hindquarters.

Being led to and from the pasture each day with its dam will quickly accustom the foal to being led. A handler for the mare and one for the foal is best.

Teaching to Stop

After the foal follows the handler readily, teach it the meaning of the word "whoa" by using that command each time you stop. Practice leading and stopping, saying "whoa" each time. The foal eventually learns the meaning of the word by associating it with the action of stopping. When the foal stops, pet and praise it. Don't keep the foal standing still for more than a few seconds. Instead, lead it forward again. After two or three times, end the lesson.

After the foal knows what is meant by "whoa," at some point it will challenge you by refusing to stop. This is the time when firmness (without roughness) is necessary. Give a slight jerk on the lead rope and repeat the command. Release the pressure on the lead rope immediately, so the foal won't react by pulling back and hurting its neck or throwing itself over backwards. Repeat the command, "Whoa!" and the light jerk on the lead rope until the foal stops. Then reward it *immediately*. The foal should soon learn that it is more pleasant to obey than to rebel.

Dangerous Reactions

Sometimes the foal reacts to pressure on the lead rope by moving backward (especially common when older foals are halterbroken). If this happens, follow the foal backward until it stops. *Do not pull on the lead rope.* If the foal rears, gently pull its head sideways and forward to keep it from losing balance and going over backwards. If it does fall, try to keep the foal from striking its head.

INTERMEDIATE TRAINING

During the young horse's first two years, it should become familiar with the activities involved in stable care. The horse should be handled daily so that it becomes accustomed to having all parts of its body touched and does not fear people. This is the "mannering" period of the young horse's life when it must be taught to behave well for all kinds of handling. Early training and handling make the young horse ready for more complicated training later.

When training the young horse, teach only one new lesson at a time. If the horse has never been bathed and clipped, for example, don't attempt to do both in the same day. Let the horse learn slowly to avoid confusion or fright.

The young horse may be frightened the first time it encounters a new situation and strange objects. Reassure it with gentle words and petting. Be careful the first time you do anything new with a horse, for its first experience will affect its behavior for the rest of its life.

Picking Up the Feet

The sooner you teach the foal to allow its feet to be touched and lifted, the better. It is more difficult (and more dangerous) to teach an older horse to allow its feet to be worked on.

Start by standing at the shoulder of the haltered foal. Facing its hindquarters, slowly run your hand down the near foreleg. If the foal takes the leg away, patiently start over and gradually work your way down the leg. Eventually, the foal will stand quietly. When it does, lift the foot.

Holding the fetlock joint, firmly lift the foot upward and slightly toward the foal's rear. Don't lift it very far off the ground and hold it only a moment before setting the hoof back on the ground. (Don't give the foal time to fight your gentle grip.) Pick up and set down the leg two or three times, holding it just a fraction longer before putting it down. Pet the foal and praise it.

Pick up each foot, eventually. However, always start with the foreleg first. Never walk up to the foal from the rear and attempt to lift the hind leg without speaking to the horse first and running your hand down the leg. You needn't pick up all four feet in the first lesson. Eventually, you will be able to lift each leg. End the lesson before the foal starts to struggle, or you will have "taught" it to struggle.

After the foal has learned this lesson, pick up each hoof daily. Then, when needed, you can clean the hoofs with a hoof pick. You can prepare the young horse for later shoeing by tapping on the bottom of the foot with the hoof pick, as a farrier will do with a hammer.

Backing

When the foal is a few months old and leads well, teach it to back up by pulling the lead line toward its chest and saying "Back." Reinforce the cue by tapping the foal's chest until it takes a step backward to get away from the pressure and the tapping. At first, be content with one backward step; praise the horse immediately. Practice backing periodically until it backs several steps on command.

Tying

It's a good idea to wait until the horse is a weanling, at least, before tying it to a stationary object. Young foals are more likely to injure themselves than older horses while learning to stand tied. Some trainers simply never tie their valuable show horses, to avoid the risk of an accident in case the horse pulls back.

Begin teaching the young horse to stand while tied *after* it has had exercise and preferably in the afternoon, when horses are naturally less active. At first, you may wish to *loop* the lead rope around a sturdy post rather than tying the rope to it, and to hold the lead rope in one hand while you groom the foal with the other hand. If the foal pulls back, you can slacken the rope immediately. If this happens, lead the horse forward again, re-loop the rope, and continue grooming. *Never* reward the horse after it pulls back by discontinuing the lesson.

Trainers sometimes tie the foal's lead rope to a deflated tire innertube that is tied to a sturdy fence post. Then, if the foal pulls back, the rubber innertube will stretch (and prevent injury to the foal) and then it will return to its shape, pulling the foal forward.

Always tie horses using a safety release knot that can be released quickly in an emergency. (See Chapter 13 for directions on tying and releasing the safety release knot.)

Eventually the horse can be tied to a solid object. Leave the horse and watch it from a slight distance, remaining handy in case you need to release the knot. If the horse pulls back, shout its name and tell it to stop. (Use whatever phrase you *usually* use to correct your horse.) When the horse stops pulling back, praise it. Don't leave a young horse tied for a long time; the longer it is tied, the more likely that it will become bored and struggle. If the horse behaves, leave it tied for gradually increasing periods of time but not so long that it becomes tired from having its head and neck in the same position.

LUNGING

Arabians should not be lunged before they are at least eighteen months old. Lunging puts uneven pressure on immature leg joints because the horse always moves in a circle, stressing one side of the leg more than the other.

In lunging, the horse moves in a large circle around the handler, changing gaits, stopping, and reversing direction on command. The handler stands in the center of an imaginary wheel, with the horse moving around the wheel's rim. The lunge line (a long rope) is the only spoke in the imaginary wheel; it connects the center and the rim (the handler and horse).

Lunging has many uses. It can take the edge off the horse's energy or serve as a warm-up period before training, riding, or showing. It can provide controlled exercise for horses that aren't ridden or driven. Lunging teaches the young horse verbal commands for changes of gait, which makes early training under saddle easier. Lunging the horse while it's wearing new equipment helps accustom it to the sound and feel of the tack before being mounted.

Equipment and Facilities Needed

The only equipment required for lunging is a sturdy halter or lunging cavesson (a headstall made especially for lunging), a lunge line (a sturdy cotton or nylon line about thirty feet long, with a heavy-duty metal snap to connect to the halter or cavesson), and a long buggy whip. The whip is used as an extension of the trainer's arm—it helps cue the horse and keep it moving.

Put splint boots on the horse's forelegs to prevent injury from interfering or playfulness while it is being lunged.

You can teach a horse to lunge anywhere, but a round ring simplifies the task because it limits the horse's range and helps keep it moving in a circle (see Chapter 12).

Training to Lunge

Hold the lead rope portion of the lunge line in one hand and figure-eight the excess line and hold it in the other hand (do *not* wrap it around your hand).

Start by saying "walk" and leading the horse in a small circle near the center of the ring with the

This young Arabian models a lunging cavesson. If a cavesson is not available, the lunge line can be attached to an ordinary halter.

Splint boots cover the cannon bones of the forelegs to prevent splints or other injuries from accidental interfering while the horse is being lunged or trained.

horse between you and the rail. Drawing out the command ("wa-a-a-lk") will help the horse learn to distinguish between the commands for "walk" and "trot," which sound similar.

As you lead the horse, play out the lunge line, gradually putting more distance between yourself and the horse. If the horse tries to stay close to you, encourage it to move away by flipping the end of the lunge line toward the animal. Gradually maneuver yourself into the center of the ring while keeping the horse moving next to the rail.

An assistant can be handy when teaching the horse to walk around you. Have your assistant lead the horse in an ever-enlarging circle as you stay in the center of the ring. Eventually, the assistant should release the horse's lead and back toward the center of the arena. If the horse follows, the assistant should put the horse back in position and then back away again.

Eventually, the horse will be moving around you on a long, fairly loose rope, as you remain in the center. Stay slightly toward the horse's rear (about even with its hip). If you stand too far toward its shoulder, the horse may slow, stop, or change direction. Always face the horse, and watch it carefully during lunging to anticipate its actions.

Don't worry if the horse breaks into a trot or canter at first—just be careful not to get run over or kicked and try to keep it moving around you on the rail. (If the horse moves toward you, flip the lunge line toward it. If that doesn't work, threaten the horse with the whip.)

If the horse breaks into a faster gait, let it tire of the gait before you ask it to slow. When the horse changes to a faster gait without being asked, act as though it were *your* idea instead. Just as the horse starts to go faster, give the verbal command for that gait. Then keep the horse moving in that gait—don't let it slow down or stop when it wants to. Keeping the horse going faster than it wants to is easier than keeping it from breaking into a faster gait. Just pop the whip behind the horse if it slows down. When *you* are ready to let the horse slow down or stop—after it would have liked to—give the command and the horse probably will be glad to rest.

After the horse has been lunged in each direction a few times, ease it into a stop with "Whoa" and a flip of the lunge line. When the horse stops, reward it. (If a safe, enclosed ring is available, the horse can be lunged without a lunge line. Free lunging prevents possible leg or neck injuries caused by pulling the horse off balance with the lunge line.)

Begin training to lunge by leading the horse in a large circle at a walk.

Gradually feed out the lunge line until the horse is moving in a wide circle around you.

After the horse has learned to walk and trot on the lunge line, he is asked to "whoa" and stand.

Horses should be sent in both directions each time they are lunged.

Here the horse is learning to reverse direction.

Teaching the Trot and Canter

In subsequent lunging lessons, you can teach the horse to change gait upon command. Teach the trot first and be sure it is well mastered before progressing to the canter. You have less control over the horse at the canter than at the slower gaits. Also, trotting builds more muscle than cantering.

When giving the verbal command "trot" make the word short and crisp, to distinguish it from the command for "walk," which should be drawn out and soothing. Say "trot" and wave the whip toward the horse's hindquarters. If the horse doesn't break into a trot, pop the whip behind it. Hit the horse with the whip only as a last resort.

When lunging, use the walk as a transition between stopping and faster gaits. Don't ask the young horse to move from a stop to a canter. Instead, progress from a walk to a trot, and a trot to a canter.

When stopping the horse, slow it gradually; then stop.

When the horse masters the trot, teach the canter the same way. Arabians usually learn verbal commands for gait changes very quickly.

Always lunge the horse for an equal period of time in each direction. If a horse is worked only in one direction, it will become "one sided" and be stiff and unwilling to work in the opposite direction. Also, lunging for an equal time in both directions helps develop the muscles on each side of the body equally.

PREPARATION FOR RIDING

Arabians seldom are ridden before they are two and a half to three years old, because they mature later than other breeds. In the case of young show horses, these age limits are sometimes pushed to prepare for performance classes. However, before starting the young horse, a veterinarian should x-ray its legs to be sure the horse is mature enough for training (see Chapter 27).

The young Arabian can learn many things before being ridden that will give it a head start on later training. From the ground, it can be taught to back and sidepass (move sideways). To teach the horse to back, give a series of short jerks on the lead line and tap the chest with the handle of the whip, while saying "back." (Backing the horse along a fence will help it back in a straight line.) For the sidepass, poke the horse's side where the rider's leg will later apply pressure for the sidepass cue, and say "over."

When the horse knows how to lunge and will consistently stop on command, you can ground drive it by attaching long reins (first to the halter; later to the bit). Then stand behind the horse out of kicking range and ask the horse to walk. Walk a few steps and then ask the horse to stop by saying "whoa" and pulling back on the reins. Use only as much pressure as necessary to get the horse to stop. To turn the horse to the right, pull back on the right rein; to make a left turn, pull the left rein.

No matter what type of performance the horse will later be trained to do, it should first wear a mild snaffle bit (a smooth, jointed mouthpiece with no shanks). Choose a bit with large rein rings (to keep the bit from being pulled into the mouth) and a thick mouthpiece. (A thin mouthpiece concentrates the pressure in a smaller area of the mouth and is therefore more severe.) Bit size is the length of the mouthpiece, measured in inches. Most Arabians wear a 4¾-inch to 5¼-inch bit; average size is probably a 5-inch snaffle. As a general guide, the bit should be adjusted high enough in the mouth to produce one wrinkle at each side of the mouth.

At first, let the horse wear the bit in its stall for short periods of time to get used to it. At first, the horse will drool and chew the bit. Later, put the bit under the halter or cavesson and lunge the horse, attaching the lunge line to the halter—*not* to the bit. Later, the horse can be ground driven with the reins attached to the bit but be careful not to pull too hard or you will cause pain and toughen the horse's mouth, making it less sensitive and responsive to the bit.

At this point, the horse is ready to start wearing the saddle. First, let the horse look at it and touch it so that the animal won't spook when it is slowly placed on the horse's back. Tighten the girth enough that the saddle will not slip and frighten the horse and remove or tie the stirrups so they won't flop. Then lunge the horse while it's wearing the saddle. When the horse has worn the saddle and bridle several times and no longer seems uncomfortable, the animal is ready to be ridden for the first time.

The First Ride

When mounting an untrained horse for the first time, it's best to have two people present in case of accident, as well as for assistance in controlling the horse. One person should hold the horse from the ground as a lightweight rider slowly mounts, being careful not to startle or kick the horse. The rider should move quietly and not too fast, but act as though no problems are expected. If the rider is nervous, the horse will think there is something to fear. Few Arabians buck if they have been handled daily from birth and if the first mounting is accomplished while gently reassuring the horse.

Under saddle, the young horse will respond to the same verbal cues it learned on the ground. The pressure on the bit will be very similar to that in ground driving. In later lessons, the horse also will learn to respond to leg pressure and to shifts in the rider's weight.

If desired, the person on the ground can lead the horse at the walk when it is first ridden. Then, when the horse seems ready, it can be ridden without being led. Expect the horse to be clumsy when first ridden, for its balance is changed by the rider's weight.

The horse is not ready for advanced training yet. The best preparation is lots of wet saddle blankets. The young horse should be ridden frequently—if taken on trails, it should go with calm, older horses that are unlikely to become alarmed and frighten the inexperienced horse. Don't rush the horse's training by expecting it to learn more difficult things like collection, head carriage, or change of leads until the basics have been thoroughly mastered. Then, over a period of time, gradually add more complex maneuvers.

A talented amateur owner may be able to personally continue his or her horse's training. If you hope to compete at advanced levels, however, you and your horse might require professional training. If you plan to train your horse by yourself, seek assistance from books and magazine articles on the subject, and—whenever possible—from skilled horsepersons. Training clinics conducted by famous professional horse trainers can be a great help because they probably have dealt with all the problems that might occur and may have several solutions to each. However, be sure that your expert trainers are experienced in training *Arabian* horses.

Neal McKinstry on Ha Rossetta, U.S. National Champion Competitive Trail Horse. *Photo courtesy of McKinstry Arabians, Craig, Colo.*

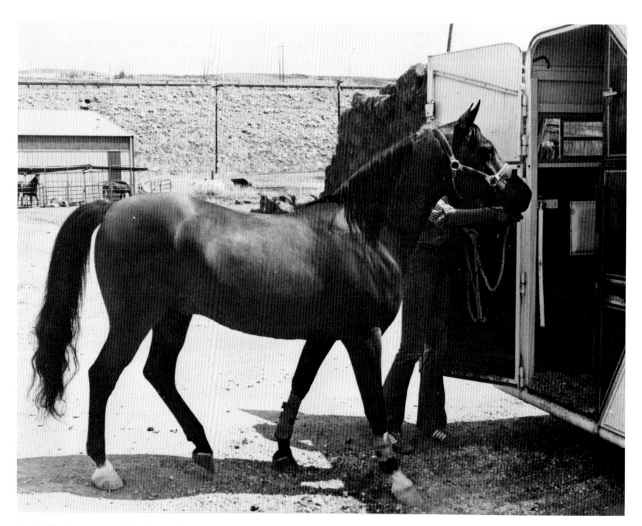

Lead the horse straight forward, toward the open trailer door. (Lead from the side, not from in front of the horse.)

29

TRAILERING

The primary considerations in trailering are the safety and comfort of the horses. This depends upon the equipment used and the method of loading and hauling horses in a horse trailer.

The best-selling style of horse trailer is the standard two-horse ("side-by-side") trailer. Seen less frequently are one-horse and two-horse "in line" trailers, where one horse rides directly behind another. Four-horse trailers, with the horses riding two abreast, also are popular. Stock trailers are long trailers used to haul various kinds of livestock. Although horses usually enter stock trailers readily because they are large and partly open, there is a danger of a horse accidentally getting a leg through the poles that make up part of the walls. Horse vans are special heavy-duty rigs used for transporting large numbers of horses; due to their expense, they are generally owned only by horse transportation companies and stables that transport large numbers of show or breeding horses.

Buyers of all styles of trailers should look for some of the same features. The trailer should be sturdy, safe, well-made, and comfortable for its occupants. It should have a strong floor, thick padding to protect the horses' bodies from injury, a smooth interior and exterior finish to prevent cuts, adequate lights inside the trailer, good ventilation, sturdy welded rings for tying horses inside the trailer, good

wiring and brakes. The trailer should pull easily and ride smoothly. Additional desirable but optional features include a tack storage and/or dressing area at the front of the trailer, an emergency escape door, removable center partitions (in trailers where horses are transported two abreast) and a loading ramp. Particularly if foals are transported, the trailer doors should close solidly all the way to the top of the trailer to prevent a loose horse from trying to jump out of the back of the trailer.

SAFETY OF THE EQUIPMENT

The construction and maintenance of the horse trailer and pulling vehicle are important to the safety of the horses being transported. The trailer must be sound and secure. Rotten floorboards can collapse, and trailer doors without good safety catches might accidentally come open during transit. There must be no sharp edges inside the trailer, and the interior should be well padded where the horse's chest, knees, and hocks may touch it.

Good six-ply tires contribute to safe hauling. A flat tire won't cause an accident if the trailer is properly made and balanced, but it can expose the horses (and people) to danger from traffic.

Check the welds on the trailer and towing vehicle to be sure there are no breaks and use a

The trailer doors close all the way to the ceiling, making it impossible for a frightened foal to try jumping over the doors. Pads at the sides and front of each trailer stall cushion the horses' chests and sides from possible injury.

An escape door at the front of a trailer allows one to enter or leave the trailer without opening the loading doors at the rear of the trailer.

Regardless of its size and style, the horse trailer should be safe and comfortable for its occupants. Large trailers like this one may be used to transport show and breeding horses.

For safety, the ball on the towing vehicle must be the proper size for the trailer hitch, and lights and brakes must be connected and tested before hauling.

strong safety chain to secure the trailer hitch. Be sure the towing ball is the proper size for the trailer hitch.

Before loading the horses, check the trailer brakes, turn indicators, and brake lights. Also inspect the towing vehicle to be sure it is in good condition.

COMFORT

Comfortable horses are under less stress during hauling and will travel better. If there is a space between the center divider and the floor of the trailer, horses will have more leg room and can brace their legs better when the trailer is moving. A center divider should always be used when hauling more than one horse, however, to prevent accidents or fighting.

The trailer must provide enough clearance for the body and legs of adult horses and the ceiling must be high enough to allow comfort and safety. A standard-size trailer is adequate for most Arabians.

Thick rubber floor mats provide the horses' hoofs with some traction, absorb concussion, help insulate from road friction heat, and protect the floor from wear and moisture. Covering the floor mats with shavings 1) encourages the horse to load because it resembles the animal's stall, 2) cushions the horse's legs, and 3) absorbs moisture. Many horses won't urinate in the trailer if urine splashes on their legs. Also, the shavings promote better traction because they absorb moisture.

The trailer should not be drafty but should have adjustments for ventilation. Be sure that the horses have enough fresh air in the trailer without being chilled.

Before loading, remove any old feed from the feeder (moldy feed may cause colic) and put good quality hay in it to encourage the horse to load and to occupy him during the trip. For easier loading, park the trailer on a level area. If the trailer has no loading ramp, parking it where its floor rests near the ground surface will make it easier for the horses to step up into the trailer. Horses also will be less reluctant to enter a trailer that they can see into, so try to park it where light illuminates the inside.

PREPARING THE HORSE

Use a sturdy, well-fitting halter and tie rope in the trailer. A cotton tie rope is best, because nylon will stretch slightly if the horse pulls against it. To prevent possible injury to the animal or damage to the tack, never leave a saddle or bridle on a horse being trailered.

If the weather is cool, blanket the horse. Protect its legs with bandages or shipping boots. If bandages are used, pad them for extra protection and be sure they aren't too tight or they will reduce circulation. Shipping boots give more padding but tend to slip. High boots covering the knees and hocks are better than those that only protect the cannon bones and pasterns. Get the horse used to shipping boots prior to hauling. Until accustomed to the boots, the horse will probably walk with short, high steps and may kick. If desired, a padded leather or plastic head bumper (helmet) may be used to protect the horse's head during trailing.

Before loading, clean the horse's hoofs with a hoof pick because mud or manure trapped inside the hoof can cause slipping in the trailer, and a stone in the hoof will make it impossible for the horse to put its full weight on that leg.

TRAINING THE HORSE TO LOAD

Don't wait until you're ready to haul the horse to teach it to enter a trailer. Allow plenty of time and patience for the lessons. Teaching the horse to enter a trailer by itself is safer and more practical than having it follow someone into the trailer. If one person trains a horse to load, only one handler will be required to load the horse in the future.

Holding the lead rope near the halter, put the end of the lead rope across the horse's neck. Standing beside the horse, use the whip to guide the animal into the trailer, repeatedly *tapping* the horse's hindquarters very gently to encourage it to step into the trailer. *Do not hit the horse* with the whip—just use a series of *light* taps.

If the horse seems frightened, stop tapping and speak soothingly to it. When not tapping, the whip should rest lightly on top of the horse's tail to discourage it from stepping backward.

If the horse angles its hindquarters away from you, straighten its body by gently tapping the hindquarters of its right (off) side with the whip. If the horse swings its hindquarters toward you, tap on its left (near) side until it steps away.

When the horse steps into the trailer for the first time, don't tie the animal. Leave it inside for a short time, speaking soothingly while the horse eats hay or grain from the feeder. Encourage the horse to stay in the trailer for a minute or two. If unloaded too soon, the horse may develop the habit of entering the trailer and then bolting backwards.

After staying in the trailer briefly, ask the horse to back out. (It should already know what "back" means, from ground training.) When the horse is unloaded, it's good to have an assistant beside the

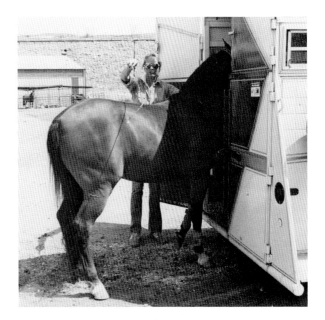

If the horse swings its hindquarters to either side, a gentle tap with the whip will straighten its body.

Hold the lead rope loosely, giving the horse enough slack in the lead line to enter the trailer. Rest the whip on the horse's hindquarters as it enters. If necessary, use a gentle tapping to encourage it to move forward.

The butt chain helps keep the horse in place until the door can be shut after the horse is loaded; it also keeps the horse from backing out the door as soon as it is opened for unloading.

trailer to catch the lead rope if the horse backs out quickly.

Pet and praise the unloaded horse. Then load it again. After the horse had been successfully loaded and unloaded a few times, it will know what to expect and not fear the trailer.

Refusal to Load

Sometimes a horse shows good sense by refusing to enter a trailer. Does the trailer rattle or shift as the horse steps into it? Is it big enough? Are the floorboards weak? If your trailer is safe and sturdy, consider the horse's background. Has it had a trailer accident or an uncomfortable trip?

Never punish a horse that is afraid or does not understand what is expected. However, if an experienced traveller throws a tantrum and refuses to load, use the whip as punishment to make the inside of the trailer more attractive than the outside. When

the horse steps into it, stop the punishment. A horse that *consistently* refuses to load may require professional retraining.

Tying in the Trailer

Fasten the butt chain and shut the trailer door before you tie the horse. If the door is still open when the horse is tied, it may try to back out. The horse is less likely to pull back if the butt chain is fastened and the door is closed.

Most horses travel better if tied. Tie the rope high—no lower than the horse's eye level. If tied too low, the horse may feel trapped and pull back. There is also more danger of getting a foreleg over a low tie rope.

About sixteen inches of rope should exist between the halter and the trailer's tie ring. Leave enough slack in the rope so that the horse can move its head but not so much that it can get its head into the other side of the trailer or get a leg over the rope.

The trailer is no place to teach a young horse to stand tied. Train the young horse to stand tied *before it* is transported for the first time (see Chapter 28).

Be sure that the rope can be reached without having to enter the trailer and always use a safety release knot or a rope with a panic snap for a quick release in an emergency. It's a good idea to keep a sharp knife handy, in case you can't get the rope untied fast enough in an emergency.

"Trailer Fighters" and Nervous Haulers

Horses that scramble and kick in the trailer are restless, cramped, and off-balance. If only one horse is being hauled, removing the center divider will give the horse more leg room and may reduce the problem. It's preferable to haul problem horses by themselves, in most cases, so they don't frighten, injure, or teach bad habits to other horses. Some horses may create less commotion if they have company, however. Some horses also will ride more quietly on one side of the trailer than on the other side.

A nervous horse may be upset by the movement of the trailer or by being confined in a small area. Wait until just before departure to load the nervous horse. When the trailer is moving, the horse will have to concentrate more on keeping its balance and probably will be more upset in a still trailer.

If the horse is extremely nervous, a mild tranquilizer may be necessary. (Beware of tranquilizing horses en route to a show, however.) The tranquilizer may be a forbidden drug (see Chapter 33.) Tranquilize immediately before loading. If you tranquilize too far in advance, the horse may become so relaxed that it is difficult to load. Some horses become better travellers with experience. Discontinue the tranquilizer if the horse becomes a better traveller; use it only when necessary.

Nervous horses sometimes sway in the trailer. Swaying may indicate lack of leg room or result from watching passing scenery. Closing or covering the trailer windows may be necessary to keep the horse from swaying. Swaying may promote motion sickness, which is manifested in horses as colic.

PULLING THE HORSE TRAILER

Remember that your towing vehicle rides much more smoothly than the horse trailer. Don't drive fast, especially on bumpy roads, and don't make frequent lane changes or fast turns. Tap your brakes gently once or twice before stopping to teach the horses to brace themselves for the stop. Always allow extra distance between vehicles—it takes a towing vehicle longer to stop.

Hauling Tips

Try to make the horses as comfortable as possible. On a long trip, stop every six hours to unload and walk the horses. Give them water and a chance to urinate.

When hauling, feed often and lightly. Don't feed grain (or greatly reduce the amount of grain, if fed). Colic can result from stress and lack of exercise during hauling.

If the horse doesn't drink a normal amount of water while travelling, reduce the amount of hay. Too much dry feed, without sufficient water, can cause impaction. Some people feed bran as a mild laxative and to increase bulk when the horses are being hauled.

A horse trailer can get hot inside even on a cool day. Be sure adequate ventilation exists and don't park in direct sun. If the weather is cold, blanket the horses; if it warms up, remove the blankets so that the horses don't sweat.

Hauling Mares and Foals

Before loading a mare and foal in a two-horse trailer, remove the center divider to create one large stall and bed the floor deeply with wood shavings.

Put the foal in first. If the foal is small, pick it up and lift it inside the trailer. If it's too big for that, put its front feet in the trailer and use a come-along to encourage its hind feet to follow (see Chapter 28).

When the foal is loaded, load and tie the mare. Be sure she is tied high enough that the foal cannot get tangled in the tie rope. Do *not* tie the foal.

A frightened foal may try to jump over a trailer door that is open at the top. If the doors are open at the top, block them with a large piece of plywood. The doors should be *solid* all the way to the ceiling.

Take extra time and care when hauling a mare and foal. Slow gradually and make slow turns to avoid throwing the foal down or causing the mare to step on it. Hauled carefully, mares seldom step on their foals in the trailer even when the foals lie down to nap.

If the foal is under a month old, make regular stops every two or three hours to let it nurse. Nursing in a moving trailer is dangerous and difficult.

UNLOADING

Before unloading the horse 1) untie the horse and throw the lead rope over its neck; 2) remove the butt chain; and 3) open the back door. (When the back door opens, many horses start to back. If still tied, they can hurt themselves.) When the door is open, ask the horse to back. Catch the lead rope when it backs out of the trailer.

AFTER THE TRIP

After unloading, walk the horse to relax it, stimulate circulation, and give it a chance to see its new surroundings. Then put the horse in a clean, comfortable place to rest. Offer fresh water, hay, and possibly a bran mash (see Chapter 14). Check the stabled horse periodically to be sure it shows no signs of colic.

After the horse has been cared for, remove soiled shavings and manure from the trailer to avoid weakening the floor. Wash out the interior, if needed, and allow it to dry before reuse.

*Sakr, U.S. National Champion Native Costume horse in 1976, 1977, 1978 and 1979. Owned by Gleannloch Farms, *Sakr also won 35 Prk Horse Championships, with a career total of 14 Top Ten and one Reserve National Championship in both performance and halter classes. Tom McNair, up. *Sparagowski photo courtesy of Tom McNair International*

30

SHOWING THE ARAB

In the United States, all-Arabian horse shows are conducted by the International Arabian Horse Association (IAHA) under the rules of the American Horse Shows Association (AHSA) for the Arabian horse division. Rule changes are introduced at the IAHA Annual Convention and, if approved by delegates from IAHA's member Arabian horse clubs, must be approved by AHSA before going into effect. In Canada, Arabian shows are held under Canadian Equestrian Federation (CEF) rules.

All-Arabian horse shows generally are conducted by Arabian horse clubs affiliated with IAHA. Both IAHA and AHSA must approve show dates and judges selected.

The sponsoring club appoints a horse show committee to plan and run its show. The committee includes, but is not limited to, a manager, secretary and treasurer. The show committee selects and hires an announcer; ring master (who assists the judge); AHSA steward (who ensures that the show is being conducted according to the AHSA rules); and the judge or judges. Conducting a horse show requires the efforts of many people; some are paid and some volunteer their labor. Typically, shows require the services of a barn manager; photographer; farrier; veterinarian(s); emergency medical technicians, who stand by in case of accident; course designers, who

plan Trail and jumping courses; trophy presenters; office workers; and a gate crew that operates the arena gate and keeps track of which horses are shown in each class. Arabian horse shows range from one to seven days in length; big shows, which last longer because they have numerous classes and entries, require large horse show staffs.

SHOW RATINGS

All-Arabian horse shows held in the United States are rated "A," "B" or "C" by the American Horse Shows Association. These ratings are based on the number of classes and total prize money offered in the various divisions of a show. Ratings are determined as follows:

Classes for	Minimum No. of Classes	Minimum Amt. of Prize Money	Rating
Arabians	7	$750.00	A
Arabians	4	$250.00	B
Half-Arabians	5	$500.00	A
Half-Arabians	3	$200.00	B
Jr. Exhibitors	3	$300.00	A
Jr. Exhibitors	3	$200.00	B

A "C" rating is given if the above minimum requirements are not met. (Some types of classes always are rated as "C" regardless of the number of classes and prize money awarded; see the *AHSA Rule Book* for more information.) One show may have several ratings, qualifying as a Class "A" show for purebred Arabian classes and as a Class "B" for Half-Arabian classes, for example.

AHSA HIGH-POINT AWARDS

The system of show ratings was designed to make competition for American Horse Shows Association awards more equitable. Horses competing for AHSA Horse of the Year awards earn points based on their show placings, with the number of points determined by each show's rating and the ribbon won. For example, wins in Class "A" events earn more points than placings in Class "B" events. Each horse placing in a class receives points, with the winner earning the most points, the second place horse earning more than the third place horse, etc.

Both Zone (area) and National Horse of the Year awards are given by breed and show division (e.g., Arabian English Pleasure Horse of the Year, etc.), with horses competing only against members of their own breed. Arabian and Half-Arabian horses earning the most points in each division receive awards. In addition, the overall high-point Arabian horse wins the prestigious King Saoud trophy.

To compete for the AHSA show awards, a horse must be enrolled by its AHSA-member owner and a recording fee must be paid to AHSA.

IAHA ACHIEVEMENT AWARDS

To earn points toward the Achievement Awards given by the International Arabian Horse Association, a horse must be enrolled by its owner in the awards program. A registration fee and annual fees are paid to IAHA by owners of enrolled horses.

Achievement Awards are given to purebred and Half-Arabian horses that attain specified numbers of points based on show placings and/or placings in Arabian races, competitive trail rides, or endurance rides. Purebreds earn points for Class "A" shows only; Half-Arabians earn points for placings

at Class "A" and Class "B" shows. (In Canada, points are awarded for CEF-recognized shows.) Details of the complex point system are explained in the *IAHA Handbook*.

Plus marks following the name of an Arabian or Half-Arabian indicate the highest IAHA achievement award it has won.[1] In ascending order, the awards are: Legion of Honor (+), Legion of Supreme Honor (+/), Legion of Merit (+ +), and Legion of Supreme Merit (+ + +). (The Legion of Supreme Honor is indicated by a plus and a slash because it was initiated later than the other awards.) Legion of Honor awards can be earned in either halter classes or performance events (performance classes at shows, races, or competitive or endurance rides) or a combination of halter and performance competition. Legion of Merit awards require points in both halter and performance (at shows, races, or rides).

To qualify for the Legion of Honor award, 75 points earned in any approved event(s) are required. To win the Legion of Supreme Honor award, a horse must earn 150 points in any approved event(s). To win the Legion of Merit award, 75 points are required (at least 30 points must be won in halter classes and at least 30 points in other events). The Legion of Supreme Merit, the highest award, requires at least 150 points (75 points earned in halter and 75 points earned in other approved events). For each award, the horse must have earned its points in at least four events (shows, races, or rides). In judged events, the horse must have competed under at least four judges, with no more than 30 points earned under any judge.

MAJOR ARABIAN HORSE SHOWS

In America and Canada, all-Arabian horse shows consist of individual rated shows, Regional Championship shows (held annually in each IAHA Region), the Canadian National Championship Show, and the U.S. National Championship Show ("the Nationals"). The "Triple Crown" of the Ara-

---

[1]*Many of the horses pictured in this book are Achievement Award winners. However, the plus marks were omitted because some of the horses undoubtedly will acquire higher awards during the life of this book, and the published symbols would then be incorrect.*

bian show season has been said to consist of the large Scottsdale (Arizona) show and the Canadian and U.S. National Championship shows. Of these, the most prestigious is the U.S. National Show.

The Nationals are held in the fall of each year, at the end of the show season. The location alternates between the eastern and western states (currently, the show is held in Louisville, Kentucky and Albuquerque, New Mexico in alternate years).

three judges' lists) become the Top Ten award winners. From these, the U.S. National Champion and the U.S. National Reserve Champion are chosen. To win the National Championship, a horse must be placed first by at least one judge. If two judges select the same horse, it becomes the Champion. If each judge chooses a different first place horse, the horse with the most points (based on all three lists) becomes National Champion. The Reserve

The "Triple Crown" of Arabian shows includes the historic Scottsdale show in Arizona. The show is now as large as the Nationals, attracting over 1,500 entries. This is the 1960 Scottsdale show.

J.F. Malony photo, courtesy of Arabian Horse Owners Foundation

About 1,500 horses are shown each year at the Nationals; this number is about 25 percent of the Arabian, Half-Arabian and Anglo-Arabians that qualify for the competition. To be shown at the U.S. or Canadian National Championships, horses first must qualify by earning points at earlier shows; the number of points varies according to the type of class. Details of the point system are covered in the *IAHA Handbook*. National Champions in performance classes achieve lifetime eligibility to be shown at the Nationals; other horses must qualify for each National show.

At present, three judges place the U.S. National Championship halter and performance classes. In the semi-finals portion of each class, the judges rank their choices from first to tenth places. The horse in first place on each list receives ten points, the second place horse gets nine points, etc. The ten horses with the most cumulative points (from all

Championship is awarded to the high-point horse among the remaining horses that were first and second on the judges' lists.

ARABIAN HORSE SHOW JUDGES

In America, any member of the American Horse Shows Association can apply to become a judge for Arabian horse shows. In Canada, judges are licensed by the Canadian Equestrian Federation (CEF).

Judges are first classed as recorded ("small r") judges. At this lower level, they may judge Class "C" or local member shows, with the exception of medal equitation classes. With special AHSA approval, they can judge Class "A" or "B" shows. "Big R" judges officiate at the larger, more prestigious Arabian shows.

In 1986, IAHA expanded its training and evaluation program for horse show judges to three parts:

1) an optional three-day training program for those who want to learn to judge Arabians and Half-Arabians; 2) a three-day Judges Evaluation Program to test judges and judge applicants; and 3) a one-day Judges Seminar to update Big R judges on rule changes and judging procedures.

All AHSA-licensed judges must attend a judges' clinic once every three years. Small r judges can meet this requirement by attending the Judges Evaluation Program once every three years. Starting in 1988, Big R judges can meet the requirement by attending a Judges Seminar once every three years. (However, *all* judges presently licensed must attend one Judges Evaluation Program between 1985 and 1987.)

All Class "A" (and CEF-approved) Arabian horse shows must choose their judges from the recommended Arabian horse judges listed in the annual *IAHA Handbook*. The *Handbook* also shows the number of "Exhibitor Report Cards on Judges" completed by exhibitors to rate each judge's performance at Class "A" or CEF shows the previous year, the number of shows judged, and the average score given the judge by exhibitors showing under him or her.

Book each year for rule changes. (Proposed changes appear in AHSA's *Horse Show* magazine.)

The *IAHA Handbook* also contains rules and amendments to the *AHSA Rule Book* for some classes. It is published annually and sent free to members of the International Arabian Horse Association. Both the *Handbook* and the *Golden Book of Arabian Horse Showing*, also published by IAHA, are recommended reading for exhibitors and show officials. *The Golden Book* is especially helpful to new exhibitors (see Bibliography).

ELIGIBILITY FOR ARABIAN HORSE SHOWS

Classes at Arabian horse shows are open to all horses and exhibitors meeting show and class requirements. Membership in the International Arabian Horse Association is required to show at all IAHA-approved shows. If an owner or exhibitor does not belong to the American Horse Shows Association, a small extra charge is assessed at the show.

To be shown in Arabian or Half Arabian classes at approved shows, Arabians must be registered by

Stable areas at Arabian horse shows are beautified by attractive stall drapes, temporary landscaping, and displays of photographs, trophies, and ribbons. The difference is apparent in this "before and after" shot at the Scottsdale Show.

HORSE SHOW RULES

In the United States, all-Arabian horse shows (and Arabian and Half-Arabian classes at other AHSA-approved shows) are regulated by the *AHSA Rule Book*. Exhibitors should study the *AHSA Rule*

the Arabian Horse Registry of America, Inc. and/or the Canadian Arabian Horse Registry; Half-Arabians and Anglo-Arabians (which are shown in Half-Arabian classes) must be registered by IAHA. To prove a horse's eligibility to be shown, entry forms require the horse's registered name and

If horses become bunched up along the rail, a rider can make a small circle toward the center of the arena and return to a less crowded place on the rail. (Equitation riders are sometimes marked down for this maneuver, however, so should attempt to avoid crowding by carefully regulating the gaits of their mounts.)

number, and its sire and dam. (If a horse is less than one year old, its registration need not be complete; however, it must qualify for registration and application for registration must have been made before the show.)

Unless the show's premium list states otherwise, purebred Arabian stallions may be shown in all but Showmanship classes (halter classes in which the junior exhibitors are judged rather than their horses), and there are no age or sex restrictions as to who may show stallions. However, Half-Arabian stallions cannot be shown at Arabian shows after they become two years old.

CLASS RESTRICTIONS

Some horse show classes are open to both professionals and amateurs, while others are limited to professionals or to amateur owners ("AOTR" or "Amateur Owner to Ride" classes). Some classes are restricted to horses of specific age or sex, and others are limited to exhibitors of specified age or sex. The premium list for each show gives class restrictions so that an exhibitor can determine his or her eligibility for each class.

"Open" classes for purebred Arabians are open to horses of all ages and sexes, and there are no qualifications for the exhibitors. Because Half-Arabian stallions cannot be shown at Arabian

shows, Half-Arabian open classes are just for mares and geldings.

"Maiden" performance classes are limited to horses that have not yet won a class at an accredited show in a particular division (e.g., "English Pleasure, Maiden" is for horses that have never won an English Pleasure class at an accredited show). When a horse wins its first class, it is said to have "broken its maiden." "Novice" performance classes are restricted to horses that have not won three classes in the particular division in which they are shown. A "limit" class restricts entries to horses that have not won six classes in that division (e.g., a horse that has won six or more blue ribbons in Western Pleasure cannot be shown in a limit Western Pleasure class).

A "Junior" exhibitor is one who has not reached his or her eighteenth birthday. Generally, "amateur" classes are open to exhibitors eighteen or older who are not paid to train or show horses or to give lessons. (It is legal for an amateur exhibitor to breed, sell, or board horses.) Qualified amateurs must have a valid AHSA amateur card in their possession (or have applied for the card with the horse show secretary at least one hour before showing). Refer to the *AHSA Rule Book*, Rule IX to determine whether you qualify as a professional or amateur.

CHAMPIONSHIP CLASSES

To compete in a championship halter class at an Arabian horse show, a horse must have won first or second place in a previous qualifying halter class at the same show and be at least two years old. Only class winners are considered for the Championship. Then the horse that placed second to the Champion in its qualifying class competes with the remaining first-place winners for the title of Reserve Champion. Separate Junior Championships also are held, with first- and second-place fillies and colts competing. If a Grand Championship is awarded for the show (such as the "Supreme Championship" held in recent years at some large shows), the Junior and Senior halter champions compete for the title.

To compete in a championship performance class, most class specifications state that the horse must have been entered, shown and judged in a previous class in the same division at the show. For example, to compete for the English Pleasure Championship, a horse must have been shown in a previous English Pleasure class at the same show. However, some shows require horses to have won a ribbon in a prior class in the same division before they qualify for the championship class.

ARABIAN AND HALF-ARABIAN SHOW CLASSES

Arabians and Half-Arabians (which includes registered Anglo-Arabians) are shown in halter and performance classes. Halter horses, which are judged mostly on type and conformation, are not ridden; horses in performance classes are judged mostly on how well they perform specific maneuvers under saddle or in harness.

Most new exhibitors first show in halter classes because they require less training and equipment. Also, young horses can be shown at halter before they are ready to compete in performance classes. Generally, if a horse is being campaigned at the national level in halter classes, it is not also shown in performance classes. Performance horses may develop different muscling than is desired in halter horses, and sometimes become slightly lower in the back from being ridden. They also are more likely to become injured or blemished. After halter careers, Arabians often go on to performance competition. (See also Chapter 33.)

PERFORMANCE CLASSES

Performance classes may be divided into two general categories: English and Western. Although some Arabians can be shown in either Western or English classes with equal success, most are better suited to one style or the other. The conformation, action, and attitude of each horse determine where its talents lie.

The horse's neck placement and shape, along with its resultant head carriage, predisposes it to either Western or English classes. A horse with a low-set neck is best suited for Western classes, where lower head carriage is needed. A longer, high-set neck with a thin throatlatch frees the horse's forelegs for higher action at the trot and allows the horse to arch its neck and bring its head toward its chest during collection, and is an important attribute in an English horse.

At large shows, Champions and Reserve Champions often remain in the arena as the rest of the awards are given and the other exhibitors are excused. Then, the winners make a "victory pass" to receive the crowd's applause.

A horse with a low trot is more likely to be a good western horse than a horse with high knee and hock action. A smooth trot is needed to help the western rider sit the jog trot comfortably, and a slower trot is more important in a western horse. The English horse should be lively, moving forward with eagerness, while the western horse should appear slower and more relaxed.

Arabian hunters, jumpers, and dressage mounts do not require as much brilliance and high action as horses shown in English Pleasure, Park, and Driving classes. They may have lower action and lower-set necks, so long as they have a smooth, ground-covering stride.

Although the gaits required for English and western classes are basically the same, the terminology is different. The slow gait for both English and western classes is the walk. English classes call for a trot while western classes specify a "jog" (a slower, less elevated trot). English classes require a canter, while western classes call it a "lope." Advanced English and western classes require a hand gallop, which is a faster canter that results from a lengthened stride.

APPOINTMENTS

Show tack and attire are together referred to as *appointments*. Appointments vary according to the show division and class specifications. The degree to which appointments are to influence a judge's selections for each class is specified by the *AHSA Rule Book* and the show's premium list.

English Appointments

At Arabian horse shows, cutback (saddle seat) English saddles are used in English Pleasure, Park, and Saddle Seat Equitation classes. Jumping (forward seat) saddles are used in Hunter and Jumper classes, and dressage saddles are used for Dressage. The cutback saddle places the rider toward the horse's loins, the jumping saddle puts the rider's weight forward over the horse's withers, and the dressage saddle places the rider about mid-way between the other two styles of English saddles.

The English Pleasure horse usually is shown in a double bridle, with four reins and two bits: a bradoon (narrow snaffle) and a curb (a bit with shanks and a leather strap or flat chain under the horse's chin). The rider wears a saddle suit consisting of a long jacket, vest, Kentucky-style jodphurs, and jodphur boots. A tailored shirt, tie, gloves, conservative accessories, and derby or soft English hat complete the attire. Conservative saddle seat attire is used for Saddle Seat Equitation classes.

Most Park Horses also are shown in a double bridle. The rider wears saddle seat attire or a more formal tuxedo jacket, matching pants, and top hat. Park Horse attire is more formal than clothing worn in English Pleasure classes, although it is similar in style.

Jumpers and hunters usually are shown in snaffle or pelham bits, with riders wearing hunt attire (jacket, tailored shirt, breeches, hunt boots, and derby or cap). Dressage horses are shown in a snaffle bit or, at advanced levels, in a full (double) bridle. Formal dressage attire consists of a long swallow-tail coat, shirt, breeches, high boots, unroweled spurs, gloves, and top hat.

In Arabian harness classes, drivers generally wear saddle seat attire for Pleasure Driving classes and Park Horse attire for Formal Driving. However, women sometimes wear long skirts instead. Roadster classes require racing silks (a jacket and matching cap) and the horse pulls a two-wheeled racing cart ("bike"). The Pleasure Driving horse pulls a light two- or four-wheel vehicle; its harness includes an overcheck (with separate overcheck bit), and/or side-check rein to hold the horse's head in place, a bridle

with blinkers, and a snaffle bit. Formal Driving horses are shown in the same equipment but are shown only to a four-wheel show vehicle.

Spurs and whips are regulated by class specifications. In most Arabian classes, they are optional.

All show attire should be clean and tailored. English clothing should be conservative in cut and color. As well as meeting class specifications, colors of clothing and tack should complement both rider and horse.

Western Appointments

Western Pleasure horses are shown in a standard stock saddle without tapaderos (stirrup covers). The show saddle usually has two cinches (girths). A western bridle without a noseband and any standard western bit may be used. Unless prohibited by the premium list, a hackamore bosal (leather noseband) or a snaffle bit may be used instead of a curb bit on horses five and under. Arabian show saddles are lightweight and most feature silver decoration on the saddle and matching bridle and reins. A matching breast collar also may be used. Tack for other western classes might not be as ornate as the silver-trimmed equipment usually seen in Western Pleasure classes for Arabian and Half-Arabian horses.

Western clothing consists of long-sleeved western shirts, western pants, chaps (often required by the premium list), western hat and boots. A western vest or jacket is optional, and a pullover sweater sometimes is worn over the western shirt. Accessories such as a western belt and neck scarf or tie may complement the rider's clothing.

All show attire should be clean and tailored; western attire is less conservative in style and color than English riding clothes. As well as meeting class specifications, tack and clothing colors should complement both horse and rider.

RING PROCEDURE FOR PERFORMANCE CLASSES

In most performance classes (such as English Pleasure, Western Pleasure, Hunter Pleasure, Native Costume, Park Horse, Ladies Side Saddle, Combination, Versatility, and Driving classes), horses perform simultaneously. However, in some classes (including

Dressage, Trail, Stock Horse, and jumping events) the entries are shown individually. In classes such as Equitation, entries perform both as a group and individually.

Ring procedure is similar for the various group performance classes. The class enters the arena and the entries circle the ring in single file at a specified gait. It is occasionally necessary for a horse to pass a slower horse on the rail or, to keep sufficient distance between horses, to make a smaller circle toward the center of the arena before returning to the rail; this is done at the rider's discretion but without breaking (changing) gait. The horses are shown at each gait required in the class specifications, with gait changes and reversals of direction requested by the announcer. After the entries have been judged in action on the rail, they are asked to line up in the center of the arena, usually facing the audience. At this time, the judge may walk behind or around the horses, examine appointments, check the exhibitor's numbers, and ask the riders to back their horses. (Backing up is a slightly advanced maneuver and not required in all classes.)

CLASS SPECIFICATIONS

Detailed specifications for appointments, gaits, and judging for each class are given in the *AHSA Rule Book*. A shorter description appears in the show premium (prize) list; a brief description also may appear in the horse show program sold to spectators.

There often are several similar classes in each division (e.g., English Pleasure, Open; English Pleasure, AOTR; and English Pleasure, Maiden classes are in the same division). Although similar, each class within a division may not be judged by exactly the same standards. The factors on which each horse is to be judged are listed in the specifications for each class in the *AHSA Rule Book*. The *Rule Book* lists them in the order of importance; the item that is to receive the most emphasis is listed first, the second most important factor is listed next, etc. Generally, there is more emphasis on the horse's manners (behavior) in amateur owner classes than in open or championship classes of the same type.

English Pleasure

The English Pleasure horse is judged at the walk, trot, strong trot (which is faster and has a longer

In many classes, horses are asked to back up during the line-up. When asked, the horse should back willingly in a straight line, without opening its mouth or throwing its head upward.

stride than the normal trot), canter (which must be a three-beat gait), and hand gallop (which has a longer stride than the canter). Open and championship classes require all five gaits; Amateur, Owner, Ladies, Gentlemen, Junior Exhibitor classes, classes for horses four years old or less, and Hack Horses are judged at the walk, trot, and canter.

English Pleasure horses are judged on manners, performance, quality and conformation; championship classes also consider the horse's presence (boldness or bearing). The English Pleasure horse's gaits are moderately collected, with the rider keeping light contact with all reins at all gaits. The English Pleasure horse's gaits must be smooth and balanced. Above all, the horse must give the impression that it is a pleasure to ride.

Hunter Pleasure

The Arabian Hunter Pleasure class was introduced in 1985. Like all pleasure horses, the hunter should appear to give an enjoyable ride. Hunters are shown on the rail at the walk, trot, canter and hand gallop. They must back readily, stand quietly, and are judged on manners, performance, suitability as hunters, quality, and conformation.

The hunter's neck should be carried lower and more relaxed than that of the English Pleasure horse, with less bend at the poll. A ground-covering stride should be shown at all gaits, including the walk. The trot should be balanced, free, and lower than that of the English Pleasure horse. The canter should be smooth and relaxed; the hand gallop should show a lengthened stride while remaining controlled and mannerly.

Park Horse

Park Horses are judged at a walk, trot and canter. They are judged on brilliant performance, presence, quality, manners, and conformation; an additional consideration in classes for Amateurs, Owners, Ladies, Gentlemen, and Junior Exhibitors is how well the horse is suited to the rider.

As the number of Arabian horses has grown, the shows have become larger and more competitive. Here, Misdee Chauncey shows *Naborr in an English Pleasure class. Today, she shows descendants of the famous Polish Stallion.
Johnny Johnston photo courtesy of Tom Chauncey Arabians, Scottsdale, Ariz.

Park Horses are judged with a much greater emphasis on high action and presence than on manners and smooth performance. All gaits should be brisk and animated, although the walk and canter are collected. The Park Horse should display more elevation of the forelegs than the English Pleasure Horse. Its trot should be *naturally* high (not result from the use of illegal training devices). The Park trot is balanced, cadensed, and characterized by good hock and shoulder action, with strong impulsion from driving hind legs. The action of the forelegs is to be "light and airy."

Driving (Pleasure and Formal)

Pleasure Driving horses are judged at the walk, normal trot and strong (extended) trot, with extreme speed penalized. They must stand quietly and back readily when asked to do so. The gaits of the Pleasure Driving horse should be like those of the English Pleasure horse. Each horse is judged on manners, quality and performance.

Formal Driving horses are judged at the walk and trot; they must stand quietly and back readily. Formal Driving gaits are like those of the Park Horse. Each horse is judged on performance, presence, manners, quality, and conformation.

Roadsters are shown at a jog trot, the fast road gait, and at speed. The class is modeled after those for Standardbreds. Entries are judged on performance, speed, quality and manners; in Amateur and Junior Exhibitor classes, the greatest emphasis is placed on manners.

Ladies Side Saddle

Each horse is shown wearing an English, western, or period (antique style) side saddle with appropriate bridle and bit. The rider wears a long skirt and other attire in keeping with the style of tack. When there are sufficient entries to do so, the class is divided into western and English sections; if the class is not divided, all styles are to receive equal consideration from the judge.

Side saddle horses are shown at the walk, normal trot (or jog trot, if shown western), and canter (or lope, if western). The class is judged on manners, performance, quality and conformation (85 percent), and appropriate attire (15 percent).

Combination (Formal and Informal)

The Formal Combination horse is shown and judged as both a Formal Driving horse in harness and as a Park Horse under saddle. The show's premium list specifies whether the rider and driver must be the same person.

The Informal Combination horse is shown and judged as a Pleasure Driving horse in harness and as an English Pleasure horse under saddle. The premium list specifies whether the rider and driver must be the same person.

have a long, ground-covering stride. The jog should be slow but relaxed. The lope should be slow and smooth; the hand gallop should display a longer stride than the lope but not be too fast.

Western Pleasure horses are shown on a light rein at all gaits and are judged on manners, performance, substance, conformation, and (in championship classes) presence. Manners are the most important consideration in judging Western Pleasure horses, except in Junior Arabian Horse classes (for horses four years old and younger), where substance receives the greatest emphasis.

Trail Horse

The (western) Trail Horse is ridden over and through obstacles (gates, simulated water, bridges, etc.), performing at a walk, jog and lope. The horse

Western Pleasure class.

Versatility (Versatile Arabian Horse)

The Versatility class is a combination of three events, two of which must be chosen from the following: Pleasure Driving, English Pleasure, and Western Pleasure. The third performance section is chosen by the show management. The premium list specifies the events included and whether the same person must show the horse in all three sections of the class.

Western Pleasure

Horses are judged at the walk, jog trot, lope, and hand gallop. The walk should be fairly fast and

is ridden on a fairly loose rein and judged on its performance and way of going, with emphasis on manners (70 percent); conformation (20 percent), and appointments (10 percent).

Stock Horse

The (western) Stock Horse is ridden on a light rein at the walk, jog trot and lope and must perform a prescribed pattern of movements including fast turns and sliding stops to demonstrate the horse's agility for working cattle. The horse is judged on "rein" (the horse's lightness and quickness of response to the rider's cues), conformation, manners, and appointments.

Dressage

Dressage horses perform tests (patterns) at various levels of difficulty to demonstrate their obedience, suppleness, and degree of training. Each horse is judged individually, receiving a point score based on how well each prescribed movement is done.

Cutting

The (western) cutting horse is worked in a reining pattern and must "cut" a cow, preventing it from returning to the herd. The cutting horse is judged on its agility and ability to control the movement of the cow. The horse receives a point score for: cow work (50 points possible), reining (50 points), conformation (20 points), manners (20 points), and appointments (10 points).

Working Cow Horse

Each horse works one cow alone in the arena, first keeping the animal at one end of the arena and then letting it run down the side. The cow must be turned in each direction against the fence and then taken to the center of the arena and circled in each direction, the horse moving around the cow. The horse is scored 60 to 80 points, based on how well it controls the movement of the cow.

Jumping Classes (Jumper and Hunter)

Jumpers are allowed a specific amount of time to cover a course of at least eight 3-foot 3-inch to 3-foot 6-inch jumps with spreads of 3-foot to 5-foot and are scored on the number of faults (striking a fence as it is jumped); a penalty is given if they exceed the allotted time to cover the course. The horses' jumping form and soundness are not emphasized; jumpers are judged on their ability to clear the fences in a limited time.

Hunters are judged on their way of going, manners and jumping style. They require an even hunting pace, moving freely and smoothly with a long stride. Hunters are shown either "under saddle" (at a walk, trot, canter and gallop, without jumping) or "over fences." A hunter course consists of at least

El Khyam, U.S. National Champion Arabian Jumper. "Khy" has taken several young riders and his owner, Judi Hook, to Nationals wins besides impressive wins in open horse shows. A versatile performer, he also won honors in classes including English Pleasure and Costume.

Photo courtesy Judi Hook

eight fences of 3-feet to 3-feet 3-inches high and up to a 3-foot spread (width).

Equitation Classes

Equitation classes are limited to junior riders and are identified by style of riding: Saddle Seat, Hunter Seat, and Stock Seat (western). Equitation riders are first judged on the rail and then perform specified individual patterns to demonstrate their riding skills. Riders are judged on seat (body and leg position), hands (how the reins are held and used), the horse's performance, appointments, and how well the horse is suited to the rider.

Native Costume

The Native Costume class is the most distinctively Arabian class, featuring a highly glamourized version of Bedouin tack and clothing. Whereas Bedouin tack and attire were plain and practical, the Native Costume horse and rider are adorned by colorful fabrics, glitter and tassels.

Most riders' costumes are based upon the general style of Bedouin clothing, including a shirt, full pantaloons, wide cumberbund, *aba* (loose robe or jacket), sandals or slippers, and *kiffieyah* (a square cloth worn as a head covering) held on by an *ighal* (cord headband). Most female riders use a slightly modified version of this male Bedouin attire, although a few women choose a "belly dancer" style. (Actual clothing of Bedouin women consisted of heavy veils and long skirts, which would be difficult to ride in; although they cared for the horses, Bedouin women seldom rode.) Professional Native Costume designers advertise in Arabian horse publications or have booths at major shows. *Arabian Costumes*, by Lois Ann Kroll (available from the International Arabian Horse Association) shows how Native Costumes and tack are made.

Despite the elaborate costuming, the Native Costume class is judged like an English Pleasure class without a trot: horses perform at the walk, canter and hand gallop. Excessive speed is penalized. Each horse must stand quietly and back readily; the horse's performance and manners are of greatest importance (75 percent), while appointments receive the balance of the judging emphasis (25 percent).

COSTS OF SHOWING

Showing at Class "A" shows is expensive. Entry fees average about $10.00 to $15.00 for regular classes and $25.00 for championship classes. Stalls and tack rooms (stalls used to store tack and feed) cost about $40.00 each. At larger, more prestigious shows, the costs may be higher.

In addition, an exhibitor has the expense of transporting the horse(s) to and from each show, plus the cost of meals and lodging during the show. A few years ago, an exhibitor who successfully trained and showed his own Arabians estimated that each horse show ribbon "cost" him about $100.00 in expenses. Today, that figure is even higher and there is no guarantee of taking ribbons home.

Additional expenses are incurred by owners who hire professionals to train and show their horses. Public trainers charge by the month to train and board show horses. Extra charges are made each time a horse is transported and shown. Large breeding farms usually have their own ("private") trainers.

All-Breed (Open) Shows

Costs of showing horses at shows open to all breeds often are lower than the costs of showing at all-Arabian shows. Small open shows also may have a more relaxed, enjoyable atmosphere than do large, competitive Arabian shows. They also offer an inexpensive way for an owner-exhibitor to practice his or her showing skills or to accustom an inexperienced horse to the show ring.

Open shows also provide an opportunity to introduce Arabian horses to people who are unfamiliar with the breed. When Arabians perform well in all-breed shows, they earn the respect of other exhibitors and help overcome misconceptions about the Arabian breed. Also, sale horses sometimes find buyers at open horse shows, especially if they are priced competitively with horses of other breeds.

Before showing at an all-breed show, read the premium list and rules carefully—the rules may be different from those of Arabian classes. Also, the quality of judging at all-breed shows varies considerably and it may be difficult to determine a judge's expertise and knowledge of the Arabian breed in advance.

In open halter classes, Arabians are judged against horses of other breeds. As a result, they usually are judged with a greater emphasis on conformation than on breed type. To compete successfully, your Arabian may need better conformation than it would to succeed in Arabian halter classes, where the greater emphasis is on Arabian type.

English Pleasure class.

INFORMATION ABOUT UPCOMING SHOWS

Arabian horse shows are advertised and listed in the "calendar" sections of Arabian horse publications, where upcoming events are listed by date. Arabian shows are also mentioned in the newsletters of IAHA-affiliated Arabian horse clubs. All shows approved by IAHA are listed in *Inside International*, the magazine sent to all IAHA members. *Horse Show* magazine, sent to AHSA members, also lists upcoming shows.

All-breed shows are advertised in general horse publications and local newspapers. Also, both all-breed and Arabian horse shows often are publicized by posters in local tack and feed stores. A list of scheduled AHSA shows appears in each *AHSA Rule Book*.

The show's premium list (prize list) and entry forms are mailed to prospective exhibitors. The premium list contains the names of show officials and gives class schedules, specifications, and showing fees. For a free premium list, contact the horse show secretary, whose name and address appears in the ads, *AHSA Rule Book*, and magazine calendar listings for the show.

PREPARING FOR YOUR FIRST SHOW

Before competing at your first Arabian horse show, study the current *AHSA Rule Book* and *IAHA Handbook*, memorizing the class specifications and rules for the classes you plan to enter. Attend at least one Arabian show as a spectator, noting the clothing and tack used in the division in which you will compete and watching successful exhibitors to learn their techniques.

Careful grooming and conditioning contribute to the sleek coat of the show horse.
Johnny Johnston photo of Fa Halima, U.S. National Champion Mare, 1980, courtesy of Dr. Robert A. Frist and Bentwood Farms, Waco, Texas

CONDITIONING FOR HALTER

Specifications for halter classes state that Arabians are to be judged on: 1) type, 2) conformation, 3) substance, and 4) quality. These factors are considered in the order listed.

Type and conformation are discussed in chapters 6 and 7. Substance refers to the bone structure and muscling of the horse. The Arabian should have substance (sufficient bone and strength) without being coarse or too chunky. Quality refers to refinement of bone and the head and to fineness of the skin and hair.

The rules also state that transmissable weaknesses (i.e., inheritable faults) are to be "counted strongly against breeding stock." (With the obvious exception of geldings, halter horses *are* breeding stock.) If your Arabian has serious conformation faults, it is not a halter prospect.

The halter horse's attitude is very important. It must be alert, vigorous, and not easily bored. It should be more "showy" than a performance horse because it must look as good standing still as it does when moving. Flashy color or unusual markings may be a bonus, for they help the horse stand out in a crowd.

To decide whether your Arabian is halter quality, have someone else stand it up and pretend that you are the judge. Try to look at the horse as though you are seeing it for the first time, viewing it from various angles and distances. Have the horse led straight toward you and away from you at the walk and the trot.

COMPARE YOUR HORSE TO THE STANDARD

Compare your Arabian to the description of Arabian type and conformation that appears in section 2 of the *AHSA Rule Book* in the rules for the Arabian Division:

(a) Comparatively small head, profile of head straight or preferably slightly concave below the eyes; small muzzle, large nostrils, extended when in action; large, round, expressive, dark eyes set well apart (glass eyes shall be penalized in breeding classes); comparatively short distance between eye and muzzle; deep jowls, wide between the branches; small ears (smaller in stallions than in mares), thin and well-shaped, tips curved slightly inwards; long, arched neck, set on high and running well back into moderately high withers; long sloping shoulder well laid over with muscle; ribs well sprung; long, broad forearm; short cannon bone with large sinew; short back; loins broad and strong; croup comparatively horizontal; natural high tail carriage. Viewed from the rear, tail should be carried straight; hips strong and round; well muscled thigh and gaskin; straight sound, flat bone; large joints, strong and well defined; sloping pasterns of good length; round feet of proportionate size. Height from 14.1 to 15.1 hands, with an occasional individual over or under.

(b) Fine coat in varying colors of bay, chestnut, grey and black. Dark skin, except under white markings.

(c) Stallions especially should have an abundance of natural vitality, spirit, suppleness and balance.[1]

Compare your Arabian not only to this ideal standard but to its competitors. How does your horse compare with the horses it will be shown against? How is your horse better, and how worse?

You may wish to carefully list your horse's faults and strengths. A series of snapshots is helpful in evaluating conformation and type. If you can *objectively* evaluate your Arabian, you can determine its potential as a halter horse. In order to show the horse as well as possible, you must know its faults and strengths. Showmanship consists of minimizing the horse's faults and emphasizing its best points.

THE CONDITIONING PROGRAM

"Condition" describes the horse's appearance. It involves weight, muscle tone, health, and grooming. Arabians are prepared for halter classes by a careful conditioning program. The well-conditioned halter horse looks as good as it *can* look.

The halter horse's overall appearance must reflect beauty, balance, symmetry, and refinement. Halter horses are heavier and in "softer condition" than performance horses but should not be too fat or flabby.

To look its best, the halter horse must *feel* its best. Health care must be adequate and up-to-date. The feeding program is very important in conditioning for halter. Record exactly what the show horse is fed, making any changes in the diet gradually to avoid colic or founder. Show horses are more prone to these problems because there is a tendency to get them too fat.

If the show horse doesn't eat all its feed, you may be feeding too much. If it is already fat, you must either reduce the feed or increase its exercise (or both). If the horse needs to gain weight, adding molasses to the grain may make it more appetizing.

Dividing the day's feed into several small feedings, instead of two larger ones, may encourage the horse to eat more. Increasing the horse's exercise also may stimulate the appetite. Check the teeth frequently to be sure the horse can get the most benefit from its feed.

The horse's manure should be moist and slightly soft. If it's watery, the diet may be too rich; in that case, reduce the grain and increase the hay (to increase fiber). Diarrhea can result from illness, parasites, or drinking excessive water. Dry manure indicates a need for a more laxative feed or that the horse isn't drinking sufficient water. Adding bran (especially as a wet mash) may help.

A "hay belly" results from feeding too much fiber (hay or grass). Because grass has more fiber than legume hay, a gradual switch from grass hay or pasture to a legume such as alfalfa hay may reduce a protruding hay belly. Switching to pelleted feed may also be helpful, and exercise at the trot will help tighten the abdominal muscles.

Exercise

Exercise is a vital part of the conditioning program. Because controlled exercise builds muscle tone, the halter horse should be exercised daily until it sweats. The horse should get controlled exercise— lunging, driving,—five or six days a week. On the days it isn't carefully exercised, the horse must be turned out for self-exercise in an arena or large paddock.

The trot requires higher lifting of the legs than other gaits, which helps build muscles. Because each leg is raised equally high, the muscles are developed equally. Cantering stimulates the circulation and exercises the heart and lungs more, and some trainers rely only on this gait to condition their halter horses.

Do not exercise the horse after it is really tired. Doing so increases the risk of injury from interfering or forging.

Free exercise — All halter horses should be allowed to run free at least once or twice a week. This gives the horse a chance to rest and play, and free exercise may use some muscles that are neglected in controlled exercise. It also helps the young horse become agile, athletic, and more graceful. There is, however, no control over the movement of a free horse, and the kind of movement also determines which muscles will be developed.

Free exercise is the safest kind for young legs. A young horse is unlikely to forge or interfere while running free but may do so when thrown off balance by a lunge line.

Ponying — A young horse (about ten months or older) can be led by a rider on a calm horse (ponied). Ponying teaches the young horse to lead better, overcome fear of unfamiliar objects, and become more surefooted across country. It also improves the horse's circulation and lung capacity, takes the edge off nervous energy, and builds muscles. An added advantage is that the horse can be exercised in straight lines instead of in circles. (Working in circles increases the possibility of injury from interfering or forging and develops muscles on one side of the body more than those on the other side.)

Lunging — Horses that are two years old or more can be lunged. It's best to lunge the young horse in a round ring without a lunge line because the free horse is less likely to lose its balance and interfere or forge. Always put splint boots on the halter horse before any controlled exercise, such as lunging, to prevent self-inflicted leg injuries.

Most halter horses are free-lunged in a round ring, working both directions an equal amount of time to develop the muscles on both sides of the body evenly. At first, the horse may work only five or ten minutes, building gradually to between fifteen and thirty minutes daily. The length of time the horse is exercised, and the gaits at which it is worked, depend upon its condition. An easy keeper may require more exercise to avoid obesity, while a horse that tends to lose weight too easily may be given less exercise.

Driving — Because driving creates less concussion to the leg bones than riding, Arabians can be safely driven before they are mature enough to ride. Like ponying, driving offers the advantage of working the horse in a straight line instead of a circle. When the horse is driven at the trot, the muscles of the gaskin, hindquarters, and shoulders are developed.

Driving also helps level the topline, whereas riding has the opposite effect by lowering the horse's back. Driving strengthens the muscles of the back and croup. The only disadvantage is that pulling weight may cause the horse's shoulder to become slightly more upright.

Swimming — Successful trainers often advocate swimming halter horses because swimming develops the muscles without placing any weight on the horse's legs. It therefore eliminates the risk of concussion-related leg injuries during conditioning. Swimming also produces long, smooth muscling instead of the bulkier muscles that result from trotting. Because the horse uses its forelegs strongly while swimming, it develops the muscling and action in the forehand.

Unfortunately, the high costs of installing and maintaining an equine swimming pool makes this conditioning method impractical for most owners.

A show horse being conditioned by swimming laps. It enters the pool by a ramp, and the handler walks around the concrete edge of the pool as the horse swims.

Mechanical Conditioning Devices

Mechanical horse walkers and treadmills are sometimes used for conditioning halter horses. However, the walker's radius is about the same as the length of a lunge line. Walking doesn't develop the muscles the way that trotting does, and it's safer to trot the horse on a straight line than a circle, which unduly stresses the joints of the legs and may lead to unsoundness or blemishes. Trotting horses on a walker also is more dangerous than trotting the horses during riding, ponying, or driving because the horses are attached to a moving mechanical arm that can cause injury in case of accident. Walkers are best reserved for cooling down halter horses after a workout, walking bathed horses to dry them, or for light exercise if a stabled horse cannot be given any other work.

Treadmills are best at developing the forearms, chest, gaskins of the legs and the hindquarters. The major problem in using them to develop the muscles of the halter horse is that continually walking on the same surface may cause soreness.

Young horses can be more safely conditioned using a treadmill than by lunging. With the treadmill, the horse walks straight ahead; lunging in circles may result in leg injuries from uneven stress along the leg bones.

Sweats

The horse's neck quickly reflects weight gain or loss. When a horse is in show condition, its extra weight is reflected by fat added to the neck, which makes the neck look shorter and thicker.

The bulk of the neck can be temporarily reduced by exercising the horse while it wears a neck sweat, a wide band of neoprene that fits around the neck. When the horse perspires under the sweat, the result is water loss from the neck tissues, which reduces the area. (To increase sweating, glycerine, an equal mixture of alcohol and glycerine, or a commercial sweating preparation is applied under the sweat.) Because this effect is only temporary, the neck must be sweated repeatedly to keep its slim appearance. After being exercised with a sweat, the horse should be cooled down before it is removed and perspiration must then be completely rinsed off to avoid dulling the hair coat.

Extra weight also can settle in the withers, making them look less prominent. To define the withers,

sweats that cover the withers can be used or the horse can be lunged wearing a lightweight saddle until the horse sweats freely.

Sweats come in various lengths to sweat the throat, neck and shoulders (to also reduce the base of the neck) so that a horse's particular problem area can be reduced. There are even hood sweats (to reduce the throatlatch, jowls, and upper face) and an entire body sweat that blankets the horse from chest to tail. The latest development is an electric neck sweat heated by a portable blow hair dryer. Sheepskin or felt throatlatch bands also are available for the horse to wear in its stall to help maintain the sweated appearance.

The Danger Of Fat

The modern Arabian show horse, sleek and too fat, presents a startling contrast to its half-starved ancestors in the desert. In adding excessive fat for beauty's sake, owners should be aware of health problems that may result.

Fat adds extra weight to the body, which puts a greater strain on the horse's heart and lungs and increases the risk of concussion-related injury to the leg bones. Fat reduces the endurance and agility of the horse.

Internal fat is even more dangerous. It can squeeze the intestines, resulting in impaction and (possibly) fatal colic. Internal fat can squeeze a mare's fallopian tubes closed, making her barren, and also may reduce a stallion's fertility. Over-fat horses are also more prone to founder than thin horses.

Successful Conditioning

The properly conditioned halter horse has a layer of fat that enhances its appearance but not so much that it looks, as author Gladys Brown Edwards said, "like a knockwurst." Its muscles are firm and well defined, and its coat is short, bright in color, and shines as a result of good health, nutrition, cleanliness, and lots of regular grooming. The horse's overall appearance reflects careful management and attention to detail.

DECONDITIONING ("LETTING DOWN")

After the show season, owners sometimes reduce feed and exercise to save money, time, labor, and to give the horse a vacation. If the horse will

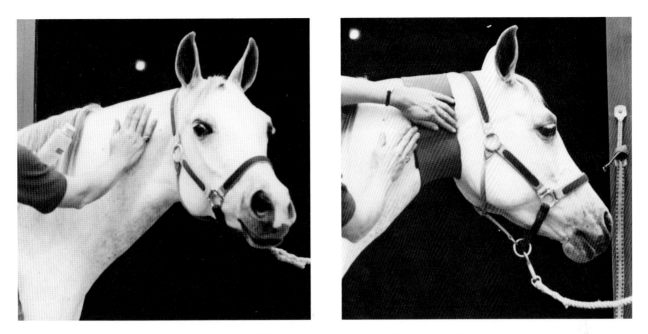

The horse's neck is prepared for sweating by rubbing on glycerine or a special commercial preparation to increase sweating. The neck sweat is then placed around the area to be reduced, and the horse is exercised to promote perspiration. Sweats come in various sizes, to cover only the throatlatch (shown) or larger areas. (By the way, this mare is just modeling. Her throatlatch is naturally fine!)

be shown next season, adequate time for re-conditioning must be allowed before the first show. It takes about four months to one year to condition a horse, depending upon its initial condition.

When letting down, make any changes in diet, stabling, and exercise *gradually*. If a horse will be turned out to pasture, begin by turning it out for only part of each day. If it won't wear a blanket in cool weather, let the horse grow a warmer coat by first switching to lighter blankets before removing the blanket completely.

Remember that long winter hair makes judging weight difficult. The only way to judge the condition of a horse with a shaggy coat is to feel its underlying fat, muscles, and bone. Start with the neck and also feel the ribs, spine, and hip bones.

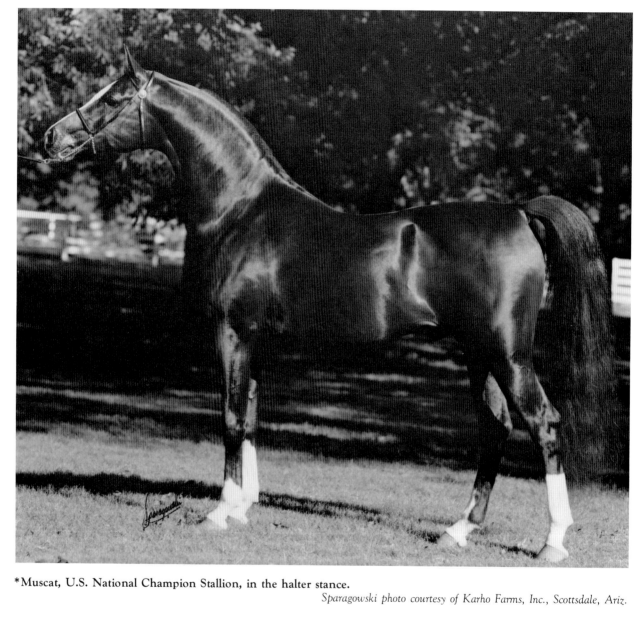

*Muscat, U.S. National Champion Stallion, in the halter stance.

Sparagowski photo courtesy of Karho Farms, Inc., Scottsdale, Ariz.

32

TRAINING FOR HALTER CLASSES

In showing the Arabian at halter, an attempt is made to recreate the level topline, high tail carriage, arched neck, and high head carriage displayed when the Arabian runs at liberty. The halter pose accentuates these traits.

In the current halter stance, one hind leg is placed slightly behind the other, the forelegs are even, the head is raised, and the neck is stretched (arched).

Seen from the side, the forelegs are approximately even with each other, but one hind leg is about ten inches behind the other hind leg. This position makes the topline appear more level. The halter rules say that *one* hind leg may be extended, but the other must be perpendicular to the ground. Arabians are not to be shown with both hind legs stretched.

In the halter pose, the Arabian's neck is extended and the head held high, making the neck appear longer and the throatlatch more refined. Raising the head and neck also makes the croup muscles tense which raises the tail and makes the croup appear more level.

This halter pose is not natural—it must be taught in a series of lessons. Once learned, however, it is never forgotten.

Whether or not the Arabian will be shown at halter, teaching the halter pose helps make the horse more attentive and responsive to the handler. The

pose also presents a prettier picture of the horse when it is shown to visitors or potential buyers.

The practice of raising the horse's head to an unnatural height is the most controversial part of the halter pose. Some trainers say that it is difficult to teach a young performance horse to carry its head in the proper position if it has first been trained to raise its head for halter classes.

TEACHING THE HALTER HORSE TO LEAD

The halter horse must be well halterbroken before show training begins. Then, it must be taught to walk and trot straight forward while remaining three to four feet from the handler. This distance gives the horse's head and neck more freedom, resulting in improved foreleg and shoulder action, and prevents blocking the judge's view of the horse.

Stand in the leading position, about three feet from the horse's left shoulder. Holding the lead high (at about the level of the horse's cheek), and leaving it slack from the halter to your hand, lead the horse forward.

If the horse moves toward you, tell it to move away. (Be sure to choose words that you don't use for another cue.) Then reinforce the verbal command by striking the front of the horse's shoulder blade (near its chest) once with the handle end of the whip. The jolt from one smart blow on this bone quickly encourages the horse to move away. (You can sample the effect by tapping your knuckles against the bony part of your arm, where your shoulder joins your body.)

When using this method, use only the degree of force necessary to teach the horse to step aside. Soon, the Arabian will learn to move away at the verbal command and the cue of the whip handle moving slightly toward the shoulder. Do not strike the horse again after teaching this lesson, unless it crowds into you. For safety's sake, the horse must keep its distance from the handler on the long lead.

THE SHOW TROT

The halter horse must trot beside the handler on a long lead. The horse's shoulder should remain even with or behind the handler. If the horse lags too far behind, tap its hocks or hindquarters lightly with a long stick or a buggy whip. If the horse pushes ahead, tap its shoulder with the whip handle.

Instead of moving forward in a straight line, horses sometimes angle their bodies when trotting. To straighten the trot, trot the horse along a fence (with the horse between you and the fence). After a time, move away from the fence. Go back to it if the horse starts angling its body again.

Professional handlers often stay well ahead of their horses and at the end of the lead line at the trot. This prevents blocking the judge's view of the horse and allows the horse more freedom, resulting in a greater display of action and spirit. However, it also is more difficult to keep the horse under control when it is behind you.

TEACHING THE HALTER POSE

Step 1: Teaching the Horse to Stop and Stand Still

Before you can train the horse to assume the proper leg position for halter, you must have the respect and attention of your horse. Therefore, the first step in training for halter is to teach the horse to stop instantly upon command and remain still. Give the first lesson after exercise, so the horse is relaxed and attentive.

Use a sturdy nylon or leather stable halter—a show halter may not be strong enough, depending on its style. A 7-foot long lead rope with a chain on the end that snaps to the halter also is needed.

Lead the horse forward a few steps, then stop, saying "Whoa!" and giving a slight jerk on the lead line. If the horse doesn't stop immediately (or stops, but moves forward again), jerk harder and firmly repeat the command. When the horse stops and stands for a few seconds, pet and praise it so it will know that it did what you wanted.

Using the chain lead — If the horse does not stop and stand, using a lead rope with an attached chain under its jaw will improve the stop. Used properly, the chain is not cruel. In fact, most show halters use chains to enhance control.

To put the chain under the horse's jaw, pass it through the halter ring on the near side, behind the chin, and through the halter ring on the other side. Then snap the chain lead to itself (to the ring where the chain connects to the lead line). If the chain is too short for this, it can be run through the halter ring, under the jaw behind the chin, and snapped to the off-side halter ring.

An alternative is to run the chain (perhaps wrapped with electrical tape to protect the nose) over the nasal bone, well above the nostrils.

Again lead the horse forward, stop, and say "Whoa!" accompanying the command with a slight jerk on the lead. If the horse stops, reward it with petting and praise. If it doesn't stop immediately, repeat the command and jerk harder on the line. Be as gentle as possible but as rough as necessary to get an immediate stop. When the horse stops, make it stand still for a few seconds. If the horse moves, repeat "Whoa!" and jerk the lead. Don't try to keep the horse standing still for too long, however. Reward your horse for good behavior *before* it gets restless and fidgets.

End the first lesson after the horse stops and stands once or twice. In later lessons, gradually increase the time you expect the horse to stand still but don't overdo it.

Step 2: Moving Away from the Standing Horse

In the show ring, the halter horse must stand still as the handler steps to either side and moves toward or away from it. The horse must be controlled from the end of the lead line.

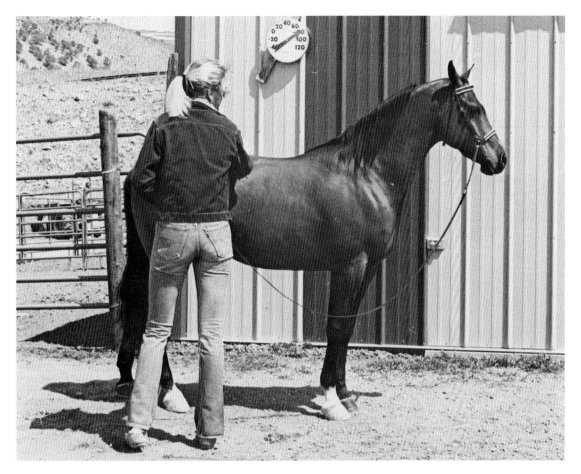

After the horse has stopped, it must be taught to stand absolutely still, no matter where you (the handler) move.

After the horse will stop and stand still on command, have it stand while you back away, repeating "Whoa!" If the horse moves toward you, repeat the command and jerk the lead. The horse must learn not to approach unless you say to. When the horse stands still as you back away, walk up to it and reward it with praise.

Next, teach the horse to stand as you walk to each side of it, again repeating "Whoa!" If the horse moves, repeat the command and jerk the lead. Always reward the horse when it stands still upon command.

At this point, the horse will stop quickly and stand still at the end of the lead line. It has learned to pay attention and obey the handler and is *now* ready to learn the halter stance.

Step 3: Teaching Hind Leg Position

To set the hind legs, the Arabian is led forward at the walk and stopped when its legs are in the proper position. To do this, decide which hind leg you want to be more *forward* when the horse is standing. Lead the horse forward and watch that leg closely. When the horse begins to lift the leg, say "Whoa!" and jerk the lead. If your timing is right, the horse will set that foot on the ground and stop with the hindlegs in the proper halter position. (If your timing was wrong, practice leading and stopping the horse until you get the hind leg position correct.)

Sometimes the wrong amount of distance occurs between the hind legs. (They should be about ten inches apart, but at whatever distance most flatters the individual's topline.) To get more space between the hind legs, lengthen the horse's stride by walking faster then stop a little slower. To get less distance between the legs, shorten the horse's stride by walking slower and asking for the stop a little quicker.

Resting a hind leg — Instead of standing squarely, horses sometimes rest the hind leg that is farthest back, placing the toe of the hoof on the ground

277

The halter pose must be taught in several lessons; it cannot be learned in one session. First: Lead the horse forward, watching its hind fee! ...

As the near hind leg begins to move forward, say "Whoa!" and jerk the lead line. The horse should complete that stride and stop with its hind legs in proper stance.

and lifting the heel of the hoof off the ground. If this happens, don't stretch the hind legs quite so far apart at first, and move slowly when setting the legs. Working on a slight incline, with the leg that was being rested going downhill, will help shift weight onto the leg. Later, the problem can be corrected after the horse has learned to elevate the head. By raising the head more, the horse must shift its weight to its hind legs. (If the leg is still being rested after the entire halter pose has been taught,

correct the problem by turning the horse's head slightly toward that side when you raise the horse's head.)

Reversing hind leg position — Some exhibitors reverse the position of the horse's hind legs when the judge moves to the other side of the horse, so that the hind leg nearest the judge is always farthest back. This gives the most flattering view of the hind legs and topline.

To do this, you must *move the horse forward exactly one step*, so that the hind leg that was originally perpendicular to the ground is now extended and the opposite leg is the one farthest forward.

It is safest to "set up" the horse in the halter pose only once and to keep it in the same position during a show class especially if either the handler or the show horse is inexperienced. Moving the horse out of position creates the risk that the horse will fail to set up again properly in the short time that the judge is watching.

Step 4: Foreleg Position

In the finished halter stance, the horse's forelegs are straight (vertical) and directly below its shoulders. However, if the horse is standing squarely with the forelegs under its shoulders when you ask the horse to use its neck in later training, the horse can be thrown off balance and pulled out of the pose. Also, its forelegs may appear to be too far under its body (toward the rear) when its weight is shifted forward.

To prevent this loss of balance and obtain a better foreleg position in the finished stance, the horse can be taught to put its forelegs just *slightly* ahead of the proper position. Then, when the neck is brought forward and the horse rolls its weight forward, the legs will be square under the shoulders. However, extreme care must be used so that the forelegs do not appear to be stretched forward, as Arabians are not shown stretched.

To move a foreleg, the handler faces the horse, standing directly in front of it. (This is the point from which the handler generally stands up a halter horse.)

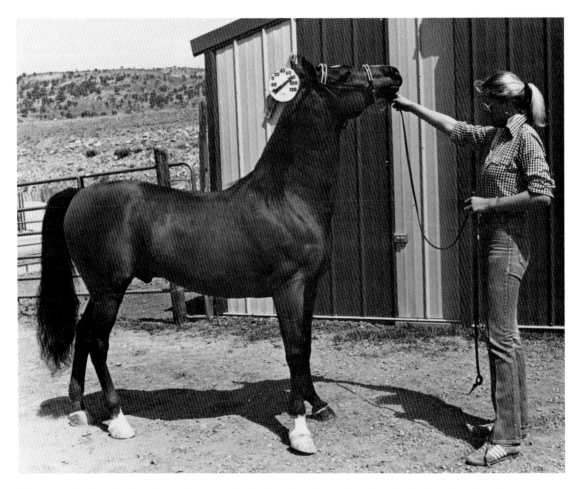

To move the horse's front foot sideways, lift the head and turn it to the side in the direction that you want the leg moved.

Moving a leg forward — The horse is taught to move a foreleg forward by pulling gently but steadily on the lead line.

The horse is taught to move each foreleg separately. To move the near foreleg forward, pull forward and just slightly toward your right. To move the off foreleg forward, pull forward and just slightly to your left. Use a gentle but steady forward pull on the lead line.

As soon as the horse lifts the foreleg, say "Whoa!" The horse should move the leg forward and set it down without taking another step.

Moving a leg sideways — When teaching the horse to move a foreleg sideways, you first take hold of the halter and apply pressure in the direction that you want the leg to go. (Apply the pressure on the same side of the halter as the leg you want moved.)

As soon as the horse lifts its foreleg to step sideways, say "Whoa!" and discontinue the sideways pressure. The horse should move the foreleg sideways one step, set it down, and not take another step.

By applying the halter pressure carefully, you can move either foreleg inward or outward. Later, transfer the cue from the halter to the lead by exerting similar pressure on the lead line.

If the horse automatically sets up properly, with its forelegs neither too far apart nor too close together, it isn't necessary to adjust the legs sideways.

Step 5: Teaching Head Position

The Arabian is trained to hold its head higher than normal when shown at halter. To begin teaching this, face the horse and lift upward on the halter. Hold the horse's head up for a few seconds, and praise and pet the animal. Repeat the lesson a few times, then raise the head and release the upward pressure on the halter. If the horse lowers its head, jerk on the lead shank. When the horse throws its head up (in response to the jerk on the chain under the chin), praise it. Hold the horse's head up again and try releasing the upward pressure. Repeat this until the horse keeps its head up after you've stopped lifting upward on the halter. *Immediately* reward the horse by praise and by ending the lesson. Don't expect the horse to hold its head up for more than a few seconds at first and reward the horse as soon as it maintains the pose. Gently *tapping* under the jaw with a stick or the whip handle will also encourage the horse to raise its head upward.

At the next lesson, transfer the upward pressure from the halter to the lead line, using the method described above. Eventually, the horse learns to raise its head when you raise the lead.

When the horse will raise its head high in response to upward pressure on the lead, step back about two feet from the horse, still holding the lead line high. If the horse lowers its head, jerk the lead.

Don't ask the horse to hold its head high for very long because this pose is tiring.

Step 6: Using the Neck

Only after the horse has been taught to elevate the head can it be taught to stretch (extend) or use (arch) the neck.

To teach the horse to extend its neck, which emphasizes the Arabian's natural arch, first elevate the head. Then, say "Whoa" as you begin a gentle, steady forward pull on the lead line. The horse knows it is not supposed to step forward because you're telling it to stop. At the same time, you are pulling its head gently toward you. Eventually the horse will remain standing still but move its muzzle toward you, resulting in the extended, arched neck position. As soon as the horse releases the pressure on the halter by breaking at the poll and stretching its head toward you, release the pressure on the lead rope, letting it form a relaxed curve between the halter and your hand.

As the horse stretches its neck forward, its weight is thrown forward ("rolled over" the shoulders). As the horse leans forward this way, it tightens its abdominal muscles and flattens its croup.

When you first ask the horse to "give" its neck, it may instead step forward. To prevent this, the whip is used as a visual barrier.

Hold the lead in one hand and the whip in the other, with the whip extending horizontally in front of the horse's neck, just above its chest. If the horse steps forward when you try to get it to reach its neck forward by pressure on the lead, say "Whoa!" and allow the whip handle to swing around and strike the horse's shoulder. The effect is like a swinging door that the horse activates by stepping forward and bumping into the whip. The horse will have already learned to move away from the whip to avoid this kind of discomfort from the whip handle, and the horse soon learns that it must not step forward when the whip is held horizontally in front of its chest.

Step 7: Completing the Pose

To complete the halter pose, the horse's ears should be forward to convey an alert expression. At the "height" of the halter pose, the horse's neck also should be arched as much as possible. Both the ears and the arched neck result from paying attention to the handler, which usually means watching the whip.

During training, a horse may watch the whip more closely if you tie a piece of bright cloth or a bit of a plastic bag to the whip's snapper (lash). The plastic is best because it is noisy as well as visual.

If the horse doesn't watch the whip, popping the whip nearby may "wake him up." Hitting a near-by wall or other object with the whip to create noise may cause the horse to watch the whip with greater interest. One trainer substitutes a household broom for the whip during training. If the horse doesn't pay attention, it is swatted on the side of its body with the flat side of the bristles. This makes a loud noise but doesn't hurt the horse. When the whip is substituted for the broom, the horse is likely to transfer its attention to the whip. Other trainers recommend blanketing the horse and popping the whip against the blanket if the horse ignores the whip.

In the show ring, the horse often is encouraged to put its ears forward and arch its neck by waving

When the legs are properly placed, the horse is taught to lift its head and hold it high.

Finally, the horse is taught to extend its neck toward the handler.

the whip slowly. (The horse can't focus its eyes on an object that moves too fast.) A common technique is to glide the whip *handle* toward the horse slowly, starting at about the handler's head level and gliding downward toward the horse. Using the whip to capture the horse's attention is an art; study the techniques of successful show exhibitors.

In training the halter horse the whip should not be used for punishment *unless* the horse has purposely misbehaved. When a horse is whipped without reason, it becomes confused, frightened, or angry. A true horseman or horsewoman can get results *without* abusing the horse's body or mind.

In addition to moving the whip, an unusual, quiet sound may be used to capture the horse's attention and cause its ears to come forward. Coins or keys can be jingled in a pocket, or you might run your thumb over the teeth of a small hair comb. In training, an aerosol can may be used to get the ears forward. When showing, some handlers make a special sound, such as a hissing or smooching noise, when they want the horse's ears up. Be sure the method used to get the horse's ears forward is *subtle* and will not interfere with other exhibitors.

When the halter horse is turned around the handler, there is a greater risk of the handler being bumped or stepped on by a frisky or frightened horse. However, the wider turn allows a more balanced appearance of the horse. For this reason, it is preferred by many professional exhibitors.

MINIMIZING LEG FAULTS

The Arabian with faulty legs can be *trained* to stand in a position that would be natural for it if its conformation were correct. This makes it more difficult for the casual observer to identify the horse's leg faults.

Table 32.1 shows how common leg faults can be partially camouflaged by subtly adjusting the way the horse stands. The well-trained halter horse automatically will assume the trained stance so that the handler is not forced to make obvious "adjustments" in the show ring.

TABLE 32.1

MINIMIZING LEG FAULTS

Fault	To Minimize:
Cow Hocks	Move the hind legs slightly farther apart.
Forelegs Toe In (Pigeon-Toed)	Move the forelegs slightly farther apart.
Forelegs Toe Out	Move the forelegs slightly closer together.
Base Wide	Move the base wide legs slightly closer together.
Base Narrow	Move the base narrow legs slightly farther apart.
Forelegs Stand Under	Move the forelegs slightly forward (under the shoulders).
Hind Legs Stand Behind (Out in the Country, Camped out)	Move the hind legs slightly forward (under the hindquarters).

TURNING THE HALTER HORSE

The horse can be turned away from or toward (around) the handler. Some professionals prefer to have the horse circle them because then the judge always has an unobstructed view of the horse. The *safest* method, however, is to pivot the horse away from you. The horse is then under better control and won't bump into you.

Turning the halter horse away from the handler, with its weight on its hindquarters, is the safest method for the handler. However, it may present an unflattering view of the horse's topline.

The horse can easily be taught to turn away from you (on its hindquarters). Tell the horse to move; then reinforce the verbal command by striking the shoulder once with the handle of the whip. Soon, the Arabian learns to watch the whip handle, and will begin to turn when you gently guide the horse away from you with light pressure on the lead and move the whip handle slightly toward the horse's shoulder (in the direction of the turn). Once the lesson is learned, the whip is just a visual cue and you need not strike the horse to make it turn.

OTHER USEFUL TRAINING FOR CLASSES

If you have enough horses, it's a good idea to have a "practice class" at home before you show in-experienced halter horses. Have several entries in the mock class. It doesn't matter whether they're really show horses or even Arabians—the idea is to get the horse used to being in the arena with other horses and handlers.

Have someone walk around your halter horse so that it won't be startled when the judge does. The "judge" also might push down the horse's tail, hold it aside, pick up a leg, run a hand over the horse's neck or body, or examine the teeth. Judges sometimes do these things, and it is a good idea to prepare the inexperienced horse in advance. Maiming a judge won't win any ribbons.

Some people also try to accustom an inexperienced horse to the sounds that will be found at a horse show by playing loud music, radio telecasts of sports events with large crowds, or even taped horse show sounds.

PRACTICING THE HALTER POSE

When the horse has first learned the halter pose, set the horse up daily. The best time to do this is when you first take your horse from its stall. As soon as the horse poses properly, reward it by not making it hold the position any longer (turn the horse out for exercise, etc.). Arabians soon learn that their reward for standing correctly is to no longer have to pose, so they assume the position immediately. This is important in the show ring when there is a limited time to show your horse to the judge.

Once the halter pose is familiar, you should only set up the horse occasionally (perhaps once a week), as a brush-up lesson. Don't pose the horse too often or expect it to maintain the complete pose for a long period of time, or it will become bored. The bored horse won't want to stretch its neck and put its ears forward—it will just want to sleep.

The proper show trot is animated. When the halter horse's head is raised, the action is elevated and the neck appears lengthened. Lisa Hardy, Spanish Hills Arabians, and Sha-Nefertaten winning the Estes Park Futurity.

Scott Trees photo

33

ſHOWING AT HALTER

In halter classes, horses are shown "in hand" (on a lead line). Halter classes for purebred Arabians are judged with primary emphasis on type, followed by conformation. Half-Arabian halter horses are judged with emphasis first on conformation, followed by type, because Half-Arabians may be of different breed types.

Generally, halter classes are divided so that horses compete against others of their sex and age. Usually, classes are for horses foaled during the same year (e.g., Fillies of 1983, Stallions of 1980, etc.). However, age groups may be combined in one class (e.g., Geldings of 1981-1983, etc.).

Futurity halter classes are for horses that were nominated to compete in them before they were foaled (actually, the pregnant dam is nominated the year before her foal is born). Horses must be nominated by their owners and annual fees paid to maintain eligibility until the year they are shown. Like most other halter classes, futurity classes are divided by sex. The National Futurities (held at the National Championship Arabian Horse Shows) are for three-year-old colts, geldings, and fillies. Futurities for younger horses also may be offered by other shows.

A Get-of-Sire class entry consists of a group of horses by the same sire; a Produce-of-Dam class entry consists of a group of horses out of the same mare. The horses in an entry may or may not be full siblings. Each group is compared to the others in the class, based on the quality (type, conformation, etc.) and similarity of its members.

Most Classic and Model classes are judged differently than other halter classes. The Most Classic Arabian class is open to horses of all sexes, but horses must be at least two years old. The horses are judged at an animated walk and trot on the rail and may be moved to the center of the arena for further evaluation. This class is judged on type, presence, animation, carriage, and conformation, with judging emphasis placed on Arabian type. In Model classes, the horses are judged (in descending order of emphasis) on type, quality, presence, and conformation. Visible blemishes and unsoundness are penalized. If the horses are trotted, it is only to judge tail carriage.

AGE OF HALTER HORSES

Halter classes are broken down by age, usually beginning with weanling foals and progressing through classes for mature horses. Although there are halter classes for weanlings and yearlings, many owners do not show young Arabians until they are at least two years old. There are several reasons for this. First, there always is a risk in transporting horses, and young horses are more likely to become frightened and injured. They also are more susceptible to viruses, which are common at horse shows. Young halter horses also may be in awkward growth stages at the time of an important show. Despite these drawbacks, some exhibitors show young horses in hope of finding buyers or to promote their sires. Also, some horses are at their best before they mature, and their best chance to achieve a show record is while they are young.

Most National Champion Stallions have achieved the title as mature stallions (usually between five and eight years old). However, most National Champion Mares only have been three or four years old at the time of their wins. This difference in ages is because mature mares are retired from showing while they are still young, to begin raising foals. This situation may change, however, if embryo transfer makes it possible for older mares to continue competing while recipient mares raise their foals (see Chapter 23).

The whip is used as an extension of the handler's arm, to attract and hold the attention of the horse, so that the animal appears alert.

CLOTHING

The handler's appearance should complement that of his or her horse. Attire is more flexible for halter classes than for performance, but clothing should be neat, clean, well-fitted, and in good taste. Dark colors are more formal and, at present, more popular.

Men generally wear a long-sleeved shirt, slacks, vest, tie. A blazer or other jacket may be added; sometimes a jacket is replaced by a pullover sweater. Gloves are optional, and hats are seldom worn.

Women may wear saddle seat attire or slacks, a long-sleeved blouse, and a blazer or pullover sweater if desired. A tie can lend a more formal appearance; gloves are optional. The woman's hair should be cut short or worn up for neatness, perhaps in the traditional "horse show bun" worn low on the back of the head. Long hair must never cover the exhibitor's number card, which is pinned on the exhibitor's back with enough pins to prevent the card from flapping. Both male and female handlers should wear appropriate low-heeled boots or shoes.

THE WHIP

A short whip (about three to four feet long) generally is used for showing at halter; however, a whip is not mandatory. When not in use, the whip usually is carried with its tip pointing toward the ground and behind the handler.

The whip is used more to attract the horse's attention and keep it looking alert while showing than for punishment. In fact, excessive use of the whip is to be penalized by the judge. Beating a horse (whip abuse) is considered to be cruelty and should be reported to show authorities.

THE SHOW HALTER

To show off their refined heads, show halters for Arabians are finer and lighter than those used for other breeds. The only specifications for show halters is that they must be "suitable" and must have a throatlatch.

Currently, four styles of Arabian show halters are popular. The oldest style still in vogue is the leather halter with silver trim. Leather or patent leather halters, usually with a colorful noseband and/or browband, also are common. Delicate-looking halters of macramé (knotted cord), sometimes with small tassels, are occasionally seen. The newest style is a plain leather halter with a thin, half or full-circle noseband made of steel wire cable. The latter style doesn't need a chain under the horse's jaw because of the severity of the full-circle steel band. Most of the other show halters incorporate a small chain under the jaw for added control. The chain fits under the horse's chin, passing through the rings at each side of the halter, and attaches to the lead. Some leads have a chain sewn in, while others have a buckle that can be attached to the chain or directly to the show halter.

The show lead is made of flat or rolled leather matching the show halter and is about seven feet in length. Most show leads have a hand stop (knob) at the end to prevent the lead from slipping through the exhibitor's hand.

At present, show halters without browbands are popular. They visually shorten the horse's head, especially the distance between the eyes and ears,

and make the forehead appear slightly broader. The major drawback is that the forelock may then become windblown, detracting from a neat appearance.

Occasionally, halter horses (most commonly stallions that need additional restraint) are shown in a headstall that includes a narrow snaffle bit (bradoon). However, jerking on the bit may create a hard mouth, which is undesirable in a performance horse.

Selecting the Show Halter

To choose a show halter that flatters your Arabian's head, check to see what horses with similar kinds of heads are wearing. If a style is attractive on them, it probably will look good on your horse. If you note that a certain style looks bad on a similar horse, avoid it.

Left: a plain head gains refinement and shape when a wide halter is used. Middle: a long head seems shorter if the noseband is placed high on the face. Right: a refined, typey head looks best in a thin halter.

Whatever its style, the show halter should be in proportion to the individual's head. A refined, typey head looks best in a delicate, narrow halter that reveals as much of the head as possible. A plainer, heavier head looks better in a halter with wider bands of leather.

Brightly colored nosebands and browbands, and reflecting surfaces, such as patent leather or silver, can call attention to a good head. Sparkle and brightness catch the observer's eye. A plain head fares better in a non-shiny material that matches the color of the horse.

If in doubt, always choose a plainer style. A halter that is too ornate can detract from a good head or attract attention to a plain one.

Adjusting the Show Halter

Most show halters are shortened or lengthened by small buckles at the cheekpiece or poll strap. Lengthening the sides of the halter lowers it on the horse's head; shortening the sides moves it higher. For the horse's comfort, the halter throatlatch should fit loosely rather than being buckled tightly at the throat. However, it should not be so loose that it looks untidy. The fashion at the time of publication of this book was an extremely fine, long (loose) throatlatch of chain or leather.

The noseband is placed at the bottom of the horse's cheek bones (jowls). This placement can make a long head appear to be slightly shorter. Moving the noseband a little lower can make a short, wide head appear slightly longer. If the horse has a camel nose, it is better to put the noseband high (to call attention to the eye) than to have it at the most arched point of the nasal bone, which will call attention to the profile.

When the halter is in place and properly adjusted, brush the horse's forelock to the side of the neck covered by the mane and tuck the forelock under the browband. If there is no browband, tuck the forelock under the cheek strap of the halter, if possible. Moving the forelock to the side and securing it under the halter reveals the horse's profile, eyes, facial markings, makes the forehead appear broader, and keeps the forelock neat. If the forelock is too short to tuck under the cheek strap of a halter that lacks a browband, oil the forelock to minimize a windblown appearance.

Arabian Halter Class Specifications
(from AHSA Rule Book, 1984-1985 Edition)*

"Horses to be shown in hand at walk and trot. Judges must require handlers to walk all horses (in the final line up) quietly on the rail prior to placing the class, except in classes judged under the European Judging System. Halter horses are not to be stretched. A horse is considered not stretched if all four feet are flat on the ground and at least one front and one rear cannon bone is perpendicular to the ground. Handled and shown throughout an entire class by only one and the same person, except that a substitute handler may be used if during a class the original handler becomes ill or is injured. Time allowed for the change of handler shall be in accordance with Rule III, Part 1, Sec. 8(A). No handler may show more than one horse per class. A suitable headstall equipped with throatlatch is mandatory. Excessive use of the whip or actions that may disturb other entries shall be penalized. Emphasis shall be placed upon type, conformation, substance and quality. Transmissible weaknesses to be counted strongly against breeding stock. Colts and stallions 2 years old and over must have both testicles descended. Horses must be serviceably sound...."

RING PROCEDURE

Exact ring procedure for halter classes is determined by the judge, so no strict patterns apply. However, the judge is supposed to evaluate each horse while the horse stands still and at the walk and trot.

Prior to the class, halter horses are lined up outside the arena in random order. They are led into the arena at a walk or brisk trot (whichever gait is specified) and move around the ring on the rail (usually clockwise). There are disadvantages to cir-

---

* Copyright 1984 by the American Horse Shows Association, Inc., and reprinted with the Association's permission. All rights strictly reserved. The reader is cautioned that Association rules are from time to time revised and amended, and is referred to the current AHSA Rule Book and amendments for a complete exposition of AHSA rules.

cling in each direction. Clockwise, the exhibitor's number cannot be seen by the judge because the horse blocks the view; counter-clockwise, the handler blocks the judge's view of the horse.

The halter horse is led in a straight line toward the judge at the specified gait (either a walk or trot, at the judge's discretion) and then stands in the halter pose to be evaluated.

Each horse enters individually, following the previous horse in line. When all are in the arena, the gate is closed, and the horses are lined up, usually "head to tail, on the rail." Then each horse is led, in turn, to the judge for an individual evaluation. The horse is led toward the judge at a specified gait (a walk or trot) and "stood up" in halter position before the judge. The judge usually walks around the horse, viewing it from both sides. Then, the horse is led away from the judge at a specified gait (if the horse was walked toward the judge, it usually trots away) and resumes its position on the rail. Judges may prefer to have the horse trotted *toward* them, which affords a better view of the action of the forelegs. Some, however, ask that the horses trot away from them.

After the judge has examined all entries, the horses selected usually are lined up in the center of the arena in order of placement so that the spectators can compare the horses. While the horses are lined up, the judge may adjust the placings by moving horses ahead or back in the line-up. The final results then are given to the announcer, who reads the names of the winning horses, owners, and handlers as each horse is presented with its award. The handler accepts the trophy and/or ribbon and leads the horse from the arena. Winners usually are photographed when the trophy is awarded. Non-winners remain in the ring until they are excused or until the ribbons have been awarded.

Exhibitor Etiquette

When showing, pay attention to the judge, ring master, and announcer. Be careful not to crowd another entry or to frighten or accidentally strike another entry or exhibitor with your whip.

If your horse becomes unruly or develops another problem that precludes finishing a class, ask permission to be excused from the ring. Never leave without being excused first; it is illegal as well as rude.

If you win a ribbon, smile and thank the presenter; men often remove their hats. If you don't get a ribbon, smile anyway. If you get a chance, congratulate the winner. The golden rule applies in showing as elsewhere. Treat others as you would like to be treated! Be pleasant to everyone at the show. Remember: you all chose to be there because of your mutual interest in Arabian horses.

If you wish to question the judge about his or her class placings or procedures, make an appointment with the judge through the AHSA steward. Do not approach the judge directly during the show.

After the judge has examined the horse in the halter pose, the horse is led in a straight line away from the judge at the specified gait. If the horse trots toward the judge, it is walked away; if it is walked toward the judge, it must be trotted away.

SHOWMANSHIP

Showmanship means presenting the halter horse to maximize its best features and to minimize its faults. Although no Arabian is perfect, good showmanship can make a horse *seem* nearly perfect. Showmanship in this context refers to professionalism and skill; it has nothing to do with the showmanship *class*, which is for junior exhibitors and requires different techniques than regular Arabian halter classes.

Good judges aren't easily fooled by tricks of showmanship. They can spot a faulty Arabian even when it is shown cleverly, and they recognize a good Arabian even when it is poorly shown. However, when two Arabians of *equal* quality compete at halter, showmanship can make the difference between winning and placing second.

Entry Position

Experienced exhibitors prefer to be either the first or last entry to enter the arena. This way, the horse initially will be directly compared to only *one* other (the horse immediately before or after it). Horses that enter between horses initially are viewed between *two* competitors.

If there are more than two horses in a class, all obviously cannot be in the desirable first and last entry positions, and jockeying for position outside the gate is poor manners. When an exhibitor cannot be first or last to enter the ring, he or she may try to enter between two horses of lower quality, thinking that his or her own horse will benefit by comparison. Some handlers stay away from outstanding competitors because they think their own

Animation

The Arabian is naturally an animated, active breed. When the Arabian halter horse enters the arena, and whenever it is led during the class, it should appear alert and energetic. Stallions, especially, are expected to show "an abundance of vitality."

In a misguided effort to show their horses' spirit, handlers sometimes overshow (overexcite) their Arabians. Causing a horse to rear, strike, kick, lunge, or become otherwise unruly is dangerous and discourteous. Showing halter horses in an overly animated manner also gives novices the misleading impression that all Arabians are too high spirited for them to handle.

The Halter Pose

Whenever the judge is looking at the entry, the Arabian halter horse should be in the correct stance and have its head up, neck arched, and ears forward. Although the horse's legs always should remain in the proper position throughout the class, don't expect the horse to "show" through the entire class.

Exhibitors ask their horses to "show"—put their ears forward and arch their necks—whenever the judge is looking at them.

horses will suffer by comparison. If, on the other hand, the exhibitor believes that his or her own horse compares favorably to the best horse in the class, the exhibitor may purposely enter next to it. Some handlers also select this position in the hope that their own horses may gain a few more glances as the judge looks at a nearby superior horse.

When the judge is not looking at your horse, let it relax somewhat. Be sure, however, that the horse does not "go to sleep" during the class. As long as it is in the arena it is being watched by *someone*. Be sure that the horse is paying attention, even when standing with its neck in a more comfortable position. Then, whenever the judge looks in your direction, "pick up" your horse, asking it to "give" its neck and ears.

Do not chat with other exhibitors or spectators during any part of a class. Instead, concentrate on showing your horse at all times. Avoid accidents in the show ring by paying attention to the actions of nearby horses and exhibitors, ring officials, and spectators on the rail who might accidentally spook a horse.

Show your horse proudly, as though it is the best horse in the class. If you're proud of your Arabian, the animal will sense it and display itself proudly. Arabians seem to know that they are beautiful and enjoy being admired.

When trotting or walking toward or away from the judge, move in a straight line. If the horse wings or paddles, it can be led at a slight angle toward or away from the judge to partly conceal its faulty action.

ETHICS

The Arabian breed is famous for its *natural* beauty. In the show ring, this natural beauty is enhanced by artificial means. However, there is a difference between enhancing and changing the appearance of the horse.

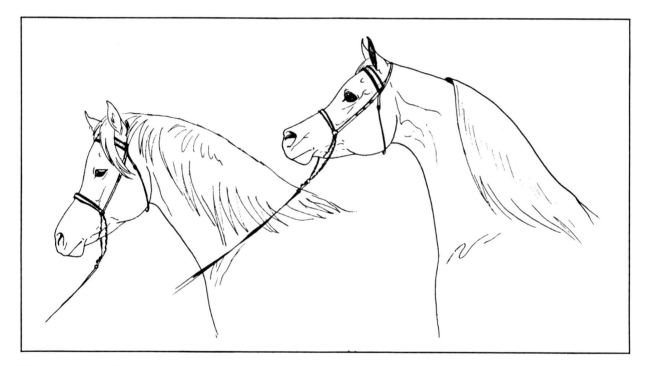

How the horse is shown can change its appearance dramatically. This is the same horse, looking sleepy and ungroomed at the left. At the right, its head is up, ears forward, eyes and nostrils wide open, and it has been clipped and carefully groomed.

The Trot

When trotting the horse, keep its head high by keeping the lead line high. This makes the neck look longer, improves the topline by tightening the muscles there, and elevates the action of the forelegs. Stay at the end of the lead line to avoid blocking the view of the horse. Letting the horse get ahead of or behind you reduces your control and distorts the head carriage of the horse.

Show rules specifically state that Arabians are to be shown with ungingered tails. (Ginger ointment, inserted into the horse's rectum to cause a burning sensation, results in higher tail carriage.) Although prohibited, ginger is often used because there is no present method of proving it has been used. However, there may be clues as to which horses have been gingered. Gingered horses may switch their tails or hold them to one side. They also are more likely to maintain a high tail carriage when relaxed. Although some Arabians keep a high tail carriage even at rest, most only raise the tail when alert or moving.

It is not legal or fair to alter the natural type or conformation of halter horses. Halter classes are for breeding stock, and unnatural alterations to the halter horse can cause deterioration in the type and conformation of the breed if that horse is chosen for breeding.

The lengths to which some exhibitors will go to unethically improve their halter horses is extreme. Reports list the following alleged practices: alteration of the teeth to conceal parrot mouth, injection of silicone to create the appearance of a normal testicle in a monorchid, surgical reduction of large or misshapen ears, surgical reduction of the eyelids, cutting tendons in the tail to correct a wry tail or raise tail carriage, and reshaping hoofs with liquid plastic to conceal toeing in or out. Although such practices are unusual, it is unfortunate that the sort of people who perpetrate them have become involved with a breed of horses known for its natural beauty.

Illegal Drugs

American Horse Shows Association Rule III, part 1, section 3 sets forth the requirements regarding drugs and medications for those competing at shows recognized by the Association. As these rules are quite specific and their violation can result in serious penalties, exhibitors should take care to read the AHSA rules in their entirety and carefully adhere to them.

The AHSA forbids the use of stimulants, depressants, tranquilizers, or local anesthetics because they can change a show horse's performance. Also forbidden are drugs that make the detection of forbidden drugs difficult. These "masking" drugs include but are not limited to injectable preparations containing polyethylene glycol or polyoxyethylated vegetable oil, injectable preparations containing

U.S. NATIONAL CHAMPION STALLIONS		
Year	National Champion	Reserve National Champion
1958	Mujahid	Synbad
1959	Synbad	Ibn Hanrah
1960	Radamason	Fadjur
1961	Ibn Habu	Bolero
1962	Bay-Abi	Saneyn
1963	Hajababa	Ibn Fadjur
1964	*Bask	Lewisfield Bold Hawk
1965	Raffon	Afari
1966	Petit Jean	Amerigo
1967	Count Bazy	Zarabo
1968	Zarabo	Fadjur
1969	Galizon	*Gwalior
1970	*Aramus	*Gwalior
1971	Ansata Ibn Sudan	*Gwalior
1972	*Elkin	Khemosabi
1973	Khemosabi	Gai-Adventure
1974	Gai Adventure	Bay-El-Bey
1975	*Asadd	*Buszmen
1976	*El Paso	Bay-El-Bey
1977	Gai Parada	Kaborr
1978	Amurath Bandolero	Erros
1979	*Aladdinn	Kaborr
1980	*Muscat	Bey Shah
1981	*Marsianin	*Czeremosz
1982	*Padron	Zarr-Hassan
1983	Arn-ett Perlane	Ruminaja Ali
1984	AAF Kaset	GG Jabask
1985	Strike	Top Contender
1986	MS Santana	Alada Baskin

U.S. NATIONAL CHAMPION MARES		
Year	National Champion	Reserve National Champion
1958	Surita	Tasliya
1959	Lallegra	Ga'Nissa
1960	Imarfa	Rose of Raswan
1961	Rominna	Imaja
1962	Chloette	Fixette
1963	Rahbana	Silver Dawn
1964	High Fashion	*Boltonka
1965	*Aristawa	*Dornaba
1966	*Dornaba	Silver Dawn
1967	Indian Genii	*Nahlah
1968	Mi-Fanci	El Malika
1969	Fame	Dancing Flame
1970	Dancing Flame	Fire Flame
1971	*Serenity Sonbolah	Gioia
1972	*Elkana	Basquelle
1973	Fire Music	SX Genii's Pride
1974	Jon-San Judizon	Amurath Bandeira
1975	Heritage Desiree	Bint Bint Hanaa
1976	Bask Melody	SX La Quinta
1977	*Wijza	T.J.'s Georgie Girl
1978	T.J.'s Georgie Girl	An Marieta
1979	*Abha Hamir	Ebony Moon
1980	Fa Halima	*Pesenka
1981	Rohara Tsultress	Alove-Note
1982	Kajora	*Penalba
1983	Bask Calonett	NH Love Potion
1984	VP Kahlua	NH Love Potion
1985	NH Love Potion	Sonoma Lady
1986	Penicylina	Amber Satin

thiamine (Vitamin B₁), dipyrone (brand name *Novin*®), furosemide (brand name *Lasix*®), sulfa drugs, or thiabendazole ("TBZ") dewormers.

Mydriatic drugs dropped into the eyes to dilate the pupils for a "wide-eyed" look also are forbidden by the rules. They also can damage the horse's vision.

Drugs only can be used to treat an illness or injury. If a forbidden drug is administered to the horse within seven days prior to a show or during a show, a medication report must be filed by the exhibitor with the AHSA steward at the show. The report must be filed within one hour after the drug is administered or within an hour after the steward comes on duty at a show. Some drugs remain in the horse's body and will be detected if the horse is selected for drug testing during a show.

The drugs and medications regulations are enforced by blood, saliva and urine tests. Any entry at an Arabian horse show may be tested for illegal drugs by the AHSA-appointed testing veterinarian. At the U.S. and Canadian National Championships, all National and Reserve National Champions must be tested, as well as one randomly selected horse in every class.

Cruelty and Abuse

Cruelty or abuse of show horses is expressly forbidden by the *AHSA Rule Book*. Known violators are barred from showing and may face other action. As described by the Rule Book, cruelty or abuse includes excessive use of a whip on a horse at the show grounds. Also cited are the use of any substance to induce temporary heat, including ginger ointment; use of an electric device in schooling or showing, including an electrical "hot shot" or cattle prod; and use of any explosive, including fire extinguishers. The rules forbid *any* inhumane treatment of a horse by anyone at the show grounds, whether or not the specific practice is identified in the *AHSA Rule Book*.

It is unfortunate that cruel exhibitors sometimes escape detection and win with abused horses, for their success may encourage others to copy their treatment of show horses in the hope of emulating their success in the show ring. Despite the rules against mistreating show horses, winning sometimes becomes the total emphasis, with the welfare of the horse ignored.

Owners who hire professionals to train and show their horses must be careful to avoid individuals who win at the expense of the animals. When a trainer's show horses consistently show indications of resentment, anger, hatred, or fear toward the trainer, an owner should not place horses in that person's hands. Winning must be secondary to the welfare of the horses whose beauty, sensitivity, and affection for people inspired the sport of Arabian horse showing.

Now, when success in the Arabian horse business often hinges upon success in the show ring, it is imperative that exhibitors maintain high ethical standards while competing at Arabian horse shows and that any witnessed cruelty or abuse of show horses is promptly reported to the horse show authorities.

The Sportsman's Charter
(from the AHSA Rule Book)

That sport is something done for the fun of doing it and that it ceases to be a sport when it becomes a business only, something done for what there is in it;

That amateurism is something of the heart and spirit—not a matter of exact technical qualifications;

That the good manners of sport are fundamentally important;

That the code must be strictly upheld;

That the whole structure of sport is not only preserved from the absurdity of undue importance, but is justified by a kind of romance which animates it, and by the positive virtues of courage, patience, good temper, and unselfishness which are demanded by the code;

That the exploitation of sport for profit alone kills the spirit and retains only the husk and semblance of the thing;

That the qualities of frankness, courage, and sincerity which mark the good sportsman in private life shall mark the discussions of his interests at a show.

Khemosabi, U.S. National Champion Stallion and U.S. National Champion Western Pleasure Horse. *Bill Macri photo courtesy of the Khemosabi Syndicate*

34

THE STALLION

No horse is more beautiful than a fiery Arabian stallion. No wonder so many people dream of owning one. However, it is impractical for most people to do so. Stallions require especially sturdy enclosures and enough exercise to take the edge off their abundant energy. The sexual urges of the stallion lie just below the surface and can erupt at any time. If a stallion gets out of control, unplanned breedings can occur. Stallions may attack geldings or other stallions, and are more likely to bite, kick, or strike at people than are mares or geldings. For these reasons, the only person who should own a stallion is the serious breeder.

LEASING STALLIONS

Breeders often can obtain temporary access to a top-quality stallion by leasing rather than buying. Leasing requires a smaller investment than an outright purchase and provides an opportunity to see how the stallion will nick with the breeders' mares and how many outside mares will be booked to him. If a breeder has enough mares to breed, leasing a good stallion might be cheaper than sending the mares to outside stallions and paying the related costs.

A young stallion sometimes can be leased quite reasonably, with the lessee assuming responsibility for training, showing, and promoting him as a show horse. This kind of "sweat equity" can be an inexpensive way for the lessee to breed to a horse whose value and reputation are expected to increase. The lessee has an opportunity to invest in the stallion's future. However, there is never any guarantee that an untried stallion will become a success in the show ring *or* in the breeding shed.

OWNING YOUR OWN STALLION(S)

Eventually, it becomes easier and less expensive for the breeder to own a stallion than to send a number of broodmares to outside stallions. If the stallion is offered at public stud, stud fees and mare care fees generate additional income for the breeding farm. A superior stallion can establish the reputation of his owner as a breeder.

Large breeding farms usually keep at least two stallions so that mares too closely related to one stallion can be bred to the other. Eventually, too many of the breeder's own mares may be related to one of the stallions; at that point, it may be necessary to sell or trade him to obtain a different stallion for outcrossing on those mares.

Arabian stallions often are more gentle than stallions of other breeds, but all stallions require more careful management than do geldings or mares.

Care of the Breeding Stallion

Like all other horses, stallions require regular health and farrier care and good nutrition. Stallions need regular strenuous exercise, which promotes fertility and makes them easier to handle.

Stallions are more content when they can see other horses from their stall and paddock. However, it usually is good to keep them out of *reach* of other horses. To prevent jealousy and attempted fighting, stallions should not be stabled next to each other.

Stallion paddocks must be surrounded by strong, high fences that are as safe as possible and will not allow stallions to go over or through them.

Number of Mares Bred

Stallions usually are test bred to a few mares (two to five) as three year olds. Occasionally a two-year-old stallion is bred. Fertility rates for young, immature stallions are lower than for mature stallions. In fact, breeding a young stallion too heavily may contribute to infertility.

Lady Wentworth advocated breeding no more than twenty-five mares per season to a four-year-old stallion in his first year at stud. Older stallions might serve thirty or forty mares per year.

Today, *few* Arabian stallions sire twenty or more foals in one year although they may be bred to more than twenty mares, for not all breedings result in live foals.

Artificial insemination makes it possible for one stallion to be bred to a larger number of mares, allowing a popular stallion to have a greater influence on the breed than in the past. If, however, too many mares are bred to one stallion, the market can soon be flooded with his foals, making them more difficult to sell and probably lowering the average sale price. Instead, Registry-approved breeding farms generally use AI to settle mares more quickly and to lower the risk of injury to the breeding stallion, rather than to increase the number of mares that can be bred to one stallion.

To attract a number of outside mares for breeding, a top quality stallion of popular bloodlines is needed. If he already has established himself as a sire of good Arabian horses, so much the better. If he is young or hasn't been promoted as a breeding stallion, it will take an investment of years and money to establish his reputation. It is possible to spend thousands of dollars to show and advertise a young stallion only to find that he is not a good sire. The young or unshown stallion will attract fewer mares and command a lower stud fee than a well-known stallion.

Breeding outside mares can be much more difficult than limiting the stallion to one's own mares. Outside mares are sometimes problem breeders; they sometimes are delivered in poor condition, and they may be ill-tempered or untrained. Because you are dealing with other people, problems will arise when breeding mares that belong to others. Stallion owners must try to foresee possible problem areas and protect themselves with adequate insurance and explicit breeding contracts.

Mare owners want their mares to be well-treated while at the breeding farm. Stallion owners who provide good mare care and settle mares promptly, returning them home in good condition, will gain repeat breedings. If a mare is neglected and sent home in poor condition or not in foal, the stallion owner risks losing her owner as a customer.

Before the mare is delivered, be sure the owner understands the kind of care the mare will receive and the costs involved. Many farms photograph the mare when she arrives at the farm and just before she goes home to protect the farm from a misunderstanding considering her condition and care—photos don't lie.

The desired result of breeding is a pregnant mare in good condition. It's better to send a mare home *slightly* overweight than too thin.

Breeding Restrictions

You can limit your stallion to "approved mares only" to prevent breeding inferior mares to your stallion. However, rejecting a mare may create bad feelings. Also, some unimpressive mares are outstanding producers. If a mare is rejected, it must be done tactfully.

advertising, training, and showing personally, costs can be reduced.

Advertising in national Arabian horse magazines is very expensive, but it is necessary to keep a stallion in the minds of the mare-owning public. Costs vary according to the publication and type of ad. Sometimes owners gain free publicity from magazine articles about their stallions and breeding programs. Advertising efforts should be followed up with brochures about the stallion, and they should be sent with a personal letter to everyone who inquires about him.

A healthy stallion requires a great deal of exercise to burn up excess vitality.
Sharon Vander Ende photo of Aulrab courtesy of Warren Park Stud, Sanger, Calif.

STALLION PROMOTION

"Promotion" means publicizing your stallion. Stallion owners have become increasingly creative and sophisticated in this area. The breeding stallion is a super star, and the breeding farm manager or owner serves as the stallion's agent or public relations person. The manager must determine how to present an image for the stallion through careful advertising, and the stallion must be visible at Arabian horse shows and related events. Movies or videotapes of the stallion often are prepared for showing at the breeding farm and at major Arabian horse events.

If a stallion is promoted heavily and professionally shown and advertised, costs can easily exceed $20,000 per year. If the manager can do some of the

Sponsoring open houses, clinics, and other events provide other opportunities to show your stallion to potential customers.

The principles of promoting a stallion are the same regardless of the amount of money available for the purpose. Instead of using an expensive four-color catalog, a black-and-white brochure may be used by the "small breeder" with a tight budget. If the important facts about the stallion are presented in a creative and attractive manner, the inexpensive brochure may be quite effective.

Incentive Plans

To attract additional outside mares for breeding, stallion owners sometimes offer various incentives to mare owners. Because it becomes increasingly difficult for the small breeder to sell foals as the number

"The Fabulous Fadjur," an Americanbred stallion, traced to the early Babson imports from both Egypt and Poland. He was a very popular sire of show horses, and many of his get were purchased for export from the U.S.

Photo courtesy of Jack Tone Ranch

of good-quality Arabian horses grows, a powerful incentive to breed to a certain stallion is the promise that his owner(s) will help sell the resulting foal.

Some big breeders allow mare owners to sell foals sired by their stallion(s) in the big breeding farm's private auctions. Other stallion owners supply free advertising for foals by their stallion(s), listing them in magazine ads and sales lists.

Some stallion owners offer special futurities, giving cash awards to owners of mares that produce champions by their stallion. The level of the championship is specified by the stallion owner, and the amount of the prizes vary. These futurities are held to attract more outside mares for breeding, attract *better* mares, and encourage the owners of the stallion's foals to show them. Major show wins by the stallion's get result in more breedings to that stallion and more potential champion get.

Most of the higher stud fees include a "live foal guarantee." Some stallion owners carry this a step further and guarantee a live *filly*. The mare is rebred free (or at a specified reduced fee) until she produces a filly by the stallion. This incentive is attractive because fillies usually sell for more money than colts.

Some stallion owners even offer a "gelding rebate," a partial refund of the stud fee, to the owner whose mare produces a colt that is gelded. As an alternative, the stallion owner may offer a free or reduced-rate rebreeding if a colt is gelded. This incentive benefits the entire Arabian horse industry because it encourages mare owners to geld colts. However, it also offers several benefits to the stallion owner. First, it encourages rebreedings and the resultant income from mare care (board). Second, it prevents most of the stallion's inferior colts from giving their sire a bad reputation (through poor breeding ability or poor showings in stallion halter classes). Finally, it reduces the number of the stallion's sons who will compete against their sire on all levels (showing, breeding, and sales of get).

STALLION SYNDICATION

Stallion syndications, although a comparatively recent innovation in the Arabian horse business, are currently becoming more common. When a stallion is syndicated, several people buy stock (breeding shares) in him. The syndicate manager usually owns the majority of the shares and gets a salary for managing the stallion.

Syndicate members share the costs of maintaining, showing, and advertising the stallion. In return, each receives a specified number of annual breedings to the stallion. These breeding rights can usually be sold (with restrictions) if the shareholder does not wish to exercise the right to breed his or her own mare(s) to the stallion. The shareholders also may sell their interest in the stallion. Usually, the price is predetermined by the terms of the syndica-

298

tion, and permission must be obtained from the other members.

Because the costs are shared among the members, a stallion might be syndicated for a million dollars' worth of shares although his sales price would never approach that amount. The syndication value of the stallion may therefore be much greater than his actual sale value.

Syndication is a complex legal procedure and must meet many government regulations. Many so-called stallion syndicates really are just partnerships that share the expenses and income from owning a breeding stallion. A true syndicate does not stand the stallion at public stud—it was formed to make the stallion exclusively available to mares owned by its members.

Pros and Cons of Syndication

The main advantages to syndication are financial. Syndicate members gain certain tax advantages. Their investment is likely to be smaller than that required to buy a good stallion outright, and their expenses are less because they are shared by the other members. The value of the stallion's foals *may* be increased by the exclusivity of syndication, and breeding shares may be sold for predetermined high prices.

Although syndicate members may benefit financially from stallion syndication, the practice could be detrimental to the Arabian breed. Syndication may severely limit the mares to which a stallion will be bred. Because the syndicate members' mares are likely to be of similar bloodlines or of the same "nationality" as the stallion, the syndicated stallion might not be bred to a sufficiently wide variety of bloodlines to discover his best possible nick. Also, some excellent Arabian mares cannot be bred to him because their owners do not belong to the syndicate or are unable to buy breeding shares.

CULLING STALLIONS

The fastest way to change a breeding program is to change stallions. It is far more difficult to sell and replace a herd of broodmares than it is to sell and replace one stallion.

Any stallion that does not sire consistently good foals should be culled from the breeding program. The stallion should sire excellent foals from excellent mares and, when bred to average mares, he should "improve on the mares" (sire foals that are better than their dams). If he doesn't, either he is a poor sire or he nicks poorly with the broodmares in the program.

Stallions with fertility problems also are a financial liability. Mares bred to a stallion should settle quickly, and the stallion's sperm should be healthy, numerous, and active.

Unlike mares, stallions usually can be used for breeding until they die of old age. However, most undergo a decline in fertility as they become elderly, and some become sterile. An old stallion may represent an economic liability to the breeder *if* the stallion is not already a famous sire of quality foals, for few outside mares may be sent to him and his foals my not find a ready market. On the other hand, a particularly valuable old stallion may be well worth the frustrations of trying to settle even a few mares. Although most old stallions are less fertile than they were in their prime, some maintain a high degree of fertility even in old age. Fertility in both stallions and mares tends to vary by family.

Remember that culling does not necessarily have a negative connotation. The stallion that is "culled" from one breeding program—for whatever reasons—may prove to be a valuable sire in a different program.

It should go without saying that all stallions should be excellent individuals. If they are not, they should not be used for breeding. Poor stallions shouldn't be culled—they should be gelded.

Geldings are great! This is El Khyam, U.S. National Champion Jumper and Canadian National Champion Hunter, as well as the winner of many classes at open horse shows. Shawnly McCoy, up.

LeRoy Weathers photo courtesy of Judi Hook, Spanaway, Wash.

35

ARAB GELDINGS

A gelding is a male horse that has been castrated. Gelding is minor surgery that can be performed anywhere by a competent veterinarian. The risk is low; most horses recover quickly and completely.

The Bedouins didn't geld their horses. Instead, mares were used for riding because they were quieter and less inclined to give away a military position by calling to other horses. Stallions were kept shackled constantly by the pastern (hobbled) when not being used for breeding. Inferior colts were sold or even abandoned to die in the desert. Life would have been much better for the Arabian stallions if the Bedouins *had* believed in gelding.

WHY GELD?

The *only* reason to keep a stallion entire is for breeding, and only the very best colts should be considered stallion prospects. If the colt lacks a superior pedigree, superior type, or superior conformation, he should be gelded. An Arabian stallion should be superior in *every* regard.

Geldings offer many advantages over stallions. They usually are much quieter, calmer, more predictable, gentler, easier to train, and more consistent performers than stallions. They can be pastured with open mares and other geldings and are far less

likely to attack and injure other horses than are stallions.

Too many stallions exist in the Arabian breed. They greatly outnumber geldings, which is unfortunate because geldings are the best pleasure and working horses.

A major reason for an owner's reluctance to geld is financial. Geldings usually sell for less than stallions because they cannot be used for breeding. In theory, a stallion can be sold for more money than a gelding and also generate income from stud fees.

In reality, so many Arabian stallions exist that the average Arabian stallion sires only a handful of purebred foals each year, and some *never* sire a purebred foal. The average stud fee also is well below the thousands of dollars demanded for famous and well-promoted stallions. The average owner will not become rich from owning an Arabian stallion.

Another reason for reluctance to geld is blind optimism. Owners have trouble being objective about their horses. Many hope unreasonably that a disappointing colt will someday blossom into a great stallion. Unfortunately, the disappointing colt will not improve with age—he'll just get bigger.

What happens if one poor stallion is bred to just three mares, each of whom produces a colt as poor as the sire? Even if all four horses are gelded at this point, we have four Arabian geldings instead of one. If they are all advertised for sale at the same time, they must compete with each other. Sales (and prices) go down in direct proportion to the increased supply of geldings. From a business standpoint, it is foolish to flood the market with inferior horses. Gelding colts before they are old enough to be used for breeding makes good business sense.

It is just as bad to flood the market with *good* Arabians. You *can* have too much of a good thing when supply exceeds demand.

Inferior colts should be gelded, but so should good colts. Only truly outstanding colts should remain stallions. Any stallion who fails to sire outstanding foals, also should be gelded. This not only curtails the rising population (to avoid further flooding the market) but makes better quality geldings available to users.

Breeders sometimes forget—possibly because they are involved in producing horses—that the *end product* of any breeding program *is the Arabian gelding*. Quality is much more important than quantity.

WHEN TO GELD

Gelding should not be done in extreme weather of any kind. In most climates, spring and fall are best. Avoid gelding during fly season since files can irritate and cause infection of the open wound.

Never geld a horse while he is in poor condition or sick. Wait until a weanling has adjusted to being separated from his dam before you geld him.

Some people think that the gravitational pull of the moon affects the rate of bleeding, and they geld according to the moon's phases, avoiding a full moon. Superstition always has played a part in horse matters, and some respected horsepersons still "geld by the moon."

Age to Geld

Gelding often is delayed until a colt is two or three years old, to "let him get his growth." Unless the colt is a breeding prospect, there is no reason to wait that long. Gelding a young colt will not stunt his growth. In fact, early gelding appears to result in greater height at maturity.

A group of California State Polytechnic University's Arabian weanlings were gelded at eight to twelve months of age. All were over fifteen hands by the age of five although their parents averaged only 14.2 hands. Horses that are gelded early *appear* to mature later (keep growing longer) and to develop greater size due to delayed closure of the growth plates in the bones of the legs.

A horse gelded at a young age also develops a lighter neck and less heavy muscling in the shoulders and hindquarters. Because he carries less extra weight in these areas, he may have greater freedom of movement. The early gelding's lighter throatlatch and neck also makes collection easier when the horse is ridden or driven.

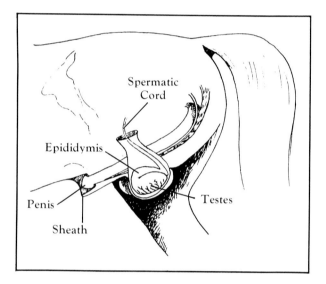

Reproductive tract of the male horse.

Gelding the young colt also is easier on the animal because the veins leading to the testes still are small, so less bleeding occurs during the operation. The weanling gelding usually heals quickly and may not even move stiffly the day after the operation. Gelding the young colt also avoids the rough play indulged in by stud colts. Some young colts tease mares and it is even possible for an eight to ten month old colt to breed and settle a mare.

Stallion behavior is partly learned behavior, and the longer the horse remains a stallion before he is gelded, the more likely he will continue such behavior after he is gelded. The sooner he becomes a gelding, the sooner he forgets his sexual urges.

Weanling colts can be gelded as soon as they have adjusted to being weaned. In fact, a colt can be gelded at almost any age although five to twelve months probably is best.

Although it's best to geld young, mature stallions usually can be safely gelded. Some stallions have been gelded and gone on to high-level show wins as geldings. (It is probably best not to geld an elderly stallion, however.)

The Gelding Operation

The two testes (testicles) produce sperm and testosterone—the male hormone that causes stallion-like behavior. The testes are in the scrotum, outside the stallion's body to provide the cooler temperature necessary for sperm life.

Immature sperm leave the testes and mature in the epididymis, an elongated tissue attached to the testicle. In gelding, the testes and the epididymis are removed through an incision in the scrotum. The *vas deferens*, a tube through which the sperm move during breeding, also is cut when the testes are removed.

Mature horses often are gelded while they are standing, but young horses are gelded while lying down since their smaller testes are more difficult to reach when they are standing.

The horse is sedated for the operation and will appear to be asleep or groggy. If the colt is lying on his left side, the right hind leg can be pulled forward and secured with a hobble or rope around the pastern. The pastern rope is attached to a rope around the lower neck or chest of the colt. Young colts are restrained easily, and the leg may simply be held back by an assistant. (If properly sedated, the horse will not feel pain or struggle.) If additional restraint is necessary, a twitch may be used.

The veterinarian cleans the horse's scrotal sac with antiseptic before making an incision. The testicle and epididymis are pulled through the incision and an emasculating instrument cuts and clamps the spermatic cord that connects the testicles to the body. (Clamping reduces bleeding.) When the emasculator is removed, the incision is left open for drainage. Both testes are removed, one at a time.

CARE AFTER GELDING

The anesthetic should wear off shortly after the brief operation, and the horse will struggle to its feet. Do not feed or water the horse for an hour or two after it gets up to prevent choking.

After the colt has been anesthetized, the veterinarian makes an incision in the scrotum. The testicles are removed one at a time.

The testicle is held prior to placement of the emasculator.

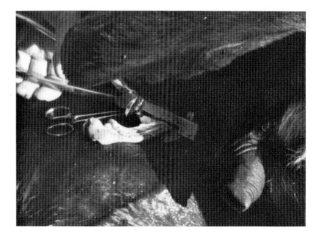

The cord is clamped with the emasculator next to the epididymis.

303

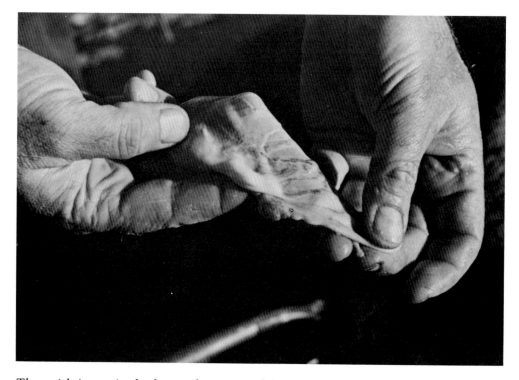

The testicle is examined to be sure the entire epididymis was removed. (Failure to do so can mean that the "gelding" will go on behaving like a stallion.)

Exercise the new gelding lightly each day after the operation. Exercise promotes drainage from the incision, which helps keep it from becoming swollen and infected. Clean off drainage to avoid attracting flies. If excessive swelling, stiffness, or bleeding occurs after the operation, consult your vet.

GELDINGS THAT "ACT LIKE" STALLIONS

If both testicles and the entire epididymis are not removed during the gelding procedure, the horse may continue to act like a stallion afterward. Such geldings usually are called "proud cut." Some geldings will continue to tease mares, etc., for a while after they have been gelded. This usually subsides within a month or two of the operation and may result from latent male hormones still present in the body or simply from learned behavior. Cryptorchids, male horses whose testes are retained in the abdomen, also will act like stallions although no testicles are visible; although they appear to be geldings, they are not.

CRYPTORCHIDS AND MONORCHIDS

Normally, testes develop inside the horse's abdomen and then move down into the scrotum.

The testes are usually down (descended into the scrotum) when the foal is born. Occasionally, they may return to the abdomen. In most colts, the testes will be down (and stay down) by the time they are six months to one year old. Both testicles must be descended before the horse can be gelded.

If the testes haven't descended by the time a colt is two, he is probably a cryptorchid. The only alternative is to surgically remove the testes from the abdomen. (If only one testicle is retained, the colt is a monorchid.)

Although cryptorchids behave like stallions, they seldom settle mares. The internal body temperature of the abdomen usually is higher than that of the scrotum and kills sperm, making them sterile. Monorchids can settle mares but shouldn't be used for breeding because the condition is inherited.

In halter classes, judges should check stallions to be sure that they are not monorchid or cryptorchid. (It is against the rules to show a stallion two or older if he doesn't have two visible testicles.) Although monorchid and cryptorchid Arabians bred in America can be registered, the Registry will not register imported horses with the defect.

Cryptorchids and monorchids should be gelded. However, this involves major surgery, with the usual risks, higher costs, and longer recovery period than normal gelding. It is unethical to geld a monorchid by removing the only visible testicle, for the horse will then appear to be a gelding but continue to act like a stallion.

Rayek, U.S. National Reserve Champion Gelding and U.S. National Champion in Native Costume. This versatile gelding owned by Gleannloch Farms has many other championships in both halter and performance. No wonder his rider (Rhita NcNair) is smiling!

Sparagowski photo courtesy of Rhita McNair

Horses that are too young to ride or breed are slow to sell, and keeping immature horses for several years is costly. Unless a youngster is a superior individual, it may be wiser to sell quickly at a low price to keep the loss relatively small.

Don Sepulvado photo courtesy of N.S.U.

36

THE HORSE BUSINESS

Any business that depends upon income related to horses is "a horse business." This includes tack and feed stores, horse trailer and barn construction companies, etc. The businesses most commonly associated with Arabian horses are professional training stables and breeding farms. Of these, breeding farms are far more numerous.

"A LOSS INDUSTRY"

Visions of selling Arabian horses for huge sums lure many people into the breeding business because high sales seem possible at some point in the near future. The truth is that although there *are* a few big winners whose success is well publicized, there are many more losers. Thomas A. Davis, Tax Counsel for the American Horse Council, says "More money goes into the horse industry than comes out." The breeder who breaks even is doing better than most, and the one who makes even a small profit is in the minority.

Because it is difficult to make a profit with a horse business, wealthy individuals sometimes invest in a horse breeding farm to reduce the amount of income taxes they must pay by "writing off" the horse expenses against their other income. Because a business must be operated with the intent of mak-

ing a profit, rather than just as a tax shelter, the Internal Revenue Service tends to view horse businesses with suspicion, especially when an individual with a large income from other sources declares large losses from a horse venture.

The horse business must conform to the various regulations governing any business as well as carefully follow current income tax laws concerning reporting income and losses. Because the tax laws related to horse farms are complex and may be changed frequently, it is wise for the owner of a horse business to be sure his or her accountant stays up-to-date concerning changes to the tax laws.

A tax manual specifically written for horse businesses and updated regularly is published by the American Horse Council, Inc., 1700 K Street, N.W., Washington, D.C. 20006.

THE HORSE BREEDING BUSINESS

Running a breeding farm requires a large investment of time, labor, and money. It also requires a wide range of skills. Every breeder needs a Certified Public Accountant (CPA) and an attorney who are familiar with the horse business and its specialized regulations. The continuing services of a good equine veterinarian and a farrier are necessary. If the horses are shown, a professional trainer may be needed. Knowledgeable and conscientious stud managers and grooms also are important to the success of a breeding farm.

Wealthy breeders can hire specialists to perform the various tasks associated with the horse business, but breeders on a restricted budget might have to fill some of these roles themselves. The owner/operator of a small breeding farm simultaneously may be a stable manager, veterinary technician, business manager, salesman, judge, trainer, ad person, pedigree researcher, office manager, and psychologist!

Costs of Doing Business

A horse business involves the usual expenses of horse ownership, plus additional costs for such items as advertising, legal and accounting services, office supplies, transportation, memberships, subscription fees, and long distance telephone calls. Although some of these expenses also are encountered by the average Arabian horse owner, the business owner usually pays *more*.

While most pleasure horse owners maintain only one or two Arabians, the breeder usually supports a herd. Show and breeding stock also require special farrier and vet care and are more expensive to feed. Veterinarian bills also are frequent and expensive due to palpating, pregnancy tests, and other costs associated with breeding.

The start-up period for a horse business is longer than for other kinds of businesses, for it takes years to produce a foal and raise it to a useable age. Most Arabians sell when they are two years old or more and can be trained. In the interim, expenses mount with little or no income.

Hobby or Business?

To deduct expenses of your horse business from your income taxes, you must prove to the Internal Revenue Service that your horses are a business instead of a hobby. The best way to do this is to make a profit. However, you can probably convince IRS that you're really *trying* to make a profit if you can demonstrate that you run your operation in a business-like manner. This means understanding the principles of business and keeping thorough written records.

Keep a written plan for each year, showing your estimated income and expenses. The more information you put in writing—to prove that you are analyzing your business progress and planning for future success—the better your chances will be of demonstrating that you are operating in a business-like way (trying to make a profit).

At the end of each year, review your income and expenses and prepare the next year's operating plan. If you lost money, analyze why in writing and propose changes that might be more successful. Compare your inventory (horses, equipment, and property) at the start of the year with the inventory at the end of the year. Show how your investment is appreciating in value for an eventual profit. Show, in writing, that you expect to make a profit, and that you *can*.

Pay an accountant to keep your financial records in order. (That, too is a deductible expense.) If you keep your own books, set up the ledgers properly and keep them current. An efficient business keeps track of its income and expenses.

If you work personally in the business, or if your family members do, keep written records of the time spent and what tasks are done. Keep up-to-date on the Arabian horse business by subscribing to magazines and buying books to increase your expertise in the field. Attend seminars and workshops related to the horse business. These costs are deductible as business expenses, and show you are really trying to succeed in your business.

When you need help, consult experts. Document their expertise in the horse business, and *take their advice*. Work closely with your CPA and your attorney to meet the tax requirements for horse breeding farms. Assume that you will someday be asked to prove your profit motive and know how to establish it.

Depreciation (Cost Recovery)

Equipment and horses that you *buy* can be depreciated over a period of time designated by the income tax laws. Horses that you produce are *not* depreciable because you've already deducted the expense of producing them.

Equipment used to operate your business may be deducted as an expense or depreciated over a period of time, depending on the type of equipment, its cost, and the existing specifications of the tax laws.

The American Horse Council (see "Other Sources of Information") publishes a helpful pamphlet entitled "Tax Tips for Horse Owners." Like the Council's comprehensive manual covering tax laws affecting the horse industry in America, it is revised whenever tax laws change.

SELLING ARABIAN HORSES

Whether you are in the horse business or not, the same principles apply to selling Arabian horses. When you meet potential buyers, be pleasant, honest, and business-like. Remember that everyone you meet is a *potential* buyer.

Age of Sale Horses

Arabians can be sold at any age. Some are even sold before birth. If you want to sell weanlings, advertise them as soon as they are born. Newborn Arabian foals are hard to resist. Weanlings and yearlings aren't quite as cute as smaller foals and are still years away from serious training, so they often are "slow sellers."

Three year old Arabians are more easily sold because they look mature and are old enough to begin using. Most buyers prefer a horse that has been started under saddle.

Horses between four and ten years old are usually the easiest to sell. Well-trained, mature Arabians usually are the most saleable horses on the market. Horses past the age of ten usually sell more slowly as they age. Elderly horses are the most difficult to sell because their useful lives may be nearing an end.

The Effect of the Horse's Sex on Its Price

Because they can give birth to foals that can be sold, mares generally sell for higher prices than male horses. Geldings usually sell for less money than stallions because they cannot generate income from stud fees or sales of get.

Bred mares, unless they happen to be in foal to a famous stallion, often do not bring much more money than open mares. However, a bred mare may sell more quickly if the buyer wants to raise a foal and likes the stallion to which the mare was bred. Sometimes a buyer prefers to buy an open broodmare to breed to the stallion of his or her own choice. Often, however, an open broodmare is viewed with suspicion; buyers may wonder if she is open because she has breeding problems. Often, a mare is advertised for sale at different prices, depending upon whether she is to be bred to the seller's stallion or left open. If a mare is pregnant

Arabian foals are hard to resist. Their friendliness and cuteness helps sell them at this age.

and has a foal at side, she is sometimes called "a three-in-one package." Mares should not be bred before they are sold unless they are good enough to be broodmares. Poor-quality mares should be priced as riding horses rather than breeding stock. If selling a broodmare, warn the customer of any known breeding problems.

When a young colt is sold, it may be gelded prior to being sold or sold entire. Colts are sometimes advertised at two prices: a higher price if the colt remains a stallion and a lower price or rebate if he is gelded by the buyer.

Stallions sell for higher prices if they are well trained, have had a successful show career, or are proven sires of quality foals. Young, unproven stallions usually are less expensive because they represent a greater risk to the buyer.

Pricing

A horse is worth exactly what a buyer will pay. An Arabian is "worth" its sales price simply because the buyer and seller agree on the amount. To determine your horse's market value, figure out what similar horses are bringing. Remember that not every horse is sold for its advertised price. The advertised price is sometimes the "asking" price. Even if the seller won't take less, he or she may not find a buyer willing to pay the price. It does little good to know how much money the seller wants to get for a horse—the important factor is what someone will pay for that horse.

Individuals and small breeders often must accept less than half the price that a famous breeder can get for a similar horse. If you are a breeder, remember that you cannot expect to make a profit on every sale. Your goal should be a profit on your breeding operation as a whole.

Before you set your sales price, know how much you've invested in the horse. Your total investment includes the initial cost of the horse plus maintenance, training, showing, etc. If you're in the business, of course, purchase prices are depreciated and other expenses are deductible.

If you need to sell a horse quickly, you may be willing to accept a lower price than if you can hold out for a higher amount. Also, it may be better to take a small loss than to wait and take a larger loss when the horse is eventually sold.

Perhaps the *best* way to price an Arabian is to ask yourself, "What would *I* really pay for this horse?"

Advertising

When possible, show your sale horses at Arabian shows. People who attend the shows obviously are interested already in Arabian horses. Post "for sale" signs and distribute sales literature.

The market for Arabian horses is still national in scope, so the best way to advertise is in national Arabian horse publications; local readers may even respond to a national ad. Serious buyers will travel long distances to obtain the right horse. Less expensive Arabian horses may be advertised locally. Start with classified ads in local newspapers and horse club newsletters. Put posters or sales lists in feed and tack stores and at local shows.

Classified Ads — Inexpensive Arabians are best advertised in classified ads, which cost less than special display advertising. Make your classified ad as interesting as possible—especially if it will appear in a national publication and must compete with other classified ads. Include the horse's age, sex, color, training, pedigree, price, and any other selling points. For best results, include both an address and a telephone number for replies.

Display Ads — Designing a display ad for an Arabian horse magazine is easy—thanks to the professionals who will convert your rough sketch into a finished ad. Look through previous magazines to find ads you like, and then use a similar format.

Send at least one *good* glossy photograph of the horse and information that will appeal to a buyer. Include the horse's name, registration number, age, sex, and price. Including the price helps in two ways. First, it prevents inquiries from people who can't or won't pay your price. Second, it will draw inquiries from people who can afford your horse but might never inquire if you don't advertise the price. (Some people assume that an unadvertised price must be high.)

Type or neatly print the information ("copy") that you want to appear in the display ad and send it with the illustrating photo(s) and a simple sketch of how you want the ad to look. Include your check for the cost of the ad plus a cover letter specifying when you want the ad to appear (check the advertising deadlines published in the magazine). Include your telephone number in case of questions about the ad. Enclose a piece of stiff cardboard to keep the photograph from being damaged and put your name and address on a stick-on label on the back of the photo.

Keep your sale horse clipped, bathed, and groomed for presentation to potential buyers, and bring it from its stall or pen in good condition. If the horse is dusty, take a moment to brush it off before showing. Put a show halter on the horse and stand it up for a brief inspection.

Responding to Inquiries

Answer all written inquiries about your sale horse(s) with speed, enthusiasm, and courtesy. Send a letter describing your horse's best qualities and include a pedigree and photographs. Invite the inquirer to telephone or visit to see the horse.

Keep sales information about the horse near the telephone. When you get a telephone inquiry, write down the caller's name and phone number first. Then ask what the buyer is looking for in a horse. If yours might meet the buyer's needs, explain how it will serve those purposes. Don't try to sell the horse to the caller unless it *will* do so. Encourage the caller to come see the horse. Be friendly but not pushy.

Presenting the Sale Horse

When a visitor comes to see your Arabian, remember that your horse is competing with others. Competition for sales is tough because more Arabians than ever are now for sale.

Call the visitor's attention to your Arabian's best points. If the horse has a poor topline but a lovely head, stress the beauty of its head. If the horse has a good topline and a plain head, point out the superior topline. If the horse has good legs, mention them. If it doesn't, don't mention the legs.

Don't point out any faults unless they affect the horse's health or performance ability. If the horse has a chronic health problem or is unsound, be sure the customer understands the situation.

Never make any claims that are not true. Many owners will present a horse with crooked legs and comment upon how correct they are. Doing so insults the intelligence of the visitor and makes the owner seem ignorant or dishonest.

Don't keep the horse standing in the halter pose for too long; after five minutes or so, it will become bored and won't look as good as when it's alert. If possible, turn the horse loose in an arena for a few minutes. The Blunts of England began the tradition of showing sale horses at liberty, and it has survived because it is highly effective. *All* Arabians look best

311

in motion—they carry their tails higher, arch their necks, and expand their nostrils, enhancing the dished appearance of the facial profile.

Afterward, if the horse is trained for riding or driving, demonstrate its abilities before asking if the customer would like to try your horse out personally.

If the customer is interested, offer to show any relatives of the sale horse that you own, show the customer the sale horse's pedigree, and provide any other pertinent information about the horse.

If the visitor is not interested in the horse, thank him or her for coming. If you treat potential buyers well, they may be future customers or refer others. If a buyer is unsure about the horse, suggest that he or she think it over and let you know later. Extend an invitation to come back to see the horse again or to call for more information.

SALES TRANSACTIONS

Cash Sales — Cash sales are best because the total price is received at once before the horse leaves your property. A certified check gives security without the risk of holding cash. If a personal check is given, keep the horse's registration certificate until the check clears.

Time Payments — Many Arabians in all price ranges are sold on time payments. In such cases, the seller keeps the horse's registration certificate until the final payment is made. However, a registration certificate is not "title" to an Arabian horse and does not serve as a lien against the horse in case of non-payment.

Have the buyer sign a sales contract or promissory note before the horse leaves. Follow your attorney's advice about content and legal recordation of the debt.

It is customary for time purchasers to insure the horse's life for enough to cover the unpaid balance on the purchase price. The policy should name the seller as "loss payee." In the event of the horse's death, the insurance settlement should be divided between buyer and seller according to the amount that each has remaining invested in the horse. Usually the insurance company only issues one check, which must be signed by both parties.

WHEN THE HORSE LEAVES

Be sure that the horse is clean and ready to be picked up or delivered. Include a clean halter and

Successful show horses can command higher sales prices and stud fees for their owner. Showing also may attract the attention of potential customers who otherwise would not see a breeder's horses.

Johnny Johnston photo of Nazmon CW (U.S. National Champion Western Pleasure Horse, AOTR) courtesy of Bentwood Farms, Waco, Texas

lead in the sale. If the horse has been paid for, give the registration certificate to the buyer. In an installment sale, provide a receipt for the down payment and a copy of the sales contract and note. The buyer should also receive a copy of the horse's pedigree and its health record. If available, provide information about the horse's show record and progeny. (Keep copies of all information for reference.)

If the buyer is unfamiliar with horses (or *Arabian* horses), you may want to make a present of a magazine subscription or a good book about Arabian horses or horse management.

These little extras—clean halter and medical record, etc.—don't cost much and will get the new owner off to a good start. Satisfied customers also will return or refer other potential buyers.

SALE CONTRACT

On this date,_____(date)_____, _(name of Seller)_____, d/b/a (name of business, if applicable), hereinafter described as Seller(s), agrees to sell to _(name of Buyer)_____, hereinafter described as Buyer(s), and Buyer(s) agrees to purchase the following described horse: (registered name)__, AHR #(registration #), sire:__(name)____, dam:___(name)_____, color:_____, sex:_____, date foaled: (date of birth) . If bred mare, dates bred: (months and days, year of breeding) to __(name of stallion)_____, AHR # (registration #)__.

Buyer and seller agree to these terms of sale: purchase price $_____.
Down payment of $_____ received on ___(date)_____
by _(method of payment/check number)_. Installment payments of $_____
per _____ due _____, with interest at rate of _____
on unpaid balance. Balance may be paid in whole or in part at any time.

Seller warrants animal to be as represented and declares the following unsoundnesses, vices if any:_____

Seller believes animal is exactly as stated, but will not assume liability for actions of animal in unforeseen circumstances or for future health problems that may develop. Buyer will indemnify and hold harmless the Seller from any losses or liabilities which may arise out of injuries to persons or property caused by the horse, or injuries to the horse, either while the horse is still in the custody of the Seller or before the final payment date.

Seller shall retain an interest in the horse equal to the unpaid balance through the life of the Contract. Upon completion of payments, Seller will deliver registration certificate and transfer complete title free and clear of any encumbrance to Buyer. Registration papers on foals produced by mares during the term of this Contract will likewise be transferred upon completion of payments. In case of breach of contract by Buyer, Seller reserves the right to repossess the horse and is entitled to retain any payments received. Buyer will not permit the attachment of any lien, encumbrance, or other charge against the horse until final payment is made.

Buyer agrees to maintain mortality insurance on horse with Seller as co-beneficiary in an amount at least equal to Seller's equity; also to provide safe quarters and adequate quality and quantity of feed and good care for the horse. Death or incapacitation of horse will not relieve Buyer of payment requirements, but an insurance settlement to the Seller in the amount of Seller's equity will be considered full payment in the event of the horse's death.

Risk of loss of animal shall be assumed by Buyer at the time of downpayment. Should Buyer be unable to assume physical possession at that time, Buyer shall then be responsible for payment to the Seller of board at the rate of $_____ per _____, plus other necessary expenses for veterinary and farrier care, foaling, etc. Seller will take proper and reasonable care of the horse while it is in the Seller's possession, but Seller will not insure the health or life of the horse.

In case of death of either Buyer or Seller, this agreement will remain in effect and will be binding upon and for the benefit of the heirs, executors, administrators, successors, and assigns of the parties.

Other provisions made a part of this contract are as follows:

_____   _____
Buyer   Seller

_____   _____
Street Address   Street Address

_____   _____
City, State, Zip Code   City, State, Zip Code

Example of a Sales Contract used by an Arabian breeding farm. Prior to use, any contract should be approved by your attorney to ensure legal protection.

Charles Craver photo of Lysander.

Courtesy of Craver Farms, Hillview, Ill.

37

FUTURE OF THE BREED

What does the future hold for the world's most ancient breed of horses? Without an ability to foresee the future, present trends are the only means to make an educated guess.

SUPPLY VS. DEMAND

Arabian horses were once in short supply, and early Arabian breeders couldn't produce them fast enough to supply the market. The breed itself was at one time in danger of extinction because it had so few living representatives.

Under these conditions, it isn't surprising that every Arabian mare became a broodmare and almost every colt also was used for breeding. Today, however, the demand isn't growing fast enough to keep up with the tremendous increase in Arabians.

In the United States, the growth of the Arabian horse population has been phenomenal. The first Arabian was registered in 1908. By 1973, that figure had jumped to 100,000 and by 1980 that figure had doubled. By 1986 300,000 purebred Arabian horses had been registered. If this fantastic growth rate continues, an additional 100,000 Arabian horses could be produced every two years!

Those in the business of breeding Arabian horses have applauded this growth rate because each year more transfers of ownership have occurred than new registrations. This sounds more promising than it actually is, however; breeders often "support each other" by buying from each other. If 100,000 new Arabians are produced every two years, all of them may not find buyers. With so many horses from which to choose, breeders must compete with a large number of rivals for sales. In such a buyer's market, prices will drop.

The present trend has been apparent for several years: the most expensive and the least expensive Arabians seem to sell fairly well while those in the mid-price range sell more slowly. More horses are offered in this mid-price range, usually reserved for horses of average or better quality, which means that the Arabian horse business is not as brisk as one might be led to believe.

There are only two ways to avoid an oversupply of Arabian horses for sale. The first is to develop new markets; the second is to reduce production.

EXPANDING MARKETS

In the past, Arabians have most often been sold for breeding and showing. In the future, they probably will become more visible in other fields. Promoting the Arabian for activities in addition to showing will make the breed more attractive to a larger variety of potential buyers.

In the future, the markets for Arabians to be used for endurance and competitive trail rides should continue to grow. As these sports grow in popularity and competition becomes keener, demand and prices for trail horses may rise.

Racing also is a promising market for Arabians, and more breeders are supporting Arabian races for that reason. The demand for racing Arabians should rise as larger purses and more races are offered.

Arabians also are being seen more often in dressage competition. This market is expected to expand as more dressage enthusiasts discover the intelligence and willing disposition of the Arabian, which suits it to dressage training.

The United States has more Arabian horses than all other countries of the world combined; many other Arabian horse-breeding countries have less than 1,000 Arabians each. America also has some of the finest Arabian horses in existence. Perhaps it is time to develop a greater international market for excess quality stock. If showing opportunities increase in other countries, a desire for quality American-bred exports should rise. American show-ring competition spurred a desire to import superior Arabian horses, and the same thing could happen abroad.

LIMITING PRODUCTION

Limiting the number of Arabian horses bred in the United States would not only insure higher prices for each horse, due to a less abundant supply, but could result in a higher standard of quality. If fewer horses were bred, horses of lesser quality could be culled and only the best Arabians kept for breeding.

The best way to limit breeding is to geld most colts. (Sooner or later, even poor stallions become sires.) Only the very best colts—and a small number of those—should remain stallions. Reducing the number of potential sires would reduce the number of potential offspring.

The best way to encourage gelding and raise the dollar value of geldings is to offer cash prizes at shows and other events. The IAHA Pentathlon, in which purebred geldings competed in five categories for a sizable cash prize, was a step in the right direction. Breeders should support such events, for if more stallions are gelded, fewer horses will be competing for sales and income from stud fees.

Only the best mares should become broodmares. A breeder can prevent an inferior mare from producing registerable purebred foals by spaying or by selling her without registration papers. When the latter is done, however, the mare cannot be shown in Arabian horse shows.

California State Polytechnic University professor Norm Dunn, an Arabian horse breeder and judge, suggests that a category for Performance Mares be created, allowing them to be shown in performance classes at Arabian horse shows but preventing their foals from being registered. This would encourage breeders to sell lower quality mares without papers (to discourage breeding them) while allowing their buyers to show them in performance classes, thus creating a larger market for such mares. This would be one way to reduce the number of poor-quality Arabian mares being bred.

As the market demand for Arabian horses drops as a result of an oversupply, more Arabians will be sold cheaply, given away, or even sold to the meat market. This tragedy might be avoidable if breeders start now to reduce the number of Arabian foals produced annually.

THE ARABIAN HORSE'S COMPETITION

Arabian sale horses compete not only with each other but with horses of other breeds. In order to sell, they must compare favorably to similar horses of other breeds and must be priced competitively.

The National Show Horse Registry (an organization for Arabian/Saddledbred crosses) has strongly affected the Arabian horse industry in a short time, for its horses compete with purebred Arabians for buyers. If the new registry continues to prosper (by offering large sums of prize money for winning National Show Horses at its shows), Arabian stallions will continue to compete with Saddlebred stallions for breedings. Some top-quality Arabian mares will no longer be used to produce purebred Arabians, being bred instead to Saddlebreds, and owners of Arabian stallions will lose income each time a mare owner chooses to breed to a Saddlebred stallion.

Due to competition from all other horse breeds, it is imperative that Arabian horse owners work together for their mutual welfare by promoting the Arabian breed. Personal prejudices and differences of opinion must be set aside to enable admirers of all types and bloodlines of Arabians to promote the breed as a whole. Enough variety exists within the Arabian breed to satisfy most potential horse buyers, and this variety actually strengthens the overall appeal of the Arabian breed.

INVESTMENTS

Like other "collectibles," horses are not a liquid asset that can be readily sold. There is a limited market for the most expensive horses, since few people

ARABIAN HORSE SHOWS

Showing probably will continue to be a popular activity among Arabian horse owners, although rising costs may prevent owners on a small budget from showing extensively. If more financial prizes are offered at shows, more exhibitors may attend. However, as the stakes become higher, the desire to win may lead to more cheating and inhumane treatment of some show horses.

It seems probable that more all-amateur Arabian horse shows will be held in the future, giving amateur owners a chance to show their own horses without competing against professionals. It has even been suggested that the U.S. National Championship Arabian Horse Show could be divided into two shows: an Open National Championship Show (for

"The Arabian...horse for all seasons." Talamontes in summer...and winter. Ridden and driven by Neal McKinstry.
Photo courtesy of McKinstry Arabians

can afford to buy them. And, because everyone does not appreciate the same type of "living art"—and because Arabian bloodlines are subject to fluctuations in popularity (and thus, in value)—one cannot be sure of a return on an investment in Arabian horses.

However, as long as investors hope to make a profit from Arabian horses, and if the United States' income tax laws remain the same, some Arabian horses will continue to be owned as investments or tax shelters.

professionals and amateurs), and an Amateur National Championship Show. This would allow amateurs a better chance at National Championship titles and reduce the problems involved in putting on a horse show that lasts a full week and attracts well over a thousand entries.

THE MARKET FOR THE AVERAGE ARABIAN

Overall, the most promising market for most Arabian horses is that of the pleasure horse. The

317

typical Arabian is well suited to being a backyard pet and riding horse. It is gentle enough for a child, spirited enough for a bold rider, and beautiful enough to please anyone.

The Arabian of the future may enjoy a resurgence of popularity for the same traits for which the breed has always been known. It may have come full circle—from pleasure horse to show horse to investment to pleasure horse again.

THE FUTURE OF THE ARABIAN BREED

Some predictions are difficult to make, but one thing is certain: Arabian horses will continue to be appreciated for their beauty, intelligence, endurance, spirit, and affectionate nature. It is up to the owners and breeders of today to insure that the Arabian horse of tomorrow retains the qualities for which it has been valued for thousands of years. The gift of kings throughout history, the Arabian horse is antiquity's gift to us, and our gift to the future.

TALK LIKE A HORSEMAN

Abortion Premature birth of the immature fetus.

AI Artificial insemination.

Action The way a horse moves its legs, especially at the trot.

Afnas Arabic word for the dished profile of the Arabian horse's head.

Afterbirth Placenta after its expulsion, following the delivery of the foal.

Aged A horse that is fifteen years or older.

Allele Any of several forms of a gene.

Amniotic fluid Liquid surrounding the fetus.

Bag Udder of the mare. (The prefoaling mare "bags up" as milk is produced.)

Barren (mare) A mare that has previously foaled but is now open.

Bloodlines Lineage; pedigree.

Bloom Good condition: sleek, shiny coat.

Board To put a horse in someone else's care; the fee for such care.

Book To arrange to breed a mare to a specific stallion; the mares bred to a stallion. The stallion's "book" is said to be full or closed if no additional mares are accepted for breeding in that season; the book is open if mares are still being accepted.

Bred Describes a mare that has been inseminated; also can mean pregnant.

Breed Group of horses descended from common ancestors and sharing traits of type.

Breeder Person who plans a mating; for purebred registration purposes, the individual owning the dam at the time of breeding, unless that person completes a special form designating another to be shown as the breeder of the horse.

Breeding Mating; the breeding privilege itself; bloodlines (e.g., "What is his breeding?")

Breeding farm Establishment that breeds horses.

Broodmare Mare used to produce foals.

Brother A male horse that shares the same sire and dam as another horse. (Horses out of different dams but by the same stallion are not brothers; they are "by the same sire.")

By Fathered by. A son of the stallion *Raffles is "by *Raffles."

Classic	An Arabian that has pronounced breed type.	**First milk**	Colostrum.
		Foal	Young horse of either sex, from birth to weaning; also, to give birth to a foal.
Coat	The horse's body hair (exclusive of the mane and tail.)		
Collection	Shortening the horse's stride by a stronger hold on the reins while pushing the horse forward with the rider's leg pressure.	**Foal heat**	Mare's first heat period after foaling.
		Foaling date	The date a horse was born (foaled).
		Follicle	Site on the mare's ovary which contains and releases the egg.
Colostrum	First milk produced by the mare for the newborn foal.	**Foundation stock**	The first horses used in a breeding program.
Colt	A stallion less than four years old.	**Gaits**	Various kinds of leg movements and speeds of movement. The walk, trot, canter, and gallop are gaits of the horse.
Conception rate	Percentage of mares bred to a specific stallion that settled.		
Condition	Overall fitness of the horse, including weight, muscle tone, and coat.		
		Geld	To castrate a male horse.
Conformation	Body structure of the horse.	**Gelding**	Castrated male horse.
Congenital	(Trait) acquired during development of the fetus, as in "congenital defect."	**Gene**	Unit of inheritance that controls a specific trait.
		Gene pool	Total genes available for inheritance.
Cover	Breeding a mare (by a stallion); the stallion's service.	**Genotype**	Genetic inheritance of a specific horse.
Cross	Two bloodlines joined by mating; usually described by sire line, e.g.: "a *Bask-*Serafix cross."	**Gestation**	Term of pregnancy.
		Get	A stallion's sons and daughters.
		Get-of-Sire Class	Halter class; each entry consists of two or more horses by the same sire, judged on reproductive similarity, type, conformation, etc.
Cryptorchid	Stallion whose testicles are retained in the abdomen instead of having descended normally into the scrotum.		
Dam	Mother.	**Grade horse**	Unregistered horse; horse with an unknown pedigree.
Dish	The concave depression in the facial profile of many Arabian horses (afnas).	**Hand**	Unit of measurement to express a horse's height from withers to ground; a hand is four inches.
Embryo	Unborn foal during early gestation.		
Embryo Transfer	Transplanting an embryo from the uterus of one mare to that of another.	**Hand breeding**	Mating horses that are under restraint.
		Heat	Estrus.
Estrus	Heat period of the mare, during which she is receptive for breeding.	**Hormone**	Chemical that is produced by a gland and carried in the blood to an organ or tissue, where it stimulates a particular effect.
Exotic	An Arabian that has pronounced breed type.		
Extreme	Used to describe the type of a horse with exaggerated breed type, especially used to refer to an ultra-typey Arabian head.	**Hybrid**	Total outcross.
		In foal	Pregnant. A mare is "in foal to" a particular stallion (pregnant by him).
Fertile	Able to reproduce.	**Inbreeding**	Mating two closely related horses; the presence of related horses in an individual's pedigree. (The amount of inbreeding may be expressed by percentage or coefficient.)
Fetus	Unborn foal.		
Filly	A female horse less than four years old.		

Infertile	Sterile; not able to reproduce.
Insemination	Implanting semen in the mare's reproductive tract.
Jibbah	Arabic word for the bulge in the forehead often seen in Arabian horses.
Linebreeding	Mating two horses that are related, but not closely related.
Maiden	Mare that has never produced a foal.
Mare	Mature female horse.
Mitbah	Arabic word for the horse's throat (the area where the head joins the bottom of the neck).
Monorchid	A stallion with only one testicle descended into the scrotum, and the other retained in the abdomen.
Near	The horse's left, as in "the near side of the horse."
Nick	A mating of two bloodlines; especially, a successful cross.
Off	The horse's right, as in "the off side of the horse."
Open	Not pregnant.
Out of	A son or daughter of a specific mare. A horse whose dam is *Rifala is "out of *Rifala." (The term is sometimes misused when describing the get of a stallion; a horse is *by* a stallion, and *out of* a mare.)
Outcrossing	Mating two horses that have no common ancestor for four or more generations. A true outcross is a mating of horses not known to be related.
Outside mare or stallion	Breeding horse owned by someone other than the owner of the horse to which it will be bred.
Ovary	Part of the mare's reproductive tract that produces the egg.
Ovulation	Release of the egg when the follicle ruptures.
Palpate	To manually examine the mare's reproductive tract.
Pasture breeding	Allowing a stallion and mare to breed naturally, without restraint (in pasture or a corral, etc.).
Pedigree	Chart of a horse's ancestors; the bloodlines or lineage of a horse.

Phenotype	An individual horse's appearance.
Placenta	Membranes in which the fetus is carried and nourished during gestation.
Prepotency	Ability of a parent to pass on its own traits to its offspring. (The foals of a prepotent stallion resemble him.)
Presence	Personality, magnetism, charisma of an individual horse. Some Arabians, especially stallions, have a lot of presence. Not all Arabians have it.
Produce	Offspring of a mare.
Produce-of-Dam class	Halter class in which each entry consists of at least two horses out of the same dam, judged on reproductive similarity, type, conformation, quality, etc.
Purebred (Arabian)	Arabian horse registered by a recognized Arabian horse registry; a horse with no outcross to breeds other than Arabian.
Quality	Overall excellence; especially refers to fine skin and hair and clean definition of bones and tendons.
Refinement	Daintiness, fineness; lack of excessive flesh or bone; lack of coarseness.
Semen	Sperm and fluids produced by the testicles of the stallion.
Service	Same as cover.
Settled	In foal. (A pregnant mare is said to have settled.)
Sire	Father. A stallion is said to sire offspring.
Sister	A female horse sharing the same sire and dam as another horse. (Mares that are out of the same dam but have different sires are not called sisters; they are *half sisters*.)
Sound	Healthy; having no disability that will interfere with the horse's intended use.
Spay	Surgical removal of the mare's ovaries, rendering her infertile.
Stallion	Mature male horse (entire).
Sterile	Unable to reproduce.
Strain	A family of Bedouin Arabian horses, traced through the tail female line; strain is sometimes

	used to mean bloodlines or "nationality" (country of recent origin of imported Arabian horses).	**Testicles**	Stallion's organs that produce sperm and testosterone, the hormone responsible for masculine appearance and behavior.
Stud	Breeding farm; a stallion used for breeding. A breeding stallion is said to "stand at stud."	**Topline**	Top outline of the horse's body in profile, especially in reference to the croup (e.g., a "level topline").
Stud book	A published record of information about individual registered horses, including pedigrees, foaling dates, colors, etc.	**Type**	Combination of physical traits that set members of a breed apart from other breeds.
Stud fee	Fee charged for breeding to a stallion.	**Typey** **Uterus**	Possessing Arabian breed type. Part of the mare's reproductive tract that contains and nourishes the fetus during gestation.
Substance	Bone structure and muscular development, related to strength and stamina.	**Vagina**	Part of the mare's reproductive tract that connects the cervix of the uterus and the vulva; the
Tack	Saddles, bridles, halters, harness, etc.		vagina is the birth canal for the foal.
Tail carriage	The way the tail is carried when the horse is alert or moving.	**Visiting mare**	See outside mare.
Tail female	The bottom line of a horse's pedigree, traced through the dam and her female ancestors.	**Vulva** **Wax**	Exterior entrance to the vagina. Thick, sticky secretation from the udder that precedes colostrum.
Tail male	Top line of the pedigree, traced through the sire and his male ancestors.	**Wean**	To separate mare and foal so the foal cannot nurse.
Tail set	Refers to where the tail connects to the body. Tail set may be described as high (desirable) or low (undesirable).	**Weanling**	Young horse that has been weaned but is less than twelve months old.
Tease	To determine a mare's receptivity for breeding.	**Wry tail** **Yearling**	Sideways carriage of the tail. Young horse between twelve and twenty-four months old.

BIBLIOGRAPHY & ſUGGESTED READING

* Especially Recommended Reading

Adams, O.R. *Lameness in Horses*. Philadelphia, Pennsylvania: Lea & Febiger, 1974.

* *AHSA Rule Book*. New York: American Horse Shows Association. *Contains showing rules and class specifications for Arabian classes; updated as horse show rules change.*

Andrist, Friedrich. *Mares, Foals and Foaling*. London: J.A. Allen.

____. *Arabian Horse Stud Book*. Denver, Colorado: Arabian Horse Registry of America, Inc.

____. *Arabian Horse Yearbook*. International Arabian Horse Association (IAHA). *Published annually for the prior show year. Lists all show results of purebred classes from All-Arabian Class "A" horse shows.*

* Archer, Rosemary, Colin Pearson and Cecil Covey. *The Crabbet Arabian Stud, Its History and Influence*. London: Alexander Heriot & Co. Ltd., 1978. *The most comprehensive history of the Crabbet Stud and its horses ever written. Many photographs of important breeding stock; traces Crabbet exports worldwide.*

* Beeman, G. Marvin, DVM. *Know First Aid for Your Horses*. Omaha, Nebraska: Farnam Horse Library, 1978. *A small, thorough reference book; handy size to accompany a first aid kit.*

Blunt, Lady Anne. *Bedouin Tribes of the Euphrates*. London: John Murray, 1879.

Blunt, Lady Anne. *A Pilgrimage to Nejd*. London: John Murray, 1881.

Brown, William Robinson. *The Horse of the Desert*. Berlin, New Hampshire: Maynesboro Arabian Stud, 1936.

Burt, Don. *As the Judge Sees It: Arabian Showing*. Covina, California: Rich Publishing, Inc., 1973.

Collins, R.W. *Grooming Horses*. Thoroughbred Record Company: 1971.

Conn, Dr. George H. *The Arabian Horse in America*. New York: A. S. Barnes & Company, 1972.

Crowell, Pers. *Cavalcade of the American Horse*. Washington, D.C.: McGraw-Hill, 1951.

Daumas, General E. *Horses of the Sahara*. Texas: Texas University Press, 1963.

Davenport, Homer. *My Quest of the Arab Horse*. London: Grant Richards, 1911.

* Davis, Thomas A. "Tax Tips for Horse Owners" (pamphlet). Washington, D.C.: American Horse Council.

* Edwards, Gladys Brown. *Anatomy and Conformation of the Horse*. Croton-on-Hudson, New York: Dreenan Press, Ltd., 1973. *Excellent small book, easily understood. Most illustrating photos are of Arabian horses.*

* Edwards, Gladys Brown. *The Arabian: War Horse to Show Horse*. Denver, Colorado: Arabian Horse Trust, 1980. *History of the breed; bloodlines; show winners. A lot of information.*

Ensminger, Dr. M.E. *Horses and Horsemanship*. Danville, Illinois: Interstate, 1977.

Ensminger, Dr. M.E. *Horses and Tack*. Boston, Massachusetts: Houghton Mifflin Company, 1977.

Forbis, Judith E. *The Classic Arabian Horse.* New York: Liveright, 1976.

* *Golden Book of Arabian Horse Showing.* International Arabian Horse Association (IAHA). *Collection of thirty-eight booklets in three sections: Judging, Horse Show Management, and Exhibiting. Booklets available separately or as a set; updated periodically.*

Goldstein, Philip. *Genetics is Easy.* New York: Lantern Press, 1967.

* Goubaux, Armand and Gustave Barrier. *The Exterior of the Horse.* London: J. B. Lippincott Co., 1892. *A classic; probably the best book ever written on conformation and anatomy of the horse, but technical and difficult reading.*

Greely, Margaret. *Arabian Exodus.* London: J. A. Allen and Company, 1975.

Hafez, E.S.E. (editor). *Reproduction in Farm Animals.* Philadelphia, Pennsylvania: Lea & Febiger, 1974.

Half-Arabian Yearbook. International Arabian Horse Association (IAHA). *Published annually for the prior show year. Lists all show results of Half-Arabian classes in Class "A" and "B" horse shows.*

Harris, Albert. *The Blood of the Arab.* Chicago, Illinois: Arabian Horse Club, 1941.

Harris, Albert. *History of the Arabian Horse Club Registry of America.* Arabian Horse Registry of America, 1950.

Hayes, M. Horace. *Stable Management and Exercise.* New York: Arco Publishing Company, Inc., 1969.

* *IAHA Handbook.* International Arabian Horse Association (IAHA). *Published annually for members. Provides extensive information about IAHA programs and services, officers and committees; lists literature, films, videotape, and slides available; gives point requirements for Special Achievement Awards; provides information on Half-Arabian and Anglo-Arabian Registries; outlines rules for National and Regional Championship classes, Arabian Racing, Competitive Trail and Endurance Rides, Dressage, Hunter and Jumper classes, Equitation classes, etc. New rules and rule changes are highlighted for easy visibility.*

Kays, D. J. The Horse. New York: Rinehart & Company, Inc., 1953.

Kidd, Jane (editor). *The Horse and Pony Manual.* Secaucus, New Jersey: Chartwell Books, Inc.

Kroll, Lois Ann. *Arabian Costumes.* California: International Arabian Horse Association, 1981. *For those interested in designing or making a costume for Arabian Mounted Native Costume classes or parades.*

Lasley, John F. *Genetic Principles in Horse Breeding.* Columbia, Missouri: 1970.

* Lose, M. Phyllis, VMD. *Blessed Are the Broodmares.* New York: Macmillan, 1978. *Probably the best book ever written on broodmares, foals. Every breeder should have and use this book.*

Nishikawa, Dr. Y. *Studies on Reproduction in Horses.* Tokyo, Japan: Japan Racing Association, 1959.

Parkinson, Mary Jane. *The Kellogg Arabian Ranch—The First 50 Years.* El Cajon, California: HHR Publications, 1977.

Raswan, Carl R. *The Arab and His Horse.* Oakland, California: 1955.

Raswan, Carl R. *The Raswan Index and Handbook for Arabian Breeders.* Mexico: 1957.

Rose, Mary. *The Horseman's Notebook.* New York: David McKay Company, Inc., 1972.

* Rossdale, Peter D. *The Horse (From Conception to Maturity).* Arcadia, California: The California Thoroughbred Breeders Association, 1972.

Simpson, William (editor). *Arabiana.* Cove, Arkansas: 1975.

Sumerhays, R. S. (editor). *Summerhays' Encyclopaedia for Horsemen.* London: Frederick Warne & Co., Ltd., 1959.

Tweedie, Major-General W. *The Arabian Horse, His Country and People.* Borden Publishing Company, 1961.

Upton, Roger D. *Newmarket and Arabia.* London: H. S. King, 1873.

Weikel, Bill (editor). Farnum Horse Library series of paperback books on many horse management and training topics.

* Wentworth, Lady. *The Authentic Arabian Horse (and his Descendants).* London: George Allen & Unwin, Ltd., 1945. *Very large volume containing writings by Lady Wentworth and her parents, Wilfrid and Lady Anne Blunt.*

Wentworth, Lady. *The World's Best Horse.* London: George Allen and Unwin, 1958.

OTHER SOURCES
OF INFORMATION

Arabian Horse Registry of America, Inc. ("The Registry"), 12000 Zuni Street, Westminster, Colo. 80234; (303) 450-4748.

Registers purebred Arabian horses; operates freeze marking programs for purebreds and registered Half-Arabians; publishes some literature about Arabian horses and the Registry's rules and services; supplies record-keeping forms for breeders; sells five-generation pedigrees; publishes the Arabian Horse Stud Book. MEMBERSHIP: Direct; annual dues. Members get a newsletter and reduced fees for services and products; membership is not required for services, however.

Arabian Horse Trust ("The Trust"), 12000 Zuni Street, Westminster, Colo. 80234; (303) 450-4710.

Formed in 1976 by the Registry; provides educational and historical services that eventually will include an extensive Arabian horse library and museum. The Trust preserves historic documents, photographs, films, books, artwork, and memorabilia related to the history of the Arabian horse breed. MEMBERSHIP: None at present; services available to everyone.

International Arabian Horse Association (IAHA), P.O. Box 33696 Denver, Colo. 80233; Telephone (303) 450-4774.

Registers Half-Arabians and Anglo-Arabians; publishes books and literature about Arabian horses and part-Arabians; oversees Arabian horse shows; manages the U.S. National Championship Arabian Horse Show; con-

ducts the education and evaluation program for Arabian horse judges; administers Achievement Awards program for show and performance horses; conducts the Arabian Horse Fair, a national educational event featuring clinics and exhibits related to Arabian horses; promotes Endurance and Competitive Trail Rides and Racing for Arabians; sponsors National halter and performance futurities, Breeders Sweepstakes, and National Arabian racing futurities; provides trophies for Arabian shows; operates youth program; puts on the National consignment sale; rents films and videotapes, promotes the breed with publicity and advertising. MEMBERSHIP: Direct or through a member Arabian horse club; annual dues. Members receive a magazine and the annual IAHA Handbook listing its rules and services; reduced fees in the Half-Arabian and Anglo-Arabian Registries; a discount on Arabian Horse Yearbooks; and the right to show at IAHA-Sanctioned horse shows. Members of local IAHA-affiliated Arabian horse clubs also may hold office in the local clubs or IAHA, serve on IAHA Committees, or be Delegates to the annual IAHA Convention that makes show rules for Arabian horses.

American Horse Council, Inc., 1700 K Street N.W., Washington, D.C. 20006.

A national organization representing the American horse industry; memberships available directly, annual dues. Provides research and statistics about the U.S. horse industry, monitors federal legislation affecting it, and provides information on federal tax laws affecting horse businesses. Formed another organization, American Horse Publications, a non-profit national organization of horse periodicals. Publishes an annual *Horse Industry Directory* that lists equine magazines and organizations as well as government sources of information of interest to horse owners; publishes the large *Horse Owners and Breeders Tax Manual* for horse business owners, attorneys, and accountants. Some publications and services are available to non-members; members receive monthly newsletters and bulletins, information on forthcoming federal legislation affecting horse interests, and assistance with income tax questions.

American Horse Shows Association, Inc. (AHSA), 220 East 42nd St., Fourth Floor, NY, NY 10017-9998; (212) 972-2472.

The United States' national horse show organization for all breeds. AHSA accredits Arabian shows; makes and enforces rules (with input from IAHA); licenses judges and AHSA Stewards for shows; administers drug testing program to prevent use of illegal drugs in show horses; operates AHSA high-point awards program; conducts clinics; rents films; publishes information on showing, including the AHSA Rule Book that contains class specifications for horse show classes and showing rules. MEMBERSHIP: Direct; annual dues. Membership at lower rate as Affiliated Member to members of IAHA, but without voting privileges. Membership is required to show at IAHA-approved Arabian horse shows, to compete for AHSA show awards, and for AHSA Committee members, show Judges and Stewards. Members receive current AHSA Rule Book and *Horse Show* magazine and free amateur cards if qualified.

Arabian Horse Owners Foundation (AHOF), P.O. Box 31391 Tucson, Ariz. 85751; (602) 326-1515.

A private, non-profit foundation (not affiliated with IAHA, Registry, or the Trust) established in 1957 to assist and educate owners of Arabian horses. In conjunction with clubs or breeders, conducts workshops on showing, judging, training, and horse management; reprints historic documents and photographs related to Arabian horses; has a mail-order gift shop; maintains the W. R. Brown Memorial Library (non-circulating) for researchers; produced the documentary film, "Skowronek: The Classic Arabian," and operated the first Arabian Horse Museum in America (no longer open). Items formerly displayed at AHOF's museum have been loaned to the Arabian Horse Trust for display in the Arabian Horse Center at Denver.

Canadian Equestrian Federation (CEF), 333 River Road, Ottawa, Ontario, Canada K1L 8B9.

Canada's national horse show organization, equivalent to the American Horse Shows Association, Inc., of the United States.

The Canadian Arabian Horse Registry, R. R. 1, Bowden, Alberta, Canada TOM OKO.

The registry for Arabian horses bred in or imported to Canada.

World Arabian Horse Organization (WAHO), 300 Greengate Road, San Luis Obispo, Calif. 93401, or: Thujas, Bisley, Surrey GU24 9AY, England.

Established in 1970 to promote Arabian horses and protect breed purity worldwide. WAHO defines "purebred Arabian" as any horse listed in any purebred Arabian stud book or registry approved by WAHO. MEMBERSHIP: Members are official national Arabian horse registries (including the Arabian Horse Registry of America, Inc.): only Member registries can vote. Associate Members are Arabian horse associations and educational facilities related to horse management or research. Individuals can also join WAHO, but cannot vote. Membership is direct and involves annual dues; members receive the WAHO newsletter.

SPECIAL INTEREST BLOODLINE GROUPS

Several special interest groups exist that should not be confused with organizations promoting the Arabian breed as a whole. Special interest groups are breeders who join together to promote specific bloodlines in which they have a mutual interest.

Bloodline groups include: *Al Khamsa* (for desert-bred lines); *CMK Breeders* (for Arabians tracing to the Crabbet, Maynesboro, and Kellogg breeding programs); *Double R Breeders* (for Arabians with Rissalix plus *Raffles and/or *Raseyn in their pedigrees); and *The Pyramid Society* (for "Straight Egyptian" Bloodlines).

These and other special interest groups advertise their horses and activities in the Arabian horse magazines.

UNIVERSITIES

Two major universities feature purebred Arabian horses in their equine programs. They are:

California State Polytechnic University
W.K. Kellogg Arabian Horse Center
3801 West Temple Boulevard
Pomona, CA 91768

and

Northwestern State University
Natchitoches, LA 71457

MAGAZINES

Arabian Horse Express, P. O. Box 845, Coffeyville, Kan. 67337.

Arabian Horse Times, R.R. 3, Waseka, Minn. 56093.

Arabian Horse World, 2650 East Bayshore Road, Palo Alto, Calif. 94303.

Canadian Arabian News, Box 101, Bowden, Alberta, TOM OKO Canada.

Equus, 656 Quince Orchard Road, Gaithersburg, Md. 20760. (All-breeds; emphasis on health, research, and management for horse owners.)

LIBRARIES

The John Crerar Library, 35 West 33rd Street, Chicago, Ill. 60616.

This is a gold mine for serious breeders and researchers with limited access to old publications about Arabian horses. The library has a collection of over 400 horse publications, including many out-of-print books about Arabian horses that were acquired with a grant from the Arabian Horse Club Registry (predecessor of the current Arabian Horse Registry of America, Inc.). Most of these can be mailed to your local library for reference use there. A list of Arabian horse books in the collection is available upon request; books must be requested by a librarian on an inter-library loan basis.

Other libraries about Arabian horses are maintained by: California State Polytechnic University, Pomona (see listing under Universities); the Arabian Horse Trust (see listing under Organizations); and the Arabian Horse Owners Foundation (see listing under Organizations). However, these books do not circulate and must be used at the facilities.

Often, desired books about Arabian horses can be ordered through your local library, if you don't find them on the shelf.

MAIL ORDER BOOK STORES

Write to the following for their current lists of books about Arabian horses:

Alexander Heriot & Co., Ltd., P.O. Box 1, Northleach, Cheltenham, Glos., England GL54 3JB.

El-Zar Book Bar, P.O. Box 1904, Cedar Rapids, Iowa 52406.

J.A. Allen & Co., 1 Lower Grosvenor Place, Buckingham Palace Road, London, England SW1W OEL.

D'Shams, Rt. 4, Box 628, Terrell, Tex. 75160.

INDEX

NOTE: Photos of horses are indicated by page numbers in bold.

AHSA, see American Horse
  Shows Association, Inc.
AI, see Artificial insemination
Abbas Pasha I, 72
*Abha Hamir, 16, **17**
Abortion, 122, 208, 209
Abu Farwa, 13
Abuse of show horses, 293
Action, 61
"Adding the Arabian," poem, 33
Adriana, 214
Advertising, 77, 310
Afari, 13
Afnas, 45
Afterbirth, see Placenta
Age
  halter horses, 285
  race horses, 20
  sale horses, 309
  to geld, 302
  to ride, 75
Al Khamsa
  legend, 2
  strains, 164
Alcock Arabian, The, 29
Alfalfa hay, 110, 112-114
Al-Marah Arabians, 13
Al-Marah Ibn Indraff, 20
American-bred Arabians, 12

American breeders, early, 10
American Horse Council,
  Inc., 27, 307, 309
American Horse Shows Associa-
  tion, Inc., 48, 255
American Quarter Horse, 30, 77
American Saddle Horse, see
  Saddlebred
Amniotic sac, 207
*AN Malik, 16
AN Marieta, 13
'Anazeh Bedouins, 1
Anazeh (the horse), 9
Andalusian breed, 29
Anglo-Arabian, 34, 83
Ansata Arabian Stud, 13
*Ansata Ibn Halima, 13, 14, **42,
  192**
*Ansata Ibn Sudan, 14, **42**
Antoniny Stud, 5
"Apple rump," 46
Arabian Exodus by Margaret
  Greeley, 46
Arabian Horse Club of America,
  The, 10
  see: Arabian Horse Registry of
  America, Inc.
Arabian horse clubs, modern, 26
  see: International Arabian

  Horse Association
Arabian Horse Registry of
  America, Inc., 32, 35, 81, 83
*Aramus, 15
*Ardahan, 15
Arenas, 95
Arn-ett Perlane, **8**
Artificial insemination, 203
*Asadd, **14**
Ascarids, 132, 135-136
Auctions, 78
Aulrab, **48, 297**
Aurik, **64**
Authentic Arabian, The, by Lady
  Wentworth, 5, 65
Aziz, 72
Azraff, 7, **166**

Babson, Henry B., 12-14
Back, 52, 76
Backing, 241, 262
*Bajram, 15
Balance, 51, 53
Bandage, 126
  chewing, 106
Barb, 29
Barnaby, **65**
Barns, 91, 92
Base narrow, 56, 64

Base wide, 56, 64
*Bask, **15**
Bathing, 147
Bay-Abi, 12-13
Bay color, 69, 70
Bedding, stall, 97, 100-101, 107, 141
Bedouin Tribes of the Euphrates by Lady Anne Blunt, 4
Bedouins, 2, 64, 67, 69, 71-72, 109, 139, 140, 229, 238
Bint Padron, 13
Bint Sahara, **184**
Bint Samiha, 14
Biting, 227
Black, 69-70
"Black bay," 69, 73
"Black Stallion, The"
    see: Cass Ole
Blankets, 103-104, 106
Bleeding, 126
Blemishes, 59
Blood, 44, 126, 132
Blood typing, 84-86, 193
Bloodworms
    see: Strongyles
"Bloody shoulder" marking, 67
Blunt, Lady Anne, 3, 69
Blunt, Wilfrid Scawen, 3, 46, 102
Bog spavin, 59
Bone spavin, 59
Bone structure, 44, 46, 52, 64
Borden, Spencer, 10
Bots, 132, 136
Bran mash, 111
"Breeder," designation of, 84
Breeding
    hand breeding, 201
    pasture breeding, 200
Breeding program, 178
Bridlepath, 150, 152
Broodmares
    care of mares, 112-114, 121-123, 136
    selecting and cost, 181-183
Brown color, 69
Brown, W. R., 10, 12, 13, 14, 21, 51
Business, horse, 307
*Buszmen, 15
Buying horses, 75, 79-81, 89
Byerly Turk, 29

CID
    see Combined

Immunodeficiency
Cal Poly
    see: California State
        Polytechnic University
Calcium, 112
Calf knees, 54-55
Caliente Babe, **34**
California State Polytechnic University, 31, 232, 302
Cal-O-Fiesta, **222**
Canadian Arabian Horse Registry, 32, 35
Cannon bone, 55-56
Canter, 61
Cass Ole, **70, 174**
Cavalry endurance rides, 3
Cell, 169
Champurrado, 7
Chestnut color, 69-70
Chicago World's Fair of 1893, 9
Chloette, 7
Chorion, 207
Chromosome, 169
Clipping, 149
    for shows, 151
Coarseness, 47
Coat, 146, 154
Coggins test, 81
Cold-blooded horses, 38-39
Colic, 75, 114, 124, 131-133, 209
Color, 2, 67, 70, 84, 88
    inheritance of color, 173
Colostrum, 220
Combined immunodeficiency, 34, 171, 193, 224
Combined training, 27
"Come-along" (rump rope), 239
Competitive Trail Rides, 22, 316
Conditioning for halter
    classes, 270
Conformation, 33, 51, 64, 76, 269
Contracts
    breeding, 195
    sale, 313
Coolers, 104
Count Bazy, **13**
Crabbet Arabian Stud, 3, 14, 102
Crabbet Arabians, 11, 13, 72
Craver, Charles III, 16
Cribbing, 107
Cross-faulting, 193
Croup, 43, 46, 54, 76, 228

Cruelty to show horses, 293
Cryptorchid, 304
Culture
    see: Uterus
Curb (unsoundness), 59
*Czubuthan, 14

Dajania, 4
Dancing Flame, 13
Darley Arabian, The, 29
Daumas, General E., 39
Daurita, **205**
Davenport Arabians, 16
Davenport, Homer, 9, 10, 12, 16
Desert-bred Arabians, 15
Deworming, 134
*Deyr, 12
Diarrhea, 223
Dickinson, General, 12, 14
Disinfecting stables, 99
Disposition, 37
Distemper, 120, 122
Domestic Arabians
    see: American-bred
Don Ibn Bask, **105**
"Double R" Arabians, 13
Draper, Joseph E., 16
Dressage, 22, 316
Driving, 23, 246, 271
*Druch, **82**
Drugs, forbidden at shows, 292
Dunn, Dr. Norman, 31, 316

EIA
    see: Equine infectious anemia
Ears, 39
Ebony Moon, 13
Edema, 209
Edwards, Gladys Brown, 44
Egyptian Arabians, 13
El Khyam, **40, 265, 300**
*El Moraduke, 16
*El Paso, 15
*Elkin, 15
Embryo transfer, 203
Encephalomyelitis, equine, 121
Endurance, 1
Endurance rides, 21-22, 316
Epiphyseal plates, 233
Equine infectious anemia, 81, 122
Estrus, 185, 188, 199
Evaluating horses
    broodmares, 181

foals, 228
immature horses, 76
sale or lease horses, 80
stallions, 190
Exercise, 104, 270
Eyes, 39
human eye, 44, 46
injuries, 126

Fa Halima, **268**
Fadjur, 13, **181, 298**
*Fadl, 12, 13, 14
*Fakher el Din, 14
Fat, danger of, 272
Fecal count, 133
Feeders, 94
creep feeder, 115
Feeds, 96
Fences, 95
Ferseyn, 6, 13
Ferzon, 13
First Aid, 125
Fleabitten grey, 67-68
Flu
see: Influenza
Fly control, 102
Foal heat, 201
Foaling, 215
preparation for, 210-212
Foals
behavior, 227
coat colors, 70
deworming, 136
evaluating, 228
halterbreaking, 238
handling and restraint, 227
health care, 223
newborn care, 219
orphans, 224
premature, 208
rejected, 226
trailering, 253
vaccinating, 121-123
weaning, 228
Forbis, Donald and Judith
see: Ansata Arabian Stud
Ford, Don, 14
Forelegs, 54-55
Forging
see: Overreaching
Founder
see: Laminitis
4-H Club, 26
Freeze marking, 84

Frisian breed, 30
Frog, 139

*GG Samir, 16
Gai Parada, 12-13
Gaits, 61
Geldings, 77, 88, 233, 301, 303, 316
Gender, inheritance of, 172
Gene, 169
Genotype, 172
Gestation, 207, 213
Ginger, 47, 291
Gleanings from the Desert of Arabia by Roger D. Upton, 9
Gleannloch Farms, 13
Godolphin Arabian, The, 29
Grains, 111
Greeley, Margaret, 46
Grey, 67, 70
Grooming, 145
Ground driving, 246
Growth patterns, 76
*Gwalior, 15
Gymkhanas, 23

Ha Rossetta, **247**
Hadban Strain, 165
Hai Karatie, **21, 50**
*Haleb, 69
Half-Arabians, 30
*Hallany Mistanny, 14
Halters
stable (work), 102
show halters, 286
Halter classes
attire and tack, 286
showing in, 285
training, 275
type and conformation
in, 48, 269
Halterbreaking, 238
*Hamrah, 10
Harris, Albert W., 21
Hay, 110
Hays, M. Horace, 102
Head, 45
Health records, 117-118
Heat period
see: Estrus
Height, 231
estimating mature size, 234
Hemolitic anemia, 220
Heterozygous, 171

"High white," 72
Hind legs, 56
Hip, 54, 76
Hocks, 56, 64
Homozygous, 170
Hoof
care, 140
color, 140
laminitis, 124
parts of, 139
picking up, 241
punctures, 126
show horse, 140-141, 157
trimming, corrective, 142
Hormones, female, 188
shots, 189, 226
"Horse Industry Directory"
see American Horse Council, Inc.
Horse of the Desert, The, by W. R. Brown, 51
Horse Shows
AHSA ratings, 255
all-Arabian, 255
all-breed, 266
future of, 317
performance classes, 261-266
rules, 258
Horses of the Sahara by General E. Daumas, 39
Horseshoes, 142
Horsewalkers
see Walkers, hot
Huntington, Randolph, 9, 30

IAHA
see: International Arabian Horse Association
Ibn Hanrah, 13
Ibn Jurdino, **24**
Illness, signs of, 123, 223
Impaction, 124, 132
Importation, approved countries, 11
Inbreeding, 179, 163
Indian Light, 7
Indraff, 7, **160**
Influenza, 121
Interfering, 62
International Arabian Horse Association, 20, 30, 34, 81, 83
Intestine, 124, 132
Investments, horses as, 317
Irex, 7

Islamic religion, 2
Ivermectin, 135

Jadaan, **12**
Jibbah, 45
Jordana, 21
Judges, training and
    evaluation, 257
Julbit, 20
Justin Morgan, 30

KJ Karaff, **66**
Kale, Howard Jr., 16
*Kareyma, 7, 61
Kasmeen (Kasmeyn), 14
Kehilan (purebred), 1, 29
Kehilan strain, 165
Kellogg Ranch, W. K. Kellogg, 6,
    11-13
Khemosabi, **12,** 13, **294**
Kicking, 107, 227
Knees, 56, 64, 76
Knot, safety release, 103
"Know First Aid for Your Horses"
    by G. Marvin Beeman,
    DVM, 125
Kontiki, **20, 195**
Kuhailan Haifi, 15

LaCroix, Dr. Eugene
    see: Lasma Arabians
Lady Fair, **68**
Laminitis, 124
Lasma Arabians, 15
Leasing, 80
*Leopard, 9
Lethal genes, 81, 171
Lice, 137
Life expectancy of Arabians, 75
Linebreeding, 179
"Listening mare," legend, 40
Loin, 52
*Lotnik, 14
Lunging, 242, 271
Lysander, **314**
Lytton, Judith Blunt
    see: Wentworth, Lady

MS Czarthan, **68**
Mane, 44
    chewing, 106
    grooming, 145
    pulling, 155
    training to lie properly, 154

Maneghi strain, 165-166
Mange, 137
Mansour, 14
Manure, 101, 134, 136, 270
"Mare care," 194
Markings, white, 70
    problems with, 71
    on registration records, 84, 88
Marshall, Douglas and Margaret
    see: Gleannloch Farms
*Marsianin, **17**
McNair, Tom, 47
*Meczet, 15
Mesaoud, **4,** 5, 67, 72
Mesenteric artery, 132
Minerals, 112
*Mirage, **3,** 12
Mohammed, Prophet, 29, 67
Moneyna, 25
Monorchid, 304
Mon-Rey, **22, 148**
Monsoon, **16**
Morab breed, 30, 33
*Morafic, 14
Morgan breed, 30
Muniqui strain, 16
*Muscat, 7, 16, **274**
*Muzelmanin, 15
Muzzle, 39, 44
Muzzle (tack), 107
My Quest of the Arabian Horse, by
    Homer Davenport, 9

*Naborr, 7, 16, **263**
Names, registered, 88
*Naomi, 9
*Napitok, 17
Napoleon Bonaparte, 3, 29
Naseel, 7
Naseem, 6, **7**
*Nasik, 12
*Nasr, 13
National Show Horse, 32-33, 316
"Nationalities," 11
Nazeer, 13, 14
Nazmon CW, **312**
Neck, 43, 51, 53, 76, 228
*Nedjme, 9, **10**
Negatiw, 7
"New Egyptian," 14
Newmarket and Arabia, by Roger
    D. Upton, 9, 21
Nicks, breeding, 180
*Nimr, 12

*Nizzam, 7
Nostrils, 39, 44
*Nurreddin, 12
Nurse mares, 225

Oaks, IAHA, 20
Ofir, 15
"Old Egyptian," 14
Onchocerca, 135
Origin of Arabian breed, 2
Our Quest, **214**
Outcrossing, 180
Overreaching, 62

Pacing (stable vice), 107
Paddling action, 62-63
*Padron, 17
Palpating
    see: Uterus
Pandemonium Angel, **31**
Parades, 25
Parasites
    external, 137
    internal, 131
Parentage verification
    see: Blood typing
Parrot mouth, 129
Pasterns, 55, 105, 142
Pasture, 110
Pawing, 107
Pedigrees, 101, 162
*Penalba, 17
Perce, Richard, DVM, 131
Periople, 141
*Pesenka, 17
Phenotype, 172
Phosphorus, 112, 114
Pietuszok, 16
*Pilot, 14
Pinworms, 132
Placenta, 124, 207, 220
*Podsnejnik, **53**
Polish Arabians, 14
Pony Clubs, Inc., The U.S., 26
Potocki, Count Joseph, 5
Pregnancy, 207
    care during, 208
    tests, 190
Premature foals, 208
Prices of Arabians, 77, 309-310
Pritzlaff, Richard, 13
Protein, 112, 141
*Prowizja, 15
Puden, **34**

Pulse rate, 124
Purpura hemorrhagica, 122

Quarter Horse breed
  see: American Quarter Horse
Queen of Sheba, 4, 69

Racing, 19, 316
*Raffles, 6, **7**, 12, **232**
Raffon, 13
Raftan, 7
*Raging Bear, **60**
Raktha, 7
Ralvon Elijah, **69**
*Ramses Fayek, 14
*Raseyn, **6**, 12, 25, 47, 61
*Rashad Ibn Nazeer, 13
*Rayek, **305**
Raymoniet, **38**
Recessive genes, 73, 129, 169-170
Red worms
  see: Strongyles
Refinement, 47
Regal Bee, **47, 116**
Registration, 83
  certificates, 81
Reproductive organs
  mares, 185, 187
  stallions, 302
Respiration rate, 124
Restraints, 117, 227
Rhinopneumonitis, 121
Richards, Alexander Keene, 9
*Rijm, 47
Rissalix, 13
Rissam, 7
Roan, 70
Roedean Rhythm 'n Blues, **28**
Rogers, John, 13
Rolo Allende-B, **98**
Roosevelt, Theodore, 9
Rose grey, 67-68
Round ring, 95
Roundworms
  see: Ascarids
Rump rope
  see: "Come-along"
Russian Arabians, 16

Saddlebred breed, 30
Saki, 24, **181**
*Sakr, 14, **254**
*Salon, 7
Salt, 109

Samiha, 14
Sanpete Sourdough, **31**
Scharif, **23, 193**
Schaun, **73**
Scours
  see: Diarrhea
"Season"
  see: Estrus
Season, breeding, 196
Seglawi strain, 165
Selby, Roger A., 7, 10, 12, 13, 61
Selling horses
  advertising, 310
  cash sales, 79, 312
  payments, 80, 89, 312
  sales contracts, 312-313
  unregistered foals, 89
  without papers, 89, 316
*Selmian, 7
Senses, 38-39
*Serafix, 7, 13, 37
*Serenity Sonbolah, 14
Sezabask, **79**
Sheykh Obeyd Stud, 4
Shock, 127
Shots, 119-122
Shoulder, 52
Shows
  see: Horse Shows
Showmanship, 289
Silver Drift, 7, 13
Silver Fire, **5**
Single-foot, 61
skin
  color, 44, 71
  thinness, 39
Skowronek, 5, **6**, 67, 72
Sleeping sickness
  see: Encephalomyelitis, equine
Sotep, 7, **173**
Spanish Arabians, 16
Spearmint, **174**
Splints, 59
Spots, body, 71-73
Stable Management and Exercise,
  by M. Horace Hays, 102
Stables, 91
  management of, 99
Stallions, 76
  Blood typing, 84, 86
  care of, 296
  Evaluating, 190
  Leasing, 295
  Promoting, 297

Stallion Reports, 83
  Syndicates, 298
Stalls, 93, 94, 101
Standardbred breed, 30
Steen, Charles, 16
Steroids, 115
Stifle, 56
"Stocking up," 104, 209
Stocks, 97
Strain, family, 164
  breeding by, 15, 165
  strain names, 167
Strangles
  see: Distemper
Stream, Jay, 16
Strongyles, 131, 136
Stud Books, 162
  foreign, abbreviations for, 11
Stud fees, 194
*Sulejman, 14
*Sultann, **191**
Sureyn, 6
"Swamp fever"
  see: Equine infectious anemia
Sweats, neck, 272

Tah Neeka, **138**
Tail
  braiding, 155, 212
  carriage, 43-44, 46, 228
  chewing, 106
  gingering, 47
  grooming, 145, 157
  wry, 46
*Talal, 14
Talamontes, **317**
Tankersley, Bazy, 13
Tapeworms, 133
Teasing, 199
Teeth, 128
  teeth bumps, 228
Temperature, 123
Tennessee Walking Horse
  breed, 30
Tetanus, 120, 126
Thoroughbred breed, 29
Threadworms
  see: Onchocerca
Ticks, 137
Toeing in, toeing out, 55-56,
  62-63, 142
Topline, 54
Torabim, **36**
Trailers

loading, 251
safety, 249
Training
  clipping, 149
  costs of, 77
  halter class, 275
  halterbreaking, 238
  lunging, 242
  principles of, 237
  trailer loading, 251
  tying, 241
Traveler's Rest Stud
  see: Dickinson, General
Treadmills, 272
Trot, 61
  floating, 64
  show horse, 65
Twitch, 119
Tying, 103, 241
Type
  Arabian, 1, 43
  definition of 1, 43
  development of, 43
  Half-Arabian, 33
  halter classes, 269
  in ancient art, 2
  and size, 232
  vs. conformation, 48

U.S. National Champions at
  Halter, 292
Underline, 54
Unsoundnesses, 59
Upton, Roger D., 9, 21
Urfah, 162
Uterus
  biopsy of, 188
  culture of, 187
  palpating, 187, 190

Vaccinations
  see: Shots
Valentino, Rudolph, 12
Veragua, Duke of, 16
Versatility, 19, 264
Vertebrae
  back, 44
  tail, 46
Vices, stable, 106
Vitamins, 113

WN Mi Kerida, 16
Walk, 61
Walk, running

see: Single-foot
Walkers, hot, 97, 271
Washington, George, 3
Water, drinking, 109
Waterers, 94
Weaning, 228-229
Weaving, 107
Weight, estimating, 235
Wentworth, Lady, 3, 5, 13, 43,
  65, 67, 72, 129, 228
White color, 69
White worms
  see: Ascarids
Wielki Szlem, 15
Winging action, 62-63
*Witez II, 14, 15
Withers, 52, 76
Witraz, 15
Wood chewing, 106, 109
Worms
  see: Parasites, internal
Wounds
  biting at, 106
  treatment of, 126

Za-Dear, **40**
*Zahid, **230**
Zarabo, 13
*Zarife, 13, 14
Zarr-Hassan, 13, 224
Zeus, **18**
Zircon Nazeer, **48, 68**